SHIPPING COMPANY LOSSES
OF THE
SECOND WORLD WAR

IAN M. MALCOLM

Cover illustrations: Front: U-boats rescuing survivors of the Laconia.
(ObltzS. Leopold Schuhmacher) Back: A convoy crossing the Atlantic, with
the Liberty ships visible in this section. (Library of Congress)

First published 2013

The History Press
The Mill, Brimscombe Port
Stroud, Gloucestershire, GL5 2QG
www.thehistorypress.co.uk

© Ian M. Malcolm, 2013

The right of Ian M. Malcolm to be identified as the Author
of this work has been asserted in accordance with the
Copyright, Designs and Patents Act 1988.

British Library Cataloguing in Publication Data.
A catalogue record for this book is available from the British Library.

ISBN 978 0 7524 9342 8

Typesetting and origination by The History Press
Printed in Great Britain

Contents

Foreword

The sacrifice in men, ships and materiel suffered by the British Merchant Navy during the Second World War is almost forgotten today. It stands alongside the losses suffered by the mercantile marines of other nations, both Allied and neutral when sailing in convoy.

Governments, being transient, forget easily, but the ignorance of a British public whose present freedoms are entirely due to victory in the Battle of Atlantic, the Mediterranean and Far East, is almost egregious. Between September 1939 and May 1943 the defensive operations of the Royal Navy, assisted by the rapidly expanding Royal Canadian Navy and joined by the navy of the United States, were largely futile against German U-boats. As an officer of an escorting corvette remarked, 'All we seem able to do is pick up the survivors.'

Thus, until tactics, technology and operational competence enabled the Allied navies to master the threat of the U-boat, the attrition suffered by the Merchant Navy was, effectively, the front line of battle in the North Atlantic Ocean.

The importance of this can scarcely be exaggerated, for besides ferrying thousands upon thousands of tons of tanks, aircraft, guns, vehicles, ammunition and that myriad of bits and pieces that constituted 'military supplies', Britain had to continue her economic life to pay for the war and sustain her daily life.

British merchant ships continued to carry essential commodities, while many vessels were requisitioned by the State for service as armed auxiliaries, troopers, transports, hospital ships and so forth. In short, the assimilation of disparate merchant shipping companies into the war effort under the leadership of Lord Leathers and his Ministry of War Transport was a major strategic achievement comparable with any initiative of a purely naval or military character.

Such a success is composed of many, many smaller triumphs and these, in turn, come at a price. In this invaluable book, Ian Malcolm has detailed the losses of fifty-three British shipping companies, ship by ship. The outcomes of many of these are epic in themselves, chronicles of individual endurance and heroism almost beyond belief when one recalls the fact that they received little recognition at the time. Today they are all but lost to us, but it is worth recalling that there are two war graves in distant Timbuktu. They are both of Merchant Seamen. Ian Malcolm's book explains why.

Captain Richard Woodman FRHistS FNI
Elder Brother, Trinity House

Author's Note

While every effort has been made to achieve accuracy, it is impossible in all cases, as the details given by various sources often differ.

DEMS gunners, both Maritime Regiment and Royal Navy, are included in the figures as they signed ships' articles and became part of the crew.

Thanks go to Stephen J. Czerwionka (Shell Group); Fred Waddington (Strick Line); A.D. Frost (Furness, Withy).

Albyn Line

THISTLEBRAE. In Trondheim in April 1940 when the Germans invaded Norway. Seized and her crew of 33 taken prisoner. Renamed *Altkirch* and then *Inster*. Sunk by the RAF off Laboe, near Kiel, on 3 May 1945.

THISTLEGARTH (Captain D. Plummer). Bound for Father Point, New Brunswick, sailing in Convoy OB.227 which left Liverpool on 11 October 1940. Dispersed from the convoy when torpedoed by U.103 (Korvettenkapitän (Krvkpt.) Viktor Schütze) at 7.33pm on the 15th. Abandoned due to taking on a heavy list, but reboarded when she remained afloat. The U-boat surfaced, but was forced to submerge again due to her gunfire being returned. Torpedoed again and sank in position 58°43′N 15°00′W. Thirty died. Nine were picked up by the corvette HMS *Heartsease* (Lt Cdr E.J.R. North).

THISTLEGLEN (Captain G.F. Dodson). Bound for Glasgow from New York, sailing in Convoy SC.42 which left Sydney, Cape Breton Island, Nova Scotia on 30 August 1941. Torpedoed by U.85 (Oberleutnant (Oblt) Eberhard Greger) at 4.42pm on 10 September and sank in position 61°59′N 39°46′W. Three died. Forty-six were picked up from 3 lifeboats and 2 rafts by the *Lorient*, which was straggling, and landed at Belfast. (For details of other ships sunk in Convoy SC.42, see under *Stonepool*, ROPNER SHIPPING CO.)

THISTLEGORM (Captain W. Ellis). Bound for Alexandria, sailing from Glasgow on 2 June 1941. In a large convoy which, after a stop at Cape Town, reached the Gulf of Suez during the third week in September. Assigned to 'Safe Anchorage F' where she remained for two weeks due to the canal entrance being blocked by 2 ships which had collided, and 2 other ships waiting to transit it. During the early hours of 6 October, bombed by 2 Heinkel He 111s, which had flown from Crete at 10.50pm on the 5th. Two bombs struck No 5 hold, ammunition in her cargo exploded, and she sank at 1.30am. Nine died and 40 taken to Suez by the light cruiser HMS *Carlisle*.

Anchor Line

BRITANNIA. Bound for Bombay, sailing independently from Liverpool on 12 March 1941. Intercepted by the German raider *Thor* (Kapitän zur See (KptzS.) Otto Kähler) at 7.45am on the 25th when about 720 miles west of Freetown. A QQQQ message was transmitted, indicating that she was being attacked by an unidentified armed merchantman (which, incidentally, was flying the Japanese flag), but the main aerial was brought down by one of the first salvoes. Returned the raider's fire until her only gun was put out of action. At

9.10am, after being repeatedly hit and with most of her lifeboats destroyed, the Master hoisted the signal that the ship was being abandoned. The *Thor*, however, continued shelling and closed to sink the ship when the lifeboats were clear, before making off without attempting to pick up the survivors. The 63 people in one of the lifeboats were rescued next morning by the *Bachi* (Sp.). The latter transferred them to the *Cilicia* on the 28th and they were landed at Freetown on the 30th. Sixty-seven in another boat were picked up by the *Raranga* (Sp.) and landed at Montevideo on 13 April. Boat No 7, with 3rd Mate William MacVicar in charge, reached the island of Curupu, Brazil, on 17 April; of its original 82 occupants (18 European and 64 Asian) only 39 remained alive. Two hundred and forty-nine died, including the Master, Goanese crew (many from the same village) and European passengers. Two hundred and forty-three survived.

CALEDONIA. Requisitioned by the Admiralty on 20 August 1939, converted into an Armed Merchant Cruiser (AMC) and renamed HMS *Scotstoun* (Captain S.K. Smyth, RN). Torpedoed at 7.15am on 13 June 1940 by U.25 (Kapitänleutnant (Kptlt) Heinz Beduhn) in position 57°00′N 09°57′W. Struck by a second torpedo at 5.30pm and sank. Six died and 346 rescued by the destroyer HMS *Echo*.

CALIFORNIA (Captain R. Smart). Requisitioned by the Admiralty in August 1939 and converted into an AMC, but became a troopship in April 1942. Under escort, and together with the troopship *Duchess of York* and the *Port Fairy*, sailed from Plymouth on 9 July 1943 bound for Freetown. Attacked by Focke-Wulf 200 Condors at about 9pm on the 11th and, on receiving two direct hits, all the passengers were sent away in lifeboats. The crew remained on board in an attempt to extinguish the fires, but when this proved impossible they took to the boats. Forty-six died. Among the survivors was William MacVicar who had commanded lifeboat No 7 of the *Britannia*. The *Duchess of York* suffered a similar fate, while the *Port Fairy*, although damaged the following day, made Casablanca. One thousand eight hundred and eighty survivors were taken on board the destroyers HMCS *Iroquois* and HMS *Douglas* and the frigates HMCS *Moyala* and HMS *Swale* which carried them to Casablanca. Both of the burning troopships were sunk by the escort at about 1.30am on the 12th. (See under *Duchess of York*, CANADIAN PACIFIC.)

ELYSIA (Captain D. Morrison). Independently bound for Karachi from Glasgow via Cape Town and nearing the southern entrance of the Mozambique Channel on the morning of 5 June 1942 when intercepted and shelled by the Japanese raiders *Aikoku Maru* and *Hokoku Maru*. Captain Morrison hoisted the signal 'I intend to abandon ship', but the shelling did not immediately stop. When everyone else was off the ship and he was preparing to leave, a small seaplane from the raiders dropped bombs on her and she sank at 9.50am in position 27°15′S 36°24′E.* The raiders departed without attempting to aid the survivors who were rescued on the evening of the same day by the hospital ship *Dorsetshire* and the minelayer HMS *Abdiel*. Out of the 136 crew and 58 passengers, 4 European crew, 18 Indian crew and 4 passengers died. Stewardess Catherine Armstrong was among those commended for their bravery.

* *A naval source claims that the ship was sunk by a Japanese submarine on the 9th in position 27°33′S 37°05′E.*

TAHSINIA (Captain C.E. Stewart). Bound for the UK, sailing independently from Colombo on 29 September 1943. Torpedoed four times by U.532 (Fregattenkapitän (Frgkpt.) Ottoheinrich Junker) between 10 and 11pm on 1 October and finally sunk by gunfire in position 06°51′N 74°38′E. The ship's motorised lifeboats took the other boat in tow, but they sailed independently after the fuel gave out. The 25 survivors, in 1 boat, were picked up by the *Nevasa* a week later and landed at Bombay on the 11th. The other 23, in the other boat, reached Mahdu Atoll in the Maldives on the 6th and were taken to Colombo by an Indian dhow. No lives lost.

TRANSYLVANIA (Captain F.N. Miles, RN). Requisitioned by the Admiralty in August 1939 and converted into an AMC. Torpedoed at 1am on 10 August 1940 by U.56 (Oblt Otto Harms) in position 55°50′N 08°03′W. Taken in tow, but foundered. Forty-eight died and the survivors were rescued by trawlers.

Athel Line

ATHELBEACH (Captain M. McIntyre). Bound for New York from Greenock, sailing in Convoy OB.293 from Liverpool on 2 March 1941 which dispersed on the 8th. Torpedoed and damaged by U.70 (Kptlt Joachim Matz) at 4.45am on the 7th. Torpedoed again by U.99 (Krvkpt. Otto Kretschmer) at 6.40am and abandoned. Shelled and torpedoed yet again by U.99 and sank in position 60°30′N 13°30′W. Seven died. Thirty-seven were picked up by the corvette HMS *Camellia* (Lt Cdr A.E. Willmot) and landed at Greenock.

OTHER SHIPS SUNK OR DAMAGED IN CONVOY OB.293

Delilian and *Mijdrecht* (Du.) (Captain J. Swart). Both damaged by U.70.

Dunaff Head (Captain R. Dicks). By U-A (Krvkpt. Hans Eckermann). Five died. Thirty-nine picked up by the destroyer HMS *Verity* (Cdr R.H. Mills) and landed at Loch Ewe.

Terje Viken (Nor.) (Captain Borchgrevink). Torpedoed and damaged by U.47 (Krvkpt. Günther Prien) and by U.99. Scuttled by gunfire from a salvage tug on the 14th. Two died. One hundred and five picked up by the destroyer HMS *Hurricane* (Lt Cdr H.C. Simms) and landed at Greenock.

U.47 sunk. Cause unknown. All 48 died.

ATHELBRAE. Bound for Demerara from Trinidad when she struck a US-laid mine and sank in position 10°02′N 61°51′W on 4 October 1942. None died.

ATHELCREST (Captain L.V.F. Evans). Bound for London from Aruba, sailing in Convoy HX.65 which left Halifax, Nova Scotia, on 12 August 1940. Torpedoed by U.48 (Krvkpt. Hans Rudolf Rösing) at 2.45am on the 25th in position 58°24′N 11°25′W. Thirty died. Scuttled by the corvette HMS *Godetia* (Lt Cdr G.V. Legassick) which picked up 6 survivors and landed them at Methil. (For details of other ships sunk in Convoy HX.65, see under *Empire Merlin*, ROPNER SHIPPING CO.)

ATHELCROWN (Captain I. Burkhill). Bound for Aruba from Cardiff, sailing in Convoy ON.56 which left Liverpool on 12 January 1942 and dispersed on the 16th in position 59°00′N 17°00′W. Torpedoed and sunk by U.82 (Kptlt Siegfried Rollmann) at 11.10pm on the 22nd in position 45°06′N 40°56′W. Five died. Twenty-three were picked up by the *Argos Hill* and landed at Halifax. Eight were picked up by a warship. After four days in a lifeboat, Apprentice C.N.T. Baptist and 3 others boarded the drifting wreck of the *Diala***** (Captain H.J.A. Peters) which had been dispersed from Convoy ON.52 and torpedoed by U.587 (Kptlt Ulrich Borcherdt) on the 15th. They were rescued 8 days later by the *Saturnus* (Swed.) which landed them at the Faroe Islands.

*See under SHELL GROUP.

OTHER SHIPS SUNK AFTER DISPERSAL OF CONVOY ON.56

Leiesten (Nor.) (Captain Nils Jespersen). By U.82. Six died. Twenty-nine picked up by the *Agios Georgios* (Gr.) and landed at Halifax on the 30th.

Pan Norway (Nor.) (Captain Johan A. Bach). By U.123 (Kptlt Reinhard Hardegen). Hardegen guided the Greek ship *Mount Aetna* (Captain Stavros Sotirchos) to the survivors in lifeboats and in the water, and rescued a wounded man. The *Mount Aetna*, neutral because she was under Swiss charter, landed all 41 at Lisbon on 6 February.

Refast (Captain A.E. Wilson). By U.582 (Kptlt Werner Schulte). Ten died. Thirty-two picked up by the *Mariposa* and landed at Halifax.

ATHELDUCHESS. On the night of 20 August 1943, in ballast, bound for New York from Swansea and in a convoy, went aground on the southern rocks of the Smalls, two tiny clusters of rocks 21 miles west of St David's Head, Pembrokeshire. When two tugs were unsuccessful in trying to pull her off at high tide, the Captain ordered 'abandon ship' and all were rescued by the Angle and St David's lifeboats. The stern section was subsequently floated off and beached, but the bow section sank. With a new bow fitted, she returned to service in 1948 as the Norwegian ship *Milford*.

ATHELDUKE (Captain J. Errett). Bound for Saltend from Fort Lauderdale, Port Everglades, Florida, in Convoy FS.1784 (Methil to Southend) when torpedoed twice and sunk by U.1274 (Oblt Hans-Hermann Fitting) at 5.32pm on 16 April 1945 in position 55°39′N 01°31′W. Senior 4th Engineer W. McKenzie died. Forty-six were picked up by the *King Neptune* and landed at Grimsby the following evening. U.1274 was subsequently depth-charged and sunk by the destroyer HMS *Viceroy* (A/Lt Cdr J.E. Manners). All 44 died.

ATHELEMPRESS (Captain W. Jackson). Bound for Trinidad from Southampton, sailing in Convoy OS.25 which left Liverpool on 12 April 1942. Dispersed from the convoy when torpedoed and sunk by gunfire by U.162 (Kptlt Jürgen Wattenberg) at 1.52am on the 30th in position 13°21′N 56°15′W. Three died. Nineteen landed at Gros Inlet Bay, St Lucia. Twenty-eight were picked up by the *Atlantic* (Nor.) and landed at Trinidad.

ATHELFOAM (Captain R.F.S. Notman). Bound for Pastelillo, Cuba, sailing in Convoy OB.294 which left Liverpool on 5 March 1941 and dispersed in position 51°29′N 20°30′W on the 9th. Intercepted and sunk by the German battleship *Scharnhorst* on the 15th in position 42°00′N 43°25′W. Two died and the others taken prisoner. (For details of the many ships sunk and captured by the *Scharnhorst* and the *Gneisenau*, see under *British Strength*, BRITISH TANKER CO. LTD.)

ATHELKING (Captain A.E. Tomkins). In ballast and bound for Soerabaja from Table Bay when intercepted by the German raider *Atlantis* (Kapitän zur See (KptzS.) Bernhard Rogge) on 9 September 1940. Ordered to stop and not use her radio, but when she complied with neither order was shelled and sunk in position 21°48′S 67°40′E. Four died and 37 taken prisoner. The prisoners from all the raider's victims were well treated and fed until, except for 23 Chinese from the *Benarty*, they were transferred to the captured Yugoslav ship *Durmitor* on 26 October. Shortly after sailing, with Lt Dehnel in command, it was discovered that there was not enough food to reach Italian Somaliland. The conditions on the *Durmitor* were deplorable. She was infested by cockroaches and rats, the prisoners slept on salt in the holds and were eventually allowed only one cup of water a day. This, plus the heat, made them so mutinous that machine guns had to be constantly trained on them. On 22 November, she arrived off the coast of Italian Somaliland and, failing to obtain a pilot, Dehnel ran her onto a reef near the village of Warsheik. She was then abandoned and all the prisoners taken to a camp at Merca, near Mogadishu, the next day. On 25 February 1941, they were freed by South African troops and taken to Mombasa by the cruiser HMS *Ceres* for repatriation to the UK. (The *Durmitor*'s passage to Somaliland is described in *The Cruise of the German Raider Atlantis* by Joseph P. Slavick.) (See also under *Scientist*, HARRISON LINE.)

ATHELKNIGHT (Captain Hugh Roberts). Bound for Trinidad from Barry, sailing in Convoy OS.28 which left Liverpool on 12 May 1942 for Freetown. Dispersed from the convoy when torpedoed by U.172 (Kptlt Carl Emmermann) at about 10.30pm on the 26th in position 28°00′N 45°40′W. An SSSS* was transmitted, but it would seem that it was not heard, and the crew got away in two lifeboats. Captain Roberts was ordered to board the U-boat where he was questioned by Emmermann and given a bag containing six loaves of bread before being returned to his boat. During the night, the U-boat shelled the ship and set her on fire and, at daybreak, sank her with another torpedo and departed. To even up the numbers in the lifeboats, some men were transferred between them. There were now 26 men in the boat with 1st Mate G.J. Davies in charge, and 25 in Captain Roberts' boat. Two days later, 2 badly wounded men died in Roberts' boat and, 2 days after that, the boats lost sight of each other. On 21 June, those in Davies' boat were picked up by the *Empire Austin* and subsequently landed at Cape Town. On 23 June, the Captain's boat landed at St Bartholomew Island, in the Leeward Islands. Nine died.

SSSS signal meant 'being attacked by a submarine'

OTHER SHIPS SUNK IN CONVOY OS.28

Montenol (Captain E.E.A. Le Sage). Badly damaged by U.159 (Kptlt Helmut Witte). Sunk by the corvette HMS *Woodruff* (Lt Cdr F.H. Gray). Three died. Sixty-one picked up by the sloop HMS *Wellington* (Lt Cdr W.F.R. Segrave) and landed at Freetown.

New Brunswick (Captain C.M. Whalley). By U.159. Three died. Twelve picked up by the sloop HMS *Totland* (Lt Cdr S.G.C. Rawson), 10 by HMS *Wellington*, 7 by the sloop HMS *Weston* (Cdr J.G. Sutton), 5 by HMS *Woodruff* and 25 by the *Inchanga*.

ATHELLAIRD (Captain Hugh Roberts). Bound for Cuba, sailing in Convoy OB.176 which left Liverpool on 29 June 1940 and dispersed in position 48°00′N 15°04′W on 2 July. Torpedoed and badly damaged by U.29 (Kptlt Otto Schuhart) at 11.52pm on the 2nd. Torpedoed again by U.29 at 2.10am on the 3rd, and sank in position 47°24′N 16°49′W. All 42 were picked up by the sloop HMS *Sandwich* (Cdr M.J. Yeatman) and landed at Greenock. (At 11.25am on the 2nd, the unescorted *Santa Margarita*, under British charter but with a Yugoslavian crew, was stopped by U.29 and sunk by gunfire at 1.45pm. All 39 survived, but 21 of them were picked up by the *King John* (Captain G.E. Smith) and 3 died when she herself was sunk by the raider *Widder* (KptzS. Helmuth von Ruckteschell) on the 13th.)

ATHELMONARCH (Captain R.J. Roberts). Bound for Alexandria from Beirut when torpedoed and sunk by U.97 (Kptlt Hans-Georg Trox) at 2.30pm on 15 June 1943 in position 32°20′N 34°39′E. Four died. Forty-seven were picked up by the Greek destroyer RHS *Aetos* and landed at Beirut.

ATHELPRINCESS (Captain E.G.B. Martin). Bound for Curaçao, sailing in Convoy UC.1 which left Liverpool on 15 February 1943. Torpedoed twice and sunk by U.522 (Kptlt Herbert Schneider) at 6.45am on the 23rd in position 32°02′N 24°38′W. One died. Fifty were picked up by the destroyer USS *Hilary P. Jones* (Cdr F.M. Stiesberg) and landed at San Juan, Puerto Rico.

OTHER SHIPS SUNK OR DAMAGED IN CONVOY UC.1 – ALL ON THE 23RD

British Fortitude. Damaged by U.202 (Kptlt Günter Poser).

Empire Norseman (Captain W.S. Smith). Damaged by U.202 and U.382. Sunk by U.558 (Kptlt Günther Krech). All 53 picked up by HMS *Totland* but transferred to the *Maaskerk*.

Esso Baton Rouge (US) (Captain J.S. Poche). By U.202. Three died. Sixty-five picked up by HMS *Totland* (Lt Cdr L.E. Woodhouse). Three badly burned men retained on the sloop and landed at Antigua on 4 March, and 62 transferred to the *Maaskerk* (Du.) which reached Trinidad on the 6th.

Murena (Du.). Damaged by U.202. One source claims it was U.382 (Kptlt Herbert Juli).

U.382. Depth-charged, badly damaged and forced to withdraw.

U.522. Depth-charged and sunk by HMS *Totland*.

ATHELQUEEN (Captain C.J.R. Roberts). Bound for Port Everglades, sailing from Hull on 9 February 1942. Torpedoed and sunk by the Italian submarine *Enrico Tazzoli* (Capitano di Fregata (C.F.) (Cdr) Carlo Conte Fecia di Cossato) on 15 March in position 26°50′N 75°40′W. Three of the survivors died on the reef just before their lifeboat landed at Elbow Cay, in the Bahamas, on the 17th. Forty-six survived. The submarine was damaged by colliding with the sinking ship and had to return to base.

ATHELSTANE (Captain H. Moore). Requisitioned by the Admiralty in 1940. In Trincomalee, Ceylon (Sri Lanka), on 8 April 1942 when the Flag Officer in Charge ordered the port to be cleared due to the threat of an air raid by Japanese carrier-based aircraft. Bound for Colombo and in company with the corvette HMS *Hollyhock* (Lt Cdr T.E. Davies) when bombed at about noon the next day and sank in position 07°30′N 81°56′E. None died. HMS *Hollyhock* was also sunk. Fifty-three, including Lt Cdr Davies, died and 16 were rescued from the sea by Captain Moore's lifeboat. (For details of other ships sunk by planes from the Japanese force commanded by Admiral Chuichi Nagumo, see under *British Sergeant*, BRITISH TANKER CO. LTD.)

ATHELSULTAN (Captain J.D. Donovan). Bound for Liverpool from Port Everglades, commodore ship of Convoy SC.100 which sailed from Halifax on 12 September 1942. Torpedoed and sunk by U.617 (Oblt Albrecht Brandi) at 0019 hours on the 23rd in position 58°42′N 33°38′W. Fifty died. Three were picked up by the corvette HMCS *Weyburn* (T/A/ Lt Cdr T.M.W. Golby), 7 by HMS *Nasturtium* (Lt C.D. Smith) and landed at Londonderry.

OTHER SHIPS SUNK IN CONVOY SC.100

Empire Hartebeeste (Captain J.F. Travis). By U.596 (Kptlt Gunter Jahn). Five died. Survivors picked up by the Norwegian ships *Norhauk* and *Rio Verde* and landed at Oban and Liverpool respectively.

Pennmar (US) (Captain S.C. Krolikowski). Straggled. By U.432 (Kptlt Heinz-Otto Schultze). Three died, including one previously killed in an accident. Sixty picked up by USCGC *Bibb* and landed at Reykjavik on 2 October.

Roumanie (Belg.) (Captain E. Morbée). Straggled. By U.617. Forty-two died. Sole survivor was Mr Suykerbuyk, the Chief Engineer, who was rescued from a raft by the U-boat and taken to St Nazaire.

Tennessee (Ex-Danish) (Captain A.H. Albrechtsen). By U.617. Fifteen died. Twelve picked up by HMS *Nasturtium*. Eight picked up from a lifeboat on the 26th by USCGC *Ingham* and landed at Reykjavik on 2 October.

Empire Soldier. Sank after colliding with the *F.J. Wolfe* on 16 September. None died.

ATHELTEMPLAR (Captain C. Ray). Sailed from Hvalfjördur, Iceland, at 6am on 7 September 1942 bound for Archangel; the next day joined Convoy PQ.18 which had left Loch Ewe on the 2nd. Convoy spotted by a German reconnaissance plane on the 12th. Attacks began on the 13th and *Atheltemplar* shot down a plane. Torpedoed by U.457 (Krvkpt. Karl Brandenburg) at 4am on the 14th and abandoned. All 61 were picked up by HMRS *Copeland* (Captain W.J. Hartley) and the destroyer HMS *Offa* (Lt Cdr R.A. Ewing) but transferred to the minesweepers HMS *Harrier* (Cdr A.D.H. Jay) and HMS *Sharpshooter* (Lt Cdr W.L. O'Mara). Sixteen later died of their injuries.* HMS *Harrier* failed in an attempt to sink the burning ship, but U.408 (Kptlt Reinhard von Hymmen) found her capsized in the afternoon and sank her by gunfire in position 76°10′N 18°00′E. U.457 was sunk by the destroyer HMS *Impulse* (Lt Cdr E.G. Roper) on the 16th. All 45 died.

* *Arnold Hague states that 3 died.*

OTHER SHIPS SUNK IN CONVOY PQ.18

13 September:
<u>By torpedo bombers</u>

Africander (Pan.) (Captain Bjarne A. Lia). All 35 rescued.

Empire Beaumont. See under WALTER RUNCIMAN & CO. LTD/MOOR LINE LTD.

Empire Stevenson. All 59 died.

John Penn (US Liberty ship) (Captain A. Johnson).Three died.

MacBeth (Pan.). None died.

Oregonian (US). Twenty-eight died.

Sukhona (USSR).

Wacosta (US). All 49 survived.

<u>By U-boats</u>

Oliver Ellsworth (US) (Captain O.E. Buford). Badly damaged by U.408. One drowned. Sixty-nine picked up by HMRS *Copeland* and the ASW trawler HMS *St Kenan* which sank the ship by gunfire.

Stalingrad (USSR) (Captain A. Sakharov). By U.408. Twenty-one died when a lifeboat capsized. Sixty-six survived, including Captain Sakharov who spent 40 minutes in the freezing water.

14 September:

Kentucky (US). Bombed. All picked up by the escort. Wreck drifted ashore and part of her cargo salvaged.

Mary Luckenbach (US). Blown up by an aerial torpedo. All 65 died.

All survivors, with the exception of those from the *Kentucky* and a few others, picked up by the escort and HMRS *Copeland*, transferred to the cruiser HMS *Scylla* and her attendant destroyers before they departed to escort Convoy QP.14 to the UK. A total of approximately 25 German planes were destroyed and U.88 (Kptlt Heino Bohmann), U.457 and U.589 (Krvkpt. Hans-Joachim Horrer) sunk.

ATHELVIKING (Captain E.G.B. Martin). Bound for the UK from Port Everglades, sailing in Convoy BX.141 which left Boston on 12 January 1945 bound for Halifax. Convoy entering Halifax in single file when torpedoed by U.1232 (Kptlt Kurt Dobratz) at 10.35am on the 14th; sank in position 44°28′N 63°28′W. Four died. Forty-seven were picked up by the motor launch HMCS *ML-102* (Lt J.K. Macdonald) and landed at Halifax.

OTHER SHIPS SUNK AND DAMAGED IN CONVOY BX.141 – ALL BY U.1232

British Freedom (Captain F.L. Morris). One died. Fifty-six picked up by the minesweeper HMS *Gaspe* (Lt A.J. Burke).

Martin Van Buren (US Liberty ship) (Captain J.H. Hiss). Damaged, abandoned and became a total loss. Three died. Sixty-six picked up from lifeboats and rafts by the minesweepers HMCS *Comox* and HMCS *Fundy*.

U.1232. Damaged when the frigate HMCS *Ettrick* ran over her conning tower and had to return to base.

In December 1941, the Athel Line acquired Tankers Ltd, a small subsidiary of British Petroleum.

TANKERS LTD SHIPS SUNK BEFORE THE ACQUISITION

SCOTTISH MAIDEN (Captain J.W.A. Gibson). Bound for Avonmouth from Curaçao, sailing in Convoy HX.83 which left Halifax on 24 October 1940. Torpedoed and sunk by U.99 (Kptlt Otto Kretschmer) at 2.55am on 5 November in position 54°36′N 14°23′W. Sixteen died. Twenty-eight were picked up by the destroyer HMS *Beagle* (Lt Cdr R.H. Wright) and landed at Liverpool.

SCOTTISH MINSTREL (Captain P. Dunn). Bound for London from New York, sailing in Convoy HX.55 which left Halifax on 3 July 1940. Torpedoed by U.61 (Oblt Jürgen Oesten) at 12.23pm on 16th in position 56°10′N 10°20′W, and sank the next day. Nine died. Thirty-two were picked up by the corvette HMS *Gardenia* (Lt Cdr T.A.O. Ellis) and landed at Folkestone. The *Manipur* (Captain R. Mallett) was sunk on the 17th by U.57. (See under BROCKLEBANK LINE.)

SCOTTISH STANDARD (Captain J. Ward). Bound for New York from the Clyde, sailing in Convoy OB.287 which left Liverpool on 16 February 1941 and dispersed on the 21st. Bombed by a single Focke-Wulf 200 Condor at 9.23am on the 21st and abandoned in position 59°19′N 16°14′W. Five died. Thirty-nine were picked up by the destroyer HMS *Montgomery* (Cdr H.F. Nash) and landed at Oban. U.96 (Kptlt Heinrich Lehmann-Willenbrock) sank her the next day, but was damaged by depth charges from a destroyer.

OTHER SHIPS IN CONVOY OB.287 SUNK OR DAMAGED BY THE PLANE

D.L. Harper. Slightly damaged, but proceeded to Halifax for repairs.

Gracian. All 48 survived.

Housatonic. Three died and 31 survived.

Rosenborg. Damaged and returned to port.

St Rosario. Damaged and returned to port.

TANKERS LTD SHIPS SUNK AFTER THE ACQUISITION

SCOTTISH CHIEF (Captain T. Thorogood). Bound for Cape Town from Bandar Abbas, Iran, when torpedoed by U.177 (Kptlt Robert Gysae) at 11.7pm on 19 November 1942, and sank within 1 minute in position 30°39′S 34°41′E. Thirty-six died. Five were picked up by the corvette HMS *Jasmine* (Lt Cdr C.D.B. Coventry), 7 by the corvette HMS *Genista* (Lt Cdr R.M. Pattinson) and landed at Durban.

Ben Line

BENALBANACH (Captain D.K.C. Macgregor). In Convoy KMS.6 which left Gibraltar on 4 January 1943 bound for Bône (Annaba) in Algeria. When about 150 miles east of Algiers during the evening of the 7th, the convoy was attacked by a single low-flying aircraft which released two torpedoes. The *Benalbanach* was struck by both and sank in less than 2 minutes. Of her 74 crew, 57 died, together with 353 of the 389 troops she carried.

BENARTY. Bound for Liverpool via Durban from Rangoon on 9 September 1942 when her Radio Officers heard a message from the tanker *Athelking* (Captain A.E. Tomkins) stating that she was being attacked by an unidentified armed merchantman. By retransmitting this message, the *Benarty* gave away her own position, resulting in her loss the following day. The raider was the *Atlantis* (KptzS. Bernhard Rogge) and when the *Benarty* was spotted, Rogge sent off an aircraft to bomb and machine-gun her. The *Benarty* began to transmit a raider warning, but transmission ceased abruptly when the main aerial was brought down. The *Atlantis* then approached and ordered the *Benarty* to stop, but when this order and a couple of shots across her bows were ignored she fired a salvo at her bridge and the ship came to a halt. The crew then abandoned the ship in two lifeboats, but when they met a boarding party heading for her, the Captain and Chief Engineer were ordered to return on board. The Germans brought the fire under control and looted the ship before setting demolition charges to sink her, and she went down shortly afterwards in position 18°32′S 70°07′E. As the radio operator on the raider believed that he had heard further transmissions from the *Benarty* after she had surrendered and been abandoned, Rogge accused the Captain of leaving a Radio Officer on board. Rogge was angry because, hoping to capture the ship, this had caused him to fire another salvo at her. But the transmission was made by another ship, relaying the *Benarty*'s original message. All 49 were taken prisoner. (For their subsequent fate see under *Athelking*, ATHEL LINE.)

BENAVON (Captain A. Thomson). In the Indian Ocean, homeward bound from Penang, when intercepted in the early morning of 11 September 1940 by the German raider *Pinguin* (KptzS. Ernst-Felix Krüder) in position 25°20′S 52°17′E. Seeing the unidentified ship flying the Norwegian flag, the *Benavon* altered course and, witnessing this, the *Pinguin* signalled her to stop and fired a warning shot. The *Benavon* returned fire with her single 4in gun and although a shell fell close to where the raider's mines were stored, it failed to explode. The *Pinguin*, now only about 500yd away, put some 60 shells into the *Benavon*. The wounded were lowered onto a raft and survivors jumped into the water from the *Benavon*, which was on fire and with her lifeboats blown away, but it was an hour later before a boat from the *Pinguin* came to their rescue. Twenty-seven died, including 2 of the wounded who were rescued, and 7 British and 18 Chinese became PoWs. When the Norwegian ship *Nordvard* was captured on the 16th, a prize crew was put on board. Some of the *Pinguin*'s prisoners were transferred to her and were landed at Bordeaux on 22 November. (See also under *Nowshera*, BRITISH INDIA STEAM NAVIGATION CO.)

BENCLEUCH (Captain W.A. Murray). Bound for the Far East via the Panama Canal, sailed from Liverpool in Convoy ON.42 on 1 December 1941. On the 11th, fire broke out in No 4 hold, but the crew were unable to contain it and when it was approaching explosives in her cargo they abandoned the ship in 4 lifeboats. The 48 men in 3 of the boats were rescued by the *Athelviscount* and the 10 in the other boat by the corvette HMCS *Nanaimo*. No lives were lost and all were landed at Halifax, Nova Scotia, on the 18th. The *Bencleuch* blew up at 1.15am on the 12th, in approximate position 53°10′N 38°00′W. As a watchman had seen an intruder emerge from a hold while the ship was loading in Leith, sabotage was suspected, but a thorough investigation had revealed nothing more than cases having been broken open.

BENCRUACHAN (Captain W.F. Riddle). Sailed from Barry bound for Alexandria via the Cape and the Suez Canal. Entering the port with four other ships in single file, on 5 July 1941, she struck an acoustic mine. Sank bow-first in shallow water so that her cargo shifted and her back was broken. Scrapped in 1950. Three men died; 21 were injured.

BENDORAN. Built in 1910. Commandeered in March 1944 to be used as a blockship in the Normandy Landings. Scuttled on 6 June to become part of the Mulberry Harbour at Arromanches.

BENLAWERS (Captain W.S. Campbell). Bound for Port Said via Durban, sailed from Swansea and joined the Milford Haven section of Convoy OB.221 which sailed from Liverpool on 29 September 1940. Owing to bad weather, straggled from the Convoy and was torpedoed and sunk shortly after 11am on 6 October by U.123 (Kptlt Karl-Heinz Moehle) in position 53°20′N 26°10′W. One Chinese was killed by the explosion, but all the others succeeded in entering the lifeboats. Seven hours later, the 16 men in one boat were picked up by the *Bengore Head*. Twelve hours after the sinking, the other 2 boats were sighted by the *Forest*. The 11 men in one boat were successfully taken on board, but the other boat, containing 23 men, was swamped by the heavy swell when coming alongside and all were lost. Twenty-four died.

BENLOMOND (Captain J. Maul). Bound independently for New York from Port Said via Cape Town and Paramaribo, and 6 hours out from the latter when torpedoed and sunk by U.172 (Kptlt Carl Emmermann) at 11.45am on 23 November 1942 in position 00°30′N 38°45′W. Out of her crew of 54, only the 2nd Steward, Poon Lim, survived, living alone for 133 days on a raft before being picked up by a Brazilian fishing boat. When the explosion occurred, Poon Lim, in his cabin, put on his lifejacket and joined others at his boat station, but a wave carried him into the sea. He managed to board a raft, but although he saw another raft with 4 other survivors on it, he was unable to get to it and the rafts gradually drifted apart. The story of his ordeal is told elsewhere in detail. On 2 April 1943, a Brazilian Negro fisherman sighted the raft east of the Salinas and went to his rescue. Although naked and unable to move, Poon Lim sang and laughed as the fisherman carried him onto his boat. By the time he was landed at Belem on the 5th, he was able to walk and was found to be suffering from nothing more than a stomach upset and dizzy spells, having gorged himself on the fisherman's red peppers.

BENMACDHUI (Captain W.S. Campbell). Sailed from Immingham on 17 December 1941 bound for Hong Kong. Left the convoy anchorage at 4pm on the 21st to proceed to the Humber light float to join a convoy, but as it could not be located in the poor visibility, Captain Campbell decided to return to the wreck buoy at the mouth of the river. When at 9.35pm a smell of burning rubber was detected, the Chief Officer and 1st Mate were sent to locate the source. And, 10 minutes later, when they were reporting their failure to do so and the ship was again turning to head for the light float, there was a violent explosion and she sank in 20 minutes. Two men died and the rest were picked up from two lifeboats and a raft by the *Peronne*. One source states that she struck a mine, while another states that it may have been sabotage.

BENMOHR (Captain D. Anderson). Sailed independently from Bombay bound for the UK via Durban and Freetown and in position 06°05′N 14°15′W when hit by 2 torpedoes fired by U.505 (Krvkpt. Axel-Olaf Loewe) at about 8pm on 4 March 1942. An SSSS message was transmitted and acknowledged by Freetown before she was abandoned and sank about 10 minutes later. The following day, an RAF Sunderland flying boat landed on the water beside the lifeboats which contained the entire crew of 56. All transferred to the Sunderland which somehow succeeded in taking off with the heavy load and carried them to Freetown. (U.505 was captured by the US Navy on 4 June 1944 and is now in the Museum of Science and Industry in Chicago.)

BENNEVIS (Captain J.D. Wilson). Ordered out of Hong Kong on 7 December 1941 when a Japanese attack seemed imminent. Bound for Singapore towing a lighter when two Japanese destroyers appeared on the 9th and signalled not to use her wireless and that she was captured. This came as a surprise to those on the *Bennevis* as they had not heard that the Japanese had declared war on Britain. The ship was taken to Hainan Island where the Chinese in the crew were set free and the Scottish crew told that they were not PoWs because Japan was not at war with Scotland. This unexpected exemption did not last long. They were sent first to Shanghai, then to Osaka, and lastly to a camp at Aomori, in northern Honshu. Throughout their captivity, they were made to work long hours on meagre rations and were flown home after the war ended in August 1945. Four died during internment. Renamed *Gyokuyo Maru*, the *Bennevis* was torpedoed and sunk by the US submarine *Swordfish* on 14 November 1944.

BENVENUE (Captain J. Struth). Sailed from the UK in Convoy OB.314 on 23 April 1941 bound for Bombay via Gibraltar and Cape Town. Sailing independently after the convoy had dispersed when torpedoed and sunk by U.105 (Kptlt Georg Schewe) at about 7.10pm on 15 May in position 04°27′N 18°25′W. All 4 lifeboats got away and those in 3 of them were picked up the following evening by the *English Trader* and landed at Freetown on the 18th. Those in the fourth lifeboat, commanded by the 1st Mate, were not so fortunate as it was not until the 26th that they were rescued by a destroyer and also taken to Freetown. Two died out of her complement of 57.

BENVORLICH (Captain E.D. Copeman). Bound for the Far East, sailed from Middlesbrough on 10 March 1941 and joined Convoy OB.298 which left Liverpool on the 16th. Attacked by a German plane at about 8am on the 19th in position 54°43′N 13°10′W, and when fire broke out after a bomb hit No 1 hold, which contained explosives, the order to abandon ship was given. Two lifeboats got away, but a Chinese lost his life when one of his hands was caught in the lower block of the falls and he was pulled into the sea. Captain Copeman, still on board and looking for a hammer to help release a raft, was knocked unconscious when an explosion occurred. Ordinary Seaman Alex Dalziel dragged him to the side, threw him overboard and kept him afloat until they were picked up by the rescue ship *Zamalek*. Twenty-four were rescued by the *Zamalek* and 12 by the destroyer HMS *Hesperus*. Nineteen died, including 4 from their injuries on the rescue ship. The survivors were landed at Greenock on the 26th.

BENVRACKIE (Captain W. Eyton-Jones). Sailed from the Tyne on 15 April 1941 bound for Beira via Cape Town and joined Convoy OB.312 which departed Liverpool on the 18th. On 9 May, when proceeding independently after the convoy had dispersed, she picked up 25 survivors from the *Lassell* (Captain A.R. Bibby) which, having dispersed from Convoy OB. 309, had been torpedoed by U.107 (Kptlt Günther Hessler) on 30 April. At about 6.30am on 13 May, the *Benvrackie* was herself torpedoed by U.105 (Kptlt Georg Schewe) in position 00°49′N 20°15′W. She went down so fast that Captain Eyton-Jones was dragged down with her, but surfaced and was taken on board the only lifeboat which got away. Originally, it contained 55, including 10 from the *Lassell*, but 2 Chinese from the *Benvrackie* died before the others were rescued by the hospital ship *Oxfordshire* at about 5am on the 26th and landed at Freetown later in the day. Ho Fook, the *Benvrackie*'s 2nd Steward, survived alone on a raft and was rescued by a Blue Star ship. Twenty-nine died – 14 from the *Benvrackie* and 15 from the *Lassell*. (See also under *Lassell*, LAMPORT & HOLT LINE.)

BENWYVIS (Captain H.J. Small). Homeward bound from Rangoon via Durban, and in Convoy SL.68 which sailed from Freetown on 13 March 1941. At 10.35pm on the 20th, the *Benwyvis* and the *Clan Ogilvy* (Captain E. Gough) were almost simultaneously hit and sunk by torpedoes fired by U.105 (Kptlt Georg Schewe) in position 20°04′N 25°45′W. Only 2 of the *Benwyvis*'s lifeboats could be launched, but one capsized and 5 men were lost.

The next morning, 20 were transferred into two lifeboats of the *Clan Ogilvy*, but Captain Small remained in his boat with 33 British and Chinese.

After 11 days together, the 3 boats decided to separate. On the evening of 1 April, those in one of the *Clan Ogilvy*'s boats were picked up by the Spanish ship *Cabo Villano* (Captain Sagardui) and taken to Santos, in Brazil, while those in the other were rescued by the *King Edgar* and landed at Freetown on the 7th. Captain Small's boat was not so fortunate. All except Cadet John Ross died of starvation and thirst. The story of the 17-year-old cadet is one of extreme hardship; he was barely able to move when rescued by the French ship *Ville de Rouen* on 17 April. Taken to Tamatave, in Madagascar, he met much kindness from British people, and although forbidden to leave by the Vichy administration, he was eventually smuggled onto a US ship and carried to Durban. Thirty-two died and 21 survived. Sixty-one on the *Clan Ogilvy* died and 21 survived.

OTHER SHIPS SUNK IN CONVOY SL.68

Andalusian. See under ELLERMAN GROUP.

Clan Macnab. See under CLAN LINE.

Jhelum. See under NOURSE LINE.

Mandalika (Du.) (Captain L.T.M. Ouwerkerk). By U.105. Three dead and 62 survived.

Medjerda (Captain C.E Banks). By U.105. All 54 died.

Tapanoeli (Du.). By U.106 (Kptlt Jürgen Oesten). All 75 survived.

(HMS *Malaya* and the Dutch merchantman *Meerkerk* damaged by U.106.)

Managed for Ministry of War Transport

EMPIRE PROTECTOR (Captain J. Cringle). Formerly called the *Pamia*, an Italian ship captured by the trawler HMS *Liffey* on 10 June 1940. Independently bound for the UK from Port Sudan via Cape Town and Freetown when torpedoed by U.38 (Kptlt Heinrich Liebe) at about 10.20am on 30 May 1941 in position 06°00′N 14°25′W. After she was abandoned, the now-surfaced U-boat put a second torpedo into her and she sank within minutes. Although an SSSS had been transmitted, it was not heard. Four died when the ship was torpedoed and 33 were picked up from 2 small lifeboats at 4.30pm by the Dutch ship *Arundo* and landed at Freetown on the 31st.

FORT BABINE. Damaged by a bomb off the coast of North Africa on 6 February 1943. Towed to Gibraltar where she spent 7 months undergoing temporary repairs. Left Gibraltar in convoy on 5 September and being towed to the UK by the tugs *Schelde* and *Prosperous* when in position 41°31′N 14°39′W on the 13th she was again struck by a bomb from a German plane. This time the Navy sank her to prevent the wreck becoming a danger to shipping. Seven died and the 16 survivors were carried to Liverpool by the sloop HMS *Woodcock*.

FORT QU'APPELLE (Captain W.A. Murray). Built in Vancouver and began her maiden voyage from there on 3 April 1942 bound for the UK via the Panama Canal and Halifax. On 7 May 1942, picked up the entire complement of 22 from the US ship *Green Island* (Captain Josef Anderson) which had been sunk the previous day by U.125 (Kptlt Ulrich Folkers). Proceeding on her way after landing the survivors at Kingston, Jamaica, the *Fort Qu'Appelle* was herself torpedoed by U.135 (Kptlt Friedrich Hermann Praetorius) at 10.45pm on the 16th when in position 39°50′N 63°30′W. Captain Murray, formerly on the *Bencleuch*, did not survive his second sinking as he was in a lifeboat being lowered when a second torpedo struck the ship directly underneath, killing all its 13 occupants and sinking the ship at 0030 hours on the 17th. At about 5pm on the 18th, the boat containing the 34 survivors was seen by a plane, and 4 hours later they were picked up by the minesweeper HMCS *Melville* (Lt Cdr R.T. Ingram) which landed them at Shelburne, Nova Scotia, the following day. Thirteen died.

SAMVERN (Captain T. McI. Blaikie). Bound for London, sailing from Antwerp on 18 January 1945, and the last in a line of 5 ships making their way through the Scheldt estuary when she struck a mine. Two lifeboats left the ship, but a full gale was blowing and one of them turned over. Some of its occupants succeeded in swimming to the other boat, but when the upturned boat drifted away, those clinging to it were lost. Sixteen died, including both the Antwerp and London pilots. Forty-seven survived.

Bibby Line

At the outbreak of war, all 11 of the Bibby Line ships were requisitioned.

YORKSHIRE (Captain V.C.P. Smalley). Bound for Liverpool, sailed from Rangoon on 13 September 1939. Joined unescorted Convoy HG.3 which left Gibraltar on 12 October. Torpedoed twice and sunk by U.37 (Krvkpt. Werner Hartmann) at 4.30pm on the 17th in position 44°52′N 14°31′W. Fifty-eight died. Two hundred and twenty-three were picked up by the *Independence Hall* (US) and landed at Bordeaux on the 20th. (For details of other ships sunk in Convoy HG.3, see under *City of Mandalay*, ELLERMAN GROUP and *Clan Chisholm*, CLAN LINE.)

SHROPSHIRE. Requisitioned by the Admiralty and her name changed to HMS *Salopian* (Captain Sir John Meynell Alleyne, RN) because there was already a Royal Navy ship of that name. Part of the escort of Convoy SC.30 which left Halifax, Nova Scotia, on 29 April 1941. Torpedoed twice at 7.20am by U.98 (Kptlt Robert Gysae). Torpedoed again at 8am and yet again at 8.50pm, but did not go down until a fifth torpedo struck at 10.43am when she broke in two and sank in position 56°43′N 38°57′W. Three died and 278 were picked up by the destroyer HMS *Impulsive* (Lt Cdr W.S. Thomas) and landed at Hvalfjördur in Iceland. (See under *Somersby*, ROPNER SHIPPING CO.)

PRÉSIDENT DOUMER (Captain Jean Paul Mantelet). An ex-French liner managed for the Ministry of War Transport (MOWT) and operated as a troopship. Sunk by U.604 (Kptlt

Horst Höltring). Out of the 345 on board, the Master, 193 crew and 63 others died. Fifty-six survivors were being taken on board the Norwegian ship *Alaska* (Captain Berge Mevatne) when she was torpedoed by U.510 (Krvkpt. Karl Neitzel). With an additional 20 survivors from the *Tasmania*, she managed to reach Lisbon on 11 November. (For details of other ships sunk in Convoy SL.125, see under *Nagpore*, P&O.)

Blue Star Line

ADELAIDE STAR. Launched at Burmeister & Wain's shipyard in Copenhagen on 30 December 1939 and seized by the Germans after they occupied Denmark in April 1940. Renamed *Seeburg* and used as a submarine depot and target practice ship until sunk by a Soviet torpedo boat in the Gulf of Danzig in December 1944. In 1947, Blue Star, which had paid almost all the instalments on the ship, sued Burmeister & Wain and the Danish War Risk Insurance for non-delivery and won their case on appeal. In 1952, the *Seeburg* was raised, repaired in Gydnia and entered the Far East Service of the Polish Ocean Lines as the *Dzierzynski*. Scrapped in 1963 after colliding with the Greek ship *Fouli* off Ushant and then breaking her back by striking a pier in the Scheldt.

AFRIC STAR (Captain C.R. Cooper). Sailed independently from Rio de Janeiro on 15 January 1941 bound for the UK via St Vincent in the Cape Verde Islands. Intercepted by the German raider *Kormoran* (Frgkpt. Theodor Detmers) on the 29th when in position 8°44′N 24°38′W. All 74 crew and 2 female passengers were picked up from the lifeboats by the *Kormoran* before she was sunk by shellfire. Some days later, the prisoners were transferred to the supply tanker *Nordmark* and subsequently to the *Portland* which landed them, and those from other ships, at Bordeaux on 14 March. The *Portland* had been captured by the Germans so that she had a prize crew on board when an attempt was made to take her over during the passage to Bordeaux. During the failed attempt, led by Able Seaman B. Lynch of the *Afric Star*, an AB and a passenger were shot dead. The *Kormoran* sank the Blue Funnel ship *Eurylocus* later on the same day that she sank the *Afric Star*.

ALMEDA STAR (Captain H.G. Howard). Damaged during an air raid on Liverpool when lying in the Mersey on 22 December 1940, but sailed independently for Buenos Aires on 15 January 1941. Torpedoed by U.96 (Kptlt Heinrich Lehmann-Willenbrock) at 7.45am on the 17th, and sank in 3 minutes in position 58°40′N 13°38′W after being shelled and receiving a fourth torpedo at 9.55am. As an SSSS message had alerted the authorities that she was under attack by a submarine, naval vessels were dispatched to the area, but not a trace of her was found. All 166 crew and 194 passengers died, including 142 members of the Fleet Air Arm.

ANDALUSIA STAR (Captain J.B. Hall). Sailed independently from Buenos Aires on 26 September 1942 bound for Liverpool via Freetown. Struck by 2 torpedoes from U.107 (Kptlt Harald Gelhaus) at 9.45pm on 6 October. All the lifeboats got away except No 2 which became suspended by its after fall, throwing its 40 occupants into the sea. Just before the last 2 boats were clear, a third torpedo struck the ship and she sank at about 10.25pm in position 06°38′N 15°46′W. Captain Hall and a few others, the last to leave, launched a raft and jumped into the sea after it. Next morning, the boats set sail for Freetown, but were picked up by the corvette HMS *Petunia* (Lt Cdr J.M. Rayner) on the morning of the 8th and landed at Freetown that evening. One passenger and 3 crew died, and 251 survived.

ARANDORA STAR (Captain E.W. Moulton). Bound for St John's, Newfoundland, sailing independently from Liverpool at about 4am on 1 July 1940 with 1,673 people on board – 174 crew, 200 guards, 479 German male internees, 86 German PoWs and 734 Italian male internees. Torpedoed in the engine room by U.47 (Kptlt Günther Prien), using her last remaining torpedo, at 6.15am on the 2nd, and sank at 7.20am in position 56°30′N 10°38′W. The ship's SSSS transmission was received by Malin Head radio station, and an RAF Coastal Command Sunderland flying boat arrived at about 9.30am to drop first aid appliances and cigarettes in watertight bags. The aircraft remained until the Canadian destroyer HMCS *St Laurent* (Cdr H.G. de Wolf) arrived at about 1pm. Eight hundred and sixty-eight people were rescued by the destroyer from 10 overcrowded lifeboats, rafts and from the oily water in which many died. The Master, 54 crew, 37 guards, 470 Italians and 243 Germans died – a total of 805. Captain Otto Burfeind, an internee and Master from the captured German ship *Adolph Woermann*, lost his life by remaining on board to help in the evacuation. The survivors were landed at Greenock, where several of the Italians had lived before internment.

The death toll of the *Arandora Star* was increased because she was overcrowded, had insufficient lifeboats, and barbed wire, placed to keep the internees in check, prevented access to the lifeboats. Captain Moulton had protested vehemently about these aspects before the ship sailed, but to no avail. It may also have been the case that there was an insufficient number of lifejackets, as many did not have one. In addition, some rafts could not be launched because they were secured by wire which required a special tool to loosen it and which could not always be found.

AUCKLAND STAR (Captain D.R. MacFarlane). Bound independently for Liverpool from Australia when sunk by 3 torpedoes from U.99 (Kptlt Otto Kretschmer) at about 5.30am on 28 July 1940 in position 52°17′N 12°32′W. Abandoned, in 4 lifeboats, after the first torpedo struck. One boat reached Slyne Head lighthouse, Co. Galway, on the 30th and the other 3 were within 12 miles of Dingle, Co. Kerry, the following day when seen by a fishing boat which towed them in. All 74 on board survived.

AVELONA STAR (Captain G.E. Hopper). Bound for London from South America, sailing in Convoy SL.36 which left Freetown on 15 June 1940. Torpedoed and sunk by U.43 (Kptlt Wilhelm Ambrosius) at about 9.30pm on 30 June in position 46°46′N 12°17′W. The survivors were picked up from the lifeboats by the *Beignon* (Captain W.J. Croome), which was herself sunk by U.30 (Kptlt Fritz-Julius Lemp) at 3am the next day. As there were insufficient lifeboats to accommodate all the survivors, many had to sit up to their waists in water on a raft or remain in the sea. An SSSS message had been sent and at about 5pm the destroyers HMS *Vesper* (Lt Cdr W.E.F. Hussey) and HMS *Windsor* (Lt Cdr P.D.H.R. Pelly) arrived to pick them up and carry them to Plymouth. The *Avelona Star* had a complement of 85. Three died when she was torpedoed and 3 more when the *Beignon* was torpedoed. Three of the *Beignon*'s complement of 30 died.

OTHER SHIPS SUNK AND DAMAGED IN CONVOY SL.36

Clan Ogilvy. Damaged by U.65 (Kptlt Hans-Gerrit von Stockhausen) but assisted by the destroyer HMS *Vesper* and the corvette HMS *Gladiolus* (Lt Cdr H.M.C. Sanders) arrived in Falmouth on 4 July.

Clearton. See under CHAPMAN, R., & SONS.

AVILA STAR (Captain J. Fisher). Sailed independently from Buenos Aires on 12 June 1942 bound for Freetown and Liverpool. On the 23rd, she picked up 3 men from a lifeboat of the *Lylepark* which had been sunk by the German raider *Michel* on the 11th. Sailed from Freetown on the 28th and torpedoed by U.201 (Kptlt Adalbert Schnee) shortly after 9pm on 5 July in position 38°04′N 22°48′W. Seven lifeboats were lowered, but some of the occupants of No 5 were thrown in the sea when it became suspended only by the bow fall and, as it was subsequently found to be leaking badly, it was abandoned. No 7 boat also came to grief when a second torpedo exploded under it, blowing its occupants into the water. When all the boats were away, the Master, the 1st Mate, the Junior 4th Engineer and a quartermaster jumped from the ship.

When, at about 9.30pm on 8 July, those in No 8 boat saw the lights of a fully illuminated ship, the 1st Officer Mr Tallack, who was in command, set off flares and signalled SOS with his torch. The ship, which turned out to be the neutral Portuguese destroyer *Lima*, picked them up and, as No 8 boat, the motorboat, had been in the company of boats 1 and 4 a few hours earlier, Mr Tallack advised Captain Rodriguez where to look for them. The boats were then found and the *Lima*, bound for Ponta Delgada in the Azores, continued on her way.

Mr Anson, the 2nd Mate, was in charge of No 2 boat and Mr Reid, the 1st Mate of the *Lylepark*, was in charge of No 6. The two boats managed to stay together until the night of the 11th. In bad weather, Mr Anson streamed his sea anchor, but, as Mr Reid was unable to stream his, the boats drifted apart. The subsequent passage of No 2 boat is a distressing one. Ten died, others had dysentery and all suffered from exposure and thirst. At 10am on 25 July, the mast of a ship was seen, and flares and burning clothing succeeded in attracting the attention of the Portuguese sloop *Pedro Nunes* which came to their rescue and landed them at Lisbon the next day.

Mr Reid's boat was never seen again and, out of a complement of 166 crew and 30 passengers (including the 3 survivors of the *Lylepark*) 73 died (including 10 in boat No 2, 1 on the *Pedro Nunes* and 2 in hospital in Lisbon). (See also under *Lylepark*, DENHOLM, J. & J., LTD.)

CALIFORNIA STAR (Captain S. Foulkes). Bound independently for Liverpool from New Zealand and Australia via the Panama Canal when struck by 2 torpedoes from U.515

(Kptlt Werner Henke) at about 7.30pm on 4 March 1943 in position 42°32′N 37°20′W. An SSSS message was immediately sent several times, but not acknowledged. A third torpedo struck when the boats were being lowered and a fourth one sank the ship at about 8pm. The U-boat then surfaced and Mr C. Stewart, the 2nd Mate, was taken prisoner before it made off. No 2 boat was being lowered when the third struck, destroying the boat and killing all its occupants. Only No 4 boat got away and all the other survivors were on rafts. Captain Foulkes, who had dived overboard, took charge of the boat and sailed it to Flores in the Azores, where they landed on the 15th. The boat originally contained 24 people, but 1 boy died during the passage and, on arrival, Captain Foulkes gave the authorities the position where they might find the rafts. But a search failed to find them. Of the ship's complement of 70 crew and 4 passengers, 51 died.

CANADIAN STAR (Captain R.D. Miller). Bound for Liverpool from Australia, sailing in Convoy HX.229 which left New York on 8 March 1943. Torpedoed twice by U.221 (Kptlt Hans-Hartwig Trojer) at about 2.40pm on the 18th and sank about half an hour later in approximate position 53°35′N 28°05′W. The after fall of No 3 boat ran free so that, hanging almost vertically, 3 passengers were tipped into the sea and lost; when it hit the rough sea, its remaining 12 occupants were also lost. Many people entered the waterlogged boat when it was righted, but most were washed out of it and only 5 or 6 of its occupants survived. No 1 boat was the only other boat which got away, and the 1st Mate Mr Hunt, in charge, rescued as many people from the rafts and the water as he could. The survivors in both lifeboats were picked up some two hours later by the corvettes HMS *Anemone* (Lt Cdr P.G.A. King) and *Pennywort* (Lt O.G. Stuart) which caught up with the convoy and subsequently landed them at Gourock. Of the 69 crew and 22 passengers on the *Canadian Star*, 32 died, including Captain Miller.

Forty-three U-boats were involved in the simultaneous attacks on Convoys HX.229 and SC.122, also bound for the UK and travelling on the same course some hours ahead. A total of 9 ships were sunk in SC.122 and 13 in HX.229. The U-boats were eventually driven off on the night of the 19th by RAF Liberators, one of which sank U.384.

OTHER SHIPS SUNK IN CONVOY HX.229

Coracero. See under DONALDSON LINE.

Elin K (Nor.) (Captain Robert Johannessen). Sunk by U.603 (Oblt Hans-Joachim Bertelsmann). All 40 picked up by HMS *Pennywort*.

Harry Luckenbach (US) (Captain Ralph McKinnon). Sunk by U.91 (Kptlt Heinz Walkerling). Abandoned in 3 lifeboats, but not picked up when seen by escorts and could not later been found by HMS *Anemone*. All 80 died.

Irénée Du Pont (US) (Captain Christian Simonson). Damaged by U.600 (Krvkpt. Bernhard Zurmühlen) and straggled. Sunk by U.91 (Kptlt Heinz Walkerling). Survivors picked up by the *Tekoa* and HMS *Mansfield*. Fourteen died and 70 survived.

James Oglethorpe (US) (Captain Albert W. Long). Liberty ship on maiden voyage. Torpedoed by U.758 (Kptlt Helmut Manseck). Forty-four abandoned ship without orders. All 14 in one boat were thrown into the water and drowned when the boat tipped in the falls, but 30 in the other boat were rescued by HMS *Pennywort*. Captain Long and the 29 men who remained on board tried to sail the ship to St John's but she was never heard of again. Forty-four died and 30 survived.

Matthew Luckenbach (US) (Captain A.N. Borden). Left the convoy the previous day because the Master thought they would be safer on their own. Found themselves in the area of Convoy SC.122. Severely damaged by U.527 (Kptlt Herbert Uhlig) and abandoned. Sunk later in the day by U.523 (Kptlt Werner Pietzsch). All 68 picked up by USCGC *Ingham* (Cdr George E. McCabe) and landed at Londonderry.

Nariva (Captain B.C Dodds). Torpedoed by U.600. Straggled and sunk by U.91. All 94 picked up by the corvette HMS *Anemone* (Lt Cdr P.G.A. King).

Southern Princess. See under SALVESEN, CHRISTIAN.

Terkoelei (Du.) Sunk by U.631 (Oblt Jürgen Krüger). Thirty-six died and 61 were picked up by HMS *Mansfield*.

Walter Q Gresham (US) (Captain B.W. Miller). Liberty ship on maiden voyage. Sunk by U.221. Twenty-seven died and 42 were picked up by HMS *Pennywort* and HMS *Anemone*.

William Eustis (US) (Captain Cecil Desmond). Torpedoed by U.435 (Kptlt Siegfried Strelow) and abandoned. All 72 were picked up by the destroyer HMS *Volunteer* which scuttled the ship.

Zaanland (Dutch with Lascar crew and British gunners) (Captain Gerardus Franken). Sunk by U.758 (Kptlt Helmut Manseck). All 53 picked up by the escorts.

U.631. Depth-charged by the corvette HMS *Sunflower* (A/Lt Cdr J. Plomer) and all 54 died.

CELTIC STAR (Captain J.H.A. Mackie). Bound independently for Montevideo from Freetown when torpedoed by Italian submarine *Giuseppe Finzi* (Tenente di Vascello (T.V.) (Lt) Mario Rossetto) at about 10.10pm on 29 March 1943 in position 04°16′N 17 °44′W. The order to vacate the engine room and abandon ship was given before a second torpedo struck, but the 3rd Engineer, Mr Nuttall, who was not on duty, risked his life by going below and stopping the engines. Two lifeboats were destroyed, but 2 others and life rafts were successfully lowered, and all from the latter, and in the sea, were transferred to the former. The submarine surfaced, but Captain Mackie managed to manoeuvre his boat so that the submarine did not see it in the darkness. It then came alongside the other boat, with the 1st Mate, Mr W. Tulip, in charge, and someone asked for the Captain. On being falsely told that he had been killed, he asked if there were any officers in the boat and, as all kept silent, took Able Seaman (AB) J. Pattison prisoner. The Italian then asked if they wanted anything and duly provided the cigarettes and matches requested. Both boats intended to sail independently for Freetown, but at 12.45pm the next day they were spotted by an

RAF Sunderland flying boat and at 5pm the anti-submarine escort trawler HMT *Wastwater* picked them up and carried them to Freetown. Of the 64 crew and 2 passengers, 2 crew died and 1 was taken prisoner.

DORIC STAR (Captain W. Stubbs). Sailing independently and bound for the UK from Sydney, Australia, via the Cape when intercepted by the *Admiral Graf Spee* (Captain Hans Langsdorff) in position 19°15′S 05°05′E on 2 December 1939. Mr W. Comber, 1st Radio Officer, immediately began sending an RRRR message indicating that the ship was being attacked by an unknown warship, until the *Admiral Graf Spee* signalled, 'Stop your wireless or I will open fire.' All were given 10 minutes to collect anything they could carry and taken to the *Admiral Graf Spee* before their ship was sunk by gunfire. On 6 December, the *Admiral Graf Spee* met the *Altmark* (Captain Dahl) and transferred most of her 196 prisoners to her, including 12 officers and 47 men from the *Doric Star*. Captain Stubbs and 4 officers were retained on the raider so that they were on board during the Battle of the River Plate which took place on the 13th. None of the prisoners was hurt during the engagement and all were released in Montevideo the following afternoon. Meanwhile, those on the *Altmark* were undergoing a miserable existence: inadequately fed, in crowded quarters and with insufficient exercise. It was not until the evening of 16 February that their ordeal ended when a party from the destroyer HMS *Cossack* (Captain P. Vian) boarded the ship illegally in Norwegian territorial waters, took them on board and landed them at Leith the following day. No lives were lost on the *Doric Star*.

DUNEDIN STAR (Captain R.B. Lee). Bound independently for the Middle East via Cape Town when on the night of 29 November 1942 she struck a submerged object which resulted in water flooding into Nos 2 and 3 holds and the engine room. As it was estimated that the ship would sink in about 3 hours, Captain Lee steered for the coast of South West Africa (Namibia), then a League of Nations territory under British mandate and administered by South Africa. An SOS was transmitted giving their position as 18°13′S 11°55′E, and acknowledged by Walvis Bay, and about three-quarters of an hour later, the ship was beached broadside on. The following morning, when the ship was rolling so that she might break her back, the motorboat succeeded in negotiating the surf and landed the passengers on the sandy beach. After a repair to the boat's rudder, it made 2 more successful trips, but, during the second of these it was caught in the surf so that it was thrown and broken up on the beach. (The ship, of course, had her non-motorised lifeboats, but the heavy surf made it impossible to use them.) The 63 on the beach, including 8 women, 3 babies and some elderly men, were now cut off from the ship with only the food and water from the motorboat and without shelter from the blazing sun.

The Norwegian ship *Temeraire* (Captain A. Toft) arrived in the evening of 1 December and, in the morning, her motorboat rescued 10 of the crew, but due to the motor stopping and the heavy swell and surf, it took the rescuers an hour and a half to row back to their ship. Utterly exhausted, they could do no more that day. The *Manchester Division* (Captain Hancock) had arrived during the early hours of the 2nd and the tug HMSAS *Sir Charles Elliot* (Captain H. Brewin) and the minesweeper HMSAS *Nerine* (Lt Van Rensburg) arrived later that day. The *Temeraire*'s motorboat then made 4 perilous journeys to take off the remaining 33 men left on board the stricken ship and carry them to the tug. Captain Lee and the Chief and Senior 2nd Engineers, the last to leave, were taken on board the *Nerine* which, short of food and water, sailed for Walvis Bay on the 4th. The others, together with those on the *Temeraire*, were put on board the *Manchester Division* and carried to Cape Town.

Everything possible was done to alleviate the harsh conditions suffered by those landed on that barren coast and with the aid of ships, land parties and the South African Air Force, all were brought to safety by the 24th. All on board the *Dunedin Star* survived, but 2 men died when the *Sir Charles Elliot* was driven ashore on her return journey.

EMPIRE JAVELIN (Managed by Blue Star for the MOWT) (Captain J. McLean). Escorted by the Free French frigate *L'Escarmouche* and bound for Le Havre from Southampton with 1,448 US troops on board when torpedoed in the afternoon of 28 December 1944. With the engine room and No 4 hold flooded, Captain McLean decided that the troops should be transferred to the escort, but when the French captain said that she was unable to come alongside, 2 lifeboats containing the wounded were sent away. However, at Captain McLean's insistence, the frigate eventually did as he asked and the order was given to abandon ship. With most of the men on board the frigate, she set about collecting those in the lifeboats, on rafts and in the water. All were then transferred to 2 landing craft which carried them to Le Havre. As a tug had been requested, Captain McLean remained on board with 6 officers and 3 men who volunteered to stay with him. But when the motionless ship was almost blown to bits by a second torpedo at about 5.15pm, all jumped into the water except the 3rd Mate, Mr David Robinson, who had gone to his cabin for something and was lost. Only 6, however, managed to reach a raft and were eventually rescued by a boat from the *L'Escarmouche*. Of the 3 Able Seamen, Douglas Southgate, Charles Shaw and William Vincent, all of whom were seen swimming from the sinking ship, only the latter survived, but I have been unable to ascertain how. None of the soldiers was lost, but 7 crew died, including 3 who had been in the engine room.

According to several sources, the *Empire Javelin* was torpedoed both times by U.772 (Kptlt Ewald Rademacher) and the U-boat herself was sunk off Portland Bill by an RCAF Wellington of No 407 Squadron on 30 December. This, however, is now refuted by the uboat.net which claims that she was depth-charged and sunk by HMS *Nyasaland* (Lt Cdr J. Scott) in the North Atlantic on 17 December 1944 in position 51°16′N 08°05′W, and that all 48 on board died.

EMPIRE LAKELAND (Managed by Blue Star for the MOWT) (Captain F. Gudgin). Sailed from New York in Convoy SC.121 on 23 February 1943 bound for the UK. Torpedoed and sunk in the late evening of 11 March when a straggler in rough seas, gales and snow squalls, by U.190 (Kptlt Max Wintermeyer) in approximate position 58°N 15°W. All 65 crew died and not a trace of the ship was found.

OTHER SHIPS SUNK IN CONVOY SC.121

Bonneville (Nor.) (Captain Finn Tessem). Commodore ship. By U.405 (Krvkpt. Rolf-Heinrich Hopman). Thirty-six died – several in the freezing water. Seven rescued, including 5 by the *Melrose Abbey* (Captain R. Good).

Coulmore. Torpedoed by U.229. Abandoned and subsequently towed to Clyde. Twenty-five died. Two picked up by HMCS *Dauphin* and 16 by USCGC *Bibb*.

Egyptian. See under ELLERMAN GROUP.

Empire Impala (Captain T.H. Munford). Ordered to pick up survivors of the *Egyptian*. Sunk by U.591 (Kptlt Hans-Jürgen Zetzsche). All 48 died.

Fort Lamy (Captain W. Evans). By U.527 (Kptlt Herbert Uhlig) when straggling. Forty-six died. Five picked up by the corvette HMS *Vervain* (Lt H.P. Crail) on the 20th and landed at St John's, Newfoundland.

Guido. See under ELLERMAN GROUP.

Leadgate (Captain E.H. Halliday). By U.642 (Kptlt Herbert Brünning) when straggling. All 26 died.

Malantic (US) (Captain P.H. Lang). By U.409. Twenty-five died. Twenty-two picked up by the *Melrose Abbey*.

Milos (Swed.). By U.530 (Kptlt Kurt Lange) when straggling. All 30 died.

Nailsea Court (Captain R.J. Lee). By U.229 (Oblt Robert Schetelig). Forty-five died. One picked up by the *Melrose Abbey* and landed at Gourock on the 13th. Three rescued by the corvette HMCS *Dauphin* (T/Lt M.H. Wallace) and landed at Gourock on the same day.

Rosewood (Captain R. Taylor). By U.409 (Oblt Hanns-Ferdinand Massmann). All 42 died.

Vojvoda Putnik (Yugo.). By U.591 (Kptlt Hans-Jürgen Zetzsche) when straggling. All 44 died.

EMPIRE STAR (Captain S.N. Capon). Sailed independently from Liverpool on 20 October 1942 bound for East London, South Africa. Torpedoed at about 3.45pm on the 23rd by U.615 (Kptlt Ralph Kapitzky) when in position 48°14′N 26°22′W. One lifeboat was destroyed, but the other 3 got away and were lying off the ship when a second torpedo struck and sank her. Captain Capon decided that the boats should stay together, but after a night of foul weather his boat had disappeared and was never seen again. Having survived the night riding to a sea anchor, during which the tiller broke and oars were used to steer and to keep the boat's head into the wind, the 1st Mate, Mr L. Vernon, could see no other boats. Later that morning, however, a boat was seen some distance away, but attempts to steer towards it failed. With the weather as wild as ever, the sea anchor was again streamed and the boat was drifting before the wind when at 6.15pm they were picked up by the sloop HMS *Black Swan*. An SSSS message had been transmitted from the ship, and the other boat, with the 3rd Mate, Mr Moscrop-Young, in charge, was also picked up by the *Black Swan*. Forty-two died, including 6 passengers; 61 survived, including 13 passengers.

IMPERIAL STAR (Captain S.J.C. Phillips). One of the 9 ships in heavily escorted Operation Halberd, Convoy GM.2, which sailed from Gibraltar during the night of 24/25 September 1941 bound for Malta. When off Cape Bon on the 27th, struck by an Italian aerial torpedo at 8.32pm and rudder and propellers blown off. Three hundred troops taken on board the destroyer HMS *Heythrop* (Lt Cdr R.S. Stafford). Taken in tow by HMS *Oribi*, but when this failed, all 141 remaining on board transferred to the destroyer before she was scuttled. No lives lost and all remaining on board landed in Malta. The battleship *Nelson* was damaged in the operation, while the other 8 ships, including the *Dunedin Star*, reached Malta.

IONIC STAR. Bound for Liverpool from Brazil when wrecked in the Mersey, where her remains can still be seen on Formby beach. No further details.

MELBOURNE STAR (Captain J.B. Hall, ex-*Andalusia Star*). Sailed independently from Greenock on 24 March 1943 bound for Australia via the Panama Canal. Torpedoed by U.129 (Krvkpt. Hans-Ludwig Witt) when in position 28°05′N 57°30′W and sank within 2 minutes, as explosives in her cargo blew up. Eleven survivors scrambled on to 2 rafts, one of which was never seen again. The other raft, with 4 men, drifted until its somewhat emaciated occupants were picked up by a US flying boat on 9 May and landed in Bermuda. One hundred and twenty-five died, including 31 passengers. Four survived.

NAPIER STAR (Captain W. Walsh). Sailed independently from Liverpool on 15 December 1940 bound for New Zealand via the Panama Canal. Torpedoed by U.100 (Kptlt Joachim Schepke) at about 4pm on the 18th when in position 58°58′N 23°13′W. Four lifeboats got away before she was sunk by a second torpedo, but only that commanded by the 2nd Mate, Mr J.W. Thompson, survived the night by baling hard and riding to an improvised sea anchor after the original one was carried away. Five people died in the boat before it was picked up by the Swedish ship *Vaalaren* on the 20th, and subsequently reached Liverpool on the 23rd. Seventy-one died, including 12 passengers. Fourteen survived.

PACIFIC STAR (Captain G.L. Evans). Bound for the UK, sailing from Freetown in Convoy SL.125 on 16 October 1942. Torpedoed by U.509 (Krvkpt. Werner Witte) at about 10.30pm on the 27th when about 170 miles north-west of the Canary Islands. Attempted to keep up with the convoy, but by 2am the next day they were alone and, as the ship was going down by the head, Captain Evans set a course for Gibraltar. At 3.30am, however, when the weather was making it impossible to steer for Gibraltar, a course was set for the Canaries. The crew did their utmost to save the stricken ship, but by the evening she was waterlogged and helpless. An SOS was transmitted, but not acknowledged, before the crew abandoned her in 3 lifeboats in position 29°21′N 19°28′W. The boats commanded by the Captain and the 2nd Mate landed at Santa Cruz de la Palma. The other boat landed at Tenerife and its 25 occupants were taken to Santa Cruz de la Palma by the Spanish ship *Ciudad de Valencia*. All 96 were carried to Gibraltar by the Spanish tanker *Campilo*. None died. (For details of ships sunk in Convoy SL.125, see under *Nagpore*, P&O.)

RODNEY STAR (Captain S.J.C. Phillips). Sailed from Buenos Aires bound for Glasgow via Santos, Brazil, and Freetown. Torpedoed by U.105 (Kptlt Georg Schewe) at 5.50am on 16 May 1941 when in position 05°03′N 19°02′W. Four lifeboats got away before a second torpedo struck, but it took a third one and shelling by the U-boat to sink the ship. Those in the boats commanded by the 2nd and 3rd Mates were picked up on the 18th by the *Batna* and landed at Dakar. The occupants of the 1st Mate's boat were picked up by a French passenger ship on the 22nd and landed at Dakar, while those in the Captain's boat were rescued on the same day by the destroyer HMS *Boreas* (Lt Cdr D.H. Maitland-Makgill Crichton) and landed at Takoradi. All 83 survived.

ROYAL STAR (Captain T.F. McDonald). Bound for Malta, sailing from Algiers during the afternoon of 20 April 1944 and joined Convoy UGS.38 at 5.50pm in position 36°54′N 03°12′E. At about 9pm, when it was almost completely dark and the convoy was in approximate position 37°02′N 03°41′E, German torpedo bombers attacked. The *Royal Star* was struck between the engine room and the stokehold. One man was killed and all except Captain McDonald abandoned ship. After the tug *Athlete* had made an unsuccessful attempt to tow the ship the following morning, the Captain jumped into the sea and was picked up and carried to Algiers by HM Motor Launch 568. One died and 72 survived.

OTHER SHIPS SUNK THAT NIGHT BY AERIAL TORPEDOES

Paul Hamilton. US Liberty troopship. All 580 died when the ship, also carrying explosives, blew up.

USS *Lansdale* (Lt Cdr Douglas M. Swift). Destroyer. Forty-seven died and 235 were picked up by the destroyers USS *Newell* (Lt Cdr Russell J. Roberts) and USS *Menges* (Lt Cdr Frank M. McCabe) and taken to Algiers. (The *Menges* was herself torpedoed and severely damaged by U.371 (Oblt Horst-Arno Fenski) on 3 May with the loss of 31 men.)

SHIPS DAMAGED THAT NIGHT BY AERIAL TORPEDOES

Samite (Captain Leonard Eccles). British Liberty ship, towed to Algiers. The author was on the *Samite* and details are given in his book *Life Aboard a Wartime Liberty Ship*.

Stephen F. Austin. US Liberty ship, towed to Algiers.

SCOTTISH STAR (Captain E.N. Rhodes). Bound for Montevideo, sailing from Liverpool on 2 February 1942 in Convoy ON.63 which dispersed in position 42°08′N 55°20′W. Sailing independently when torpedoed, shelled and sunk by the Italian submarine *Luigi Torelli* (Capitano di Corvetta (C.C.) (Lt Cdr) Antonio De Giacomo) shortly after 9am on the 19th in position 13°24′N 49°36′W. Survivors in 3 of the lifeboats were picked up by the cruiser HMS *Diomede* and landed at Port of Spain, Trinidad. The other boat, commanded by Mr M.C. Watson, the 1st Mate, reached Barbados on the 27th. Four engine room staff died; 69 survived.

SULTAN STAR (Captain W.H. Bevan). Sailed independently from Buenos Aires on 27 January 1940 bound for Liverpool. Torpedoed and sunk by U.48 (Kptlt Herbert Schultze) shortly before 5pm on 14 February in position 48°54′N 10°03′W. One man died. As an SSSS message had been sent and acknowledged, 71 were picked up from the lifeboats about half an hour later by the destroyers HMS *Whitshed* (Cdr E.R. Conder) and HMS *Vesper* (Lt Cdr W.F.E. Hussey) which landed them at Plymouth. The 1st Radio Officer, Mr P.G. Winsor, who almost went down with the ship, later lost his life on the *Empire Lakeland*.

TACOMA STAR (Captain R.G. Whitehead). Sailed independently from Montevideo on 4 January 1942 bound for Liverpool via Hampton Roads and Halifax, Nova Scotia. Torpedoed and sunk by U.109 (Kptlt Heinrich Bleichrodt) at 3.30am on 1 February in position 37°33′N 69°21′W. In response to her SSSS message, the destroyer USS *Roe* sought survivors without success. All 94 died.

TUSCAN STAR (Captain E.N. Rhodes). Sailed independently from Santos bound for Liverpool via Freetown when torpedoed and sunk by U.109 at about 11.30pm on 6 September 1942 in position 01°34′N 11°39′W. The U-boat picked up the 2nd Radio Officer, Mr G.H. Gill, from the water and took him prisoner, and noticing women and children in one of the lifeboats, supplied tinned food. Those in the Captain's boat were picked up by the *Otranto* at about 4.30pm the following day and landed at Freetown on the 10th. The other 2 boats, commanded by the 1st and 3rd Mates, reached the coast of Liberia. Fifty crew and 3 passengers died, 1 was taken prisoner and 60 survived.

VIKING STAR (Captain J.E. Mills). Sailed independently from Montevideo on 9 August 1942 bound for Liverpool via Freetown. Torpedoed at about 7.45pm on 25 August by U.130 (Krvkpt. Ernst Kals) in position 06°00′N 14°00′W. The ship was abandoned and the survivors were in 2 lifeboats, one of which was damaged and had to be discarded, and on rafts when a second torpedo sank the ship. As they had communicated with a Sunderland flying boat some 5 hours earlier, Mr F MacQuiston, the 1st Mate and officer in charge, decided to remain where they were for 24 hours. There were 2 rafts beside the boat and in the morning these were lashed together to act as a sea anchor. Two other rafts had been seen some distance away during the evening, but these had disappeared and the one containing Captain Mills was never heard of again.

As the African coast was 150 miles to the east, the boat left the rafts on the morning of the 27th in an attempt to reach it and summon help for those on the rafts. At 3am on the 29th, the boat and its 36 occupants were hurtled on to a sandy beach in Sierra Leone. It was a desolate part of the coast, but after many vicissitudes they sailed home from Freetown on the *Otranto*, along with the survivors of the *Tuscan Star*.

Mr J. Rigiani, the 3rd Mate, who had 11 men under his command on the rafts, set an eastern course and as one of the rafts was waterlogged they took 6-hour spells on each raft. Food, including malted milk tablets, and drink were strictly rationed and the occasional fish that they caught was eaten raw. On the morning of 1 September, another raft was in sight and after 4 hours' hard paddling they took Able Seaman R. Boardman off it. The raft was then lashed to the other 2 and was a bonus as it contained food and water. At daylight on 4 September, when they were about half a mile from the shore, they broke up one of the rafts in order to use its floorboards as paddles. When a breaker caught them and flung them towards the steeply shelving beach, they swam for it. Sadly, Mr Boardman did not reach it; perhaps he was struck by a raft being thrown among them. Locals who found them lying exhausted on the beach told them they were in Liberia and took them to their village where they supplied them with food and drink. Next day, when walking towards the village of Latia, they caught up with Mr P. Sullivan, the 1st Radio Officer, who had been alone on a raft until it drifted ashore. From Latia, they were taken by a Pan-American

Airways launch to the town of Cape Mount for repatriation. Eight died and 53 survived.

WELLINGTON STAR (Captain T. Williams). Sailed independently from Melbourne on 12 May 1940 bound for the UK via the Panama Canal. Left Las Palmas on 13 June and was torpedoed at about 11am on the 16th by U.101 (Kptlt Fritz Frauenheim) in position 42°39′N 17°01′W. After the crew had abandoned ship in 4 lifeboats, the U-boat put 3 more torpedoes into her and shelled her before she sank. Those in 3 of the boats were picked up on the 24th by the French ship *Pierre LD* and landed at Casablanca, while the 17 in the other boat reached Figueira da Foz, near Oporto, the same day. All 69 survived.

Booth Line

ANSELM (Captain A. Elliott). Troopship bound for Freetown from Gourock accompanied by the survey ship HMS *Challenger* (Cdr W.C. Jenk), AMC HMS *Cathay* (Captain C. McC. Merewether), and corvettes HMS *Petunia* (Lt Cdr G.V. Legassick), HMS *Lavender* (Lt Cdr J. Whayman) and HMS *Starwort* (Lt Cdr N.W. Duck). Torpedoed twice and sunk by U.96 (Kptlt Heinrich Lehmann-Willenbrock) on the morning of 5 July 1941 in position 44°25′N 28°35′W. Two hundred and fifty-four died. One thousand and sixty-two carried to Lagos by HMS *Cathay*. U.96 was depth-charged and severely damaged by HMS *Petunia* and HMS *Lavender*.

CRISPIN. Requisitioned by the Admiralty and became ocean boarding vessel HMS *Crispin* (A/Cdr B. Moloney). Together with the corvette HMS *Arbutus* (Lt Cdr H. Lloyd-Williams), the armed yacht HMS *Philante* and the rescue ship *Copeland*, detached from Convoy OB.280 to join Convoy SC.20 when torpedoed by U.107 (Krvkpt. Günther Hessler) at 11.33pm on 3 February 1941. Abandoned and sank the next day in position 56°38′N 20°05′W. Twenty died. Eight were picked up by the *Copeland* and 113 by the destroyer HMS *Harvester* (Lt Cdr M. Thornton) and landed at Liverpool. *Ringhorn* (Nor.) (Captain Trygve Terkelsen), a straggler from Convoy OB.280, was torpedoed and sunk by U.52 (Kptlt Otto Salman). Fourteen died. Five were picked up by the corvette HMS *Camellia* (Lt Cdr A.E. Willmot) and landed at Greenock on 9 February.

FORT LA MAUNE (Managed for the MOWT) (Captain J.W. Binns). Sailed independently from New York bound for Bari, Italy, and India via the Suez Canal. Torpedoed and sunk by U.188 (Kptlt Siegfried Lüdden) at 8.16pm on 25 January 1944 in position 13°04′N 56°30′E. All 56 spent 14 days in a lifeboat and landed in Yemen. Seen by a Catalina flying boat so that HMS *Nigella* (T/Lt C.L.L. Davies) picked them up and landed them at Aden on 6 February.

POLYCARP (Captain A. Allan). Bound independently for Heysham and Liverpool from Para, Brazil, when torpedoed and sunk by U.101 (Kptlt Fritz Frauenheim) at 3.05am on 2 June 1940 in position 49°19′N 05°35′W. All 43 were picked up by the *Espiguette* (Fr.) and landed at Newlyn.

Bristol City Line

(CHARLES HILL & SONS, BRISTOL)

BRISTOL CITY (Captain A.L. Webb). Bound for New York from Bristol, sailed from Milford Haven on 21 April 1943 and joined Convoy OBS.5. Torpedoed and sunk by U.358 (Kptlt Rolf Manke) at about 4.25am on 5 May when in position 54°00′N 43°55′W. Fifteen died. Thirty-four were picked up by the corvette HMS *Loosestrife* (Lt H.A. Stonehouse) and landed at St John's, Newfoundland. (For details of other ships sunk in Convoy OBS.5 see under *Dolius*, HOLT, ALFRED, & CO.)

MONTREAL CITY (Captain E.R.W. Chanter). Straggling from Convoy ON.152 on 21 December 1942 when torpedoed twice by U.591 (Kptlt Hans-Jürgen Zetzsche) and sank at 4.09am in position 50°23′N 38°00′W. The U-boat witnessed the crew abandoning the ship in 3 lifeboats, but they were never seen again. All 40 died. *Oropos* (Gr.) straggled from Convoy ON.152 and went missing. Believed to be the ship torpedoed and sunk by U.621 (Oblt Max Kruschka) at about 2.30am on 18 December in approximate position 51°N 37°W. All 34 died.

TORONTO CITY (Captain E.J. Garlick). A weather reporting ship sailing independently when torpedoed and sunk by U.108 (Krvkpt. Klaus Scholtz) at 6.25pm on 1 July 1941 in position 47°03′N 30°00′W. The Germans questioned survivors on rafts and clinging to debris, but they were never seen again. All 43 died.

British India Steam Navigation Co. (BI)

ASKA. Having called at Freetown a fortnight earlier, the *Aska*, capable of 20 knots and unescorted, sailed from Bathurst on 7 September 1940 bound for London and carrying 350 French troops. She was attacked by a German aircraft and struck by 3 bombs when between Rathlin Island and Maiden's Rock at 2am on the 16th. Survivors were picked up from lifeboats by trawlers but transferred to the minesweeper HMS *Jason* which took them to Greenock. No lives lost.

BANKURA. Arrived in Tobruk, from Alexandria, with ammunition and stores at 10am on 21 April 1941. Air-raid sirens sounded as she was discharging, but it was 6.30pm before German dive bombers attacked. A bomb blew a large hole in the side of No 1 hold, filling it with water, and the Master ran the ship ashore. When she was further damaged by bombs the next day, the naval authorities ordered the crew to abandon her. All were taken to Alexandria on a small schooner captured from the Italians. No lives were lost.

BARODA. In Bombay on 14 April 1944 when at about 1.30pm the *Fort Stikine*, loaded with explosives, went on fire. At 4.06pm an explosion occurred on the latter, showering the *Baroda* with debris and causing a fire, and a second one at 4.33pm destroyed her. Owing to the Lascar crew being paid off earlier in the day, only a few officers remained on the *Baroda*, and the Chief Engineer, Mr J. Stewart, was the only man killed. (For details of the carnage caused by the explosion, see under *Fort Stikine*, PORT LINE.)

CALABRIA (Managed for the MOWT) (Captain D. Lonie). Bound for Liverpool from Calcutta, sailing in Convoy SL.56 which left Freetown on 21 November 1940. Straggling when torpedoed three times by U.103 (Krvkpt. Viktor Schütze) between 8.58pm and 9.06pm on 8 December 1940 and sank in position 52°43′N 18°07′W. All 360 died, including 230 Lascars who were to crew other ships.

CHAKDINA. Requisitioned by the Admiralty, HMS *Chakdina* carried men of the Black Watch from Alexandria to reinforce Tobruk. She landed them on 4 December 1941 and fully illuminated to identify her as a hospital ship, which she was not, sailed for Alexandria the next day with 380 wounded, medical staff and about 100 prisoners, including General Von Ravenstein of the Afrika Korps. She was torpedoed by an Italian plane at 9am and sank within minutes in position 32°11′N 24°30′E. Survivors were picked up by the destroyer HMS *Farndale* (Cdr S.H. Carlill) and landed at Alexandria on the 7th. All but one of the medical staff survived. Seventy-nine died.

CHAKLA. Converted into a naval auxiliary. HMS *Chakla* was at anchor in Tobruk harbour when bombed and sunk on 29 April 1941. No further details.

CHANTALA. Converted into a naval auxiliary. HMS *Chantala* was mined and sunk off Tobruk on 7 December 1941. No further details.

CHILKA (Captain W. Bird). A troopship on her way to Padang in Sumatra to embark refugees when on 11 March 1942 she was fired upon by a Japanese submarine in position 00°23′N 95°41′E. *Chilka* returned the fire, but after the submarine had scored several hits and further resistance was futile, Captain Bird ran up the signal 'I am about to abandon ship'. The firing then ceased and 5 lifeboats got away. One man died in Captain Bird's boat before it sailed 8 miles up a creek on Nias Island early on the 16th. After several hours resting, they set out on foot and carrying the wounded at 1am the next day. Eventually, they reached the Mission Hospital at Batak Nias Zending where the wounded were cared for. Those from 2 other boats were already at the hospital and, on the 23rd, the occupants of the remaining 2 boats joined them.

Japanese airborne troops had landed at Palembang on 14 February and the Dutch East Indies had surrendered to the Japanese on 9 March; Captain Bird knew their troops would soon be arriving on Nias, so he procured a steel lifeboat from the District Officer. Together with some engineers, the ship's surgeon and a gunner, they set sail on 31 March and, on 4 May, were picked up by a Greek ship 35 miles east of Madras and taken to Karachi. Seven died. Although the Japanese were noted for their barbarity, the seacunny in No 5 boat reported that the crew of the submarine gave them water and biscuits and told them the course to steer.

CRANFIELD. On passage from Calcutta to Suez via Madras on 23 November 1942 when torpedoed and sunk by the Japanese submarine I-166 in position 08°26′N 76°42′E. When a second torpedo destroyed her engine room, killing its occupants, the survivors took to the lifeboats and rafts. These were taken in tow by fishing canoes and landed at the village of Varkala in Travancore. No further details.

DEVON. Bound for New Zealand from Newcastle upon Tyne when intercepted on 19 August 1941 by the German raider *Komet* (KptzS. Robert Eyssen) in approximate position 4°S 92°W. Before she was sunk by the raider, all 144 were permitted to leave. The 31 Europeans were taken on board the *Komet* and the 113 Lascars to the captured Dutch ship *Kota Nopan*. On leaving the area, both ships were refuelled by the tanker and supply ship *Münsterland* and after rendezvousing with the raider *Atlantis* (KptzS. Bernhard Rogge) east of New Zealand, set sail for home via Cape Horn on 24 September. On 17 October, the two ships parted company, the *Kota Nopan* reaching Bordeaux on 17 November. The slower *Komet* reached Le Havre on the 27th, and while being escorted by motor torpedo boats and minesweepers was attacked by British bombers and MTBs. One bomb hit the ship, but did little damage, and she arrived at Cuxhaven at 7.15am on the 29th, where the prisoners were landed.

DUMANA (Captain O. West). Ferrying RAF personnel to various places on the West African coast, sailed from Freetown in Convoy STL.8 on 23 December 1943 bound for Takoradi. At 8.33pm on Christmas Eve, torpedoed and sunk by U.515 (Kptlt Werner Henke) in position 04°27′N 06°58′W. Thirty-nine died and the survivors spent the night in lifeboats, on rafts and clinging to anything that floated. The Master, 114 crew and 15 RAF men were picked up by the trawler HMS *Arran* (Lt W.G.N. Aplin) and the whaler HMS *Southern Pride* (Lt G.B. Angus) and landed at Takoradi on Christmas Day.

DUMRA (Captain W.C. Cripps). Unescorted and bound for Durban from Tulear in Madagascar when torpedoed by U.198 (KptzS. Werner Hartmann) at 7.50am on 5 June 1943 in position 28°15′S 33°20′E. The lifeboats were lowered, but those in them were ordered to stand by in case the ship did not sink. When a second torpedo struck about 10 minutes later, the men still on board were flung into the sea and the ship sank immediately. With the exception of the 5th Engineer, Mr S.G. Barnes, all were picked up by the lifeboats, but some died from their wounds, including Captain Cripps. The boats landed at Santa Lucia Bay, Natal, the next morning. Twenty-six died and 67 survived.

The Chief Engineer, Mr H.T. Graham, had been taken prisoner by the U-boat and when it sank the US Liberty ship *William King* the next day, Captain O.H. Reed joined him. Both were transferred to the German supply ship *Charlotte Schliemann* on the 26th and subsequently handed over to the Japanese in Batavia (Djakarta). On 18 September 1944, they were on the hell ship *Junyo Maru*, en route from Tanjung Priok (the port for Batavia) to Padang in Sumatra, when she was torpedoed and sunk by the submarine HMS *Tradewind* (Lt Cdr S.L.C. Maydon) in position 2°52′S 101°12′E. Of the 4,200 slave labourers on board, only about 200 survived; of the 2,300 Allied prisoners, only about 680 survived. Mr Graham and Captain Reed were among those who died.

ERINPURA (Captain P.F. Cotter). Commodore ship of a convoy of 23 ships bound for Malta from Alexandria. On the evening of 1 May 1943, two single enemy planes were driven off before the main attacks began at 7.50pm. The tanker *British Trust* (Captain J. Hall) was sunk by a torpedo bomber prior to the *Erinpura* being struck by a bomb which exploded in a forward hold. Water flooded in and she sank within 5 minutes. Sixty-five of the 190 crew died, and of the 1,025 troops on board only 203 survived, including 67 of the 700 Basuto soldiers of the African Auxiliary Pioneer Corps. The high loss of life among the troops was due to their being ordered below decks for protection during the attacks. Using their searchlights, escort ships picked up survivors who were landed at Benghazi the following morning.

FULTALA. Torpedoed and sunk by the Japanese submarine I-3 in Indian Ocean on 7 April 1942 in position 06°52′N 76°54′E. Survivors were picked up after 10 days in a lifeboat. No further details.

GAIRSOPPA (Captain G. Hyland). Bound for London from Calcutta, sailing from Freetown in Convoy SL.64 on 30 January 1941. In bad weather, left the convoy on 14 February when making for the nearest port to replenish her coal bunkers was torpedoed and sunk by U.101 (Kptlt Ernst Mengersen) at 0008 hours on the 17th in position 50°00′N 14°00′W. Owing to the foremast being brought down and carrying away the aerials, an SSSS message could not be transmitted. Two or three lifeboats were launched, but only the one commanded by Mr R.H. Ayres, the 2nd Mate, was heard of again. Although it originally contained 35, only 3 Europeans and 4 Lascars remained alive when The Lizard was sighted on 1 March. But while the exhausted men were trying to reach a beach between cliffs in the rough sea, the boat capsized and all but Mr Ayres and another European were drowned. The latter succeeded in swimming to rocks, but was washed off and disappeared. Four evacuee girls had seen what was happening and alerted the authorities. Lifeboat men dragged Mr Ayres out of the surf and he was taken to Helston Cottage Hospital. Eighty-four died. The *Simaloer* (Du.) detached from the convoy on 2 March and was sunk by German aircraft on the 3rd. Two died.

GAMBHIRI. Sunk as a blockship at Scapa Flow on 5 November 1939.

GANDARA. In Calcutta when due to a false threat of Japanese air raids the authorities ordered all ships to clear the port. Sailed for the UK via the Cape on 5 April 1942 in an unescorted convoy of 6 ships, all of which were sunk and which included the *Indora* and the *Malda*. The Blue Funnel ship *Dardanus* (Captain A. English) which had left Calcutta on the 2nd was damaged by planes from the Japanese carrier *Ryujo* on the 5th and, later that day, the *Gandara* began towing her to Madras. At 7.30pm on the 6th, however, a high-level plane bombed the ships and shortly afterwards warships approached and began shelling from a distance of about 3 miles. The *Gandara* slipped the tow and when shells from the cruisers *Mogami* and *Mikuma* repeatedly hit both ships they were abandoned. The warships then closed and sank both ships in position 16°00′N 82°20′E. Thirteen of *Gandara*'s crew died, but all on the *Dardanus* survived. The *Shinkuang*, managed by BI for the MOWT, was sunk by the Japanese warships on the same day.

GARMULA (Captain R.C. Brown). Homeward bound from Melbourne, sailing independently for Freetown from Cape Town on 6 July 1942. Torpedoed and sunk by U.752 (Krvkpt. Karl-Ernst Schroeter) on the 23rd in position 05°32′N 14°45′W. Twenty-one died. Sixty-seven were picked up by the trawler HMS *Pict* (Lt Cdr W.N.H. Faichney) and landed at Freetown.

GHARINDA (Captain R. Stone). On passage from Glasgow to New York in Convoy ONS.5 when torpedoed and sunk at 9.50pm on 5 May 1943 by U.266 (Kptlt Ralf von Jessen) in position 53°10′N 44°40′W. All 91 were picked up by the frigate HMS *Tay* (Lt Cdr R.E. Sherwood) and landed at St John's, Newfoundland. (For details of other ships lost in Convoy ONS.5, see under *Dolius*, HOLT, ALFRED, & CO.)

GOALPARA. Having brought a cargo from Alexandria to Piraeus, she was damaged when the *Clan Fraser* was bombed during a German air raid on the port and blew up at about 3.30am on 7 April 1941. Bombed and beached when in Eleusis Bay on the 15th; the crew, led by the 1st Mate, Mr G.R. Mudford, walked through Athens and then to the Corinth Canal, 40 miles away. A ship carried them to Crete from where another vessel took them back to Alexandria. All survived. (See under *Clan Fraser*, CLAN LINE, and under *Quiloa* below.)

GOGRA (Captain J. Drummond). Sailed from Glasgow in Convoy OS.45 on 26 March 1943 bound for Bombay and Karachi. At 6.55pm on 2 April, torpedoed and sunk by U.124 (Krvkpt. Johann Mohr) in position 41°02′N 15°39′W. She went down in about a minute, taking her extra 1st Mate, Mr G.R. Mudford (ex-*Goalpara*), with her. But on rising to the surface he survived over 3 hours in the freezing water before being picked up by HMS *La Malouine* (Lt V.D.F. Bidwell) and landed at Freetown. Eighty-two died, including Captain Drummond. Eight were picked up by the *Danby* but transferred to the Canadian ship *New Northland* and landed at Freetown. U.124 also sank the *Katha*. (See under HENDERSON LINE.)

GOLCONDA. Went aground in the Karnafuli River near Chittagong on 24 February 1940, and became a total loss.

HARESFIELD (Captain T.E.C. Earl). On passage from Aden to Calcutta and sailing independently when torpedoed and sunk by the Japanese submarine I-29 on 9 September 1942 in position 13°05′N 54°35′E. No 1 lifeboat, commanded by the 1st Mate, Mr G.E. Hopkins, reached Karachi on the 23rd. Those in No 3 boat, commanded by Captain Earl, were picked up by the *Jalaratna* on the 25th and taken to Aden. No 6 boat was taken in tow by an Arab dhow on the 15th and landed at Muscat. On reaching land, after 10 days on their own, those in No 5 boat, commanded by the 2nd Mate, Mr M.G. Brookfield, received assistance from Arabs, trekked overland and were taken to Muscat by a dhow. They were then carried to Karachi by a Chinese coastal steamer. All survived.

HATIMURA (Captain W. Putt). In Convoy SC.107 bound for the UK from North America when torpedoed and severely damaged by U.132 (Kptlt Ernst Vogelsang) at 0015 hours on 4 November 1942. On fire and abandoned when sunk about 3 hours later by U.442 (Frgkpt. Hans-Joachim Hesse). U.132 was still close by, and when the high explosives on the *Hatimura* exploded as she went under, she too went down with her crew of 47. Three of the *Hatimura*'s crew died. Eighty-seven were picked up by the US Navy tugs *Pessacus* and *Uncas* and transferred to the rescue ship *Stockport* (Captain Ernest Fea) which landed them at Reykjavik on the 8th. (For details of other ships sunk in Convoy SC.107, see under *Jeypore*, P&O.)

HOMEFIELD (Captain S. Kiely). Having discharged military supplies at Piraeus, the *Homefield* was returning to Port Said in Convoy AS.23 when it was attacked by 9 German bombers on 2 April 1941. Struck by 2 bombs, she was abandoned and then sunk by the destroyer HMS *Nubian*. Survivors were picked up by the destroyer HMAS *Voyager*. No further details. The Greek ship *Coulouras Xenos* suffered a similar fate.

INDORA. Bound for Mauritius, sailing from Calcutta on 5 April 1942, in the same unescorted convoy as the *Gandara* and *Malda*. Attacked by a Japanese cruiser squadron the next day, and seeing other ships being shelled and sunk, her Master ordered the ship to be abandoned. It was a wise decision, as the lifeboats had just pulled clear when the cruisers *Mikuma* and *Mogami* and the destroyer *Amagiri* sank the ship. After picking up survivors from the *Malda* and the Blue Funnel ship *Autolycus*, the Master set a course for Chandbali, north of False Point in Orissa, where he knew there were smooth landings; a factor which he considered important because two Chinese were seriously wounded. There were now 53 in his boat and because some Lascars from other ships gave trouble, he landed at the nearest place. The troublemakers immediately absconded and when the others reached Rajpara the next day, arrangements were made for their return to Calcutta. Lives were lost, but no details ascertained.

JUNA. Converted into a naval auxiliary and renamed HMS *Fiona*. Plying between Alexandria and Sidi Barrani, bombed and sunk on 18 April 1941. Several killed, but no details.

KARANJA. Took part in Operation Torch (the invasion of North Africa) and one of the troopships which sailed from the Clyde in Convoy KMF.1 on 26 October 1942. Landed troops at Sidi Ferruch and after a brief call at Algiers was commodore ship of a convoy to Bougie where air raids began as the troops were being ferried ashore on 11 November. When the *Awatea* and *Cathay* were sunk, many survivors of the latter made for and were taken on board the *Karanja*. At dawn the next morning, bombs struck the *Karanja*, destroying the engine room, killing those in it and setting her on fire. The survivors were taken to the Ecole Supérieure where they remained until boarding the *Strathnaver* for the passage back to the Clyde. No details of casualties. (See also under *Cathay*, P&O.)

MALDA (Captain H.M. Edmondson). Bound for Colombo, sailing from Calcutta on 5 April 1942 in the same unescorted convoy as the *Gandara* and *Indora*. Attacked, but undamaged, the next day by a plane from a carrier in the Japanese cruiser squadron. Shelled by the cruisers *Suzuya* and *Kumano* and destroyer *Shirakumo* which caused many to be killed and seriously wounded. Most of the lifeboats were destroyed, but at least 2 got away and when one landed at a sandy beach in Orissa in the early evening, they joined about 200 survivors from other ships. An RAF Hurricane passed low over them and rocked its wings to indicate that help would be arriving. The following morning a police inspector and a guide arrived and, carrying their wounded, they trudged through jungle and swamps to a small group of huts along the coast to find those from Captain Edmondson's boat already there. The stretcher cases were given morphine before being taken upstream in native dugouts and then to a hospital by bus. After another night in the open, the fit and walking-wounded trudged on to Cuttack where the latter went into the hospital and from where the former went on by train to Calcutta. Two engineers and 23 Lascars died.

MASHOBRA. Requisitioned as a Fleet Air Arm depot ship and became HMS *Mashobra*, stationed at Scapa Flow until May 1940. Arrived in Norwegian waters on 11 May and survived air attacks until she was hit by a bomb at Gangsaas, Halstad, on the 25th. Beached and her guns and stores removed, but had to be scuttled by the Royal Navy when Narvik was being evacuated. No further details. The tanker *Oleander*, struck by a bomb on the 26th, suffered a similar experience.

MUNDRA. Carrying survivors from other ships when sunk by the Japanese submarine I-18 (Cdr Kiyonori Otani) on 6 July 1942, off the coast of Natal, South Africa, in position 28°45′S 32°20′E. Of those on board, 94 died and 155 survived. No further details.

NAGINA (Captain W. Bird, ex-*Chilka*). Homeward bound from Calcutta, sailing from Takoradi in Convoy TS.37 on 18 April 1943. Torpedoed and sunk by U.515 (Kptlt Werner Henke) at 9pm on the 30th in position 07°19′N 13°50′W. The Chinese carpenter and 2nd Radio Officer L. Burby were killed, the latter by being struck on the head by a lifeboat. The 113 others were picked up by the trawler HMS *Birdlip* (Lt E.N. Groom) and landed at Freetown the next day.

OTHER SHIPS SUNK IN CONVOY TS.37 – ALL BY U.515

Bandashapour (Captain W.A. Chappell). One died and 77 picked up by HMS *Birdlip*.

City of Singapore (Captain A.G. Freeman). See under ELLERMAN GROUP.

Clan Macpherson (Captain E. Gough). See under CLAN LINE.

Corabella (Captain P. Leggett). Nine died and 39 picked up by HMS *Birdlip*.

Kota Tjandi (Du.) (Captain A.S. Tendijck). Six died and 71 survived.

Mokambo (Belg.) (Captain E. Huys). Being towed to Freetown by the tugs HMS *Aimwell* and HMS *Oriana* when capsized and sank on 2 May. All 57 survived.

The Masters of all the ships in the convoy had protested at the inadequacy of the escort, as U-boats were known to be in the vicinity.

NALGORA (Captain A.D. Davies). Bound for Alexandria via the Cape, sailing from the UK in Convoy OB.261 which dispersed on 22 December 1941. Torpedoed, shelled and sunk by U.65 (Krvkpt. Hans-Gerrit von Stockhausen) shortly after 10pm on 2 January in position 22°24′N 21°11′W. Some were picked up by the *Nolisement* and landed at Freetown, while others were picked up by the *Umgeni* and landed at Glasgow on the 13th. Captain Davies' boat landed at San Antonio in the Cape Verde Islands on 30 December. All survived.

NARDANA (Captain C.E. White). Homeward bound from Bombay via Cape Town and Freetown. Sailed from Freetown on 1 March 1941 in Convoy SL.67. Torpedoed and sunk by U.124 (Kptlt Georg-Wilhelm Schulz) at about 6am on the 8th in position 20°51′N 20°32′W. Three Europeans and 16 Lascars died. One hundred and seven were picked up the next day by the destroyers HMS *Faulknor* (Captain A.F. de Salis) and HMS *Forester* (Lt Cdr E.B. Tancock) and landed at Gibraltar on the 16th.

OTHER SHIPS SUNK IN CONVOY SL.67

Harmodius (Captain R. Parry). Sunk by U.105 (Kptlt Georg Schewe). Thirteen died. Sixty-one picked up by destroyer HMS *Faulknor* but transferred to HMS *Forester*.

Hindpool (Captain M.V.A. Tinnock). Sunk by U.124. Twenty eight died. Six picked up by HMS *Faulknor* and 6 by the *Guido*.

Lahore (Captain G.S. Stable). Sunk by U.124. All 82 picked up by HMS *Forester*.

Tielbank (Captain W. Broome). Sunk by U.124. Four died and 62 picked up by HMS *Forester*.

NEURALIA. On passage from Split in Yugoslavia to Taranto, to embark German PoWs, when she struck a mine off southern Italy on 1 May 1945. Four died, but no further details.

NIRPURA (Captain T.G. Hodgkinson). Sailed from Durban in Convoy DN.21 bound for Karachi with 39 South African troops, 667 mules, 35 horses and 35 donkeys when torpedoed and sunk by U.160 (Kptlt Georg Lassen) at 11.22pm on 3 March 1943 in position 32°47′S 30°48′E. Thirty-eight died. Eighty-eight were picked up; those in the lifeboats by the Argentinian ship *Ombu*; the others, after being in the water for about 18 hours, by a trawler. U.160 also sank the US Liberty ship *Harvey W. Scott* (Captain A.E. Uldall). All 61 saved. The Dutch tanker *Tibia* (Captain H. Veldhuis) was damaged by U.160, but returned to Durban on the 4th. None died.

NOWSHERA (Captain J.N. Collins). Bound for Durban and the UK from Adelaide when intercepted by the German raider *Pinguin* (KptzS. Ernst-Felix Krüder) towards midnight of 18 November 1940 and all allowed to leave her before she was sunk by aircraft bombs suspended against her hull and detonated. On board the *Pinguin,* they received poor rations, but were kept below in reasonable conditions and allowed on deck for 2 hours every day, but it was very different when they were transferred to the captured Norwegian tanker *Storstadt* (renamed *Falkenjell* by the Germans). When, on 9 December, in a position south-east of Madagascar, the *Falkenjell* rendezvoused with the raider *Atlantis* (KptzS. Bernard Rogge) to collect the survivors of the *Automedon*, she already had on board those from the *Storstadt, Port Brisbane, Port Wellington, Benavon, Domingo de Larringa, British Commander* and *Maimoa*.

The conditions on the *Falkenjell* were appalling. The sanitary arrangements were bad and, as she was carrying approximately 500 prisoners, the space was totally inadequate. The food too was bad and, for the fortnight before she reached Bordeaux on 5 February, the prisoners were kept below decks with an allowance of only one cup of water a day.

They arrived at Front-Stalag 221 at 10.30pm on the day of their arrival and remained there until the morning of 12 March when they boarded a train to take them to Germany. The prisoners were well guarded, but at about 1.30am on the 13th, when the train slowed down to about 35mph, Mr Bellew, the 5th Engineer, together with Mr Harper, the 4th Engineer of the *Automedon*, and Messrs Howlett and Dunshea, the 4th and 5th Engineers of the *Maimoa*, jumped from it. Their ensuing adventure is a story in itself, but greatly assisted by the French people after they crossed into unoccupied France, they succeeded in reaching Marseille on the 18th where they received further assistance from the Rev. Donald Caskie, the padre of the Seamen's Mission. From Marseille, Messrs Harper and Dunshea crossed the Pyrenees into Franco's Spain together and eventually reached Gibraltar on the 31st. It appears that Mr Bellew went on his own and eventually reached Gibraltar from where a ship carried him to Greenock. All spent time in Spanish jails and received rough treatment from the Falangists. There is no information on what happened to Mr Howlett or of casualties on the *Nowshera*.

QUILOA (Captain S.C. Brown). Sailed from Alexandria with a regiment of muleteers, their mules, stores and 500 tons of train rails. Although she was being subjected to German air attacks, the mules were discharged at a jetty in Scaramanga near Athens before she was hit, at much the same time as the *Goalpara,* in Eleusis Bay on 15 April 1941. After being beached, the deck officers made and fitted a large cement box over a hole in the side of the ship, but in spite of the train rails being jettisoned, the corvettes HMS *Hyacinth* and HMS *Salvia* were unable to refloat her. The crew made their way to Nauplion from where a ship carried them to Crete. There, they met the crew of the *Goalpara* and all returned to Alexandria on the same ship. All survived. (See also under *Goalpara*.)

ROHNA (Captain T.J. Murphy). Requisitioned as a troopship in 1939. Bound for India, sailing from Oran, with 1,770 US troops on board at 12.30pm on 25 November 1943, to join Convoy KMF.26 which had left the Clyde on the 15th. At about 4.30pm on the 26th, when the convoy was off Bougie, it was attacked by about 30 Heinkel 177s and Junkers 88s, armed with Hs.293 radio-controlled glider bombs, and a number of torpedo bombers. At about 5.30pm, the *Rohna* was struck in the engine room by a glider bomb; a fire ensued, all electrical equipment was put out of action, No 4 bulkhead collapsed, and she sank about an hour and a half later. The *Rohna* was the only ship hit, while at least 2 planes were shot down and several damaged. Hampered by the darkness and rough seas, the rescue work continued until 2.15am on the 27th. Survivors were picked up by the minesweeper USS *Pioneer*, *Clan Campbell*, the destroyer HMS *Atherstone* and the tug HMS *Mindful*. Some were landed at Philippeville (Skikda) and others at Bougie. Out of the *Rohna*'s total complement of 1,965, 1,135 died – 5 of her officers, 115 Lascars, and 1,015 US troops.

SANTHIA. With West African troops on board, she went on fire, capsized and sank at No 3 Garden Reach Jetty in Calcutta on 25 November 1943, blocking the berth until she was raised in April 1945. No lives lost.

SIRDHANA (Captain P. Fairbairn). Leaving Singapore on 13 November 1939, and about 3 miles off the port, when she hit a mine which had broken loose from the naval defence field. Among her many passengers were 137 Chinese deportees who had to be released from a forward hold but were later recaptured. Twenty Asian deck passengers died.

SURADA (Captain E.H. Brady). Homeward bound from Calcutta via Colombo when torpedoed and sunk by U.188 (Kptlt Siegfried Lüdden) at 4.48pm on 26 January 1944 in position 13°00′N 55°15′E. The U-boat surfaced and asked for the Master, but on being falsely informed he had gone down with the ship, asked if anyone was injured and if they had food and water. After giving the survivors the course to steer for the island of Socotra, it departed. All 103 were picked up by the *Darro* the following day and landed at Aden on the 29th.

TALAMBA. A hospital ship engaged in Operation Husky (the invasion of Sicily) when deliberately targeted and sunk in a German air attack while fully illuminated and embarking wounded about 5 miles off Avola anchorage at 10pm on 10 July 1943. Survivors were taken off or picked up by various vessels including HMS *Tartar* (Cdr StJ.R. Tyrwhitt), HMS *Eskimo*, the BI hospital ship *Tairea* and the Norwegian ship *Bergensfjord*. Five died. The planes also attacked the fully illuminated hospital ships *Dorsetshire* and *Aba* and sank the US Liberty ship *Robert Rowan* which, loaded with ammunition, was abandoned before she exploded.

TILAWA (Captain F. Robinson). Bound for Mombasa, sailing independently from Bombay on 20 November 1942 with 17 European and 895 Asian passengers. Torpedoed by the Japanese submarine JP-29 in the early hours of the 23rd and such panic ensued among the deck passengers, who took to the lifeboats or jumped into the sea, that Captain Robinson stopped the engines. Boats and rafts were all round the ship, which was down by the head, when a second torpedo struck and she sank in about 5 minutes. The Captain and the 1st Mate were swept into the sea. Both succeeded in reaching a raft and later transferred to lifeboats, but Mr E.B. Duncan, her 1st Radio Officer, who was still sending distress messages, went down with the ship. His transmissions, however, were heard by the cruiser HMS *Birmingham*.

On the morning of the 25th, a Swordfish from the *Birmingham* sighted survivors and at 8.45pm the cruiser arrived to begin picking up them up; most having to be assisted or carried on board and many requiring the care of the ship's medical staff. When the *Birmingham* arrived at Ballard Pier in Bombay at 5pm on the 27th, the quay was packed with anxious relatives. A massive reception was given to the survivors, with tables laid out with food, refreshments and warm clothing. Two hundred and eighty-five passengers and 28 crew died.

UMARIA (Captain A.D. Davies, ex-*Nalgora*). Homeward bound from Bombay via Colombo, Cape Town and Freetown. Sailed from Freetown in Convoy SL.126 on 12 March 1943. Torpedoed by U.662 (Kptlt Heinz-Eberhard Müller) shortly before 11pm on the 29th, but proceeded until struck by a second torpedo from U.662 at about 4am the next day in position 46°44′N 16°38′W. All 103 were picked up by the frigate HMS *Wear* (Lt G.D. Edwards) which sank the ship by gunfire and carried the survivors to Liverpool.

OTHER SHIPS SUNK IN CONVOY SL.126

Empire Bowman (Captain C.H. Cranch). Sunk by U.404. Four died and 46 picked up by HMS *Wear*.

Empire Whale. See under DONALDSON LINE.

Sagara (Captain P. Cooper). Sunk by U.404 (Kptlt Otto von Bülow). Taken in tow by the tug HMS *Dexterous*, but sank on 4 April. All 97 picked up by HMS *Wear*.

(*Ocean Viceroy* damaged by U.662.)

URLANA. Homeward bound from Buenos Aires and in Convoy SL.135MK when she ran aground in bad weather at about 2am on 5 September 1943, near Idrigill Point on the NW coast of Skye. Pounded by heavy seas, she broke up in about half an hour. The *Thurland Castle*, which was standing by, took off 108 and landed them at Loch Ewe the same day.

British Tanker Co. Ltd

BRITISH ADVOCATE. Bound for Cape Town and the UK from Abadan when intercepted by the pocket battleship *Admiral Scheer* (KptzS. Theodor Krancke) west of the Seychelles on 20 February 1941. Pretending to be a British warship, the *Scheer* exchanged messages with the tanker until she was close and then signalled that she would blow her out of the water if the wireless was used. When the ship stopped, the crew were transferred to the *Scheer* and, with a prize crew on board, she sailed for Bordeaux on the 27th, arriving on 29 April. Under the name *Nordstern* she was sunk in Nantes on 25 September 1941, but was raised and again sunk, on 23 July 1944, in Donges. Raised again in 1947, she was sold for scrap.

BRITISH ARDOUR (Captain T. Copeman). Bound for Greenock, sailing in Convoy HX.231 which left New York on 25 March 1943. Torpedoed and damaged by U.706 (Krvkpt. Alexander von Zitzewitz) at 4.45pm on 5 April when in position 58°08′N 34°04′W. Scuttled by the destroyer HMS *Vidette* (Lt Cdr R. Hart) and the corvette HMS *Snowflake* (Lt Cdr Chesterman). All 62 crew were picked up by the *Snowflake* and landed at Londonderry on the 9th. (For details of other ships sunk in Convoy HX.231, see under *Shillong*, P&O.)

BRITISH CAPTAIN. Mined and sunk 15 miles east of Aldeburgh, Suffolk, on 2 December 1941. One died and 53 rescued.

BRITISH CHIVALRY (Captain Hill). Bound for Abadan from Melbourne when torpedoed and sunk by the Japanese submarine I-37 (Lt Cdr Hajime Nakagawa) on 22 February 1944 in position 00°50′S 68°00′E. After Captain Hill was taken prisoner, he was forced to watch as the submarine machine-gunned the men in the two lifeboats, on rafts and in the water, while a photographer filmed the proceedings. Twenty died and 38 were picked up 37 days later by the *Delane* in position 04°55′S 65°00′E and landed at Durban.

Nakagawa committed similar acts of barbarity against survivors of the *Sutlej* and *Ascot*, sunk later the same month. Also, in the early hours of 14 May 1943, he sank the fully illuminated Australian hospital ship *Centaur* off the coast of Queensland when 269 lives were lost. Subsequently tried as a war criminal, he was not held responsible for the sinking of the *Centaur* on the grounds of insufficient evidence. He was sentenced to 8 years' hard labour for the other crimes but served only 6 and died at the age of 84 in 1986. (See under *Sutlej*, NOURSE LINE and *Centaur*, HOLT, ALFRED, & CO.)

BRITISH COLONY (Captain R. Wood-Thorburn). Bound independently for Gibraltar from Trinidad when torpedoed and sunk by U.162 (Kptlt Jürgen Wattenberg) at 2am on 13 May 1942 in position 13°12′N 58°10′W. Four died and 43 were landed 13 miles north of Bridgetown, Barbados.

BRITISH COMMANDER (Captain Thornton). Intercepted by the German raider *Pinguin* (KptzS. Ernst-Felix Krüder) at 4.20pm on 27 August 1940 and ordered to stop. Captain Thornton complied, but the Radio Officer continued to transmit a QQQQ message until the ship was shelled and abandoned. None died. All 46 taken on board the *Pinguin* which then sank the ship in position 29′37′S 45′50′E. The crew, together with prisoners from other ships, were eventually transferred to the captured Norwegian ship *Storstadt*. They had been reasonably well treated on the *Pinguin*, but the conditions on the *Storstadt* were appalling and for the fortnight before they reached Bordeaux on 5 February 1941 they were given only one cup of water a day and never allowed on deck. On 12 March, they boarded a train which took them to prison camps in Germany. (See also under *Nowshera*, BRITISH INDIA STEAM NAVIGATION CO.)

BRITISH CONSUL (Captain J. Kennedy). In Port of Spain, Trinidad, when torpedoed and sunk in shallow water at 5am on 19 February 1942 by U.161 (Kptlt Albrecht Achilles). (The *Mokihana* (US) (Captain C. Porta) was also sunk in shallow water by the U-boat at the same time.) Raised and repaired and bound for Key West in Convoy TAW(S) when torpedoed and sunk by U.564 (Kptlt Reinhard Suhren) shortly after 10am on 19 August in position 11°58′N 62°38′W. Two died. Forty were picked up by the corvette HMS *Clarkia* (Lt Cdr F.J.G. Jones) and landed at Guantanamo Bay.

> **OTHER SHIPS SUNK IN CONVOY TAW(S)**
>
> *Empire Cloud* (Captain C.C. Brown). By U.564. Three died. Taken in tow by the tug *Roode Zee* (Du.), but sank on the 21st. Fifty-one picked up by ships in the convoy and landed at Key West and Mobile.
>
> *West Celina* (US) (Captain B.V. Mirkin). By U.162 (Kptlt Jürgen Wattenberg). One died. Forty-three landed at Margarita Island from two lifeboats on the 21st and 22nd.

BRITISH COUNCILLOR. In coastal Convoy FS.84 when badly damaged by an E-boat on 2 February 1940, and sank the next day in position 53°48′N 00°34′E. All crew rescued by the destroyer HMS *Gallant* and landed at Rosyth. (A conflicting report by 1st Radio Officer Anthony Cox states, 'We hit two mines after leaving South Shields at 4.20pm on February 2nd 1940. Survivors were picked up by the destroyer HMS *Whitby*.')

BRITISH DOMINION (Captain J.D. Millar). Bound for Gibraltar from Curaçao via Trinidad and straggling from Convoy TM.1 when struck by three torpedoes fired by U.522 (Kptlt Herbert Schneider) at 0040 hours on 11 January 1943. Abandoned when torpedoed and sunk by U.620 (Kptlt Heinz Stein) at 3am in position 30°30′N 19°55′W. Thirty-eight died. Sixteen were picked up by the corvette HMS *Godetia* (Lt A.H. Pierce) and landed at Gibraltar.

OTHER SHIPS SUNK IN CONVOY TM.1

Albert L Ellsworth (Nor.) (Captain Thorvald Solheim). By U.436 (Kptlt Günther Seibicke). All 42 picked up by the corvette HMS *Havelock* (Cdr R.C. Boyle) and landed at Gibraltar.

British Vigilance. See below.

Empire Lytton (Captain J.W. Andrews). By U.442 (Krvkpt. Hans-Joachim Hesse). Fourteen died. Thirty-four picked up by the corvette HMS *Saxifrage* (Lt N.L. Knight) and landed at Gibraltar.

Minister Wedel (Nor.) (Captain W.J. Wilhelmsen). By U.522. All 38 picked up by HMS *Havelock*.

Norvik (Pan.). By U.522. Two died and 43 survived.

Oltenia II. See below, under Managed for Ministry of War Transport.

BRITISH EMPEROR. Bound for Durban from Abadan when intercepted by the raider *Pinguin* (KptzS. Ernst-Felix Krüder) at 4am on 7 May 1941 in position 8°30′N 56°25′E. As the Master ignored the signals to stop, the raider shelled her until she was on fire and sinking while the Radio Officer continued transmitting a QQQQ message until the radio room was hit. Aware of the transmissions, Krüder hurried from the scene, disguising his ship as the Norwegian ship *Tamerlane*.

The RFA oiler *British Genius*, in the Seychelles, received and re-transmitted the QQQQ message which was picked up by stations in Colombo and Mombasa. The cruiser HMS *Cornwall* (Captain P.C.W. Manwaring), in Mombasa, was then sent to the area, and the following morning her seaplanes flew over the *Pinguin* which they reported to be flying the Norwegian flag. When the cruiser made up on her shortly after 4pm, she behaved as the real *Tamerlane* would have done and sent off a QQQQ message indicating that she was being challenged by an unknown ship and giving her position. This put doubt in Captain Manwaring's mind; still suspicious, he fired shots across her bows and ordered her to stop. Krüder ignored the order, but when the ships closed she turned and struck the German naval ensign. A battle ensued and the *Pinguin* was sunk. Three hundred and thirty-two Germans, including Krüder, and 200 prisoners, mostly Indian, died. Sixty Germans and 22 prisoners were rescued by HMS *Cornwall* which proceeded to Durban for repairs, having received direct hits. There are no details of *British Emperor*'s casualties, but only a few of her crew of 45 survived. Nor are there details of the casualties suffered by the *Cornwall*.

BRITISH ENDEAVOUR (Captain T. Weatherhead). Bound for Abadan from Glasgow and in Convoy OGF.19 when torpedoed and sunk by U.50 (Kptlt Max-Hermann Bauer) at 0020 hours on 22 February 1940 in position 42°11′N 11°35′W. Five died. Thirty-three were picked up by the *Bodnant* and landed at Funchal, Madeira, on the 26th.

BRITISH FAME. Bound for Abadan from Avonmouth, sailing in Convoy OB.193 which left Liverpool on 4 August and dispersed on 7 August 1940. Torpedoed and sunk by the Italian submarine *Alessandro Malaspina* (C.F. Mario Leoni) on the 12th in position 37°44′N 22°56′W. It took five torpedoes to sink the tanker and at one point her gunfire forced the *Malaspina* to submerge. Three died and one taken prisoner. No details of casualties, but 45 survived.

BRITISH FORTUNE. Bombed and sunk one mile from Aldeburgh Light Buoy on 31 October 1941. No further details.

BRITISH FREEDOM (Captain F.L. Morris). Bound for Halifax, Nova Scotia, and the UK from New York and in Convoy BX.141 when torpedoed and sunk by U.1232 (Kpt. Kurt Dobratz) at 10.45am on 14 January 1945 in position 44°28′N 63°28′W. One died. Fifty-six were picked up by the minesweeper HMCS *Gaspé* (Lt A.J. Burke) and landed at Halifax. (For other ships sunk and damaged at the same time by U.1232, see under *Athel Viking*, ATHEL LINE.)

BRITISH GENERAL (Captain F.O. Armstrong). Bound for Abadan from the Tyne, sailing in Convoy OA.222 which left Methil on 30 September 1940. Dispersed from the convoy when torpedoed and sunk by U.37 (Kptlt Victor Oehrn) shortly after 6pm on 6 October in position 51°42′N 24°03′W. All 47 died.

BRITISH GRENADIER (Captain H.G. Jeary). Bound for Curaçao from Freetown and sailing independently when torpedoed by U.103 (Krvkpt. Viktor Schütze) at 10.52pm on 22 May 1941 in position 06°15′N 12°59′W. None died. Forty-six were picked up by the *Ganda* (Port.) and by the *Jose Calvo Sotelo* (Sp.) and landed at Freetown. The ship later sank in position 06°20′N 12°50′W.

BRITISH GUNNER (Captain J.W. Kemp). Bound for Aruba from Swansea, sailing in Convoy OB.289 which left Liverpool on 20 February 1941. Torpedoed by U.97 (Kptlt Udo Heilmann) at 6.24am on the 24th and although Captain Kemp considered that the ship could make port under tow, Lt Cdr G.V. Legassick in the corvette *Petunia* ordered that the ship be abandoned in position 61°16′N 12°20′W. Three died. Forty-one were taken on board the *Petunia* and landed at Stornoway.

OTHER SHIPS SUNK IN CONVOY OB.289 – ALL BY U.97

Jonathan Holt (Captain W. Stephenson). Fifty-one died. Three picked up by the *Petunia*; 3 by the rescue ship *Copeland* (Captain W.J. Hartley) and landed at Greenock.

Mansepool (Captain H.R. Clark). Two died. Seventeen picked up by the *Petunia*; 22 by the *Thomas Holt*, but transferred to the *Petunia*.

(*G.C. Brøvig* (Nor.). Damaged and towed to Stornoway by the *Petunia*.)

BRITISH INFLUENCE (Captain I.H. McMichael). Bound for Hull from Abadan and sailing independently when stopped by U.29 (Kptlt Otto Schuhart) at 2.15pm on 14 September

1939 in position 49°43′N 12°49′W. Schuhart ordered the crew to leave the ship before he sank her. He then sent off rockets to attract rescuers and stopped the *Ida Bakke* (Nor.) to inform the Master (Captain Anton Zakariassen) of their plight. The *Ida Bakke* picked them up; they were transferred to the Courtmacsherry lifeboat the next day and landed at Kinsale harbour. All 42 survived.

BRITISH INVENTOR. Mined off St Alban's Head, Dorset, on 12 June 1940 and became a total loss. No further details.

BRITISH LIBERTY (Captain T. Templeton). Bound for Dunkirk from Haifa when she struck a mine in an Allied minefield and sank 4 miles north-east of the Dyck Light Vessel on 6 January 1940. Twenty-six died, including Captain Templeton.

BRITISH LOYALTY (Captain R. Wastell). In Diego Suarez, Madagascar, on 30 May 1942 when torpedoed and sunk in shallow water by a midget submarine (Lt Saburo Akieda) from the Japanese submarine I-20 (Lt Cdr Takashi Yamada). Refloated and taken to Addu Atoll where she was repaired and used as a storage hulk. Anchored off the SW entrance to Addu Atoll at 8am on 9 March 1944 when torpedoed by U.183 (Kptlt Fritz Schneewind). Again sunk in shallow water, she was raised and used as a hulk until scuttled on 5 January 1946 in position 00°38′S 73°07′E. Several casualties, but no details.

BRITISH MARINER (Captain H. Beattie). Bound for Curaçao from Freetown and in company with two tankers and an escort when torpedoed by U.126 (Kptlt Ernst Bauer) shortly before 6am on 20 October 1941 in position 07°43′N 14°20′W. Abandoned, but towed to Freetown by the tugs *Donau* (Du.) and HMS *Hudson*. Used as an oil storage hulk until scuttled in 1946. Three died. Forty-eight were picked up by HMS *Hudson* and landed at Freetown.

BRITISH MONARCH (Captain J.F. Scott). Bound for Glasgow from Bougie, Algeria, with a cargo of iron ore, sailing in Convoy HGF.34 which left Gibraltar on 13 June 1940. Torpedoed and sunk by U.48 (Krvkpt. Hans Rudolf Rösing) at 3.46am on the 19th in position 45°00′N 11°21′W. All 40 died.

OTHER SHIPS SUNK IN CONVOY HGF.34

Baron Loudoun. See under HOGARTH, H., & CO./BARON LINE.

Otterpool. See under ROPNER SHIPPING CO.

Tudor (Nor.) (Captain Hans Bjønnes). By U.48. One died. The remaining 39 picked up from lifeboats by the corvettes HMS *Arabis* (Lt Cdr B. Blewitt) and HMS *Calendula* (Lt Cdr A.D. Bruford) which landed them at Plymouth on 21 and 22 June respectively.

BRITISH MOTORIST (Captain G.C. Bates). Received two direct hits during an air raid on Darwin, Northern Territory, Australia, on 19 February 1942 and sank. Raised in 1959 and towed to Japan to be scrapped. The Master and 17-year-old 2nd Radio Officer J.H. Webster were killed. Twenty other ships were sunk or badly damaged. One hundred and seventy-seven were killed and 107 wounded on these ships and there were many casualties, both military and civilian, on shore.

BRITISH OFFICER. Nearing the entrance to the Tyne at the end of her passage from Sheerness when she set off a mine and became a total loss on 1 December 1940. Fifteen died. Thirty-two survived.

RRITISH PETROL. Bound for Trinidad in ballast when intercepted and shelled by the German raider *Widder* (KptzS. Helmuth von Ruckteschell) on 13 June 1940 in position 20°N 50°W. As the radio room was destroyed, no RRRR message was sent. Two died and the remainder of the crew were picked up from lifeboats by the raider before the ship was sunk. The *Widder* returned to Brest on 31 October. Walter Leonard Skett, the 1st Radio Officer, was shot and killed by a German guard in Milag Nord PoW Camp at 11.20pm on 13 May 1942. The Germans claimed that he was trying to escape, although he was wearing only pyjamas and slippers. (See also under *Davisian*, HARRISON LINE.)

OTHER SHIPS SUNK BY THE WIDDER BETWEEN 5 MAY AND 31 OCTOBER 1940

Krossfonn (Nor.), *Davisian*, *King John*, *Beaulieu* (Nor.) *Oostplein* (Du.) *Killoran*, *Anglo Saxon*, *Cymbeline* and *Antonios Chandris* (Gr.).

BRITISH PREMIER (Captain F. Dalziel). Bound for Swansea from Abadan via Freetown. Straggling from Convoy SLS.60 when torpedoed and sunk by U.65 (Krvkpt. Hans-Gerrit von Stockhausen) at 4.41pm on 24 December 1940 in position 06°20′N 13°20′W. Thirty-two died. Nine were picked up by the cruiser HMS *Hawkins* (Captain H.P.K. Oram) on 3 January and landed at Freetown. Four rescued off the West Coast of Africa, after 41 days in an open boat (the last 25 days without food) by the destroyer HMS *Faulknor* (Captain A.F. de Salis) and landed at Freetown.

BRITISH PROGRESS. Torpedoed by an E-boat off Norfolk in position 52°55′N 2°00′E. Towed into port and scrapped. No further details.

BRITISH PRUDENCE (Captain G.A. Dickson). Bound for the Clyde from Trinidad, sailing in Convoy HX.181 which left Halifax on 21 March 1942. Straggling when torpedoed and sunk by U.754 (Kptlt Hans Oestermann) at 3.31pm on the 23rd in position 45°28′N 56°13′W. Three died. Forty-seven were picked up by the destroyer HMS *Witherington* (Lt R. Horncastle) and landed at Halifax the next day.

BRITISH RELIANCE (Captain A. Henney). Bound for the UK, sailing in Convoy SC.26 which left Halifax, Nova Scotia, on 20 March 1941. Torpedoed by U.46 (Oblt Engelbert Endrass) at about 11.30pm on 2 April and sank in position 58°25′N 28°21′W. All 50 were picked up by the *Tennessee* and landed at Reykjavik from where they were carried to Gourock on the *Royal Ulsterman*. (For details of other ships sunk in Convoy SC.26, see under *British Viscount* and *Westpool*, under ROPNER SHIPPING CO.)

BRITISH RESOURCE (Captain J. Kennedy). Bound for the UK via Halifax from Curaçao and sailing independently when torpedoed by U.124 (Kptlt Johann Mohr) at 9.18pm on

14 March 1942. Sunk by a second torpedo fired at 9.33pm in position 36°04′N 65°38′W. Forty-five died. Four were picked up by the corvette HMS *Clarkia* (Lt Cdr F.J.G. Jones) and landed at Hamilton, Bermuda.

BRITISH SCIENCE. Bound for Piraeus from Haifa when sunk by German aircraft in position 36°06′N 24°00′E, north of the Kithera Channel, on 18 April 1941. All were picked up by the destroyer HMS *Hero* (Cdr H.W. Biggs) and landed at Suda Bay, Crete.

BRITISH SECURITY (Captain A.J. Akers). Bound for the Clyde from Curaçao, sailing in Convoy HX.126 which left Halifax on 10 May 1941. Torpedoed by U.556 (Kptlt Herbert Wohlfarth) at about 3pm on the 20th and blew up in position 57°28′N 41°07′W. All 53 died. (For details of other ships sunk in Convoy HX.126, see under *Elusa*, SHELL GROUP.)

BRITISH SERGEANT. In Trincomalee, Ceylon (Sri Lanka), on 8 April 1942 when the Flag Officer in Charge ordered the port to be cleared due to the threat of an air raid by Japanese carrier-based aircraft. Bombed the following morning, broke in two and sank in position 8°00′N 81°38′E. None died.

ALSO SUNK ON THE 9TH BY PLANES FROM THE JAPANESE FORCE COMMANDED BY ADMIRAL CHUICHI NAGUMO

HMAS *Athelstane* (Captain H. Moore). Depot ship. None died.

HMAS *Vampire* (Cdr W.T.A. Moran). Destroyer. Nine died, including Cdr Moran.

HMS *Hermes* (Captain R.J.F. Onslow). Aircraft carrier. Three hundred and seven died, including Captain Onslow. (Because she had been undergoing repairs, HMS *Hermes* had no planes on board.)

HMS *Hollyhock* (Lt Cdr T.E. Davies). Corvette. Fifty-three died, including Lt Cdr Davies.

(HMHS *Vita* picked up about 600 survivors from the above ships.)

Norviken (Nor.) (Captain Pareli Berg). Captain Berg and 3 Chinese ratings died. Forty-two reached the shore in a lifeboat and on rafts, but the ship later ran aground near Timkovie and eventually broke in two. Unlike the other ships, the *Norviken* did not come out of Trincomalee, but was on passage from Madras to Bombay.

BRITISH SPLENDOUR (Captain J. Hall, ex-*British Trust*). On passage from Houston, Texas, to join a convoy to the UK, and escorted by the ASW trawlers HMS *St Zeno* (Lt J.K. Craig) and HMS *Hertfordshire* (Cdr J.A. Shater). Torpedoed and sunk at 4.17am on 7 April 1942 by U.552 (Kptlt Erich Topp) in position 35°07′N 75°19′W. Twelve died. Forty-one were picked up by HMS *St Zeno* and landed at Norfolk, Virginia.

BRITISH STRENGTH. Sailed in Convoy OB.294 which left Liverpool on 5 March 1941 and dispersed in position 51°29′N 20°30′W on the 9th. Sunk by the *Scharnhorst* on the 15th in approximate position 42°00′N 43°00′W. Two died and the others were taken prisoner.

OTHER SHIPS SUNK AND CAPTURED

Sunk by the *Scharnhorst*

Athelfoam. See under ATHEL LINE.

Demeterton. See under CHAPMAN, R., & SONS.

Mangkai (Du.) Thirty-six died and 9 taken prisoner.

Sardinian Prince. See under FURNESS, WITHY GROUP.

Silverfir. See under SILVER LINE.

Captured by the *Gneisenau*

Bianca (Nor.). (Captain Arne Grønningseter). All taken prisoner, including the Captain's wife and small son.

San Casimiro. Under prize crews, the *Bianca* and *San Casimiro* sailed for France. Both, however, were intercepted by the battle cruiser HMS *Renown* on 20 March and all 46 prisoners and prize crews taken on board the warship before the ships sank due to scuttling by the Germans. See under *San Casimiro*, SHELL GROUP.

Polykarp (Nor.) (Captain L. B. Guttormsen). Under a prize crew, arrived in the Gironde on 24 March. Apart from the Master and a gunner, all her original crew remained on board. After being held on the *Scharnhorst* for 4 days, the former were taken to Brest on a German tanker. None died.

Sunk by the *Gneisenau* – flagship of Admiral Günther Lütjens

Chilean Reefer. See under HOLT, ALFRED, & CO.

Empire Industry (Captain D.A. Addison). All 38 taken prisoner.

Granli (Nor.) (Captain Leif Thorbjørnsen). All 16 taken prisoner.

Myson. See under REARDON SMITH LINE.

Rio Dorado (Captain A.J. Clare). All 39 died.

Royal Crown. All 39 taken prisoner.

Simnia. See under SHELL GROUP.

(Having worked in tandem, the *Scharnhorst* and the *Gneisenau* returned to Brest on 22 March.)

BRITISH TRIUMPH. Bound for Aruba from Hull, mined and sunk off the Norfolk coast on 12 February 1940 in position 53°06′N 1°25′E. Four died.

BRITISH TRUST (Captain J. Hall). Bound for Benghazi from Alexandria and in a convoy of 23 ships which was attacked by German planes 25 miles north of Benghazi at about 8pm on 1 May 1943. Torpedoed by a Heinkel He 111 and sank in 3 minutes. Ten died. Using searchlights, escort ships picked up survivors and landed them at Benghazi the next morning.

(The *Erinpura* was sunk in the same attack. See under BRITISH INDIA STEAM NAVIGATION CO.)

BRITISH UNION. Bound for Curaçao from Gibraltar and sailing independently when shelled by the raider *Kormoran* (Krvkpt. Theodor Detmers) on the night of 18 January 1941 in position 26°34′N 30°58′W. Exchanged fire with the raider, but set on fire and abandoned while being machine-gunned and a torpedo sank the ship. As an RRRR message had been transmitted, the *Kormoran* had to leave the scene quickly. Twenty-eight were taken prisoner and 7 picked up by the AMC HMS *Arawa* the following day. Nine died.

BRITISH VENTURE (Captain D.C. Baron). Sailing independently when sunk by the Japanese submarine I-27 (Lt Cdr Toshiaki Fukumura) on 24 June 1943 in position 25°13′N 58°02′E. Forty-two died and 19 were rescued by the *Varela*. (See also under *Fort Mumford*, REARDON SMITH LINE and *Sambridge*, BROCKLEBANK LINE.)

BRITISH VIGILANCE (Captain E.O. Evans). Bound for Trinidad and Gibraltar from Curaçao and straggling from Convoy TM.1 when torpedoed and badly damaged by U.514 (Kptlt Hans-Jürgen Auffermann) shortly before 11pm on 3 January 1943 in position 20°58′N 44°40′W. Twenty-seven died. Twenty-seven were picked up by HMS *Saxifrage* and landed at Gibraltar. The burning tanker remained afloat until sunk by U.105 (Kptlt Jürgen Nissen) 3 weeks later. (Details of other losses in Convoy TM.1 are given under *British Dominion*.)

BRITISH VISCOUNT (Captain W.C. Baikie). Bound for Scapa Flow from Curaçao and dispersed from Convoy SC.26 when torpedoed by U.73 (Kptlt Helmut Rosenbaum) at 8.32am on 3 April 1941. Abandoned and sank in position 58°18′N 27°50′W. Twenty-eight died and 20 were picked up by the destroyer HMS *Havelock* (Cdr E.H. Thomas). (See also under *British Reliance*.)

BRITISH WORKMAN (Captain A.W. Wilson). Bound for Galveston from Greenock, sailing in Convoy ON.89 which left Liverpool on 23 April 1942. Straggling when torpedoed and sunk by U.455 (Kptlt Hans-Heinrich Giessler) at 6.38am on 3 May in position 44°07′N 51°53′W. Six died. Forty-seven were picked up by the destroyer HMCS *Assiniboine* (A/Lt Cdr J.H. Stubbs) and the corvette HMCS *Alberni* (T/Lt A.W. Ford) and landed at St John's, Newfoundland.

BRITISH YEOMAN (Captain E.P.S. Attewill). Bound for Gibraltar, sailing independently from Curaçao on 1 July 1942. Torpedoed and then sunk by gunfire by U.201 (Kptlt Adalbert Schnee) at 1.46am on the 15th in position 26°42′N 24°20′W. Forty-three died. Ten were picked up by the *Castillo Almenara* (Sp.) and landed at St Vincent, Cape Verde Islands.

Managed for Ministry of War Transport

EMPIRE CORPORAL (Captain G.E. Hodgson). Formerly the *British Corporal*, bound for Key West from Curaçao in Convoy TAW.12 when torpedoed and sunk by U.598 (Oblt Gottfried Holtorf) shortly before midnight on 14 August 1942 in position 21°45′N 76°10′W. Six died. Forty-nine, picked up by the US motor torpedo boat 498, transferred to the destroyer USS *Fletcher* (Cdr W.M. Cole) and landed at Guantanamo Bay, Cuba. (The *Michael Jebsen* (Captain R. Nielsen) was also sunk by U.598. Seven died. Forty were picked up and landed at Guantanamo Bay.)

EMPIRE GEM (Captain F.R. Broad). Bound for the UK via Halifax from Port Arthur, Texas; sailing independently when torpedoed by U.66 (Krvkpt. Richard Zapp) at 2.40am on 24 January 1942 and sank in position 35°02′N 75°33′W. Forty-nine died. The Master and a Radio Officer were rescued by a US coastguard ship and landed at Hatteras Inlet the next day.

EMPIRE METAL. In Bône, Algeria, during an air raid on 2 January 1943. Discharging into the depot when hit in the bow by a bomb dropped by a Focke-Wulf 190, and a mass of flame shot into the air. In an attempt to stop the oil burning, the destroyer HMS *Laforey* sank the tanker on the 6th, but the oil on the water continued to burn for days and lit up the port at night. Several died, but no details.

JOSEFINA THORDEN. Bound for Shell Haven from Curaçao, crossed the Atlantic in Convoy SC.123 which sailed from New York on 14 March 1943. Sailed to Methil from Loch Ewe in coastal Convoy WN.410 and then heading independently for Shell Haven when, on 6 April, she struck a mine in the Thames estuary in position 51°47′N 01°28′E. The after part sank, but the fore part was taken in tow and its oil discharged at Shell Haven before it was broken up. Fifteen died and 40 survived.

MELPOMENE. Bound for Baton Rouge, sailing in a convoy which left Falmouth in February 1942 and dispersed from it some days later. Torpedoed and sunk by the Italian submarine *Giuseppe Finzi* (C.C. Alberto Dominici) during the evening of 6 March 1942 in position 23°35′N 62°39′W. All 49 were picked up from 3 lifeboats by a US Navy ship on the 9th and landed at San Juan, Porto Rico.

OLTENIA II (Captain A. Ladle). Bound for North Africa from Trinidad and sailing in Convoy TM.1 when torpedoed and sunk by U.436 (Kptlt Günther Seibicke) at 10.37pm on 8 January 1943 in position 27°59′N 28°50′W. Seventeen died. Forty-three were picked up by HMS *Havelock*. (Details of other losses in Convoy TM.1 are given under *British Dominion*.)

Brocklebank Line

MAGDAPUR (Captain A.G. Dixon). Sailed independently from South Shields at 7.30pm on 9 September 1939 bound for Southampton. Struck a mine at 3.15pm on the 10th when between the Sizewell Buoy and Aldeburgh Napes. The bridge, 4 lifeboats and the radio room wrecked. Mr Bell, the Radio Officer, Mr H. Atherton, the 2nd Mate, and 4 Lascars died, and Captain Dixon was so severely wounded in the legs that he was forced into retirement. The 75 survivors were picked up and taken to Aldeburgh by the Aldeburgh lifeboat.

MAHANADA (Captain J. Owen). In Convoy OB.290 which sailed from Liverpool on 23 February 1941. Between midnight and 2am on the 26th, the convoy was attacked by U.47 (Krvkpt. Günther Prien) when in position 55°36′N 13°42′W and 3 ships were sunk. At 10am it was attacked by a single Focke-Wulf 200 Condor and then, at 6.45pm, by 4 Heinkels. The *Mahanada* was raked with machine-gun bullets and struck in the stern by

2 bombs. With No 1 hold flooding and a fire in No 2, the crew took to the lifeboats, but 2 quartermasters who had been in the fo'c'sle were never seen again. The *Mahanada*, on fire, was seen by an escort the next day, but she had disappeared by the 28th. Those in Nos 3 and 4 boats were picked up by the sloop HMS *Weston* and landed at Londonderry on 1 March. Those in boats 1, 2 and 5 were picked up by destroyer HMS *Vanquisher* and landed at Liverpool on the 2nd. Three died.

OTHER SHIPS SUNK IN CONVOY OB.290

Amstelland (Du.) (Captain C.S.T. van Rietbergen). Captain van Rietbergen was the only casualty.

Baltistan. See under STRICK LINE.

Beursplein (Du.). Twenty-one died.

Borgland (Nor.) (Captain Anders Andersen). Torpedoed by U.47. All 32 picked up by the corvette HMS *Pimpernel* (Lt F.H. Thornton).

Kasongo (Belg.) (Captain E. Mathieu). Torpedoed by U.47. Six died and 40 picked up by the corvette HMS *Campanula* (Lt Cdr R.V.E. Case).

Kyriakoula (Gr.). All 28 survived.

Llanwern. See under RADCLIFFE SHIPPING CO.

Rydboholm (Swed.). Torpedoed by U.47. All 28 picked up by HMS *Pimpernel*.

Solferino (Nor.) (Captain Rudolf Nyegård). The Captain and 2 others died. Survivors picked up by the Swedish ship *Gdynia* which turned round and landed a total of 93 survivors at Greenock on 1 March.

Swinburne. Bombed, but later sunk by an escort. All survived.

Six other ships were damaged and the convoy dispersed after the attack ended. U.47 went missing on 7 or 8 March in approximate position 60°00′N 19°00′W. All 45 died, cause unknown.

MAHRATTA (Captain W. Hill). Sailed from Calcutta on 12 August 1939 and from Gibraltar in Convoy HG.1 on 26 September 1939 bound for London. During the night of 6 October she detached from the convoy to pick up a pilot and grounded on the Goodwin Sands. Taken in tow by 6 tugs, but broke up over the very spot where the first *Mahratta* had sunk in 1909. All the crew were landed at Dover.

MAHRONDA (Captain W. Hill – See *Mahratta*). Torpedoed and sunk by the Japanese submarine I-20 (Lt Cdr Takashi Yamada) on 11 June 1942 in position 14°37′S 40°58′E. Five lifeboats got away and all landed on the coast of Mozambique. No casualties. (The coaster *Hellenic Trader* (Captain Metaxas), flying the Panamanian flag and which witnessed the torpedoing of the *Mahronda*, was also sunk by I-20, using a large-calibre gun. Captain Metaxas drifted ashore on a raft, but no further details.)

MAHSEER. Struck a mine and sank in the Thames estuary on 18 October 1941. All survived.

MAHSUD. When anchored at Gibraltar on 8 May 1943, the bottom was blown out of her engine room by a limpet mine placed by Italian frogmen operating from the old Italian tanker *Olterra* based at Algeciras in Spain. Two years later she was raised, strengthened and towed home for repair. No casualties. Other ships damaged in the attack were the US Liberty ship *Pat Harrison* (2 killed) and the *Camerata*. None died on the *Mahsud*.

MAIDAN (Captain C.L. Miller). Loaded a cargo of explosives in the USA and joined Convoy HX.84 which sailed from Halifax on 28 October 1940. The convoy was intercepted by the German pocket battleship *Admiral Scheer* (Captain Theodor Krancke) at 4.30pm on 5 November when in position 52°48′N 32°15′W. The *Maidan* was shelled and blew up with the loss of all 91 on board.

Owing to the courageous action of AMC HMS *Jervis Bay* (Captain E.S. Fogerty Fegen), the convoy's only escort, the other 33 ships had time to scatter and escape. Although out-gunned, she headed straight for the *Scheer*, at the same time laying a smokescreen, and was sunk. One hundred and ninety died and 65 crew were picked up by the equally courageous Captain Sven Olander of the Swedish ship *Stureholm*, who risked his ship by doing so. (See under *Jervis Bay*, SHAW SAVILL & ALBION and *Rotorua*, FEDERAL STEAM NAVIGATION CO.)

The tanker *San Demetrio* (Captain G. Waite) was damaged, on fire, and abandoned, but later boarded on the 7th by Mr A.G. Hawkins, the 2nd Mate, Mr C. Pollard, the Chief Engineer, and the 14 others in their lifeboat. Devoid of any navigational aids, the *San Demetrio* sailed into the Clyde on 16 November under her own steam. Her only casualty was Fireman John Boyle who had been injured by falling into the boat and died en route to the Clyde. The lifeboat with Captain Waite and 25 others was picked up and taken to Newfoundland. (For details of other ships sunk in Convoy HX.84, see under *Fresno City (I)*, REARDON SMITH LINE.)

MAKALLA (Captain A.S. Bain). Sailed from London on 18 August 1940 bound for Calcutta. Joined Convoy OA.203 which was attacked by German planes at about 10pm on the 23rd when about 20 miles south-east of Duncansby Head. Several bombs struck the ship and she eventually sank at 2.30am the next day in approximate position 58°17′N 02°27′W. Survivors were picked up from lifeboats and a raft by HMS *Leith*, but the 3rd Mate, Mr K.W. Sabin, after spending all night alone on a raft, was rescued by the Norwegian ship *Don*. Mr R. Malcolm, the 5th Engineer, Mr F. Irving, a quartermaster, and 9 Lascars died. The *Llanishen* (Captain J.E. Thomas) was also sunk and 8 died.

MALABAR (Captain H.H. Armstrong). Commodore ship of Convoy HX.5 which sailed from Halifax, Nova Scotia, on 17 October 1939 bound for the UK. In the company of 2 other ships, dispersed from the convoy on the 28th and torpedoed and sunk by U.34 (Kptlt Wilhelm Rollmann) at 2.55am on the 29th in position 49°57′N 07°37′W. Mr W. Adams, the 3rd Engineer, and 4 Lascars died. Seventy-six were picked up from lifeboats by HMS *Grafton* (Cdr M.S. Thomas) and landed at Plymouth. The *Cairnmona* (Captain F.W. Fairley) also dispersed from the convoy, was torpedoed on the 30th by U.13 (Kptlt Karl Daublebsky von Eichhain) in position 57°38′N 01°45′W. Three died and 42 were picked up by the Aberdeen drifter HMS *River Lossie* (Skipper J.C. Spence).

MALAKAND (Captain Kinley). In Huskisson Dock, Liverpool, when an air raid began at 10pm on 3 May 1941. Hit by incendiary bombs and set on fire. The crew fought the fires, but with 350 tons of bombs in the holds becoming hotter all the time they left at midnight. A mobile fire unit took over at 1am, but finding it difficult to get near the ship due to the heat they too were unsuccessful and the *Malakand* blew up at 7.30am. No casualties.

MANAAR (I) (Captain Campbell Shaw). Sailed independently from Liverpool on 2 September 1939 bound for Calcutta. Intercepted by the surfaced U.38 (Kptlt Heinrich Liebe) shortly after 5am on the 6th when in position 38°28′N 10°50′W. Abandoned after being repeatedly struck by shells. The shelling continued while the boats were being lowered and the U-boat eventually used torpedoes to sink the ship. Those in the lifeboat commanded by Captain Shaw and containing 29 others, including a dead Lascar, were picked up by the Dutch ship *Mars* and landed at Lisbon on the 8th. Sixteen Lascars in another boat were picked up by the Portuguese ship *Carvalho Araujo* and also landed at Lisbon on the same day. Those in the boat commanded by the 2nd Mate and containing 22 others, were picked up by the Italian vessel *Castel Bianca* on the 7th and landed at Gibraltar on the 8th. The 12 in the boat commanded by the 3rd Mate were picked up by the Italian ship *Traviata* and landed at Cardiff on the 13th. Mr A. Craig, the 2nd Engineer, and 9 Lascars died; 78 survived. Mr J.G.M. Turner, the Radio Officer, was awarded the OBE for gallantry.

MANAAR (II) (Captain R. Mallet). Bound independently for the UK from East Africa when torpedoed by the Italian submarine *Leonardo da Vinci* (T.V. Gianfranco Gazzana-Priaroggia) at 3.15am on 18 April 1943 in position 31°30′S 33°30′E. After the crew had taken to 4 lifeboats, a second torpedo struck the ship, but she was later sunk by shellfire from the submarine which took the 2nd Mate, Mr Robert Gray, prisoner. The 2 boats, commanded by Mr S.S. Slade, the 1st Mate, and Mr A.R. Barrow, the 3rd Mate, landed together at Isilimela, South Africa, on the 21st and the survivors eventually went on to Durban. Captain Mallet's boat landed at Port St John's and Quartermaster W. Mackenzie's boat landed somewhere farther south. None died.

On 22 May, the *Leonardo da Vinci* was heading for Bordeaux when she transmitted a message stating she was returning to the base. This was heard by the British and her position found by direction finding. On being sent to the area, the destroyer HMS *Active* and the frigate HMS *Ness* heard the sound of her engines on their ASDIC machines at about noon on the 23rd and, after intensive depth-charging, she sank in approximate position 42°16′N 15°40′W. All died, including the prisoner, Mr Gray.

MANDASOR (Captain W. Hill). Sailed independently from Calcutta on 13 January 1941 bound for the UK via Durban. When in position 06°23′S 61°40′E on the 24th she was bombed and machine-gunned by a seaplane which, by dragging a wire behind it, carried away the ship's main and emergency aerials. The German raider *Atlantis* (KptzS. Bernhard Rogge) then appeared and, while she was shelling the *Mandasor*, the main aerial was repaired and hoisted and a QQQQ message transmitted. One man had been killed and several wounded by the plane, but now a shell killed Mr J.B. Leigh, the 2nd Mate, and Mr J.G.M. Turner, the 1st Radio Officer. (See *Manaar I*.) The lifeboats got away, but Captain

Hill was still on the *Mandasor* when a party from the *Atlantis* boarded to search for food and to set time bombs in the engine room. Afterwards he joined the other survivors on the raider, which incidentally lost its seaplane, but not its crew, as the guns of the *Mandasor* had scored several hits.

The *Speybank* (Captain A. Morrow) was captured on the 31st, and the Norwegian tanker *Ketty Brøvig* (Captain E. Møller), which furnished the *Atlantis* with badly needed fuel, on 2 February. On 21 March, the *Atlantis* rendezvoused with the supply ship *Tannenfels* (Captain Stroheim). The prisoners were transferred to her and, disguised as the Norwegian ship *Tarrongo*, she reached Bordeaux on 20 April. On 12 May, the prisoners were herded into cattle trucks for the journey to Germany, but while en route during the night the 3rd Mate, Mr E.S. Livingstone, jumped off the train. Next day, with the help of French people, he crossed into unoccupied France and eventually reached Marseille. On crossing the Pyrenees on the 23rd, he was arrested by the Spanish police. The *Mandasor* had a complement of 88, but I have no details of casualties. Under a prize crew the *Speybank* reached Bordeaux on 10 May.

MANGALORE (Captain W. Ison). Left Hull on 23 November 1939 and was mined at 7.30am the next day when at anchor in the Hawke Roads, Spurn. Broke in two and abandoned. All 77 survived.

MANIPUR (Captain R. Mallett). In Convoy HX.55 which sailed from Halifax on 3 July 1940 bound for the UK. During the night of the 17th, struck by 2 torpedoes fired by U.57 (Oblt Erich Topp) and sank in about 5 minutes in position 58°41′N 0°14′W. Fourteen died. Sixty-five were picked up by the destroyer HMCS *Skeena* (Lt Cdr J.C. Hibbard) and landed at Rosyth. (The tanker *Scottish Minstrel* (Captain P. Dunn) was torpedoed by U.61. See under ATHEL LINE.)

MATHERAN (Captain J. Greenall). Bound for Liverpool and in Convoy HX.79 which sailed from Halifax on 8 October 1940. Torpedoed by U.38 (Kptlt Heinrich Liebe) at 9.15pm on the 19th and sank within 10 minutes in approximate position 57°N 17°W. With great difficulty, due the rough seas, 72 survivors were picked up from the lifeboats by the rescue ship *Loch Lomond* (Captain W.J. Park) but the latter, straggling behind the convoy, was herself torpedoed at 6.15am the next day by U.100 (Kptlt Joachim Schepke). All the survivors of the *Matheran* survived their second sinking and, together with those of the *Loch Lomond* and men from two other sunken ships, were rescued by the minesweeper HMS *Jason* (Lt Cdr R.E. Terry) and landed at Methil on the 24th. Captain Greenall and 6 others died. One died on the *Loch Lomond* and 39 survived. (For details of other ships sunk and damaged in Convoy HX.79, see under *Wandby*, ROPNER SHIPPING CO.)

MATRA (Captain J. Butterworth). Crossed the Atlantic in Convoy HXF.7, but sunk by a mine off the East Tongue Light Ship in the Thames estuary on 13 November 1939. Sixteen died and the survivors were picked up by the Margate lifeboat.

SAMBRIDGE (Captain A.S. Bain – see *Makalla*). A Liberty ship on her maiden voyage, managed for the MOWT, sailing independently from Madras on 8 November 1943 bound for Aden. Torpedoed in the Arabian Sea by the Japanese submarine I-27 (Lt Cdr Toshiaki Fukumura) at about 7pm on the 18th. All in the engine room were killed, some blown overboard and others badly burned, before a second torpedo struck and the ship sank within minutes. The submarine then surfaced and, when her officers became angry at not being able to locate the Captain, Mr H. Scurr, the 2nd Mate, volunteered to become their prisoner and was taken on board. Those in the lifeboats and on rafts heard a burst of machine-gun fire before the submarine departed, but it is doubtful if any were hit. Early the following morning, the 4th Engineer, Mr T.G. McGlone, who had kept himself afloat all night without a lifejacket, was rescued by the *Tarantia*. Some hours later the *Tarantia* picked up 38 men from Captain Bain's boat and all were landed at Aden on the 20th. Also that day, those in the other boat were picked up by a frigate. Five died and 48 survived. Mr Scurr was taken to Penang, but nothing was known about his fate until New Year's Day 1945 when his mother received a postcard from him saying he was alive and in a prison camp in Japan. (After sinking the *Khedive Ismail* on 12 February 1944, with the loss of 1,383 lives, I-27 was sunk by the escorting destroyer *Petard* (Cdr R. Egan) and all hands, including Fukamura, perished.)

SOLON II (Captain J. Robinson). A captured French ship, managed for the MOWT, sailing independently when torpedoed by U.508 (Kptlt Georg Staats) at midnight on 3 December 1942 in position 07°45′N 56°30′W. Carrying manganese ore and copper, she sank in minutes. Seventy-five died, but a lifeboat containing the 4th Engineer, Mr A. Macfarlane, and 6 Lascars reached British Guiana (now Guyana) on the 7th.

TASMANIA (Captain Hans Christian Roder). Ex-Danish and managed for the MOWT, in Convoy SL.125 which sailed from Freetown on 16 October 1942. U-boats began to attack on the evening of the 26th. During the morning of the 28th, the *Tasmania* stopped to pick up survivors of the *Hope Castle* (Captain Dugald McGilp) and hurriedly caught up with the convoy again. Damaged by a torpedo fired by U.659 (Krvkpt. Hans Stock) at about 10pm on the 30th, but able to continue. At about 0010 hours on the 31st, struck and sunk by 2 torpedoes fired by U.103 (Kptlt Gustav-Adolf Janssen) in position 36°06′N 16°59′W. Forty-one in one boat were picked up by the *Mano* and landed at Greenock on 9 November. Forty-four in the other boat were picked up by the Norwegian ship *Alaska* (Captain Berge Mevatne) shortly before she too was torpedoed, by U.510 (Frgkpt. Karl Neitzel), but managed to reach Lisbon on 11 November. The *Baron Elgin* (Captain J.S. Cameron) stopped and, after taking 40 minutes to rescue a man from the water, she came across one of the *Tasmania*'s boats and took 40 on board, including 16 from the *Hope Castle*. She then went on to pick up the entire 49 from the *Baron Vernon* (Captain Peter Liston) sunk by U.604 (Kptlt Horst Höltring), and all were landed at Funchal, Madeira. Two died. (For details of other ships sunk in Convoy SL.125, see under *Nagpore*, P&O.)

Canadian Pacific Line/Canadian Pacific Railway (CPR)

BEAVERBRAE (Captain B.L. Leslie). Bound for Saint John, New Brunswick, from Liverpool when attacked 3 times by a single Focke-Wulf 200 Condor from 8.05am on 25 March 1941. Badly damaged, set on fire and men scalded in the engine room when 2 bombs struck the after deck. The crew abandoned ship at 8.45am, but Captain Leslie remained on board until 10am. During the day, an RAF plane dropped supplies to the lifeboats and at 5.15pm the destroyers HMS *Gurkha* (Cdr C.N. Lentaigne) and HMS *Tartar* arrived to carry all 86 to Scapa Flow. The *Beaverbrae* sank the following day in position 60°12′N 9°00′W.

BEAVERBURN (Captain T. Jones). Bound for Saint John, New Brunswick, sailing in Convoy OA.84 which left Southend on 2 February 1940 and dispersed on the 5th. Torpedoed and sunk by U.41 (Kptlt Gustav-Adolf Mugler) at 1.10pm on the 5th in position 49°20′N 10°07′W. One died. Seventy-six were picked up by the *Narragansett* and landed at Falmouth. During a second attack on the convoy on the 5th, U.41 was depth-charged and sunk by the destroyer HMS *Antelope* (Lt Cdr R.T. White). All 49 died. At 3.30am that same day, U.41 torpedoed and damaged the unescorted Dutch tanker *Ceramic*, but she succeeded in reaching Rotterdam.

BEAVERDALE (Captain C. Draper). Bound independently for Liverpool, sailing from Saint John on 18 March 1941 and from Halifax on the 26th. Torpedoed by U.48 (Kptlt Herbert Schultze) at 1am on 2 April, shelled at 1.25am, and blew up and sank 35 minutes later in position 60°50′N 29°19′W. All 79 abandoned ship; as one lifeboat, with the 1st Mate, R.W. Barker, in charge and containing 21 men, was never seen again it is thought that it may have been hit when the ship was being shelled. The remaining 2 boats set out for Iceland and Captain Draper's boat landed at Öndverdarnes on the 8th. Those in the other boat, commanded by the 2nd, Mate G. Mansell, were picked up by the trawler *Gulltoppur* (Ice.) and landed at Reykjavik. All 58 survivors subsequently boarded the *Royal Scot* and *Royal Ulsterman* which landed them at Greenock on 17 April. Twenty-one died. (U.48 was damaged by the explosion and had to return to base.)

BEAVERFORD (Captain E. Pettigrew). In Convoy HX.84 which sailed from Halifax on 28 October 1940 bound for the UK. Sunk by the German pocket battleship *Admiral Scheer* (KptzS. Theodor Krancke) during the late afternoon of 5 November. All 77 died. (For details of other ships sunk in Convoy HX.84 sunk by the Scheer, see under *Fresno City (I)*, REARDON SMITH LINE.)

BEAVERHILL. In Saint John and setting out to join a convoy for the UK when shortly after leaving her loading berth on 24 November 1944 she broke away from a tug and came to grief on the small rocky outcrop known as Hillyards Reef in the middle of the harbour. With her back broken, she lay there until disposed of in December 1946.

DUCHESS OF ATHOLL (Captain A.H.A. Moore). Troopship bound for Glasgow from Durban, sailing independently from Cape Town on 3 October 1942. Torpedoed by U.178 (Kptlt Hans Ibbeken) at 6.35am and 6.55am on the 10th. Abandoned when a third torpedo struck at 7.25am, sinking at 9.25am in position 07°03'S 11°12'W. At 9.15am, the U-boat surfaced among the lifeboats, questioned their occupants, apologised for sinking the ship and remained in the vicinity all day and most of the following night. As the main transmitter was put out of action, an RRRR message was sent using the lower-powered emergency one, but no acknowledgement was heard. However, further transmissions from a lifeboat transmitter were heard, very faintly, by the naval radio station on Ascension Island and by the ocean boarding vessel HMS *Corinthian* (Cdr E.J.R. Pollitt) which used her Direction Finder to locate them. She arrived on the scene at 8.30am on the 11th; all 821 survivors, including women and children, were on board her by 1.30pm and landed at Freetown on the 15th.

DUCHESS OF YORK (Captain W.G Busk-Wood). Accompanied by the troopship *California*, sailed from Greenock on 8 July 1943 bound for the Mediterranean. The ammunition ship *Port Fairy*, bound for Australia via Freetown, joined them the following morning and Convoy Faith consisted of only the three ships. On sailing from the Clyde, the escort was the destroyer HMS *Douglas* and the frigate HMS *Moyola*, but HMCS *Iroquois* (Cdr W.B.L. Holms) joined them on the 10th. At about 9.10pm on the 11th, the convoy was attacked by 3 Focke-Wulf 200 Condors. Both troopships were hit by bombs, set ablaze and abandoned. Because the flames might be seen by U-boats, the troopships were torpedoed and sunk by the escort off the coast of Spain at about 1.35pm on the 12th in position 41°51'N 15°24'W. When the frigate HMS *Swale* (Lt Cdr J. Jackson) arrived from Gibraltar at 10.35pm on the 11th, the survivors of the troopships were being picked up from lifeboats, rafts and from the water by the *Douglas, Moyola* and *Iroquois*. At 1.17am on the 12th, however, the *Swale* was ordered to escort the *Port Fairy* to Casablanca and that evening, when the two ships were attacked by two Condors, the *Port Fairy* was hit by a bomb and set on fire. With the help of the *Swale* the fire was extinguished and both ships reached their destination. Thirty-four died on the *Duchess of York* and the survivors, picked up by the naval ships, landed at Casablanca. (See under *California*, ANCHOR LINE.)

EMPRESS OF ASIA (Captain A.B. Smith). Troopship bound for Bombay and Singapore, sailing in Convoy WS.12ZB which left the Clyde on 12 November 1941, and from Freetown on the 28th. Arrived in Durban on 18 December and sailed for Bombay on the 24th. Arrived in Bombay on 14 January 1942 and having disembarked the troops and embarked 2,235 others, sailing in Convoy BM.12 on the 23rd, bound for Singapore. The other ships in the convoy were the *Félix Roussel* (157 troops), the *Devonshire* (1,673 troops) and the *Plancius* (Du.) (987 troops). Shortly after sailing, Convoy BM.12 joined up with a convoy of about 8 ships heading for Tanjung Priok, Batavia, but on nearing that port one of these ships, the *City of Canterbury*, remained with the Singapore section. At 11am on 4 February the convoy was in the Banka Strait when it was bombed by Japanese planes, flying at about 5,000ft. The *Empress of Asia* suffered five near misses, but although the ship was badly shaken, only 2 lifeboats were damaged. Later that day the *Devonshire* and the *Plancius* went on ahead of the other 3 ships as they were capable of a faster speed than the convoy's 12½ knots.

About 11am on the 5th, when nearing Sultan Shoal, approximately 11 miles from Singapore city, and sailing at reduced speed as they were about to take pilots on board, the convoy was bombed by about 24 Japanese planes. The *Empress of Asia*, their main target, was hit by at least 3 bombs and when it proved impossible to control the fires, she anchored near Sultan Shoal Lighthouse and was abandoned. Small boats came and ferried men from the ship to the lighthouse, while warships participated in the rescue. In particular, the sloop HMAS *Yarra* (Lt Cdr W.H. Harrington) took off about 1,800, and the ship was clear by 1pm. Fifteen troops died, but the only casualty out of the crew of 416, was the Canadian Pantryman D.R. Elworthy, who died from his injuries in a Singapore hospital.

The majority of the troops subsequently became prisoners of the Japanese. When the catering staff were asked to help with medical work in hospitals, 147 volunteered and most of them, too, are likely to have been taken prisoner. The remainder of the crew manned 3 small ships which sailed for Batavia on the 11th. Two of them arrived there on the 15th and at least some of the men were brought home on other ships. The other small ship, which put into Palembang on the 13th because of a shortage of fuel, appears to have succeeded in reaching Australia. The *Félix Roussel* (Captain Snowling) was also hit during the air attack on the 5th, but reached Singapore. Under a different commander, HMAS *Yarra* was sunk on 4 March and 138 died.

EMPRESS OF BRITAIN (Captain C.H. Sapsworth). Troopship bound independently for Liverpool from Port Tewfik and Cape Town when hit by two bombs delivered by a Focke-Wulf 200 Condor (Oblt Bernhard Jope) at about 9.20am on 26 October 1940. Set on fire and, about half an hour later, abandoned by all but a skeleton crew. Crew and passengers were picked up by the destroyers HMS *Echo* (Cdr S.H.K. Spurgeon) and ORP *Burza* (Pol.) (Kpt. Antoni Doroszkowski), and the A/S trawler HMS *Cape Arcona*. Under tow, and with both a sea and air escort, when torpedoed twice by U.32 (Oblt Hans Jenisch). The tow lines were then slipped by the tugs HMS *Seaman* and HMS *Raider* and she sank at 2.05am on the 28th in position 55°16′N 9°50′W. Twenty-five crew and 20 passengers died. Five hundred and ninety-eight survived. Two days later, U.32 was depth-charged and sunk by the destroyers HMS *Harvester* (Lt Cdr M. Thornton) and HMS *Highlander* (Cdr W.A. Dallmeyer). Nine died and 33 survived.

EMPRESS OF CANADA. (Captain G. Gould). Troopship bound independently for Takoradi and the UK from Durban when torpedoed by the Italian submarine *Leonardo da Vinci* (T.V. Gianfranco Gazzana-Priaroggia) at 11.50pm on 13 March 1943. Gazzana-Priaroggia then allowed time for the ship to be abandoned before putting a second torpedo into her about an hour later and she sank in position 01°13′S 09°57′W.

Owing to the ship listing heavily, the lifeboats on one side could not be lowered. Many were therefore left clinging to wreckage and some taken by sharks. Of the 1,346 on board 392 died, including 499 Italian PoWs and Greek and Polish refugees, among whom were 90 women and 44 crew. Approximately half of the casualties were Italian prisoners because the naval officer in charge of them failed to pass on the message to abandon ship. When the surviving prisoners learned this they threw him overboard, an action which brought no repercussions. It was 3 days later before the *Corinthian*, the destroyer HMS *Boreas* and the corvettes HMS *Petunia* and HMS *Crocus* arrived to pick up the survivors and take them to Takoradi and Freetown. (See also under *Manaar (II)*, BROCKLEBANK LINE and *Doryssa*, SHELL GROUP.)

MONTROSE. Converted into an Armed Merchant Cruiser and renamed HMS *Forfar* (Captain N.A.C. Hardy). Shortly after leaving Convoy HX.90 to join Convoy OB.251 on 2 December 1940, torpedoed 5 times between 5.46am and 6.57am by U.99 (Kptlt Otto Kretschmer) and sank in position 54°35′N 18°18′W. One hundred and seventy-two died and 159 were rescued: 13 picked up by the destroyer HMCS *St Laurent* (Lt H.S. Rayner) and landed at Gourock, 59 by the destroyer HMS *Viscount* and landed at Liverpool, and 87 by the *Dunsley* and landed at Oban. (See also under *Tasso*, ELLERMAN GROUP.)

NIAGARA. Jointly owned by Canadian Pacific and Union Steam Ship Co. of New Zealand, bound for Vancouver from Auckland. On 18 June 1940, when off Bream Head, Whangarei, struck a mine laid by the German raider *Orion* (Krvkpt. Kurt Weyher) and sank in position 35°53′S 174°54′E. No further details.

PRINCESS MARGUERITE (Captain R.A. Leicester). Troopship. Bound for Famagusta from Port Said in a convoy consisting of only one other merchantman and three warships when torpedoed twice by U.83 (Kptlt Hans-Werner Kraus) at 2.08pm on 17 August 1942. As the torpedoes hit her fuel tanks she was immediately set ablaze and the order given to abandon ship. When the fire spread to ammunition stores there was an explosion and she sank in position 32°03′N 32°47′E. Abandoning was hazardous as only 5 lifeboats could be lowered and there was burning oil on the water into which the majority had to jump. Five crew and 44 troops died. One thousand seven hundred and four were picked up by the destroyers HMS *Hero* (Lt W. Scott) and HMS *Kelvin* (Cdr M.S. Townsend) and landed at Port Said.

RUTHENIA. An oil hulk in Singapore when captured by the Japanese in 1942 and renamed *Choran Maru*. Returned to the owners in 1945.

Chapman, R., & Sons

BRIGHTON. Bound for Dunkirk from Immingham, struck a mine and sank as she approached the port on 6 May 1940. All 34 saved.

CARLTON (Captain W. Learmont). Sailed in Convoy OB.260 which left Liverpool on 16 December 1940 and dispersed on the 19th. Torpedoed and sunk by the Italian submarine *Calvi* (C.C. Giuseppe Caridi) on the 20th in position 55°18′N 18°49′W. Twenty-nine died. One lifeboat overturned when being launched and only 4 remained alive in the other boat when it was found 18 days later. (See also under *Jumna*, NOURSE LINE.)

CLEARTON (Captain J.E. Elsdon). Bound for Manchester from Rosario, sailing in Convoy SL.36 which left Freetown on 15 June 1940. Damaged by U.102 (Kptlt Harro von Klot-Heydenfeldt) at 11.55am on 1 July. Straggling when torpedoed again by U.102 at 1.25pm and sank in position 47°53′N 09°30′W. Eight died and 26 were picked up by the destroyer HMS *Vansittart* (Lt Cdr R.G. Knowling) which landed them at Plymouth. HMS *Vansittart* sank U.102 shortly before rescuing the survivors and all 43 on board died.

DEMETERTON. Sailed in Convoy OB.294 which left Liverpool on 5 March 1941 and dispersed on the 9th in position 51°29′N 20°30′W. Shelled by the German battleship

Scharnhorst on the 16th and sank in position 45°58′N 44°00′W. All taken prisoner. (For details of other ships sunk by the *Scharnhorst*, see under *British Strength*, BRITISH TANKER CO. LTD.)

EARLSTON (Captain H.J. Stenwich). Sailed in Convoy PQ.17 which left Hvalfjördur, Iceland, bound for Archangel, on 27 June 1942, but was ordered by the Admiralty to disperse on 4 July due to erroneous information they had received that heavy units of the German Navy had sailed from Norwegian ports. Damaged by bombs from Junkers 88s on the 5th. Torpedoed twice by U.334 (Kptlt Hilmar Siemon) at 5.47pm that same day and sank in position 74°54′N 37°40′E. None died. Captain Stenwich and 3 gunners taken prisoner. Twenty-seven landed on the Norwegian coast, while 21 landed on the Rybachy Peninsula (USSR) a week later.

SUNK BEFORE DISPERSAL

Christopher Newport (US), *Navarino** and *William Hooper* (US).

SUNK AFTER DISPERSAL

Alcoa Ranger (US), *Aldersdale*, *Bolton Castle*,* *Carlton* (US), *Daniel Morgan* (US), *El Capitan* (Pan.), *Empire Byron*, *Fairfield City** (US), *Hartlebury*, *Honomu* (US), *Hoosier* (US), *John Witherspoon* (US), *Olopana* (US), *Pan Atlantic** (US), *Pan Kraft** (US), *Peter Kerr** (US), *Paulus Potter* (Du.), *River Afton* (Commodore ship), *Washington** (US) and *Zaafaran*.*

**By the Luftwaffe for the loss of 5 planes.*

SHIPS THAT GOT THROUGH

9 July:

Bellingham, *Donbass* (USSR) and rescue ship *Rathlin*.

24 July:

Azerbaidjan (USSR), *Empire Tide*, *Ironclad* (US), *Silver Sword* (US) and *Troubadour* (Pan) – arrived under a naval escort.

28 July:

Winston-Salem (US).

FRUMENTON. Bound for London, crossed the Atlantic in Convoy SC.69 which left Halifax on 10 February 1942. Sunk by a mine off Orford Ness, Suffolk, on 4 March. No further details.

INNERTON. Requisitioned by the MOWT and sunk to become part of Mulberry Harbour at Gold Beach, Normandy, on 9 June 1944.

KORANTON (Captain C.E. Howard). Bound for Hull from Philadelphia with a cargo of pig iron, sailing in Convoy SC.25 which left Halifax on 10 March 1941. Straggling when torpedoed and sunk by U.98 (Kptlt Robert Gysae) at 1.50pm on the 27th in position 58°51′N 22°36′W. All 36 died.

MABRITON (Captain R. Patrick). Bound for Father Point, New Brunswick, sailing in Convoy OB.216 which left Liverpool on 19 September 1940 and dispersed in position 53°00′N 17°05′W on the 23rd. Torpedoed and sunk by U.32 (Oblt Hans Jenisch) at 3.25am on the 25th in position 56°12′N 23°00′W. Twelve died. Eighteen were picked up by the minesweeper HMS *Jason* (Lt Cdr R.E. Terry). Seven picked up by the sloop HMS *Rochester* (Cdr G.E. Renwick) on the 30th and were landed at Londonderry. (For details of other ships sunk after dispersal of Convoy OB.216, see under *City of Simla*, ELLERMAN GROUP.)

PETERTON (Captain T.W. Marrie). Bound for Buenos Aires, sailing in Convoy OG.89 which left Liverpool on 31 August 1942. Sailing independently when torpedoed 3 times and sunk by U.109 (Kptlt Heinrich Bleichrodt) at 1.14pm on 17 September in position 18°45′N 29°15′W. Nine died and Captain Marrie was taken prisoner by the U-boat. Twelve were picked up 8 days later by the *Empire Whimbrel* and landed at Buenos Aires. Twenty-two picked up 49 days later by the ASW trawler HMS *Canna* (T/Lt W.N. Bishop-Laggett) were landed at Freetown. In addition to the 9 who died at the outset, 15-year-old Apprentice Edward Briggs Hyde died on 16 November from bronchial pneumonia in the hospital in Freetown, where he is buried.

RIVERTON. Sunk at Narvik on 20 April 1940. (See under *Mersington Court,* COURT LINE.)

TIBERTON (Captain H. Mason). Bound independently for Middlesbrough from Narvik with a cargo of iron ore when torpedoed by U.23 (Kptlt Otto Kretschmer) at 4.05am on 19 February 1940, and sank in 30 seconds in position 58°55′N 01°53′W. All 34 died.

Managed for Ministry of War Transport

EMPIRE COWPER. Commodore ship of Convoy PQ.13 which arrived at Murmansk on 31 March 1942. Returning to the UK in Convoy QP.10 which sailed from Kola Inlet on 10 April. Bombed by a Junkers 88 the next day and abandoned. Hit again and sank in position 71°01′N 36°00′E. Nine died.

OTHER SHIPS SUNK AND DAMAGED IN CONVOY QP.10

Harpalion. Sunk by aircraft at the same time as the *Empire Cowper*.

Kiev (USSR). Damaged by aircraft and sunk by U.435 (Kptlt Siegfried Strelow).

El Occidente (Pan.). Sunk by U.435.

Stone Street (Pan.). Damaged by aircraft and returned to Kola.

Survivors were picked up by the ASW trawlers HMS *Paynter* (Lt R.H. Nossiter) and HMS *Blackfly* (Ty/Lt A.P. Hughes). On arrival at Iceland, they were transferred to the light cruiser HMS *Liverpool* which carried them to Scapa Flow from where they were taken to Scrabster by ferry. Because they may have been spies, rifles were trained on them as they landed and, because they were not members of the armed forces, the Salvation Army refused to serve them.

EMPIRE CURZON. Ran aground on the coast of Normandy in bad weather on 2 September 1944. Refloated and towed to Southampton, but subsequently scrapped in Briton Ferry.

EMPIRE DEW (Captain J.E. Elsdon). Bound independently for Father Point, New Brunswick, when torpedoed and sunk by U.48 (Kptlt Herbert Schultze) at 2.51am on 12 June 1941 in position 51°09′N 30°16′W. Twenty-three died. Nineteen were picked up by the destroyer HNoMS *St Albans* (Lt Cdr Gunnar Hovdenak) and landed at Liverpool.

FORT GOOD HOPE (Captain H. Gentles). On her maiden voyage, bound for Garston from Vancouver, when torpedoed and sunk by U.159 (Kptlt Helmut Witte) at 4.45am on 11 June 1942 in position 10°19′N 80°16′W. Two died. Forty-five were picked up by the gunboat USS *Erie* and landed at Cristobal.

China Navigation Co. (Butterfield & Swire)

ANKING. Requisitioned by the Admiralty in December 1941 and became a depot ship, HMS *Anking* (Captain J.P.L. Reid). At midnight on 27 February 1942, sailed from Batavia (Djakarta) in a convoy of 3 ships, escorted by the sloops HMIS *Jumna* and HMAS *Yarra*, bound for Tjilatjap on the south coast of Java. Arrived off Tjilatjap at 11am on 2 March, but ordered not to enter the port. HMIS *Jumna* was to proceed to Colombo, while the convoy was to make for Fremantle escorted by HMAS *Yarra* (Lt Cdr R.W. Rankin). On the morning of the 3rd, the *Yarra* picked up survivors of the *Parigi* (Du.) from two lifeboats.

When Japanese warships were seen on the 4th, Lt Cdr Rankin ordered the convoy to scatter while his ship engaged the enemy. HMS *Anking*, the motor minesweeper *MMS51* and HMAS *Yarra* were then sunk by the cruisers *Atago*, *Takao* and *Maya*, while the destroyers *Arashi* and *Nowaki* sank the RFA tanker *Francol* (Captain J.H. Burman). The *Yarra* was the last to sink. Of her complement of 151, 117 died in action, including her Captain, 21 died on rafts and 13 were picked up from a raft by the Dutch submarine K11 on the 9th. Twenty-six died on the *Anking* which carried Royal Australian Navy personnel. Fifty-seven were picked up on the evening of the sinking by the *Tawali* (Du.). Fourteen from *MMS51* were picked up from 2 Carley floats by the *Tjimanjoek* (Du.) on the 7th. Some survivors of the *Francol* were picked up from the water by the Japanese. One source states that they were never heard of again, but the RFA Association claims that 4 were killed and a fifth died later as a PoW.

ANSHUN (Captain Miller). Using her searchlights, the cruiser *Tatsuta*, assigned with other warships to evacuate surviving Japanese troops from Milne Bay, Papua New Guinea, bombarded the Gili Gili Wharves on the night of 6 September 1942, and sank the *Anshun*. There were casualties, but no details available. Survivors were picked up by HMAS *Arunta* and landed at Townsville, Queensland. Raised and towed to Sydney in 1944, and eventually sold.

CHANG-NING. Tug, captured by the Japanese at Ichang (Yichang) on the Yangtze in 1941. Trace lost.

CHANGLO. Tug, captured by the Japanese at Shanghai in 1941.

CHANGSHA. Captured by the Japanese in the China Sea in December 1941 and renamed *Ryuzan Maru*. Sunk by a mine off Hankow on 27 January 1945.

CHANGTEH. Tug, requisitioned by the Admiralty in 1941 and became HMS *Changteh*, an auxiliary minesweeper. With military personnel on board, sailed from Singapore on 13 February 1942. Bombed and sunk by Japanese planes in the Durian Strait on the 14th. Forty got away in a lifeboat, but 10 died while trying to land at Sumatra. It would appear that the survivors then walked from the mouth of the River Indragiri to Rengat. From Rengat, they were taken to Padang where they embarked on the cruiser HMS *Danae* which carried them to Tjilatjap. Over 100 died.

CHEKIANG. Captured by the Japanese near Shanghai on 8 December 1941 and renamed *Sekko Maru*. Torpedoed and sunk off Formosa (Taiwan) by the submarine USS *Sculpin* (Lt Cdr L.H. Chappell) on 9 August 1943 in position 24°55′N 122°00′E.

CHENGLING. Tug, captured by the Japanese at Ichang in December 1941. Trace lost.

CHENGTU. Scuttled at Hong Kong on Christmas Day 1941 to avoid capture by the Japanese. Raised in 1942 and sailed as the *Seito Maru* until sunk by a mine off Kota Bharu, Malaya, on 26 October 1944.

CHENYANG. Tug, captured by the Japanese at Hankow on 8 December 1941. Returned to owners in 1946.

CHINKONG. Tug, captured by the Japanese at Hankow in December 1941. Returned to owners after the war.

CHUTING. Tug, lost at Singapore on 15 February 1942.

FATSHAN. Captured by the Japanese at Canton (Guangzhou) on 8 December 1941 and renamed *Koto Maru*. Returned to owners in 1945.

HOIHOW (Captain W.M. Christie). Sailed independently from Port Louis, Mauritius, on the morning of 2 July 1943 bound for Tamatave, Madagascar. Torpedoed twice and sunk by U.181 (Krvkpt. Wolfgang Lüth) at 9.07pm that same day and sank within 3 minutes in position 19°30′S 55°30′E. One hundred and forty-five died. Three crew and one passenger were picked up by the *Mormacswan* (US) and landed at Montevideo on the 25th.

HSIN PEKING. Bound for Hong Kong from Tongku, NE China, when captured by the Japanese on 8 December 1941. Renamed *Rakuzan Maru*. Bombed and sunk by US carrier-based aircraft on 9 August 1945, off the east coast of Korea in position 42°30′N 129°45′E.

KALGAN. Captured by the Japanese at Bangkok on 12 December 1941. Renamed *Nishi Maru*. Bombed and sunk by US carrier-based aircraft off Manila on 13 November 1944.

KANCHOW. Scuttled at Hong Kong on Christmas Day 1941 to avoid capture by the Japanese. Raised in 1943 and called *Kanshu Maru* when she struck a mine off Hakata Bay, Kyushu, in October 1945. Beached and scrapped.

KAYING (Captain R.H. Fairley). Bound for Tripoli and Alexandria in a small convoy, sailed from Benghazi on 9 March 1943. Torpedoed and sunk by U.593 (Kptlt Gerd Kelbling) at 8.34pm on the 18th in position 32°59′N 22°21′E. Nine died. Seventy-two rescued and landed at Alexandria. U.593 also sank the *Dafila* (Captain G. Mugford). Twenty died and 3 wounded. Fifteen were picked up by the armed whaler HMSAS *Southern Maid* and landed at Derna.

KIANGSU. Captured by the Japanese when trying to escape from Hong Kong on the night of 8 December 1941. Renamed *Kinmon Maru*. Gutted by fire in Singapore on 10 June 1944.

KINGYUAN. One of the 11 ships lost when the *Fort Stikine*, loaded with explosives, blew up in Bombay on 14 April 1944. Sixteen other ships were seriously damaged. No details of casualties on the *Kingyuan*. (See under *Fort Stikine*, PORT LINE.)

KINTANG. Captured by the Japanese in Shanghai on 8 December 1941. Found damaged in Japan in September 1945, towed to Shanghai and broken up there in 1948.

KWANGTUNG. Carrying 98 crew and 35 military personnel when shelled and sunk by the Japanese submarine I-156 (Lt Cdr Katsuo Ohashi) on 5 January 1942, south of Java in position 09°12'S 111°10'E. The submarine machine-gunned and rammed the lifeboats, and only 35 were picked up the next day.

LI WO. Requisitioned by the Admiralty and became HMS *Li Wo* (T/Lt T. Wilkinson, RNR). Sailed from Singapore on 13 February 1942 bound for Tanjung Priok carrying military and civilian personnel, fleeing the beleaguered island. Having survived 4 air attacks after sailing, she came across two Japanese convoys escorted by a cruiser and destroyers on the 14th. Lt Wilkinson, with the approval of all on board, engaged the enemy. A transport ship was damaged, set ablaze and abandoned. Herself on fire and mortally wounded, the *Li Wo* rammed the transport and probably sank her. Seventy-seven died. Seven became PoWs.

LIANGCHOW. Blown ashore in a storm at Benghazi on 8 January 1943 and lost. No further details.

MING CHUAN. Captured by the Japanese in 1938 and renamed *Mari Maru*. Returned to owners in 1945.

NANNING. Scuttled at Hong Kong on 11 December 1941 to avoid capture, but raised by the Japanese and renamed *Nannin Maru*. Sunk by a mine when off Yawata (now part of Kitakyushu, in north Kyushu) on 16 July 1945.

PEKIN. Used as accommodation ship at Wuhu for 30 years, but disappeared from the records.

SAINGTAN. Captured in a damaged condition by the Japanese at Ichang on 8 December 1941. Repaired and renamed *Kinko Maru*. Sunk off Hankow by US planes in September 1944.

SHASI. Captured by the Japanese on 8 December 1941 and renamed *Rijo Maru*. Damaged off Ube, Japan, in an air attack on 15 July 1945, but returned to owners after the war.

SHUNTIEN (Captain W.L. Shinn). In Convoy TA.5 bound for Alexandria from Tobruk with hundreds of Italian and German PoWs on board when torpedoed and sunk by U.559 (Kptlt Hans Heidtmann) at 7.02pm on 23 December 1941 in position 32°6'N 24°46'E. Approximately 50 were picked up by the corvette HMS *Salvia* (Lt Cdr J.I. Miller), but when she herself was torpedoed and sunk by U.568 (Kptlt Joachim Preuss) at 1.35am the next day, all died together with the entire crew of 58. Nineteen were rescued by the destroyer HMS *Heythrop* (Lt Cdr R.S. Stafford), but over 700 died.

SINKIANG. Bound for Colombo from Calcutta when bombed and sunk by planes from the Japanese aircraft carrier *Ryujo* on 6 April 1942. There were casualties, but no details available.

SIUSHAN. Lost during evacuation of Singapore in February 1942, but no details.

SOOCHOW. Scuttled at Hong Kong on 8 December 1941 to avoid capture, but raised by the Japanese in 1942 and renamed *Tosan Maru*. Bound for Moji, sailing in Convoy HI.68 which left Manila on 24 July 1944. Torpedoed and sunk by the submarines USS *Flasher* (Cdr R.T. Whitaker) and USS *Crevalle* (Lt Cdr F.D. Walker) on the 26th in position 18°24′N 118°02′E.

SUITING. Lost to the Japanese on 8 December 1941, but no details.

SUIYANG. Struck a mine near Bangkok on 27 March 1946. Beached and became a total loss. No details.

SZECHUEN. Bound for Port Said from Haifa with a cargo of aviation spirit when she exploded and sank on 27 November 1942. Casualties, but no details.

TAIYUAN. Scuttled at Soerabaja on 2 March 1942 to avoid capture by the Japanese.

TATUNG. Scuttled south of Singapore on 17 February 1942 to avoid capture. Raised by the Japanese and renamed *Taito Maru*. Found unusable in Singapore in August 1945 and scrapped in 1947.

WAN YUAN. Requisitioned by the Admiralty in December 1941. Scuttled at Singapore on 12 February 1942 to avoid capture.

WANHSIEN. Scuttled at Hong Kong in February 1941 to avoid capture. Raised and scrapped in 1946.

WANTUNG. Captured by the Japanese in Shanghai on 8 December 1941 and renamed *Heizan Maru*. Sunk during a US air attack near Anking on 28 December 1943.

WENCHOW. Captured by the Japanese near Shanghai on 8 December 1941 and renamed *Hachigan Maru*. Torpedoed and sunk by the submarine USS *Seawolf* (Lt Cdr F.B. Warder) off Kudat, Borneo, on 14 August 1942.

WOOSUNG. Captured at sea by the Japanese on 8 December 1941 and the Master taken prisoner. Renamed *Reizan Maru*. Struck a mine and sank in the Yangtze on 18 January 1945.

WUHU. Captured by the Japanese on 8 December 1941, and renamed *Kakuzan Maru*. Sunk during a US air attack near Anking on 29 December 1943.

WULIN. Sunk in a Japanese air attack at Johore on 11 January 1942, but raised and renamed *Unryu Maru*. Torpedoed and sunk by the submarine HMS *Shakespeare* (Lt D. Swanston) east of Port Blair in the Andaman Islands on 31 December 1944 in position 11°40′N 93°15′E.

Clan Line

(INCLUDING THE SCOTTISH SHIRE LINE AND THE HOUSTON LINE, ALSO OWNED BY CAYZER, IRVINE & CO.)

BANFFSHIRE (Houston Line) (Captain H. Evans). Bound for the UK from Colombo and Aden when torpedoed and sunk by U.532 (Frgkpt. Ottoheinrich Junker) at 8.56pm on 29 September 1943 in position 09°26′N 71°20′E. One died. Ninety-nine were picked up by the minesweeper HMIS *Rajputana* (Lt W.G. Coltham) and landed at Colombo.

BERWICKSHIRE (Scottish Shire Line) (Captain J. McCrone). Bound for Tamatave, Madagascar, sailing in Convoy DN.68 which left Durban on 18 August 1944. Torpedoed and sunk by U.861 (Kptlt Jürgen Oesten) at 0038 hours on the 20th in position 30°58′S 38°50′E. Eight died. Ninety-four were picked up by the ASW trawler HMS *Norwich City* (Lt R.A. Groom) and landed at Durban. The tanker *Daronia*, also in the convoy, was damaged by U.861 and returned to Durban.

CLAN ALPINE (Captain J.H. Crellin). Bound for Walvis Bay and Port Sudan, sailing in Convoy OS.44 which left Liverpool on 6 March 1943. Torpedoed by U.107 (Kptlt Harald Gelhaus) at 5.30am on the 13th in position 42°45′N 13°31′W and subsequently scuttled by the sloop HMS *Scarborough* (Lt Cdr E.B. Carnduff). Twenty-eight died. Sixty-six were picked up by the sloop but transferred to the *Pendeen* and landed at Gibraltar. (For details of other ships sunk in Convoy OS.44, see under *Oporto*, ELLERMAN GROUP.)

CLAN BUCHANAN (Captain D. Davenport Jones). Sailing independently from Durban to Colombo when intercepted and shelled by the armed merchant raider *Pinquin* (KptzS. Ernst-Felix Krüder) in position 5°24′N 62°46′E on the morning of 28 April 1941. With her radio room destroyed, her steering gear out of action and her 4.7in gun blown in the engine room, she had little choice but to stop. After all had been taken on board the raider, she was scuttled. Her radio signals, although apparently weak, were nevertheless heard and triggered the search for the *Pinguin*. When she was sunk by the cruiser HMS *Cornwall* on 7 May, only 13 of the *Clan Buchanan*'s complement of 104 survived. (See under *British Emperor*, BRITISH TANKER CO. LTD.)

CLAN CAMPBELL (Captain J.F. Vooght). Bound for Malta, sailing from Alexandria on 20 March 1942 in the heavily escorted Convoy MW.10 which consisted of only 3 other ships – *Breconshire*, *Pampas* and *Talabot* (Nor.). On the 22nd the convoy came through an air attack relatively unscathed and in the evening the ships were ordered to proceed independently, each ship accompanied by a destroyer. The *Clan Campbell*, escorted by HMS *Eridge* (Lt Cdr W.F.N. Gregory-Smith) was bombed and sunk at 10.30am the next day when nearing her destination. Ten died, including Captain Vooght. The weather was bad and it took HMS *Eridge* 2½ hours to pick up the 112 survivors, some of whom also died. (See under *Pampas*, ROYAL MAIL LINE and *Breconshire*, HOLT, ALFRED, & CO.)

CLAN CHATTAN. In Convoy MW.9 which left Alexandria bound for Malta on 12 February 1942 escorted by 2 cruisers, 8 destroyers and an anti-aircraft ship. Bombed and sunk on the 14th. None died. (See under *Rowallan Castle*, UNION CASTLE LINE.)

CLAN CHISHOLM (Captain F.T. Stenson). Homeward bound from Calcutta, sailing in unescorted Convoy HG.3 which left Gibraltar on 12 October 1939. Torpedoed and sunk by U.48 (Kptlt Herbert Schultze). Four died. Forty-two were picked up by the *Bardaland* (Swed.) and landed at Kirkwall, 17 by the *Skud* (Nor.) and 15 by the *Warwick Castle*. (For details of other ships sunk in Convoy HG.3, see under *City of Mandalay*, ELLERMAN GROUP and *Yorkshire*, BIBBY LINE.)

CLAN CUMMING. Although in a heavily escorted convoy, she was torpedoed and damaged by the Italian submarine *Neghelli* on 18 January 1941 in position 37°15′N 24°04′E. Returned to Piraeus, where she had discharged her outward cargo, to undergo repairs in dry dock. The first German air raid took place on 6 April and when the *Clan Fraser* blew up while discharging ammunition, the *Clan Cumming* rolled on to her beam ends, a steel plate measuring 23ft by 3ft landing on her bridge top, and half of a windlass crashing through No 4 hatch which started a fire. With repairs completed, she sailed from Piraeus, but after shooting down a German plane, she was sunk by a mine in the Gulf of Athens on the 14th. Survivors were picked up by a Greek destroyer, but no further details. The *Neghelli* was depth-charged and sunk by the destroyer HMS *Greyhound* (Cdr W.R. Marshall-A'Deane) on 19 January. (See under *Clan Fraser*.)

CLAN FERGUSON (Captain A.N. Cossar). In Convoy WS.21S (Operation Pedestal) which sailed from Gibraltar on 10 August 1942 in an attempt to relieve Malta. Struck by an aerial torpedo at dusk on the 12th and, loaded with 2,000 tons of aviation spirit and 1,500 tons of explosives in her cargo, blew up. Eighteen died. Ninety-six landed in Tunisia and were interned by the Vichy French. (For details of Convoy WS.21S, see under *Waimarama* and *Empire Hope*, SHAW SAVILL & ALBION, *Deucalion* and *Glenorchy*, HOLT, ALFRED, & CO., *Dorset*, FEDERAL STEAM NAVIGATION CO. and *Ohio*, SHELL GROUP.)

CLAN FRASER (Captain J.H. Giles). Sailed in Convoy ANF.24 which left Alexandria on 1 April 1941 and arrived in Piraeus on the 4th. The Germans invaded Greece on the 6th and shortly after 9pm Junkers 88s operating from Catania in Sicily bombed shipping in the harbour. With 250 tons of TNT still to be discharged out of the 350 tons she had brought from Alexandria, she was struck by 3 bombs, set ablaze and abandoned. Six men were killed and 9 wounded. When she blew up at about 3.30am on the 7th, merchant seamen, service personnel and civilians were killed, the entire port was devastated and the violent explosion was felt in Athens, 15 miles away.

OTHER BRITISH SHIPS SUNK

City of Roubaix. See under ELLERMAN GROUP.

Cyprian Prince. See under FURNESS, WITHY GROUP.

Patris, *Surf* (armed yacht) and *Viking* (salvage ship).

BRITISH SHIPS DAMAGED

Cingalese Prince, *Clan Cumming*, *Devis* and *Katie Moller*.

Goalpara. See under BRITISH INDIA STEAM NAVIGATION CO.

GREEK SHIPS SUNK

Acropolis, *Elpis*, *Evoikos*, *Halcyon*, *Kyrapanagia II* and *Syyliani*.

The *Petalli*, set on fire by the explosion, was towed out of the harbour and sunk.

GREEK SHIPS DAMAGED

Agailiani and *Constantinos Louloudis*.

CLAN MACALISTER (Captain R.W. Mackie). At the Dunkirk evacuation had embarked 750 troops from the beaches by boat when hit by 3 bombs on 29 May 1940. Badly damaged and heavy casualties. Troops and wounded crew taken off by the destroyer HMS *Malcolm* (Captain T.E. Halsey); Captain Mackie and 12 crew were later taken off by the minesweeper HMS *Pangbourne* (Cdr D. Watson). As the ship then sank upright in shallow water, she continued to be the subject of attack.

CLAN MACARTHUR (Captain J.D. Matthews). Dispersed from Convoy DN.55 and bound for Port Louis, Mauritius, from Glasgow and Durban when torpedoed 3 times by U.181 (Frgkpt. Wolfgang Lüth) between 3am and 4am on 12 August 1943 and sank in position 23°00′S 53°11′E. Fifty-three died. After a fortnight, the lifeboats and raft were spotted by a Catalina flying boat which brought the Free French sloop *Savorgnan de Brazza* to their assistance and took the 77 survivors, some of whom were wounded, to Tamatave in Madagascar.

CLAN MACDOUGALL (Captain C.H. Parfitt). Bound independently for East London, South Africa, when torpedoed by U.106 (Kptlt Jürgen Oesten) at 3.13am and again at 3.34am on 31 May 1941; sank in position 16°50′N 25°19′W. Two died. Eighty-five landed at Santo Antão, Cape Verde Islands.

CLAN MACFADYEN (Captain P.E. Williams). Bound independently for Trinidad and the UK from Port Louis, Cape Town and Pernambuco when torpedoed and sunk by U.508 (Kptlt Georg Staats) at 0002 hours on 27 November 1942. Broke in two and sank within 4 minutes in position 08°57′N 59°48′W. Eighty-two died. Four were picked up from a raft by the sailing ship *Harvard* and landed at Port of Spain on the 31st. Six on another raft landed at Trinidad on 1 December.

CLAN MACFARLANE (Captain F.J. Houghton). Bound for Mombasa from Glasgow when collided with the *Ganges* on 17 July 1940 and sank in position 12°38′N 55°31′E, near the island of Socotra. The weather was bad and the ships were sailing in opposite directions without lights when the bow of the *Ganges* ploughed into the port side of the *Clan Macfarlane*. Forty-one died. Forty-seven survived. The *Ganges* remained afloat.

CLAN MACINDOE. With aviation spirit in her cargo, she went on fire in Alexandria on 15 April 1943. Beached near the port on the 27th and declared a total loss.

CLAN MACKINLAY. Bound for London from Bombay and in Convoy WN.31 when bombed and sunk by a German plane in position 58°35′N 02°53′W, off Noss Head, Wick, on 6 November 1940. Five died. When the author was on holiday in Keiss some years ago, there was a bale of rubber protruding from the sand which was thought to have come from the wreck. (The *Harborough*, also in Convoy WN.31, was damaged, set on fire and towed to Scapa Flow. One died: 18-year-old 2nd Radio Officer Frank West.)

CLAN MACNAB (Captain P.G. de Gruchy). In Convoy SL.68 which sailed from Freetown on 13 March 1941 bound for the UK. At about 11.20pm on the 17th, she altered course to starboard instead of to port as ordered and collided with the Norwegian tanker *Strix* in position 17°13′N 21°22′W. As she was taking in water, she detached from the convoy at 1.16pm the next day and set a course for St Vincent but shortly afterwards reported that she was sinking. The corvette HMS *Crocus* picked up 36 from a lifeboat, and another boat with over 30 landed at Silvao Bay, St Vincent, Cape Verde, on the evening of the 21st. Sixteen died: James Rice, 3rd Engineer; Walter Swift, Purser; and 14 Lascars. (For details of other ships sunk in Convoy SL.68, see under *Benwyvis*, BEN LINE.)

CLAN MACNAUGHTON (Captain R.J.W. Bennett). Bound independently for Trinidad from Alexandria and Freetown when torpedoed twice and sunk by U.155 (Kptlt Adolf Cornelius Piening) at 6pm on 1 August 1942 in position 11°54′N 54°25′W. Five died. Twenty-nine landed at the island of Tobago and 23 at Trinidad. Twenty-five were picked up by the *Empire Bede* (Captain T.E. Daniel) and landed at Port of Spain on the 5th. (The *Empire Bede* was torpedoed and sunk by U.553 (Krvkpt. Karl Thurmann) on the 18th.)

CLAN MACPHEE (Captain T.P.B. Cranwell). Bound for Bombay and in Convoy OB.197 which left Liverpool on 13 August 1940. Torpedoed and sunk by U.30 (Kptlt Fritz-Julius Lemp) at 7.32pm on the 16th, after the convoy had dispersed in position 57°30′N 17°14′W. Sixty-seven died. Forty-one were picked up by the *Kelet* (Hung.) which was herself torpedoed, shelled and sunk by UA (Kptlt Hans Cohausz) on the 19th. Six from the *Clan Macphee* died and the remaining 35, together with the 33 crew of the *Kelet*, were picked up by the *Varegg* (Nor.) and landed at Galway on the 26th.

OTHER SHIPS SUNK AND DAMAGED IN CONVOY OB.197

Alcinous (Du.) (Captain Jakob Kool). Torpedoed and damaged by U.46 (Oblt Engelbert Endrass). Towed to Gourock.

Hedrun (Swed.). Torpedoed and sunk by U.48 (Krvkpt. Hans Rudolf Rösing) shortly after noon on the 16th. Ten died.

CLAN MACPHERSON (Captain E. Gough, ex-*Clan Skene*). Homeward bound from Calcutta via Durban, sailing in Convoy TS.37 which left Takoradi on 18 April 1943. Torpedoed and sunk by U.515 (Kptlt Werner Henke) at about 5.45am on 1 May in position 07°58′N 14°14′W. Four died. One hundred and thirty-six were picked up by the MS trawler HMS *Arran* (T/Lt D.S. Hutton) and landed at Freetown on the same day. (For details of other ships sunk in Convoy TS.37, see under *Nagina*, BRITISH INDIA STEAM NAVIGATION CO.)

CLAN MACQUARRIE. Bound for New York from Durban when torpedoed, shelled and sunk by the Italian submarine *Leonardo da Vinci* (C.C. Luigi Angelo Longanesi-Cattani) on 13 June 1942 in position 05°30′N 23°30′W. One died. Sixty-one were picked up by the *Desirade* (Fr.) and landed at Cape Town. Twenty-eight landed at Trinidad.

CLAN MACTAVISH (Captain E.E. Arthur). Bound independently for Trinidad and New York from Beira and Durban. Picked up 35 survivors of the *Boringia* (Captain Sofus Heinrick Konard Kolls) at about 7am on 8 October 1942. The *Boringia* had been sunk by U.159 (Kptlt Helmut Witte) about 7 hours earlier with the loss of 25. The *Clan Mactavish* torpedoed and sunk by U.159 at 9.07am, also on the 8th, in position 34°53′S 16°45′E. Fifty-four died. The U-boat surfaced to question the survivors, but dived when a plane appeared and the *Matheran*, directed by the plane, picked up 67 from lifeboats. (See also under *Kalewa*, HENDERSON LINE.)

CLAN MACWHIRTER (Captain R.S. Masters). Bound for Hull from Bombay and Durban, sailing in Convoy SL.119 which left Freetown on 14 August 1942. Straggling when torpedoed twice by U.156 (Krvkpt. Werner Hartenstein) at 1am on the 27th in position 35°45′N 18°45′W. Sank when the lifeboats were being launched, but 3 boats got away. Twelve died. The U-boat surfaced and after questioning the survivors gave them the course and distance to the nearest land before leaving. The boats picked up men from the sea, clinging to wreckage and from rafts and when daylight came, set sail for Madeira. A gale separated the boats on the 28th, but when they were nearing Madeira on the 30th, the 2nd Mate succeeded in using a lifeboat transmitter to send a message which was heard by the Portuguese authorities. The sloop *Pedro Nunes* eventually found all 3 boats and carried their 74 occupants to Funchal. (For details of other ships sunk in Convoy SL.119, see under *City of Cardiff*, ELLERMAN GROUP.)

CLAN MENZIES (Captain W.J. Hughes). Sailed independently from Melbourne bound for Liverpool via the Panama Canal. Torpedoed and sunk by U.99 (Kptlt Otto Kretschmer) at 2.15am on 29 July 1940 in position 54°10′N 12°00′W. Six died and 88 landed at Enniscrone, Co. Sligo.

CLAN MONROE (Captain C.W. Banbury). Bound for the Tees from Cochin, Kerala, India, when she struck a mine off Harwich on 29 July 1940 in position 51°52′N 01°48′E. Beached in Hollesley Bay and declared a total loss. Thirteen died.

CLAN MORRISON. Bound for Blyth from Southampton, sailing in Convoy FN.102 when she struck a mine and sank off Cromer on 24 February 1940 in position 53°07′N 01°22′E. Survivors were picked up by the minesweeping trawler HMS *Nogi*. The *Jevington Court*, in Convoy FS.103, was mined and sunk off Cromer on the same day. All were picked up from lifeboats by the minesweeper HMS *Dunoon*.

CLAN OGILVY (Captain E. Gough). Homeward board from Chittagong, sailing in Convoy SL.68 which left Freetown on 13 March 1941. Torpedoed and sunk at almost the same time as the *Benwyvis* by U.105 (Kptlt Georg Schewe) at 10.35pm on the 20th in position 20°04′N 25°45′W. Sixty-one died and 21 rescued. (See also under *Benwyvis*, BEN LINE.)

CLAN ROSS. Bound independently for Cochin from Liverpool when torpedoed twice and sunk by the Japanese submarine I-6 (Lt Cdr Inaba Michimune) at about 2pm on 2 April 1942 in position 15°58′N 68°24′E. The submarine surfaced, provided the survivors with water and biscuits and the course to set for Bombay, and her crew saluted them and wished them 'Bon Voyage'. Eleven died and 3 wounded. Thirty-eight were picked up by the *L.A. Christensen* (Nor.) (Captain Arne Høst Olsen).

CLAN SKENE (Captain E. Gough). Bound independently for New York from Beira and Cape Town when torpedoed twice and sunk by U.333 (Kptlt Peter-Erich Cremer) at 9.05am on 10 May 1942 in position 31°43′N 70°43′W. Nine died. Seventy-three were picked up by the destroyer USS *McKean* and landed at San Juan, Puerto Rico.

CLAN STUART. Bound for Beira from the Tyne. In Convoy OA.107, and in fog, when the *Orlock Head*, bound for Rouen and Dunkirk and also in a convoy, ran into and sank her about 18 miles south-east of Start Point on 11 March 1940. Seventy-five were picked up by the French trawler *Notre Dame de Montlignon* and landed at Plymouth. The *Orlock Head* remained afloat.

STIRLINGSHIRE (Scottish Shire Line) (Captain C.E. O'Byrne). Bound for Liverpool from Australia and Bermuda, sailing in Convoy HX.90 which left Halifax on 21 November 1940. Torpedoed and sunk by U.94 (Kptlt Herbert Kuppisch) at 6.23 pm on 2 December in position 55°36'N 16°22'W. All 74 were picked up by the *Empire Puma* and landed at Liverpool. (For details of other ships sunk in Convoy HX.90, see under *Tasso*, ELLERMAN GROUP.)

Court Line

(OWNED BY HALDIN & PHILIPPS)

ALDINGTON COURT (Captain A. Stuart). Sailed independently on 8 October 1942 for Saldanha Bay, South Africa, and Alexandria. Torpedoed and sunk by U.172 (Kptlt Carl Emmermann) at 10.20pm on the 31st in position 30°20'S 02°10'W. Thirty-three in one lifeboat were never found. Eleven were picked up by the *City of Christiania* and landed at Montevideo on 25 November. Thirty-four died.

ARLINGTON COURT (Captain C. Hurst). Bound for Hull from Rosario, sailing in Convoy SL.7 which left Freetown on 31 October 1939. On 16 November, straggling when torpedoed twice between 2pm and 3pm by U.43 (Kptlt Wilhelm Ambrosius) and sank in position 48°14'N 11°42'W. Twelve died. Twenty-two were picked up by the *Algenib* (Du.) and landed at Queenstown. Six were picked up by the *Spinanger* (Nor.) and landed at Dover.

BONNINGTON COURT. Bound for the Tyne for repairs, in Convoy FN.388 which left Southend on 19 January 1941. Bombed and sunk that day by German planes, 9.5 cables 275° from Sunk Light Vessel in the Thames estuary. Two died: 2nd Engineer R.W. Lindemere and 3rd Engineer W.R. Shaw.

CEDRINGTON COURT. Sailed from Buenos Aires on 22 November 1939 and in Convoy SL.13 which left Freetown on 18 December. Detached from convoy when, on 7 January 1940, she struck a mine laid by a German destroyer and sank in position 51°23'N 1°35'E, 2 miles north-east of North Goodwin Lightship. All 34 survived.

CRESSINGTON COURT (Captain W.J. Pace). Bound independently for Cape Town, Durban and Alexandria, sailing from Trinidad on 14 August 1942. Torpedoed and sunk by U.510 (Krvkpt. Karl Neitzel) at 9.07am on the 19th in position 07°58'N 46°00'W. Eight died. Thirty-six were picked up by the *Woensdrecht* (Du.) which was torpedoed and sunk by U.515 (Kptlt Werner Henke) on 12 September. The only casualty was one of the crew of the *Cressington Court* and all the others were picked up the next night by two US patrol ships and landed at Port of Spain, Trinidad.

DARLINGTON COURT (Captain C. Hurst, ex-*Arlington Court*). Sailed in Convoy HX.126 which left Halifax on 10 May 1941. Torpedoed twice by U.556 (Kptlt Herbert Wohlfarth) at about 1pm on the 20th and capsized and sank in position 57°28′N 41°07′W. Twenty-eight died. Twelve were picked up by the rescue ship *Hontestroom* (Du.) at 7am on the 21st, and she landed a total of 70 survivors at Reykjavik on the 27th. (For details of other ships sunk in Convoy HX.126, see under *Elusa*, SHELL GROUP.)

DORINGTON COURT (Captain E.D.A. Gibbs). Sailed independently from Madras on 4 November 1942 bound for Lourenço Marques (Maputo), Durban and the UK. Torpedoed, shelled and sunk by U.181 (Kptlt Wolfgang Lüth) during the evening of the 24th in position 27°00′S 34°45′E. Four died. On the morning of the 26th, a lifeboat containing 23 men and towing a dinghy containing another 16 arrived off Inhaca Island from where a tug towed them into Lourenço Marques.

HANNINGTON COURT. Bound for the UK, sailing from Table Bay on 12 July 1941. An explosion occurred in the engine room the next morning, killing 2 engineers. She went on fire and was abandoned when the fire got out of control; the crew were picked up by the *Burdwan*. Taken in tow by the *Burdwan*, but the tow parted. After more attempts to tow her, by minesweepers and an Admiralty tug, a last attempt was made by the tug *T.S. McEven*, but as this was discontinued because the tug was running out of fuel, the still-burning ship was shelled and sunk by the light cruiser HMS *Dragon* on the 19th in position 34°46′N 19°23′E.

ILVINGTON COURT. Bound for Glasgow from Pepel, Sierra Leone, with a cargo of iron ore. Torpedoed by the Italian submarine *Dandola* (C.C. Ricardo Boris) on 26 August 1940 and sank in 5 minutes in position 37°14′N 21°52′W. Eight died and 19 survived. No further details.

JEVINGTON COURT. In Convoy FS.103 which left the Tyne on 23 February 1940 bound for Southend. Struck a mine the next day when 8¼ miles 161° from Cromer Knoll Light Vessel in position 53°08′N 01°22′E. All were picked up by the minesweeper HMS *Dunoon* (Lt Cdr H.A. Barclay) which was herself mined on 30 April while sweeping off Great Yarmouth and sank in position 52°45′N 2°23′E. Twenty-six died and 47 were rescued.

KENSINGTON COURT (Captain J. Scofield). Bound independently for Birkenhead from Rosario when shelled by U.32 (Kptlt Paul Büchel) at 12.38pm on 18 September 1939. Torpedoed at 2pm and sank in position 50°31′N 08°27′W. All 35 were picked up by two Sunderland flying boats piloted by F/Lts T.M.F. Smith and J. Barrett who were both awarded the DFC.

LAVINGTON COURT (Captain J.W. Sutherland). Bound for Cape Town and the Middle East from Leith and Oban, sailing in Convoy OS.34 which left Liverpool on 11 July 1942. Torpedoed by U.564 (Kptlt Reinhard Suhren) at 2.30am on the 19th. Towed by two tugs, but foundered in position 49°40′N 18°04′S on 1 August. Seven died. Forty-one were picked up by the sloop HMS *Wellington* (Lt Cdr W.F.R. Segrave) and landed at Londonderry. *Empire Hawksbill* (Captain H.T. Lamb) was torpedoed by U.564 at the same time as the *Lavington Court*. All 47 died.

MARSA. In Convoy MKS.30G which originated at Port Said and rendezvoused with Convoy SL.139 on 16 November 1943. Straggling in position 46°40′N 18°18′W when bombed and sunk by a German plane on the 21st. One died and 47 survived. The sloop HMS *Chanticleer* (Lt Cdr R.H. Bristowe), torpedoed by U.515 (Kptlt Werner Henke) on the 18th, was towed to the Azores and declared a total loss. Twenty-eight died. The *Delius* was damaged during another air attack on the 22nd.

MERSINGTON COURT. When the German invasion of Norway began on the night of 8/9 April 1940, the *Mersington Court* was loading iron ore in Narvik, as were the *Peverton, Blythmoor, Romanby* and *Riverton*. On 10 and 13 April, the first and second battles of Narvik were fought between the Royal Navy and the Kriegsmarine and both won by the former. A force consisting of British, French and Polish troops began to land on the 15th and, assisted by Norwegian troops, caused the much smaller force of Germans and Austrians to withdraw on 30 May. Owing to the serious situation in France, however, which culminated in Dunkirk, the British could not afford to have forces in Norway, so 25,000 Allied troops were evacuated from Narvik between 4 and 8 June.

The crew of the *Mersington Court*, together with those of the other ships mentioned above and survivors from the destroyers HMS *Hunter* and HMS *Hardy*, were taken prisoner. Held in a school, they were extremely cold and received insufficient food. Then forced to walk through deep snow and over rough ground to Sweden, they were released by the Germans but interned by the Swedes. Thirteen tried to escape on the Norwegian ships *Charente* and *Gudvang* which, attempting to run the German blockade, were caught and the men taken to the Milag Nord camp in Germany. Others embarked on ships which succeeded in reaching Kirkwall on 23 January 1941. (See also under *Romanby*, ROPNER SHIPPING CO.) The *Mersington Court*, scuttled by the Germans on 15 April 1940, was broken up in Antwerp in October 1952.

OVINGTON COURT (Captain G. Linsell). On the night of 25/26 November 1940, at anchor at Durban awaiting entry to the port, her anchors dragged and as seawater had entered the engine room through open hatches, there was insufficient pressure in the boiler to move the ship. The tug *T. Erikson* was dispatched too late to be of any assistance. A lifeboat made it safely to the beach, but a second one carrying 12 men capsized in the heavy surf. All were recovered but 4, including 15-year-old Cabin Boy Gordon Hunter, died later in Addington Hospital. Others were rescued by breeches buoy, and Captain Linsell, the last to remain on board, left by this means, carrying the ship's monkey. Four died and 34 were rescued.

PENNINGTON COURT (Captain J. Horne). Bound for Belfast from Saint John, New Brunswick, sailing in Convoy SC.103 which left New York on 26 September 1942. Straggling when torpedoed twice by U.254 (Kptlt Odo Loewe) at 9pm on 9 October. Struck by a third torpedo at 11.10pm and sank in position 58°18′N 27°55′W. The U-boat saw survivors in lifeboats, but they were never seen again. All 45 died.

ROSSINGTON COURT. Bound for the Tyne from New Westminster, British Columbia, sailing in Convoy HX.26 which left Halifax on 9 March 1940. When about 400 miles east of Halifax on the 13th, was rammed in the engine room by the *Athelviking*, whose steering gear had jammed, and sank. All 36 were picked up from a lifeboat and landed at Falmouth. The *Athelviking* returned to port.

Cunard White Star Ltd

ANDANIA. Requisitioned by the Admiralty and converted to the Armed Merchant Cruiser HMS *Andania* (Captain D.K. Bain). On patrol when torpedoed by UA (Kptlt Hans Cohausz) at 0009 hours on 16 June 1940 and sank in position 62°36′N 15°09′W. All 347, including 2 injured, were taken off by the trawler *Skallagrimur* (Ice.), transferred to the destroyer HMS *Forester* (Lt Cdr E.B. Tancock) and landed at Scapa Flow on the 17th.

BOSNIA (Captain W.H. Poole). Bound independently for Manchester from Sicily when fired upon by U.47 (Kptlt Günther Prien) at 8.15am on 5 September 1939. Torpedoed at 9.38am and sank in position 45°29′N 09°45′W. One died. Thirty-one were picked up by the *Eidanger* (Nor.) (Captain Johannes Presthus) and landed at Lisbon the following day.

CARINTHIA. Requisitioned by the Admiralty and converted to the AMC HMS *Carinthia* (Captain J.F.B. Barrett). Bound for the UK, sailed from Gibraltar on 1 June 1940. Torpedoed by U.46 (Oblt Engelbert Endrass) at 1.13pm on the 5th in position 53°13′N 10°40′W. Taken in tow the next morning by the tugs HMS *Marauder* (Lt W.J. Hammond) and HMS *Brigand*, but sank off Tory Island, Co. Donegal, at 7pm. Four died. Remainder were picked up by the destroyers HMS *Volunteer* (Lt Cdr N. Lanyon), HMS *Wren* (Lt Cdr F.W.G. Harker), HMS *Berkeley* (Lt Cdr H.G. Walters) and the minesweeper HMS *Gleaner* (Lt Cdr H.P. Price).

LACONIA (Captain Rudolph Sharp, ex-*Lancastria*). Troopship bound for Canada from Port Tewfik, Aden, Mombasa and Durban, sailed independently from Cape Town on 1 September 1942 with 2,741 on board, made up of the crew, military personnel, civilians (mainly women and children), 1,809 Italian PoWs and their Polish guards. Shortly after 10pm on 12 October, she was torpedoed twice by U.156 (Krvkpt. Werner Hartenstein) and sank an hour later in position 05°05′S 11°38′W. When the second torpedo struck a hold containing 450 Italians most were killed and the ship took on a list to starboard. The order to abandon ship was given and the Polish guards saved many lives by preventing the remaining Italians rushing the undamaged lifeboats.

U.156 immediately took part in the rescue of survivors and was later assisted by U.506 (Kptlt Erich Würdemann), U.507 (Krvkpt. Harro Schacht) and the Italian submarine *Cappellini* (T.V. Marco Revedin). With lifeboats in tow and hundreds of survivors standing on their decks, they headed for the African coast. The Vichy French warships *Gloire*, *Dumont d'Urville* and *Annamite* had been ordered out of Senegal and Dahomey to rendezvous with them. The survivors were transferred to the French ships which subsequently landed 1,083 survivors, including 415 Italians, at Dakar. One thousand six hundred and fifty-eight died, including Captain Sharp.

Although U.156 announced that any ships participating in the rescue would not be attacked and displayed a white sheet with a red cross painted on it, this and another U-boat were attacked by a US B-24 Liberator based at Ascension Island. U.156 had 151 survivors on board at the time – 142 on them on deck – and several were killed. She dived and suffered no damage. As it had also been subjected to an attack by this plane the previous day, this resulted in what became known as the Laconia Order, issued by Grand

Admiral Karl Dönitz: 'All efforts to save survivors of sunken ships, such as the fishing out of swimming men and putting them on board lifeboats, the righting of overturned lifeboats, or the handing over of food and water, must stop ...'

LANCASTRIA (Captain Rudolph Sharp). Troopship, sailed from Liverpool on 14 June 1940 to participate in the evacuation of military personnel and civilians from St Nazaire. Anchored 11 miles south-west of the port when an air attack began at 1.50pm on the 17th. As she had embarked the maximum she could carry, the destroyer HMS *Havelock* advised Captain Sharp to leave. This he declined to do as, without a naval escort, his ship would be at the mercy of U-boats. She was struck by three bombs at 3.48pm, rolled over and sank within 20 minutes. Over 1,400 tons of fuel oil leaked into the sea, many choked on it and were drowned, while others were killed by planes which targeted the people in the water. Between 3,000 and 6,000 died, and 2,477 were rescued by other ships taking part in the evacuation.

LAURENTIC. Requisitioned by the Admiralty and converted into an AMC. (See under *Patroclus*, HOLT, ALFRED, & CO.)

Denholm, J. & J., Ltd

BROOMPARK (Captain J.L. Sinclair). Bound for New York from the Tyne, sailing in Convoy ON.113 which left Liverpool on 17 July 1942. Torpedoed and damaged by U.552 (Kptlt Erich Topp) shortly before 4am on the 25th in position 49°02′N 40°26′W. Sank at 6am on the 28th when being towed to St John's, Newfoundland, by the tug USS *Cherokee*. Four died. Forty-five were picked up by the corvette HMCS *Brandon* (Lt J.C. Littler) and landed at St John's. (For details of other ships sunk in Convoy ON.113, see under *Empire Rainbow*, ROPNER SHIPPING CO.)

DENPARK (Captain J. McCreadie). Homeward bound from Takoradi, sailing in Convoy SL.109 which left Freetown on 4 May 1942. Torpedoed and sunk by U.128 (Kptlt Ulrich Heyse) at 0028 hours on the 13th in position 22°28′N 28°10′W. Twenty-one died. Twenty-five were picked up by the *Nordlys* (Dan.) and the *City of Windsor*, and landed at the Clyde.

EARLSPARK (Captain E.J. Williams). Sailing independently and on passage from Sunderland to Bordeaux when torpedoed and sunk by U.101 (Kptlt Fritz Frauenheim) shortly after noon on 12 June 1940 in position 42°26′N 11°33′W. Seven died. Thirty-one were picked up by the sloop HMS *Enchantress* (Cdr A.K. Scott-Moncrieff).

ELDONPARK. Bound for Port Talbot from Bône (Annaba) in Algeria when stranded on the Helwick (a sandbank running along the south Gower coast and about 1km off the shore at Port Eynon) in bad weather on 7 February 1940. Beached at Port Eynon and the crew sheltered in the wheelhouse, the only part of the ship above water. All 37 taken off by the Mumbles lifeboat (Coxswain W.E. Davies) when the ebb tide brought better conditions.

GRANGEPARK (Captain J.S. Webster). Bound for Oran, sailed from the Clyde on 8 November 1942 in Convoy KMS.3. Torpedoed and sunk by U.263 (Kptlt Kurt Nölke) shortly after 10am on the 20th in position 35°55´N 10°14´W. Four died. Sixty-seven were picked up by the sloop HMS *Fowey* (Cdr L.B.A. Majendie) and landed at Gibraltar.

OTHER SHIPS SUNK IN CONVOY KMS.3

Prins Harald (Nor.) (Captain Westbye Foss-Sørensen). Torpedoed by U.263 at the same time as the *Grangepark*. Three died. Survivors picked up by the rescue ship and landed at Gibraltar.

Trentbank. By an aerial torpedo on the 24th. (See under WEIR, ANDREW, & CO./ BANK LINE.)

(A torpedo fired by U.263 was caught and exploded in the anti-torpedo net of the *Ocean Pilgrim*.)

HOLMPARK (Captain A. Cromarty). Bound independently for Trinidad and Philadelphia from Lourenço Marques and Cape Town when torpedoed and sunk by U.516 (Kptlt Gerhard Wiebe) at 11.07am on 24 October 1942 in position 13°11´N 47°00´W. Mr A.F. Hargreaves, the Chief Steward, and DEMS Gunner W. Hunt, RN, died. Forty-nine landed at Port Dennery, St Lucia on 8 November. On the 13th, Deck Boy W.E. Addy died in hospital in St Lucia where he is buried.

LYLEPARK (Captain C.S. Low). Bound independently for Cape Town from New York when intercepted, shelled and sunk by the German raider *Michel* (KptzS. Helmuth von Ruckteschell) on 11 June 1942 in approximate position 14°00´W 10°00´W. Thirty-six died and 3 wounded. Twenty-two taken prisoner by the *Michel* but transferred to the supply ship *Doggerbank* (ex-*Speybank*, captured by the *Atlantis*) which took them to Japan where they spent the remainder of the war in Camp Fukuoka.

In order to avoid captivity, Captain Low and the 1st Mate Mr Reid remained on the burning ship and slid down the falls into a damaged lifeboat. When it sank, they succeeded in boarding separate rafts. Captain Low, spotted by a plane from the carrier HMS *Archer*, was picked up and taken to Freetown, while Mr Reid and the 2nd Mate were also brought there by the *Avila Star*, and all were returning to the UK on her when she was torpedoed and sunk on 6 July. Along with others, Captain Low, with a wounded arm and shoulder, was picked up from a lifeboat by the Portuguese destroyer *Lima* and taken to Ponta Delgada in the Azores. Mr Reid was in charge of one of the *Avila Star's* lifeboats which was never seen again. (See also under *Avila Star*, BLUE STAR LINE, *Patella*, SHELL GROUP, *Arabistan*, STRICK LINE, *Empire Dawn*, RUNCIMAN, WALTER, & CO. LTD/MOOR LINE LTD and *Gloucester Castle*, UNION-CASTLE LINE.)

MOUNTPARK (Captain J. Edwards). Bound for Manchester from Bahia Blanca, sailing in Convoy SL.69 which left Freetown on 23 March 1941. Bombed and sunk by a Focke-Wulf 200 Condor when in position 55°21´N 12°21´W. Six died and 5 wounded. (See also under *Swedru*, ELDER DEMPSTER LINE.)

WELLPARK (Captain A. Cant). Bound independently for Alexandria from Canada when a plane from the German cruiser *Thor* (KptzS. Günther Gumprich) brought down her aerial by means of a hook at the end of a wire at about 3pm on 30 March 1942. Shelled by the *Thor* and scuttled after being abandoned in approximate position 25°00'S 10°00'W. Seven died. Forty-one taken prisoner on board the *Thor,* but later transferred to the supply ship *Regensburg* for transportation to Japan. (See under *Kirkpool*, ROPNER SHIPPING CO.)

Donaldson Line

ATHENIA (Captain James Cook). Bound for Montreal, sailing independently from Liverpool on 2 September 1939. War was declared at 11am on the 3rd and at 9.45pm the ship was torpedoed by U.30 (Oblt Fritz-Julius Lemp) and sank at 11am on the 4th in position 56°44'N 14°05'W. Of the 1,103 passengers and 329 crew, 112 died. Of the survivors, 602 were picked up by the *Knute Nelson* (Nor.) (Captain Carl Johan Anderssen) and landed at Galway. Two hundred and twenty-three, picked up by the illuminated motor yacht *Southern Cross* (Swed.), transferred to the *City of Flint* (US) (Captain J.A. Gainard) and landed at Halifax, Nova Scotia. Four hundred and ninety-five were picked up by the destroyers HMS *Electra* (Lt Cdr S.A. Buss) and HMS *Escort* (Lt Cdr J. Bostock) and landed at Greenock. As U-boat commanders were instructed to observe the Hague Convention, which stated that merchant ships were not to be sunk without warning, Lemp contravened the instruction. This infuriated Hitler as many of the *Athenia*'s passengers were US citizens and the sinking might have brought the United States into the war.

CORACERO (Captain R.C. Young). Bound for Liverpool from Buenos Aires, sailing in Convoy HX.229 which left New York on 8 March 1943. Torpedoed and sunk by U.384 (Oblt Hans-Achim von Rosenberg-Gruszcynski) shortly after 2pm on the 17th in position 51°04'N 33°20'W. Five died. Fifty-three were picked up by the destroyer HMS *Mansfield* (Lt Cdr L.C. Hill) and landed at Gourock. U.384 was sunk by an RAF B-17 Flying Fortress when off the south-west of Ireland on the 19th. All 47 died. (For details of other ships sunk in Convoy HX.229, see under *Canadian Star*, BLUE STAR LINE.)

CORINALDO (Captain W. Anderson). Bound for Glasgow from Buenos Aires, sailing in Convoy SL.125 which left Freetown on 16 October 1942. Torpedoed and damaged by U.509 (Krvkpt. Werner Witte) at 10.16pm on the 29th, dropped out of the convoy and abandoned. Damaged again by U.659 (Krvkpt. Hans Stock) shortly after 2am on the 30th. Torpedoed and shelled by U.203 (Kptlt Hermann Kottmann) just over 2 hours later and sank in position 33°12'N 18°24'W. Eight died. Fifty were picked up by HMS *Cowslip* and landed at Gibraltar. (For details of other ships sunk in Convoy SL.125, see under *Nagpore*, P&O.)

CORRIENTES (Captain T.H.Y. Stewart). Bound for Montreal from Glasgow, sailing in Convoy OB. 217 which left Liverpool on 21 September 1940 and dispersed at noon on the 25th. Torpedoed in the engine room by U.32 (Oblt Hans Jenisch) shortly after 2.30am on the 26th and abandoned. Torpedoed and shelled by U.37 (Kptlt Victor Oehrn) between 8pm and 9.40pm on the 28th and sank in position 53°49'N 24°19'W. All 50 were picked up by the *Kolsnaren* (Swed.) and landed at Philadelphia. (For details of other ships sunk after the dispersal of Convoy OB.217, see under *Eurymedon*, HOLT, ALFRED, & CO.)

CORTONA (Captain M.M. Brown). Bound for Buenos Aires, sailing in Convoy OS.33 which left Liverpool on 1 July 1942 bound for Freetown. Dispersed from the convoy when torpedoed by U.116 (Krvkpt. Werner von Schmidt) at 0022 hours on the 12th. Shortly afterwards, torpedoed 3 times by U.201 (Kptlt Adalbert Schnee) and sank in position 32°45′N 24°45′W. Twenty-three were picked up from a lifeboat on the 22nd by the destroyer HMS *Pathfinder* (Cdr E.A. Gibbs) and landed at Londonderry. Thirty-one in another lifeboat were never heard of again.

OTHER SHIPS SUNK AFTER DISPERSING FROM CONVOY OS.33

Empire Attendant. See under WEIR, ANDREW, & CO./BANK LINE.

Port Hunter. See under PORT LINE.

Shaftesbury (Captain U. Eynon). By U.116. Captain taken prisoner by the U-boat and landed at Lorient on 23 August. Twenty-three picked up on the 23rd by the *Tuscan Star* were transferred to HMS *Folkestone* (Cdr J.G.C. Gibson) and landed at Freetown. Twenty-one landed from a lifeboat at Villa Cisneros, in Spanish Sahara. All 45 survived.

Siris. See under ROYAL MAIL LINE.

Sithonia (Captain C.C. Brown). By U.201. After 14 days in a lifeboat, 25 picked up by a Spanish fishing boat and landed at Las Palmas on 7 August. After 18 days in a lifeboat, 21 landed at Timiris in Senegal and interned by the Vichy authorities. Seven died.

U.136 (Kptlt Heinrich Zimmermann) was depth-charged and sunk by the French destroyer *Léopard*, the frigate HMS *Spey* and the sloop HMS *Pelican*. All 45 died.

ESMOND (Captain J.B.M. Macaffert). Bound for Sydney, Cape Breton, from the Tyne, sailing in Convoy OB.318 which left Liverpool on 2 May 1941. Torpedoed by U.110 (Kptlt Fritz-Julius Lemp) at about noon on the 9th and sank in position 60°45′N 33°02′W. Twenty-two were picked up by the *Borgfred* (Nor.). Twenty-seven were picked up by the *Aelybryn* and landed at Sydney on the 18th. One was picked up by the corvette HMS *Aubretia* (Lt Cdr V.F. Smith) and landed at Reykjavik. None died. (For details of other ships sunk in Convoy OB.318, see *Gregalia* (below) and under *Ixion*, HOLT, ALFRED, & CO.)

GERALDINE MARY (Captain G.M. Sime). Bound for Manchester from Botwood, Newfoundland, sailing in Convoy HX.60 which left Halifax on 23 July 1940. Torpedoed by U.52 (Kptlt Otto Salman) at 9.22am on 4 August and sank about 2 hours later in position 56°46′N 15°48′W. Three died. Twenty-eight were picked up by one of the escort ships and landed at Methil on the 8th. Six others were picked up and landed at Liverpool. Fourteen landed at Uig on the Isle of Lewis.

OTHER SHIPS SUNK IN CONVOY HX.60 – ALSO BY U.52 ON 4 AUGUST

Gogovale (Captain F.S. Passmore). All 37 picked up by HMS *Vanoc*.

King Alfred (Captain R. Storm). Seven died. Thirty-four picked up by the destroyer HMS *Vanoc* (Lt Cdr J.G.W. Deneys) and landed at Liverpool. The stern of the *King Alfred* remained afloat and was sunk by the destroyer.

GRACIA. In Convoy OB.287 which sailed from Liverpool on 16 February 1941. A single Focke-Wulf 200 Condor attacked the convoy on the 19th, 20th and 21st, and the *Gracia* was bombed and sunk at 1.25pm on the 19th in position 59°34′N 07°18′W. All 48 rescued.

OTHER SHIPS SUNK AND DAMAGED IN CONVOY OB.287

Housatonic. Bombed at the same time as the *Gracia* and sank the next day. Three died. Thirty-one survived.

St Rosario and *Rosenborg*. Damaged at 11am on the 20th and both returned to port.

Scottish Standard (Captain J. Ward). Bombed at 9.23am on the 21st and abandoned. Five died. Thirty-nine picked up by the destroyer HMS *Montgomery* (Cdr H.F. Nash) and landed at Oban. Torpedoed and sunk the next day by U.96 (Kptlt Heinrich Lehmann-Willenbrock) which was depth-charged and damaged by HMS *Montgomery*.

GREGALIA (Captain A. Bankier). Bound for Buenos Aires from Glasgow, sailing in Convoy OB.318 which left Liverpool on 2 May 1941. Torpedoed and sunk by U.201 (Kptlt Adalbert Schnee) at about 2.30pm on the 9th in position 60°24′N 32°37′W. All 66 were picked up by HMT *Daneman*. Fifty-two were subsequently transferred to the *Aelybryn* and 14 to the *Borgfred* (Nor.). (For details of other ships sunk in Convoy OB.318, see *Esmond* (above) and under *Ixion*, HOLT, ALFRED, & CO.)

MODAVIA. Having crossed the Atlantic in an ocean convoy, joined Convoy WP.300 which left Milford Haven on 25 February 1943 bound for the Solent. Off Berry Head, at the southern end of Torbay, torpedoed by an E-boat at 1.20am on 27 February 1943, but continued in a north-easterly direction for about half an hour before capsizing in approximate position 50°24′N 03°01′W. All 54 rescued.

OTHER SHIPS SUNK IN CONVOY WP.300

Harstad (Nor.). Minesweeper. Twenty-two died. Arne Johnsen, the sole survivor, was wounded and spent some time in the freezing water before being rescued.

HMS *Lord Hailsham* (T/Lt P.H.G. Clark). ASW trawler. Eighteen died.

LST-381. Landing Tank Ship. Some sources claim that this LST was sunk, but a US source outlines the history of this vessel which survived the war.

PARTHENIA. In Convoy HX.76 which sailed from Halifax, Nova Scotia, on 26 September 1940. On 9 November, when proceeding up the Clyde estuary, sunk in collision with the outward bound *Robert F Hand*. At least one man, W.H. Graham, died. The ships were on almost reciprocal courses and the *Robert F Hand* survived the collision.

ROTHERMERE (Captain G. M. Sime, ex-*Geraldine Mary*). Bound for London from Botwood, Newfoundland, sailing in Convoy HX.126 which left Halifax on 10 May 1941. Owing to the ships being sunk by U-boats, the commodore gave the signal to scatter at about 12.50pm on the 20th. Torpedoed by U.98 (Kptlt Robert Gysae) at about 3.30pm and 3.50pm on the 20th and sank in position 57°48′N 41°36′W. Twenty-two died. Thirty-four were picked up from 2 lifeboats by the *Brúarfoss* (Ice.) at 11pm on the 23rd and landed at Reykjavik on the 27th. (For details of other ships sunk in Convoy HX.126, see under *Elusa*, SHELL GROUP.)

SULAIRIA (Captain R.C. Young). Bound for Montreal from Glasgow, sailing in Convoy OB. 217 which left Liverpool on 21 September 1940 and dispersed at noon on the 25th. Torpedoed by U.43 (Kptlt Wilhelm Ambrosius) at 1.30pm on the 25th and sank in position 53°43′N 20°10′W. One died. Fifty-six were picked up by HMCS *Ottawa* and landed at Gourock on the 27th. (For details of other ships sunk after the dispersal of Convoy OB.217, see *Corrientes* (above) and under *Eurymedon*, HOLT, ALFRED, & CO.)

Managed for Ministry of War Transport

EMPIRE REDSHANK (Captain J.H. Clinton). Bound for Galveston from Cardiff, sailing in Convoy ON.166 which left Liverpool on 11 February 1943. Torpedoed by U.606 (Oblt Hans-Heinrich Döhler) at 10.20pm on the 22nd when in position 46°53′N 34°32′W. So badly damaged that she was sunk by HMCS *Trillium* which picked up all 47 and landed them at St John's, Newfoundland. (For details of ships sunk in Convoy ON.166, see under *Eulima*, SHELL GROUP.)

EMPIRE SPRING (Captain A. McKechan). CAM ship – Catapult Aircraft Merchantman – bound for Halifax from Manchester, commodore ship of Convoy ON.63 which left Liverpool on 2 February 1942 and dispersed on the 13th in position 42°08′N 55°20′W. Torpedoed and sunk by U.576 (Kptlt Hans-Dieter Heinicke) at 3.37am on the 14th in approximate position 42°00′N 55°00′W. All 53 died. Corvette HMS *Arbutus* (T/Lt A.L.W. Warren), escorting Convoy ON.63, was torpedoed by U.136 (Kptlt Heinrich Zimmermann) at 10.36pm on the 5th, broke in two and sank in position 55°05′N 18°43′W. Forty-three died and 47 survived.

EMPIRE WHALE (Captain J.T. Davitt). Bound for the Tyne from Pepel, Sierra Leone, sailing in Convoy SL.126 which left Freetown on 12 March 1943. Torpedoed and sunk by U.662 (Kptlt Heinz-Eberhard Müller) at 10.50pm on the 29th in position 46°44′N 16°38′W. Forty-seven died. Ten were picked up by the frigate HMS *Spey* (Cdr H.G. Boys-Smith) and landed at Londonderry. (For details of ships sunk in Convoy SL.126, see under *Umaria*, BRITISH INDIA STEAM NAVIGATION CO.)

Elder Dempster Line

ABOSSO (Captain R.W. Tate). Sailed independently from Cape Town on 8 October 1942 bound for Liverpool with a crew of 182 and 189 passengers. Between 10.13 and 10.28pm on the 29th torpedoed twice by U.575 (Kptlt Günther Heydemann). As an SSSS message was transmitted, and heard, before she sank in position 48°30′N 28°50′W, the authorities were alerted. Thirty-one in No 5 boat were picked up by the sloop HMS *Bideford* (Lt Cdr W.J. Moore) on 2 November and landed at Gibraltar. Three hundred and forty died, including 28 of the 33 Dutch submariners being carried as passengers.

ACCRA (Captain J.J. Smith). Bound for West Africa, sailing in Convoy OB.188 which left Liverpool on 23 July 1940. Torpedoed by U.34 (Kptlt Wilhelm Rollmann) at 2.47pm on the 26th and sank an hour and a quarter later in position 55°40′N 16°28′W. Nineteen died when a motorboat capsized in the choppy sea. Four hundred and seventy-seven were picked up by the *Hollinside*, the *Loke* (Nor.), the sloop HMS *Enchantress* (Cdr A.K. Scott-Moncrieff) and the corvette HMS *Clarkia* (Lt Cdr F.J.G. Jones). (For details of other ships sunk in Convoy OB.188, see under *Thiara*, SHELL GROUP.)

ADDA (Captain J.T. Marshall). Bound for West Africa, commodore ship of Convoy OB.323 which left Liverpool on 17 May 1941 and dispersed on the 25th. When nearing Freetown torpedoed and sunk by U.107 (Kptlt Günther Hessler) at 4.42am on 8 June in position 08°30′N 14°39′W. Ten crew and 2 passengers died. Four hundred and eighty-eight were picked up by the corvette HMS *Cyclamen* (Lt H.N. Lawson) and landed at Freetown on the same day.

ALFRED JONES (Captain H. Harding). Bound for Takoradi, commodore ship of Convoy OB.320 which left Liverpool on 8 May 1941 and dispersed on the 14th. Torpedoed by U.107 (Kptlt Günther Hessler) at 2.09pm on 1 June and after another torpedo struck about half an hour later, sank in approximate position 08°N 15°W. No boats could be lowered. Fourteen died. Sixty-two were picked up by the corvette HMS *Marguerite* (Lt Cdr A.N. Blundell) and landed at Freetown.

APAPA (Captain E.V. Davies). Bound for Liverpool, sailing from Freetown in Convoy SL.53 on 27 October 1940. At about 9.25am on 15 November the convoy was attacked by Focke-Wulf 200 Condors. The *Apapa* was hit, set ablaze, abandoned and sank at noon in position 54°34′N 16°47′W. Twenty-three died. Two hundred and twenty-nine rescued by the *Mary Kingsley*, *New Colombia*, *Boulderpool*, and the corvette HMS *Broke*. Some passengers were able to jump across to the *Mary Kingsley* when her Master brought the stern of his ship close to the stern of the *Apapa*.

OTHER SHIPS SUNK IN CONVOY SL.53

Cree (Captain R.H. Twentyman). With a cargo of iron ore, straggling when torpedoed and sunk by U.123 (Kptlt Karl-Heinz Moehle) at 0021 hours on the 22nd in position 54°39′N 18°50′W. All 44 died.

> *Lilian Moller*. Dispersed from the convoy when torpedoed and sunk by the Italian submarine.
>
> *Maggiore Baracca* (C.C. Entico Bertarelli). Sunk on the 18th in position 53°57′N 18°05′W. All British officers and Chinese crew died.
>
> *Planter* (Captain D.H. Bryant). Straggling when torpedoed and sunk by U.137 (Kptlt Herbert Wohltarth) on the 16th, in position 55°38′N 08°28′W. Thirteen died. Sixty picked up by the destroyer HMS *Clare* (Lt Cdr C. Gwinner) on the 17th and landed at Londonderry the next day.

BASSA (Captain G.E. Anderson). Bound for New York, sailing in Convoy OB.218 which left Liverpool on 24 September 1940. Dispersed from the convoy when torpedoed and sunk by U.32 (Oblt Hans Jenisch) at 0053 hours on the 29th in approximate position 54°N 21°W. Lifeboats left the ship but were never seen again. All 50 died.

> **OTHER SHIPS SUNK AND DAMAGED IN CONVOY OB.218**
>
> *Empire Ocelot* (Captain P. Bonar). Dispersed from the convoy. By U.32. Two died. Thirty-two picked up by the destroyer HMS *Havelock* (Captain E.B.K. Stevens) and landed at Liverpool.
>
> *Manchester Brigade* (Captain F.L. Clough). See under MANCHESTER LINERS.
>
> *Stratford* (Captain J.R. Murray). By U.137. Two died. Fifteen picked up by the corvette HMS *Gloxinia* (Lt Cdr A.J.C. Pomeroy) and 17 by the ASW trawler HMS *Wolves* (Skipper B. Pile).
>
> *Vestvard* (Nor.) (Captain O.N. Brástad). Dispersed from convoy. Torpedoed twice by U.31 (Kptlt Wilfried Prellberg). One drowned after jumping overboard. The other 30 landed near Slane Head Light in Galway on 1 October.
>
> (*Ashantian*. Damaged by U.137 and escorted to Belfast by HMS *Gloxinia* and HMS *Wolves*. Four died.)

BEREBY (Captain H. Harding, ex-*Bodnant* and *Alfred Jones*). Bound for Takoradi, sailing in Convoy OS.7 which left Liverpool on 23 September 1941. Ran aground at Ringford Point, Co. Down, the following day and became a total loss. None died and her cargo was salvaged. The *Nailsea Manor* (Captain J.H. Hewitt), also in the convoy, was torpedoed and sunk by U.126 (Kptlt Ernst Bauer) on 10 October in position 18°45′N 2°18′W. All 42 were picked up by the corvette HMS *Violet* (Lt Cdr K.M. Nicholson), transferred to the *City of Hong Kong*, and landed at Freetown on the 14th.

BODNANT (Captain H. Harding). Bound for Freetown and Lagos, sailing in Convoy OB.265 which left Liverpool on 26 December 1940. On the 30th she was in collision with the *City of Bedford*, commodore ship of Convoy HX.97, sailing in the opposite direction and sank in approximate position 60°03′N 23°01′W. None died. The *City of Bedford* also sank with the loss of 48 lives. (See also under ELLERMAN GROUP.)

BOMA (Captain C.E. Anders). Bound for Lagos, sailing in Convoy OB.193 which left Liverpool on 4 August 1940. Torpedoed and sunk by U.56 (Oblt Otto Harms) at 9.38pm the following day in position 55°44′N 08°04′W. Three died. Fifty were picked up by the *Vilja* (Nor.), transferred to the destroyer HMS *Viscount* (Lt Cdr M.S. Townsend) and landed at Liverpool.

DAGOMBA (Captain J.T. Marshall, ex-*Adda*). Bound for Trinidad, sailing in Convoy TS.23 which left Takoradi on 29 October 1942. Dispersed from the convoy when torpedoed twice by the Italian submarine *Ammiraglio Cagni* (C.C. Carlo Liannazza) at 5.52pm on 3 November and sank 3 minutes later in position 2°29′N 19°00′W. No SSSS message sent as wireless room wrecked. Captain Marshall, Mr Frost, the Chief Engineer, Mr Ellis, the Bosun, and Mr Court, an AB, went down with the ship, but all were recovered from the water. The submarine surfaced, her commander apologised for sinking the ship, provided the survivors with provisions and told them the course to steer for Freetown. Twenty-five in No 4 boat, with the 3rd Mate Mr Wicksteed in charge, were picked up by the Vichy French minesweeper *Aviso Annamite* on 11 November, taken to Dakar and interned. They were subsequently released and arrived in Bathurst (Banjul), The Gambia, on 13 December. Twenty-one in No 2 boat, with the 1st Mate Mr Bird in charge, were picked up by the Portuguese sloop *Bartolomeu Dias* on 14 November and landed at Luanda, Angola, on the 21st. Taken from there by mail boat, they arrived in Freetown on the 30th. Seven died, including the 2nd Mate Mr Mail, in No 4 boat, and 3 on rescue ships.

Some were of the opinion that the *Dagomba* was sunk by a submarine wearing a wolf's head as a device; when a survivor of U.164 was questioned in the US in 1943, he claimed that this was U.513 whose commanding officer was called Wolf. U.513, however, was commanded by Krvkpt. Rolf Rüggeberg; the captured German had never heard of him, and Rüggeberg did not claim the kill.

DARU (Captain W. Rowlands). Bound for the UK, sailing in Convoy SL.85 which left Freetown on 25 August 1941 and joined up with Convoy HG.72. Bombed by a German plane when off the SE coast of Ireland on 15 September and sank in position 51°57′N 05°58′W. All 56 rescued.

DIXCOVE (Captain R. Jones). Bound for the Liverpool, sailing in Convoy SL.87 which contained 11 ships and left Freetown on 14 September 1941. Torpedoed and sunk by U.107 (Krvkpt. Günther Hessler) at 6.31am on the 24th in position 31°12′N 23°4′W. One died. Fifty-one were picked up by the *Ashby* and the *Fana* (Nor.) (Captain Nic Knudsen) but transferred to the sloops HMS *Gorleston* (Cdr R.W. Keymer) and HMS *Lulworth* (Lt Cdr C. Gwinner), and landed at Londonderry on 4 October.

OTHER SHIPS SUNK IN CONVOY SL.87

Edward Blyden. See below.

John Holt (Captain C.G. Hime). By U.107. One died. Sixty-eight picked up by HMS *Gorleston* and landed at Ponta Delgada.

Niceto de Larrinaga (Captain F.M. Milnes). By U.103 (Kptlt Werner Winter). Three died. Forty-two picked up by HMS *Lulworth*. Eleven picked up by the corvette HMS *Gardenia* (Lt Cdr H. Hill) and landed at Ponta Delgada in the Azores.

St Clair II. See under UNITED AFRICA CO. LTD.

Silverbelle. See under SILVER LINE.

DUNKWA (Captain J.W. Andrew). Bound for Opobo, Nigeria, from Glasgow, sailing in Convoy OB.310 which left Liverpool on 13 April 1941 and dispersed on the 18th. Torpedoed and sunk by U.103 (Krvkpt. Viktor Schütze) at 5.17pm on 6 May in position 08°43′N 17°13′W. Seven died. Schütze had an overturned lifeboat righted and provided the 39 survivors with water. They were subsequently picked up by the *Polydorus* (Du.) and landed at Oban, Cameroon. Two days earlier, the *Japan* (Swed.), also dispersed from the convoy, was sunk by U.38 (Kptlt Heinrich Liebe). All 54 landed in Vichy French territory and interned.

EDWARD BLYDEN (Captain W. Exley). In Convoy SL.87. Torpedoed twice by U.103 (Kptlt Werner Winter) at 11.46pm on 22 September 1941 and sank in position 27°36′N 24°29′W. All 63 were picked up by the sloop HMS *Bideford* (Lt Cdr W.J. Moore) and landed at Londonderry on 5 October. (For other ships sunk in Convoy SL.87, see under *Dixcove* above.)

HENRY STANLEY (Captain R. Jones, ex-*Dixcove*). Bound for Freetown, sailing in Convoy ON.149 which left Liverpool on 26 November 1942. Dispersed from the convoy when torpedoed by U.103 (Oblt Gustav-Adolf Janssen) at midnight on 6 December and again at 1.30am, and sank in position 40°35′N 39°40′W. Sole survivor was Captain Jones, taken prisoner by the U-boat and released from captivity in April 1945. Sixty-two died, in 4 lifeboats, and are presumed to have perished in a gale.

OTHER SHIPS SUNK AFTER DISPERSING FROM CONVOY ON.149

Ceramic. See under SHAW SAVILL & ALBION.

Serooskerk (Du.) (Captain D. de Boer). By U.155 (Kptlt Adolf Comelius Piening). No lifeboats launched and all 83 died.

ILORIN (Captain C.H. Bott). Unescorted, when nearing Takoradi from Lagos and with her navigational lights on, torpedoed and sunk by U.125 (Kptlt Ulrich Folkers) at 10.06pm on 1 September 1942 in approximate position 05°N 01°W. Sank within 3 minutes; all 30 died.

MARY SLESSOR (Captain C.H. Sweeny, ex-*Mattawin*). Bound for Liverpool from Algiers in Convoy MKS.7 which at about midnight on 7 February 1943 ran into a minefield laid by U.118 (Krvkpt. Werner Czygan) 5 or 6 days previously. Struck two mines and sank in position 35°55′N 6°02′W. Thirty-two died. Forty-eight picked up by the sloop HMS *Landguard* (Lt Cdr T.S.L. Fox-Pitt) and landed at Liverpool.

OTHER SHIPS IN CONVOY MKS.7 SUNK BY MINES AT THE SAME TIME

Baltonia (Captain J.A. Prosser). Eleven died. Fifty-one picked up by the *Kingsland*, transferred to the corvette HMCS *Alberni* (Lt A.W. Ford), and landed at Londonderry.

Empire Mordred (Captain H. Mackinnon). Fifteen died. Fifty-five picked up by the sloop HMS *Scarborough* (Lt Cdr E.B. Carnduff) and landed at Londonderry.

MATTAWIN (Captain C.H. Sweeny). Bound for Alexandria via Cape Town and Durban, sailing from New York on 29 May 1942. Torpedoed twice by U.553 (Kptlt Karl Thurmann) between 7.18am and 7.30am on 2 June and sank in position 40°14′N 66°01′W. All 71 rescued: 37 by the *Torvanger* (Nor.) (Captain Leif Danielsen) and landed at Halifax, and 34 by the USCGC *General Greene* and landed at Cape Cod. The *Torvanger* was herself torpedoed and sunk by U.84 (Oblt Horst Uphoff) on 23 June. Four died and 33 survived.

NEW BRUNSWICK (Captain C.M. Whalley). Bound for Lagos, sailing from Glasgow on 12 May 1942 and joined Convoy OS.28. Torpedoed by U.159 (Kptlt Helmut Witte) at about 3.25am on the 21st and sank in position 36°53′N 22°55′W. Three died. Twelve were picked up by the sloop HMS *Totland* (Lt Cdr S.G.C. Rawson), 10 by the sloop HMS *Wellington* (Lt Cdr W.F.R. Segrave), 7 by the sloop HMS *Weston* (Cdr J.G. Sutton), 5 by the corvette HMS *Woodruff* (Lt Cdr F.H. Gray) and 25 by the *Inchanga*. U.159 depth-charged and slightly damaged. (For other ships sunk in Convoy OS.28, see under *Athelknight*, ATHEL LINE.)

NEW COLUMBIA (Captain F.B. Kent). Bound independently for Lagos from Matadi and Libreville when torpedoed twice by U.68 (Oblt Albert Lauzemis) between 9.14pm and 9.44pm on 31 October 1943 and sank in position 04°25′N 05°03′E. All 65 crew and 19 Kroo men were picked up by the *Conakrian* and landed at Lagos.

NEW TORONTO (Captain C.J. Kewley). Bound for Liverpool from Forcados, Nigeria, via Lagos and Accra when torpedoed and sunk by U.126 (Kptlt Ernst Bauer) at 9pm on 5 November 1942 in position 05°57′N 02°30′E. Three crew and a cattleman died. Fifty-seven crew, 28 cattlemen and 17 Kroo men were picked up by the motor launch HMS ML-263.

SEAFORTH (Captain W. Minns). Bound independently for West Africa from Liverpool when torpedoed twice by U.103 (Krvkpt. Viktor Schütze) between 9.33pm and 9.50pm on 18 February 1941 and sank in position 58°48′N 18°17′W. All 59 died although lifeboats were seen to be launched after the first strike.

SWEDRU (Captain Little). In Convoy SL.69 which sailed from Freetown on 23 March 1941 bound for the UK. Set on fire and badly damaged when bombed by a Focke-Wulf 200 Condor on 16 April in position 55°21′N 12°50′W. Abandoned on the 19th and sunk by the escort in position 54°44′N 11°02′W. Seventeen crew and 7 passengers died; 37 survived. (See also under *Mountpark*, DENHOLM, J. & J., LTD.)

WILLIAM WILBERFORCE (Captain J.W. Andrew, ex-*Dunkwa*). Bound independently for Liverpool from Lagos and Takoradi when torpedoed and sunk by U.511 (Oblt Fritz Schneewind) at 9.42pm on 9 January 1943 in position 29°20′N 26°53′W. Three died. Sixty were picked up by the *Monte Arnabal* (Sp.) and landed at Las Palmas.

Managed for Ministry of War Transport

EMPIRE ABILITY (Captain H. Flowerdew). Formerly the German ship *Uhenfels*, captured by HMS *Hereford* (Lt Cdr C.W. Greening) in November 1939. Bound for Liverpool from Port Louis, Mauritius, sailing in Convoy SL.78 which left Freetown on 18 June 1941. Torpedoed and sunk by U 69 (Kptlt Jost Metzler) at 1.19am on the 27th in position 23°50′N 21°10′W. Two died. One hundred and seven were picked up by the *Amerika*, transferred to the corvette HMS *Burdock* (Lt H.J. Fellowes) and landed at Milford Haven. (For details of other ships sunk in Convoy SL.78, see under *Criton*, ROPNER SHIPPING CO.)

LAFONIA (Captain M.O.V. Whitfield). Bound for Greenock in ballast, sailing in a convoy which left the Thames on 24 March 1943. The convoy was in fog when at about 0032 hours on the 26th it encountered a convoy proceeding in the opposite direction. The *Lafonia* collided with the oncoming *Como* in position 55°21′N 01°22′W and sank some hours later. Quartermaster James Brown died and the others were rescued by the *Monkstone*. The *Como* remained afloat and suffered no casualties.

MACON (Captain A. English). Sailed from Liverpool on 27 January 1941 bound for Freetown but experienced engine trouble and put in for repairs at Ponta Delgada in the Azores. Resumed her voyage on 22 July and was torpedoed by the Italian submarine *Barbarigo* (C.C. Francesco Murzi) at 10.30pm on the 24th. Two lifeboats got away and were standing off the ship when the submarine sank her by gunfire in position 32°48′N 26°12′W. Of the original 19 in No 1 boat, with Captain English in charge, only 17 remained alive when they were picked up at 1.30am on 3 August by the sloop HMS *Londonderry*, as the Chief Engineer and Chief Steward had died. Also on the 3rd, those in No 3 boat, with 2nd Mate Mr Butler in charge, were picked up by the *Clan Macpherson* (Captain C.M. O'Byrne). Four died.

POINT PLEASANT PARK (Captain Owen Owens and Canadian crew). Bound independently for Cape Town and Durban from Saint John, New Brunswick, when torpedoed by U.510 (Kptlt Alfred Eick) at 2pm on 23 February 1945. Eight men killed outright and many injured. An SSSS message was transmitted and although the main aerial had been brought down when the torpedo struck, it was heard by two shore stations. The crew abandoned the ship in 3 lifeboats; after the U-boat, now on the surface, put several rounds into her she sank in position 29°42′S 09°58′E. Those in No 3 lifeboat, with 2nd Mate R.S. Taylor in charge, were picked up by the fishing vessel *Boy Russell* (Captain Veer) off Mercury Island at noon on 2 March and taken to Lüderitz in South West Africa (Namibia). Nos 2 and 4 boats, which managed to keep in company, sighted the mine-sweeping trawler HMSAS *Africana* when near Conception Bay at 4pm on 4 March and, after succeeding in attracting her attention, all were taken on board and taken to Walvis Bay, with both boats in tow. Nine died, including Greaser R. Munroe in No 3 boat at 2am on 24 February. Forty-nine survived.

Elders & Fyffes

ARACATACA (Captain S. Brown). Bound for Avonmouth, sailing independently from Port Antonio, Jamaica, on 16 November and from Halifax on 21 November 1940. Torpedoed by U.101 (Kptlt Ernst Mengersen) at 0041 hours on the 30th. Abandoned, but reboarded. Torpedoed again at 1.11am and again abandoned. Struck by a third torpedo at 2.04am and sank in position 57°08′N 20°50′W. Thirty-six died. Eighteen were picked up by the *Potaro* and landed at Buenos Aires on 23 December. Fifteen picked up by the *Djurdjura* were landed at St John's, Newfoundland.

CAMITO. Requisitioned by the Admiralty in 1940 and converted into an ocean boarding vessel, HMS *Camito* (A/Cdr A.A. Barnet). Escorting the captured Italian tanker *Sangro* to the UK when torpedoed and sunk by U.97 (Kptlt Udo Heilmann) at 2.40am on 6 May 1941 in position 50°40′N 21°30′W. U.97 then chased and sank the *Sangro*. Twenty-eight died on HMS *Camito* and the survivors of both ships were picked up by corvette HMS *Orchis* (Lt H. Vernon, RNR) and landed at Greenock.

CARARE. Bound for Jamaica and Santa Marta, Colombia, sailing from Avonmouth on 28 May 1940 with a complement of 97 crew and 29 passengers. Struck a mine when off Countisbury Head, near Lynmouth, and sank in about 20 minutes. Seven died. Survivors were picked up by a naval patrol vessel and landed at Barry Dock.

CASANARE (Captain J.A. Moore). Bound for Garston, sailed independently from Victoria, Cameroon, on 18 October 1940. Torpedoed and sunk by U.99 (Kptlt Otto Kretschmer) at 9.40pm on 3 November when in position 53°58′N 14°13′W. Nine died. Fifty-four were picked up by the destroyer HMS *Beagle* (Lt Cdr R.H. Wright) and landed at Greenock. (See under *Patroclus*, HOLT, ALFRED, & CO.)

CHAGRES. Bound for Garston from Victoria, Cameroon, when sunk by a magnetic mine in Liverpool Bay on 9 February 1940. Two died and 60 survived. Mines were laid off the Bar Lightship on 6 January by U.30 (Oblt Fritz-Julius Lemp). The *El Oso*, *Cairnross*, *Munster* and *British Councillor* were also sunk by them and the *Gracia* damaged.

CRISTALES (Captain H. Roberts). Bound for Halifax, sailing in Convoy ON.92 which left Loch Ewe on 6 May 1942. Torpedoed by U.124 (Kptlt Johann Mohr) shortly before 4am on the 12th when in position 52°55′N 29°50′W. All 82 survived: 37 were picked up by the corvette HMCS *Shediac* (Lt J.E. Clayton) and landed at St John's, Newfoundland, on the 16th, 45 by USCGC *Spencer* and landed at Boston. The wrecked *Cristales* was sunk by the *Shediac*. (For details of other ships sunk in Convoy ON.92, see under *Llanover*, RADCLIFFE SHIPPING CO.)

MANISTEE. Requisitioned by the Admiralty in 1940 and converted into an ocean boarding vessel, HMS *Manistee* (Lt Cdr E.H. Smith). Part of the escort of Convoy OB.288 which sailed from Liverpool on 18 February 1941 and was bombed and machine-gunned by a Focke-Wulf 200 Condor on the 22nd when the *Keila* and *Kingston Hill* were damaged and returned to port. The escort left during the forenoon of the 23rd and the convoy dispersed in approximate position 59°30′N 21°15′W at 9pm that same day. Torpedoed and damaged by U.107 (Kptlt Günther Hessler) at 10.22pm on the 23rd and sunk by her at about 8am the next day in position 58°55′N 20°50′W. All 141 died. (For details of ships sunk and damaged in Convoy OB.288, see under *Sirikishna*, SALVESEN, CHRISTIAN.)

MATINA (Captain D.A. Jack). Independently bound for Garston from Port Antonio, Jamaica, when severely damaged by a torpedo and gunfire from U.28 (Kptlt Günter Kuhnke) at 4.32am on 26 October 1940. The U-boat witnessed the ship being abandoned, but nothing was seen of her complement of 69 again. The drifting wreck was torpedoed and sunk by U.31 (Kptlt Wilfried Prellberg) at 10pm on the 29th in position 57°30′N 16°31′W.

MOPAN (Captain S.A. Sapsworth). Homeward bound from the West Indies and sailing unescorted when intercepted by the pocket battleship *Admiral Scheer* (Captain Theodor Krancke) on the afternoon of 5 November 1940. Complied with Krancke's order to stop and not use her wireless, and her 68 crew rowed across to become prisoners of the *Scheer* before their ship was sunk in position 52°48′N 32°15′W. Together with prisoners from other victims of the *Scheer*, those from the *Mopan* were transferred to the captured Norwegian tanker *Sandefjord* on 24 January 1941 and which arrived at Bordeaux on 28 February. Eight men escaped when being taken to Germany by train in March, but only 2 reached Spain and, eventually, the UK. Shortly after sinking the *Mopan*, the *Scheer* intercepted Convoy HX.84, the Jarvis Bay Convoy, which had sailed from Halifax on 28 October. (For details see under *Maidan*, BROCKLEBANK LINE.)

NICOYA (Captain E.H. Brice). Bound for Avonmouth, sailing independently from Montreal on 10 May 1942. Torpedoed and sunk by U.553 (Kptlt Karl Thurmann) at 5.52am on the 12th in the Gulf of St Lawrence in position 49°19′N 64°51′W. Six died. Eighty-two, including 10 passengers, landed at Fame Point Lighthouse, Gaspé Peninsula, Quebec.

PATIA. Requisitioned by the Admiralty and converted into a Fighter Catapult ship, HMS *Patia* (Cdr D.M.B. Baker). Bound for Belfast from the Tyne and on her way to collect her first aircraft, she was machine-gunned, bombed and sunk near 20G Buoy, Coquet Island, Northumberland, on 27 April 1941 in position 55°34′N 1° 27′W. The ship's gunners shot down the attacking plane. Thirty-nine died. Thirty-one, including the wounded, landed near the village of Boulmer from a lifeboat. The local lifeboat rescued 3 survivors from the German plane.

ROSENBORG (Captain P.V. Petersen). Ex-Danish and managed for the MOWT, bound for Belfast and Swansea, sailing from Reykjavik in Convoy RU.71 on 22 April 1943. Straggling when torpedoed twice by U.386 (Oblt Hans-Albrecht Kandler) at 1.43am on the 25th and sank within a minute in approximate position 61°N 15°W. Twenty-eight died, including 2 passengers. Two were picked up by the rescue ship *Goodwin* (Captain G.L. Campbell) and landed at the Clyde on the 28th.

SAMALA (Captain A.E. Harvey). Independently bound for Garston from Kingston, Jamaica, when torpedoed and shelled by U.37 (Kptlt Victor Oehrn) at 10.13am on 30 September 1940 and sank in approximate position 53°N 18°W. The U-boat witnessed the ship being abandoned, but nothing was seen again of her complement of 68, including 2 passengers.

SULACO (Captain H.C. Bower). Bound for Victoria, Cameroon, sailing in Convoy OB.229 which left Liverpool on 15 October 1940 and dispersed on the 18th. Torpedoed and sunk by U.124 (Kptlt Georg-Wilhelm Schulz) at 2.29am on the 20th when in position

57°25′N 25°00′W. Sixty-five died. Sole survivor was James Harvey, the Chief Cook. Less than an hour previously, U.124 had sunk the Norwegian ship *Cubano* (Captain H. Martinsen), also from Convoy OB.229, and it was one of her lifeboats which picked up James Harvey from a raft. Two died on the *Cubano*. Thirty, plus James Harvey, were picked up by the destroyer HMCS *Saguenay* (Cdr G.R. Miles) on the 21st and landed at Greenock on the 23rd.

TUCURINCA (Captain J.A. Moore, ex-*Casanare*). Bound for Avonmouth, in the Halifax section of Convoy HX.228 which sailed on 3 March 1943 and joined up with the New York section which sailed on 28 February. Torpedoed and sunk by U.221 (Oblt Hans-Hartwig Trojer) at 9.26pm on 10 March in position 51°00′N 30°10′W. Sole casualty was the 3rd Engineer. Eighty-one, including 10 RCAF officers, were picked up by the Free French corvette *Roselys* and landed at Gourock.

OTHER SHIPS SUNK AND DAMAGED IN CONVOY HX.228

Andrea F Luckenbach (US) (Captain Rolf Neslund). By U.221. Twenty-one died. Sixty-four picked up by the Admiralty tanker *Orangeleaf* and landed at the Clyde.

Brant County (Nor.) (Captain Norvald Breivik). By U.86 (Kptlt Walter Schug). Twenty-eight crew and 8 soldier passengers died. Twenty-two crew picked up by the *Stuart Prince*, but one died from burns.

HMS *Harvester* (Cdr A.A. Tait). Depth-charged and then rammed by U.444 (Oblt Albert Langfeld) when she surfaced. In a damaged condition when torpedoed and sunk by U.432 (Kptlt Hermann Eckhardt). One hundred and forty-four died, including 39 of the 51 survivors of the *William C Gorgas*. Sixty, plus 12 from the *William C Gorgas*, picked up by the Free French corvette *Aconit*.

Lawton B Evans (US). Damaged by U.221.

Jamaica Producer. Damaged by U.590 (Kptlt Heinrich Müller-Edzards).

William C Gorgas (US) (Captain J.C. Ellis). By U.757 (Kptlt Friedrich Deetz). Twenty-two died. Fifty-one picked up by the destroyer HMS *Harvester*. (See above.)

U.444, disabled and unable to dive, was rammed for a second time, this time by the *Aconit*. Forty died when she sank and 4 picked up by the *Aconit*.

U.432. Sunk by the *Aconit*. Twenty-six died and 20 picked up by the *Aconit*.

Ellerman Group

ALBANO. Struck a mine 7.6 miles from Coquet Light, midway between Blyth and Sunderland, on 2 March 1940. Nine died. Twenty-nine were picked up by the destroyer HMS *Wallace* (Cdr B.I. Robertshaw) and the armed patrol trawler *Stella Carino*.

ANDALUSIAN (Captain H.B. McHugh). In Convoy SL.68 sailing from Freetown to the UK when torpedoed and sunk by U.106 (Kptlt Jürgen Oesten) at 9.07pm on 17 March 1941 in position 14°33′N 21°06′W. All 42 landed at Boa Vista in the Cape

Verde Islands. (For details of other ships sunk and damaged in Convoy SL.68, see under *Benwyvis*, BEN LINE.)

ARIOSTO (Captain H. Hill). Bound for Liverpool from Lisbon, and commodore ship of Convoy HG.75, homeward bound from Gibraltar. Torpedoed and sunk by U.564 (Oblt Reinhard Suhren) at 6.40am on 24 October 1941 in position 36°20′N 10°50′W. Six died. Thirty-eight were picked up by the *Pacific* (Swed.) and landed at Barrow. Seven picked up by the destroyer HMS *Lamerton* (Lt Cdr H.C. Simms) were landed at Gibraltar.

OTHER SHIPS SUNK IN CONVOY HG.75

Alhama (Captain A. Cameron). By U.564. All 33 survived.

Carsbreck (Captain J.D. Muir). By U.564 on the 24th. Twenty-four died. Eighteen picked up by Free French minesweeper *Commandant Duboc* but transferred to the fighter catapult ship HMS *Ariguani* (Cdr R.A. Thorburn). Two days later, HMS *Ariguani* was torpedoed and severely damaged by U.83 (Oblt Hans-Werner Kraus) and abandoned. Two died. The 18 from the *Carsbreck* were then picked up by the corvette HMS *Campion* (Lt Cdr A. Johnston), transferred to the destroyer HMS *Vidette* (Lt Cdr E.N. Walmsley) and landed at Gibraltar. HMS *Ariguani* was reboarded and towed to Gibraltar.

HMS *Cossack* (Captain E.L. Berthon). Destroyer. Severely damaged by U.563 (Oblt Klaus Bargsten) at about 0045 hours on the 24th and abandoned. Reboarded by a skeleton crew and being towed to Gibraltar by the tug HMS *Thames* when, due to bad weather on the 27th, the tow was slipped, the crew taken off and she sank. One hundred and fifty-nine died and 60 survived.

Ulea (Captain F.O. Ambrose). By U.432 (Oblt Heinz-Otto Schultze). Nineteen died. Nine picked up by the corvettes HMS *La Malouine* (T/Lt V.D.H. Bidwell) and HMS *Bluebell* (Lt Cdr R.E. Sherwood) and landed at Liverpool.

ASSYRIAN (Captain R.S. Kearson). Homeward bound from New Orleans and commodore ship of Convoy SC.7 (Sydney, Cape Breton, to UK) which sailed on 5 October 1940. Torpedoed and sunk by U.101 (Kptlt Fritz Frauenheim) at 1.22am on the 19th in position 57°12′N 10°43′W. Seventeen died. Thirty-four were picked up by the sloop HMS *Leith* (Cdr R.C. Allen) and landed at Liverpool. (For details of other ships sunk and damaged in Convoy SC.7 see under *Sedgepool*, ROPNER SHIPPING CO.)

BASSANO (Captain D.H. Casson). Bound for Hull from New York and sailing independently when torpedoed twice by U.105 (Kptlt Georg Schewe) at 6.14pm on 9 January 1941 in position 57°57′N 17°42′W. One died. Fifty-six were picked up by the destroyer HMS *Wild Swan* (Lt Cdr C.E.L. Sclater) and landed at Liverpool.

BELGRAVIAN (Captain R.S. Kearson). Bound for Hull and in Convoy SL.81 which sailed from Freetown on 15 July 1941. Torpedoed and sunk by U.372 (Oblt Heinz-Joachim Neumann) at about 2am on 5 August in position 53°03′N 15°54′W. Three died.

Forty-seven were picked up by the corvette HMS *Bluebell* (Lt Cdr R.E. Sherwood) and landed at Greenock. (For details of other ships sunk and damaged in Convoy SL.81 see under *Swiftpool*, ROPNER SHIPPING CO.)

CASTILIAN (Captain J. Every). Bound for Lisbon, sailing independently from Eastham Locks (Manchester Ship Canal) on 11 February 1943 to join a convoy at Holyhead. Captain Every had been ordered to anchor in Church Bay for the night, but chose to anchor off Holyhead breakwater. When the anchors began to drag, he took the ship farther out to sea, ran aground on the East Platters Rocks near the Skerries, Anglesey, at 3.20am on the 12th, and she became a total loss. All 47 taken off by the Holyhead lifeboat.

CAVALLO. In Nauplia, in the Peloponnese, during the evacuation of Greece. Subjected to an air attack on 23 April 1941 and abandoned although not hit. Badly damaged on the 24th and sank the next day. None died, but no further details.

CITY OF ADELAIDE (Captain R.J. Ross-Rickets). Bound independently from Karachi to Fremantle when sunk by a torpedo and gunfire from the Japanese submarine I-8 at dusk on 30 March 1944 in position 12°01′S 80°27′E. The crew abandoned the ship in the 6 lifeboats which kept together until picked up by the US Liberty ship *Carole Lombard* three days later. The *Carole Lombard*, on passage from Fremantle to Colombo, had heard the SSSS message transmitted by the *City of Adelaide*, but after a spell spent looking for lifeboats, resumed her normal course. No information of any casualties. The Captain of I-8 was Cdr Tetsunosuke Ariizumi who also sank the Dutch ship *Tjisalak* on 26 March 1944 and the US Liberty ship *Jean Nicolet* (Captain D.N. Nilsson) on 2 July 1944. As he murdered most of the personnel from both these ships, it may be that he failed to act the same way towards those on the *City of Adelaide* because he was unable to locate their lifeboats in the dark. After the war, light prison sentences, later commuted, were given to some of I-8's crew, but Ariizumi was never caught.

CITY OF ATHENS (Captain J.A. Kinley). Sailed independently from Glasgow bound for Alexandria via Takoradi and Cape Town when torpedoed by U.179 (Frgkpt. Ernst Sobe) at 4.07pm on 8 October 1942. The ship was abandoned because she had explosives in her cargo, but not before an SSSS message had been transmitted and acknowledged. Struck by a second torpedo at 4.31am, she sank within 10 minutes in position 33°40′S 17°03′E. One died and the 98 survivors, plus the ship's cat which they rescued from a raft, were picked up at 7pm from 6 lifeboats by the destroyer HMS *Active* (Lt Cdr M.W. Tomkinson). At about midnight, a radar contact was made by HMS *Active* and, by star shells and searchlight, she illuminated the surfaced U.179. The U-boat crash-dived but was depth-charged and all 61 on board her died. HMS *Active* landed the survivors of the *City of Athens* at Cape Town the following day. A week later, a crew member and 3 DBS (Distressed British Seamen) were shipped out on the *City of Corinth*. (See below.)

CITY OF BAGHDAD (Captain J.A. White). Bound for Penang from the UK when intercepted by the German raider *Atlantis* (KptzS. Bernhard Rogge) disguised as the Norwegian ship *Tarifa* on 11 July 1940. When ordered to stop, the Radio Officer of the *City of Baghdad* began to send a QQQQ message, indicating that she was being attacked by an unidentified armed merchantman but the transmission abruptly ceased when a shell demolished the radio room. The ship was then brought to a halt and the crew and passengers taken aboard the *Atlantis* from lifeboats. A boarding party was put aboard and she was scuttled in position 00°16′S 90°0′0E. Fifteen died.

It is not clear what happened to all the passengers and crew of the *City of Baghdad*, but at midnight on 5 August the captured Norwegian ship *Tirranna*, under a prize crew, set sail for St Nazaire with 274 of the 365 prisoners held by the *Atlantis*, many of whom were sick and wounded. During the passage, however, her prize captain Lt Waldman decided it was safer to make for somewhere in unoccupied France, but when they anchored off Cape Ferrat on 22 September, the unhelpful Vichy authorities advised him to proceed to Bordeaux. On 23 September, when the *Tirranna* was anchored in the Gironde, she was torpedoed and sunk by the submarine HMS *Tuna* (Lt Cdr M.K. Cavanagh-Mainwaring) and 60 prisoners died, including women and children.

After sinking the *King City*, *Athelking*, *Benarty* and *Commissaire Ramel*, the *Atlantis* had 293 prisoners on board. Rogge was anxious to get rid of them and when the neutral Yugoslav ship *Durmitor* was captured on 22 October, she suited his purpose. Two hundred and sixty prisoners, including those from the *Scientist* sunk on 3 May, were transferred to her and, under a prize crew, she sailed for Italian Somaliland on the 26th. (See under *Athelking*, ATHEL LINE.)

CITY OF BARODA (Captain C.S. Nelson). Bound for Calcutta from London via Trinidad, Walvis Bay, Durban and Colombo. Sailed from Walvis Bay on 1 April 1943 in Convoy NC.9 (Walvis Bay to Cape Town). Torpedoed and severely damaged by U.509 (Kptlt Werner Witte) at 10pm on the 2nd in position 22°56′S 15°21′E. Towed to Lüderitz Bay, South West Africa, and beached, but later broke in two and declared a total loss. One crew and 7 passengers died. One hundred and twenty-nine crew and 196 passengers were picked up by the ASW trawler HMS *Cape Warwick* (Lt W.E. Goggin) and taken to Cape Town.

CITY OF BATH (Captain T.V. Birkett). Sailed from Mombasa and unescorted when on passage from Pernambuco to the UK via Trinidad when torpedoed and sunk by U.508 (Kptlt Georg Staats) at 1.43am on 2 December 1942 in position 09°29′N 59°35′W. Three died. Fifty-two were picked up the next day by the *City of Dunkirk* and landed at Trinidad. Twenty-eight landed at Trinidad on the 5th.

CITY OF BEDFORD. Commodore ship of Convoy HX.97 from Halifax to the UK which sailed on 18 December 1940. On the night of 30 December, the convoy met Convoy OB.265 travelling in the opposite direction. It was dark, there was a force 7 wind and a thick fog. The *City of Bedford* collided with the *Bodnant*, in Convoy OB.265, and sank in 20 seconds in position 60°03′N 23°01′W. Forty-eight died. The *Bodnant* also sank, but none died. No details of those rescued. (See also under ELDER DEMPSTER LINE.)

CITY OF BENARES (Captain Landles Nicoll). Bound for Quebec, sailing in Convoy OB.213 outward from Liverpool on 13 September 1940. Torpedoed and sunk by U.48 (Kptlt Heinrich Bleichrodt) at 10.8pm on the 17th in position 56°43′N 21°15′W and 9 hours after the departure of the RN escort. One hundred and twenty-three crew died, along with 51 private passengers (including 4 children), 77 of the 90 children who were being taken to Canada for safety under the government scheme organised by the Children's Overseas

Reception Board (CORB) scheme and 6 of their escorts. One hundred and four were picked up by the destroyer HMS *Hurricane* (Lt Cdr H.C. Simms) and landed at Greenock. Forty-five, who spent 8 days adrift in a lifeboat, were spotted by a Sunderland flying boat and picked up by the destroyer HMS *Anthony* (Lt Cdr N.J.V. Thew) but one Indian seaman died before the ship reached Gourock.

CITY OF BIRMINGHAM. Struck a mine off Spurn Head when approaching Hull on 16 August 1940 and sank in position 53°32′N 15°30′E. None died, but no further details.

CITY OF BOMBAY (Captain F.W. Penderworthy). Unescorted and bound for Karachi from Liverpool via Trinidad and Saldanha Bay (north-west of Cape Town) when torpedoed by U.159 (Kptlt Helmut Witte) at 10.05pm on 13 December 1942. The U-boat surfaced and tried to sink her by gunfire, but it was only after a second torpedo was put in her at 3.11am that she went down. Twenty-four died. One hundred and thirty were picked up: 24 by the *Star of Cairo* (Egyp.) and landed at Cape Town, 92 by the *Cape Breton* on the 19th and landed at Recife on the 29th, and 14 by the corvette USS *Tenacity* and landed at Pernambuco.

CITY OF BRISBANE. Bombed by German planes when off the South Longsands Buoy in the Thames estuary on 2 August 1940. Eight died.

CITY OF CANTON (Captain E. Scrymgeour). Unescorted and on passage from Beira to Mombasa when torpedoed by U.178 (Krvkpt. Wilhelm Dommes), at 0001 hours on 17 July 1943. Abandoned and broke in two when a second torpedo struck about half an hour later and sank in position 13°52′S 41°10′E.

Accounts of what happened to the survivors differ widely, but that of Cadet Christopher Tulitt must be correct as far as his own experience goes. He was in the 3rd Mate's lifeboat which landed on the coast of Mozambique during the afternoon of the 17th. The following day, they sailed down the coast to Baixe Pinda Lighthouse, where the keeper and his wife fed them, and they subsequently travelled to Durban. Because the U-boat was unable to find the Master, it took 2nd Mate R.M. Broadbent prisoner but handed him into the hands of the Japanese at the Andaman Islands and it is not known if he survived. According to Mr Tulitt, Captain Scrymgeour and the Storekeeper drifted on a raft for 6 days before being picked up by the French cruiser *Suffren* and it seems that many others were rescued by this warship which landed them at Durban. Nineteen more were picked up by the Portuguese ship *Luabo* and landed in Mozambique. Eight died and 95 survived.

CITY OF CAIRO (Captain W.A. Rogerson). Sailed independently from Bombay on 1 October 1942 bound for Durban, Cape Town, Pernambuco and the UK. Left Cape Town on 1 November, torpedoed twice by U.68 (Krvkpt. Karl-Friedrich Merten) between 8.30pm and 8.40pm on the 6th and sank 10 minutes later in position 23°30′S 05°30′W. The U-boat surfaced and Merten gave the survivors directions and apologised for sinking the ship.

When a count was made the following morning, it was learned that 6 people were missing, and 292 were distributed in 6 boats. Captain Rogerson ordered the boats to keep together and set a course for St Helena, travelling by day and lying roped together at night. On the 8th, 1st Mate S. Britt, in charge of No 1 boat, asked permission to proceed independently, but it was only after another bad night that the Captain gave in to Mr Britt's insistence. That same night, Daniel McNeill fell over the side of No 8 boat when urinating and was lost.

During the night of the 12th/13th, No 6 boat, with 1st Radio Officer G. Nutter, of the Bibby Line, in charge, drifted away from the group, and at 4.30am on the 19th, when a ship was seen from No 6, flares were sent up and Mr Nutter signalled SOS on his torch. This brought the *Clan Alpine* (Captain C.W. Banbury) to their rescue, boats 7 and 5 were subsequently located and 150 survivors landed at Jamestown, St Helena, that afternoon. Those in No 8 boat, with 1st Mate T. Green, of British India Steam Navigation Co., in charge, were picked up that same day by the *Bendoran* (Captain W.C. Wilson) and taken to Cape Town.

When it set off on its own, Mr Britt's boat contained 54 people. When it was picked up by the German ship *Rhakotis* (KptzS. Jacobs) on 12 December only Quartermaster Angus MacDonald, 3rd Steward Jack Edmead, and 21-year-old Diana Jarman (a passenger) remained. Their boat was waterlogged, they had to be hoisted on board, and when being operated on during the 17th, Diana Jarman died. On 1 January 1943, when the *Rhakotis* was sunk by the cruiser HMS *Scylla* (Captain I.A.P. MacIntyre), Angus MacDonald and Jack Edmead got away in two different lifeboats. Jack's boat was towed into Corunna by a Spanish trawler on the 3rd and he was eventually repatriated to the UK. Along with 79 others, Angus was picked up by U.410 (Kptlt Kurt Sturm) on the 4th and landed at St Nazaire. He was released from a German prison camp when the war ended.

Boat No 4, a smaller one, originally contained 17 people, but only 3rd Mate J.A. Whyte and Australian Margaret Gordon (a passenger) remained alive to be picked up by the Brazilian minelayer *Caravelas* on 27 December. After a spell in hospital in New York, Mr Whyte was travelling home on the unescorted *City of Pretoria* (Captain F. Deighton) when she was sunk by U.172 (Kptlt Carl Emmermann) on 4 March 1943, and there were no survivors. Out of the *City of Cairo*'s original complement of 298, 104 died: 6 when she was sunk, 89 in the lifeboats and 9 after being rescued.

CITY OF CARDIFF (Captain R.L. Stewart). Bound for Manchester via Beira, sailing in Convoy SL.119 which left Freetown on 14 August 1942. Torpedoed by U.566 (Oblt Gerhard Remus) at 7.08pm on the 28th and abandoned, not sinking until two days later. Twenty-one died. Sixty-three were picked up by the sloop HMS *Rochester* (Cdr C.B. Allen) and landed at Londonderry.

OTHER SHIPS SUNK IN CONVOY SL.119

Clan MacWhirter. See under CLAN LINE.

Zuiderkerk (Du.). Torpedoed by U.156 at the same time as the *City of Cardiff*. Rejoined the convoy, but had to be abandoned. All 68 picked up by the sloop HMS *Leith* (Lt Cdr E.C. Hulton) and the ship scuttled by the sloop HMS *Erne* (Lt Cdr E.D.J. Abbot) the following day.

CITY OF CHRISTCHURCH. In Convoy KMS.11G (UK to Mediterranean Slow) which sailed from the Clyde on 14 March 1943. Attacked by German aircraft when off the Portuguese coast on the 21st and badly damaged. Detached from the convoy and making for Lisbon the following day when it became clear she was sinking. All taken off by the corvette HMCS *Morden* (T/LT. J.J. Hodgkinson) and sank at 7pm.

CITY OF CORINTH (Captain G.J. Law). Bound for the UK from Calcutta via Cape Town, Pernambuco and Trinidad. Sailed independently from Pernambuco on 7 November 1942. Torpedoed by U.508 (Kptlt Georg Staats) at 8.54am on the 17th, but drifted and sank later in position 10°52'N 61°03'W. Fourteen died. Seventy-three were picked up by the submarine chaser USS PC-536 and landed at Port of Spain.

CITY OF GUILDFORD (Captain C. Collard). In Convoy XT.7 from Alexandria to Tripoli when torpedoed and sunk by U.593 (Kptlt Gerd Kelbling) at 3.24pm on 27 March 1943 in position 33°00'N 22°50'E. One hundred and twenty-three died, including 46 army personnel. Eight crew and 5 soldiers were picked up by the destroyer HMS *Exmoor* (Lt D.T. McBarnett) and landed at Benghazi.

CITY OF HANKOW. On passage from Liverpool to Durban and Beira via Saldanha Bay, South Africa. In thick fog, ran aground at South Point, 4 miles north of Saldanha Bay, at 4.40am (GMT) on 18 December 1942 and became a total loss.

CITY OF JOHANNESBURG (Captain W.A. Owen). Bound for the UK from Calcutta via Colombo and Cape Town. Sailed independently from Colombo on 6 October 1942; torpedoed and sunk by U.504 (Krvkpt. Hans-Georg Friedrich Poske) at 11.12pm on the 23rd in position 33°20'N 29°30'E. Four died and 83 survived; they were picked up by the *Zypenberg* (Du.), *Fort George* and *King Edward*, and landed at Durban, Port Elizabeth and Cape Town respectively.

CITY OF KARACHI. Bound for Volos, Crete, sailing in Convoy AG.11 (Alexandria to Greece) which left on 7 April 1941. On 12 April she and the Norwegian ship *Brattdal* (Captain Kristian Hartvik) were told to rendezvous with an escort outside the torpedo net, but as an escort could not be found both returned to the port in the morning. It transpired that the escort had been wiped out by the Germans and shortly after the ships returned to Volos they were subjected to an air attack during which the *City of Karachi* was damaged. It was not, however, until the 15th that the Luftwaffe finished her off. One died, but no further details. After being hit twice, the *Brattdal* limped to Almira Bay and then on to Gardiki Bay in the Strait of Oreos on the evening of the 15th. The ship was unsuccessfully attacked the following morning, but on the 17th she was hit and sank. All 28 survived, but the Galley Boy was last seen on the quay at Aegeos on 26 April and may have drowned when one of the motorboats transporting them to the cruiser HMS *Orion*, for passage to Alexandria, capsized.

CITY OF KOBE (Captain W.S. Craig). In Convoy FS.56 sailing from the Firth of Forth to the Thames. On 19 December 1939 she struck a mine, laid by U.60 (Kptlt Georg Schewe) on the 15th, and sank off the coast of Suffolk in position 52°35'N 01°59'E. One died. Thirty were picked up by the MS trawler HMS *Tumby* (Skipper J.W. Greengrass) and the coasters *Corinia* and *Faxfleet*.

CITY OF MANCHESTER (Captain H. Johnson). On passage from Pekan in Malaya to Tjilatjap (Cilacap), on the south coast of Java, when torpedoed twice, shelled and sunk by the Japanese submarine I-53 (later renumbered I-153) (Lt Nakamura) on 28 February 1942 in position 08°16'S 108°52'E. Crew machine-gunned while abandoning ship. While searching for survivors of the sunken seaplane *Langley*, the US minesweeper USS *Whippoorwill* found and picked up those from the *City of Manchester*. The US gunboat *Tulsa*, which was similarly engaged and had medical facilities, embarked and treated 10 wounded, and both ships returned to Tjilatjap. During the evening of 1 March, the Dutch vessel *Zaandam* (Captain Stamperius) crammed with evacuees, including 100 from the *City of Manchester*, some of whom were wounded, sailed for Fremantle and arrived there on the 6th. No doubt because it was a panic situation, the story of the *City of Manchester* is confusing. She apparently had a complement of 161. Nine died and 6 became prisoners of the Japanese.

CITY OF MANDALAY (Captain A.G. Melville). Homeward bound from Saigon and intermediate ports, sailing in unescorted Convoy HG.3 which left Gibraltar on 12 October 1939. Torpedoed and sunk by U.46 (Kptlt Herbert Sohler) at 4.50pm on the 17th and sank in position 44°57′N 13°36′W. Two died. Seventy-eight were picked up by the *Independence Hall* (US) and landed at Bordeaux on the 20th.

OTHER SHIPS SUNK IN CONVOY HG.3 – ALSO ON THE 17TH

Clan Chisholm. See under CLAN LINE.

Yorkshire. See under BIBBY LINE.

CITY OF MANILA (Captain A.S. Reay). In Convoy SL.118 which left Freetown on 4 August 1942 bound for Liverpool. Torpedoed by U.406 (Kptlt Horst Dieterichs) at 4.22pm on the 19th in position 43°21′N 18°20′W and abandoned. Reboarded by some of the crew the next day, but broke in two, was again abandoned and sank. One died. Forty-six were picked up by the *Empire Voice* and landed at Loch Ewe. Forty-nine picked up by the sloop HMS *Gorleston* (Cdr R.W. Keymer) were landed at Londonderry.

OTHER SHIPS SUNK IN CONVOY SL.118

Balingkar (Du.). By U.214 (Kptlt Günther Reeder) on the 18th. Two Lascars died – one when the ship was torpedoed and the other after being rescued. Ninety-one rescued.

Hatarana (Captain P.A.C. James). Damaged by U.214 at the same time as the *Balingkar* and scuttled by the corvette HMS *Cheshire* (A/Captain H.G. Hopper). Torpedoed and damaged by U.214 at the same time as the *Balingkar* and *Hatarana*, and abandoned. Two hundred and twenty rescued by the destroyer HMCS *Skeena* (Lt Cdr J.C. Hibbard) and the corvette HMS *Periwinkle* (Lt Cdr P.G. MacIver). HMS *Cheshire* was towed to Belfast Lough and beached, and later repaired in Liverpool. No details of casualties.

HMS *Penstemon* (Lt Cdr J. Byron). None died. Twenty picked up by HMS *Penstemon* and landed at Londonderry. Eighty-eight picked up by the *Corabella*.

Triton (Nor.) (Captain Einar Tholvsen). By U.566 (Kptlt Gerhard Remus) on the 17th. All 43 picked up by the *Baron Dunmore* and landed at Loch Ewe on the 26th.

CITY OF MARSEILLES. Ran aground near Batticaloa on the east coast of Ceylon (Sri Lanka) on 21 January 1943. Refloated and broken up in 1947. No lives lost.

CITY OF MELBOURNE (Captain H.G.T. Booth). Bound independently for New York from Beira via Cape Town, sailing from Cape Town on 23 April 1942. Torpedoed by U.156 (Kptlt Werner Hartenstein) at 10.05pm on 13 May. Subjected to gunfire from the U-boat, broke in two and sank at 0026 hours on the 14th in position 15°00′N 54°40′W. One died and 86 landed at Barbados.

CITY OF MOBILE. Bombed and sunk by German planes in the Irish Channel on 16 September 1940. No further details.

CITY OF NAGPUR (Captain D.L. Lloyd). Sailed independently from Glasgow for Karachi via Freetown, Natal and Bombay. Torpedoed by U.75 (Kptlt Hermuth Ringelmann) at 2.29am on 29 April 1941 and abandoned in position 52°30′N 26°00′W. After an unsuccessful attempt to sink the ship by gunfire, the U-boat fired another torpedo at 3.33pm, but as this caused her only to list, it took a final torpedo, fired at 6am, to sink her. An SSSS message had been sent after the first torpedo struck. Sixteen died. Later in the day, the lifeboats were spotted by a Catalina flying boat and during the evening 452 were picked up by the destroyer HMS *Hurricane* (Lt Cdr H.C. Simms) and landed at Greenock on 1 May.

CITY OF ORAN (Captain F.W. Letton). Bound for Colombo via Mombasa, sailing from Durban in Convoy CB.1 (Cape Town to Beira) on 26 July 1943. Torpedoed by U.196 (Krvkpt. Eitel-Friedrich Kentrat) at 0024 hours on 3 August in position 13°45′S 41°16′E. Sunk by the rescue tug HMS *Masterful* which picked up all 84 and landed them at Mombasa.

CITY OF OXFORD (Captain A. Norbury). Bound for Garston, sailing from Lisbon on 11 June 1942 to join Convoy HG.84 which left Gibraltar on the 10th. Torpedoed and sunk by U.552 (Kptlt Erich Topp) at 4.33am on the 15th in position 43°42′N 18°12′W. One died. Forty-three were picked up by the rescue ship *Copeland* (Captain W.J. Hartley). All subsequently transferred to the corvette HMS *Marigold* (Lt J.A.S. Halcrow) and then to the sloop HMS *Stork* (Cdr F.J Walker) which landed them at Liverpool.

OTHER SHIPS SUNK IN CONVOY HG.84 – ALL BY U.552 ON THE 15TH

Etrib (Captain B. McMillan). Four died. Forty-one picked up by HMS *Marigold*. Transferred to the *Copeland* and landed at Gourock on the 20th.

Pelayo (Captain R.H. Williams). Commodore ship. Seventeen died. Thirty picked up by the *Copeland*.

Slemdal (Nor.) (Captain J.M. Pedersen). All 37 picked up by the *Copeland*.

Thurso (Captain W. Walker). Thirteen died. Twenty-nine picked up by HMS *Marigold* and landed at Greenock.

CITY OF PERTH (Captain J. Blewitt). Bound for Liverpool, sailing from Bône (Annaba) in Convoy MKS.10 (Mediterranean to UK Slow) on 23 March 1943. Torpedoed by U.431 (Oberleutnant zur See (ObltzS.) Dietrich Schöneboom) at 0042 hours on the 26th in position 35°50′N 01°41′W. Taken in tow by the armed trawler HMS *Man O' War* (Lt G.L. Coles), beached south of Cape Figalo, west of Oran, and became a total loss. Two died. Ninety landed at Gibraltar by HMS *Man O' War* on the 28th.

CITY OF PITTSBURG. Bound for Alexandria from Montreal via the Cape and Suez Canal when wrecked in the Great Pass, the entrance to the western harbour at Alexandria, on 11 January 1942. Her cargo was salvaged, but there are no further details.

CITY OF PRETORIA (Captain F. Deighton). Sailed independently from New York bound for Liverpool on 27 February 1943. In position 41°45′N 42°30′W when torpedoed twice by U.172 (Kptlt Carl Emmermann) at 6.09am on 4 March and blew up, owing to having ammunition in her cargo. All 145 died.

CITY OF RIPON (Captain J.E. Robinson). Sailed from Port Said bound for New York via Cape Town and Trinidad. Left Cape Town on 18 October 1942 and sailing independently when torpedoed three times and sunk by U.160 (Kptlt Georg Lassen) shortly after 8am on 11 November in position 08°40′N 59°20′W. Sixty-two died. Sixteen were picked up by the *Midosi* (Braz.) and landed at Port of Spain.

CITY OF ROUBAIX. Sailed in Convoy AN.21 which left Alexandria on 18 March 1941 and arrived in Piraeus on the 22nd. At anchor near the *Clan Fraser* when the latter was bombed during a German air raid on the port at 9pm on 6 April and blew up at about 3.30am on the 7th. Similar to the *Clan Fraser*, she was loaded with ammunition and when the fire spread to her she was abandoned and also blew up. None died. (See under *Clan Fraser*, CLAN LINE.)

CITY OF SHANGHAI (Captain A.F. Goring). Bound for Cape Town and Turkey from the Tyne, sailing in Convoy OB.313 which left Liverpool on 22 April 1941 and dispersed on the 28th. Torpedoed by U.103 (Krvkpt. Viktor Schütze) at 1.30am on 11 May and sunk by gunfire in position 06°40′N 27°50′W. Six died. Twenty-eight were picked up by the *Stad Arnhem* (Du.) and landed at Freetown. Seventeen picked up by the *Richmond Castle* were landed at Glasgow. Twenty-two picked up by the *Josefina S* (Arg.) were landed at Pernambuco.

CITY OF SIMLA (Captain H. Percival). Bound for Bombay via Cape Town, sailing in Convoy OB.216 which left Liverpool on 19 September 1940 and dispersed in position 53°00′N 17°05′W on the 23rd. Torpedoed and sunk by U.138 (Oblt Wolfgang Lüth) at 9.20pm on the 20th and sank in position 55°59′N 08°16′W. Three died. Three hundred and eighteen were picked up by the *Guinean*, transferred to the destroyer HMS *Vanquisher* (Lt A.P. Northey) and landed at Londonderry on the 22nd. Twenty-nine picked up by the trawler *Van Dyke* (Belg.) were landed at Liverpool.

OTHER SHIPS SUNK IN CONVOY OB.216

Boka (Pan.). By U.138. Eight died. Twenty-six picked up by HMS *Arabis*.

Empire Adventure. See under RUNCIMAN, WALTER, & CO. LTD/MOOR LINE LTD.

Mabriton. See under CHAPMAN, R., & SONS.

New Sevilla. See under SALVESEN, CHRISTIAN.

CITY OF SINGAPORE (Captain A.G. Freeman). Bound for Liverpool from Calcutta, sailing in Convoy TS.37 to Freetown which left Takoradi on 26 April 1943. Torpedoed by U.515 (Kptlt Werner Henke) at 5.40am on 1 May in position 07°55′N 14°16′W. All 97 were picked up by the C/S trawlers HMS *Arran* (Lt D.S. Sutton) and HMS *Birdlip* (Lt E.N. Groom) and landed at Freetown that same day. (For details of other ships sunk in Convoy TS.37, see under *Nagina*, BRITISH INDIA STEAM NAVIGATION CO.)

CITY OF VENICE (Captain J. Wyper). Bound for Algiers, sailing from the Clyde on 24 June 1943 carrying military cargo and 292 Canadian troops who were to take part in Operation Husky, the invasion of Sicily. In Convoy KMS.18B, which passed Gibraltar on 3 July, when torpedoed and sunk by U.375 (Kptlt Jürgen Könenkamp) at 9.40pm on the 4th in position 36°44′N 01°31′E. Twenty-one died. Four hundred and sixty-one were picked up by the corvettes HMS *Honeysuckle* (Lt H.H.G. MacKillican) and HMS *Rhododendron* (Lt O.B. Medley), the frigate HMS *Teviot* (Cdr T. Taylor) and the tug HMS *Restive* (Lt D.M. Richards) and landed at Algiers.

OTHER SHIPS SUNK IN CONVOY KMS.18B

Devis (Captain W. Denson). Commodore ship. By U.593 (Kptlt Gerd Kelbling) at 3.43pm on the 5th. Fifty-one soldiers died and many were badly burned. (She had 264 Canadian and some British troops on board.) Two hundred and ninety-one, including Captain Denson, were picked up by the destroyer HMS *Cleveland* (Lt J.K. Hamilton) and landed at Bougie. (On 30 July all 46 on board U.375 perished when she was depth-charged and sunk by the submarine chaser USS PC-624 in position 36°40′N 12°28′E.)

St Essylt (Captain S. Diggins). By U.375. One crew member and a soldier died. (She had 320 troops on board.) Three hundred and ninety-seven picked up by the same naval vessels as the *City of Venice*.

CITY OF WELLINGTON (Captain M. Martyn). Sailed independently from Lourenço Marques bound for the UK via Mossel Bay and Freetown. Torpedoed and sunk by U.506 (Kptlt Erich Würdemann) at 10.43pm on 21 August 1942 in position 07°29′N 14°40′W. Seven died. Sixty-six were picked up by the destroyer HMS *Velox* (Lt G.B. Barston) and landed at Freetown the following day.

CITY OF WINCHESTER (Captain W.S. Coughlan). Dispersed from Convoy OB.313 when torpedoed three times by U.103 and sank in position 08°20′N 26°14′W at 11.46pm on 9 May 1941. Six died. Ninety-two were picked up by the *Herma* (Nor.) and landed at Takoradi. (See *City of Shanghai* above.)

CRESSADO. Bound for Preston from Leixões in Portugal, sailing in Convoy HG.82 which left Gibraltar on 27 April 1942. In collision with anti-aircraft ship HMS *Pozarica* when off the Skerries and sank. None died, but no further details.

DAGO. Sailed independently from Gibraltar bound for Liverpool via Lisbon and Leixões. En route from Lisbon to Leixões when attacked by a Focke-Wulf 200 Condor shortly after

6pm on 15 March 1942. Struck by 3 bombs, abandoned and sank in about 5 minutes. An hour later, a Portuguese motorised lifeboat came out from Peniche and towed the lifeboats, containing all 37, into the port.

DARINO (Captain W.J.E. Colgan). Independently bound for Liverpool from Lisbon, Oporto and Cadiz when torpedoed and sunk by U.41 (Kptlt Gustav-Adolf Mugler) at 1.50am on 18 November 1939 In position 44°12′N 11°07′W. Sixteen died. Eleven were picked up by the U-boat but transferred to the *Caterina Gerolimich* (It.) and landed at Dover.

DIDO. Abandoned and seized on 18 June 1940, during the fall of France. None died, but no further details.

DOMINO. Berthed at South Canada Dock, Liverpool, when sunk during a German air raid on 4 May 1941. None died.

OTHER SHIPS DAMAGED OR SUNK* IN THE LUFTWAFFE BLITZ ON LIVERPOOL ON 3 AND 4 MAY

Adda, Argos, Asiatic, Australia Star, Baron Inchcape, Bra-Kar (Nor.),* *Cantal, Clan Macinnes, Corbet, Elstree Grange, Empire Bronze, Europa, Flint,* HMS *Adventure,* HMS *Maplin, Kadin, Kydoniefs, Leopold, Lobos, Malakand* (carrying bombs and blew up),* *Mimosa, Roxburgh Castle, Salland, Silver Sandal, Stromboli,* Tacoma Star, Talthybius, Trentino* (see below), *Walvera,* Ferry *Royal Daffodil,* Lightship *Sirius,** Trawler *Van Orley,* Tugs *Bison,* Bonita,* Enid Blanche, Hornby, Skirmisher* and *Wapiti.*

DRACO. In Tobruk on 11 April 1941, during the German siege of the port. Attacked by aircraft, beached and abandoned. Attacked again on the 21st and became a constructive total loss. All 32 rescued, but DEMS Gunner Reginald Good, RNR, P/X 7734, died of his wounds. Refloated in 1948 and taken to Valencia for breaking up.

DYNAMO. Bound for Hull from London when she struck a mine and sank in the Thames estuary on 17 April 1943. Seven died, but no further details.

EGYPTIAN (Captain D.V. Murphy). Sailed from New York on 23 February 1943 and in Convoy SC.121 bound for the UK when torpedoed and sunk by U.230 (Kptlt Paul Siegmann) shortly after 2am on 7 March in position 56°25′N 37°38′W. Forty-four died; 4 were picked up by the corvette HMCS *Rosthern* (Lt R.J.G. Johnson) and landed at Londonderry. The *Empire Impala* (Captain T.H. Munford), which had been ordered to pick up survivors, was herself torpedoed and sunk by U.591 (Kptlt Hans-Jürgen Zetzsche) 7 hours later in position 57°00′N 36°00′W. All 46 died. (For details of other ships sunk in Convoy SC.121, see under *Empire Lakeland*, BLUE STAR LINE.)

ERATO (Captain G.D. Smail). Bound for Oporto and Gibraltar, sailing in Convoy OG.69 (outward to Gibraltar) which left Liverpool on 20 July 1941. Torpedoed and sunk by U.126 (Kptlt Ernst Bauer) shortly before midnight on the 27th in position 43°10′N 17°30′W. Nine died. Twenty-seven were picked up by the corvette HMS *Begonia* (Lt T.A.R. Muir) and landed at Gibraltar.

OTHER SHIPS SUNK IN CONVOY OG.69

Hawkinge (Captain W.A. Isaksson). By U.203 (Kptlt Rolf Mützelburg). Fifteen died. Six picked up by the corvette HMS *Sunflower* (Lt Cdr J.T. Jones) and landed at Londonderry. Ten picked up by the destroyer HMS *Vanoc* (Lt Cdr J.G.W. Deneys) and landed at Liverpool.

Inga I (Nor.) (Captain L. Tvedt). By U.126. Three died. Sixteen picked up by an escort ship and landed at Gibraltar on the 30th.

Kellwyn (Captain A. McLean). By U.79 (Kptlt Wolfgang Kaufmann). Fourteen died. Nine picked up by the armed trawler HMS *St Nectan* (Lt Cdr H.B. Phillips) and landed at Gibraltar on 1 August.

Wrotham (Captain J.G. Davies). By U.561 (Oblt Robert Bartels). None died. Twenty-six picked up by the corvettes HMS *Fleur de Lys* (Lt A. Collins) and HMS *Rhododendron* (Lt Cdr W.N.H. Faichney) and landed at Gibraltar.

Lapland (Captain J.S. Brown). By U.203. All 26 picked up by HMS *Rhododendron*.

Norita (Swed.). By U.203. Two died. Eighteen picked up.

ESTRELLANO (Captain F. Bird). Bound for Liverpool from Leixões, sailing in Convoy HG.53 which left Gibraltar on 6 February 1941. Torpedoed and sunk by U.37 (Oblt Asmus Nicolai Clausen) at 4.30am on the 7th in position 35°53′N 13°13′W. Twenty-one were picked up by the sloop HMS *Deptford* (Lt Cdr D.A. Thring). Six died, including one who died of his wounds on board HMS *Deptford*.

OTHER SHIPS SUNK IN CONVOY HG.53 – ALSO BY U.37

Courland (Captain R.C. Smith). Three died. Twenty-seven picked up by the *Brandenburg*.

Brandenburg (Captain W. Henderson). All her crew of 23 died, plus all but one of the 27 survivors of the *Courland*. The sole survivor of the *Courland* was picked up by the destroyer HMS *Velox* (Lt Cdr E.G. Roper) and landed at Gibraltar.

FABIAN (Captain M. Hocking). Bound for Istanbul via Cape Town and the Suez Canal, sailing in Convoy OB.234 which left Liverpool on 24 October 1940 and dispersed on the 30th. Torpedoed by U.65 (Krvkpt. Hans-Geritt von Stockhausen) at 2.29pm on 16 November and sunk by gunfire in position 02°49′N 15°29′W. The surfaced U-boat provided the lifeboats with food and water and treated two injured men. Six died. Thirty-three were picked up by the *British Statesman* and landed at Freetown.

FLORIAN (Captain L.R. Mann). Bound for New York from Hull and sailing independently but reported missing after 20 January 1941. At 0042 hours on the 20th, U.94 (Kptlt Herbert Kuppisch) torpedoed an unknown ship which sank within a minute, and it is deduced that she was the *Florian*. All 41 died.

GUIDO (Captain G. Mussared). Bound for Greenock from St Kitts, sailing in Convoy SC.121 which left New York on 23 February 1943. Romping when torpedoed and sunk by U.633 (Oblt Bernhard Müller) at 8.55am on 8 March in position 58°08′N 32°20′W. Ten died. After about an hour, 35 were picked up by USCGC *Spencer* and landed at Londonderry on the 13th. (For details of other ships sunk in Convoy SC.121, see *Empire Lakeland*, BLUE STAR LINE.)

IONIAN (Captain W.S. Smith). Bound for Hull from Crete and London and in Convoy FN 43 (Forth North, Thames to Firth of Forth) when she struck a mine laid by U.20 (Kptlt Karl-Heinz Moehle) on 22 November 1939 at 1.30am on the 29th in position 52°45′N 01°56′E. All 37 were picked up by the sloop HMS *Hastings* (Cdr E.H. Vincent) and landed at South Shields.

KELSO (Captain A. Hinchcliff). Bound for Liverpool from New York, sailing in Convoy SC.94 which left Sydney, Cape Breton, on 31 July 1942. Torpedoed and sunk by U.176 (Kptlt Reiner Dierksen) at 3.20pm on 8 August in position 56°30′N 32°14′W. Three died. Forty-one were picked up by the corvette HMCS *Battleford* (T/Lt R.J. Roberts) and landed at Greenock.

OTHER SHIPS SUNK IN CONVOY SC.94

Anneberg (Captain C.L. Bullock). By U.379 (Kptlt Paul-Hugo Kettner). None died. Seventeen picked up by HMCS *Battleford*, 14 by HMS *Nasturtium* and 7 by the corvette HMS *Primrose* (Lt Cdr A. Ayre), landed at Londonderry on 13 August.

Cape Race. See under LYLE SHIPPING CO.

Condylis (Gr.). By U.438 (Kptlt Rudolf Franzius) after being damaged by U.660 (Oblt Götz Baur). Nine died and 26 rescued.

Empire Reindeer (Captain W.E. Bacon). By U.660. All 65 picked up by HMS *Nasturtium* and HMS *Dianthus*.

Kaimoku (US) (Captain T.H. Cunningham). By U.379. Four died. Forty-six picked up by HMCS *Battleford*.

Mount Kassion (Gr.). By U.176. All 54 rescued.

Oregon (Captain S. Edmondson). By U.438 after being damaged by U.660. Two died. Thirty-seven picked up by the corvette HMS *Dianthus* (Lt Cdr C.E. Bridgeman). Three picked up by HMS *Nasturtium* landed at Liverpool on 14 August.

Radchurch (Captain J. Lewin). By U.176. Two died. Forty picked up by HMCS *Battleford*.

Spar (Du.). By U.593 (Kptlt Gerd Kelbling). Three died. Thirty-six picked up by the corvette HMS *Nasturtium* (Lt C.D. Smith) or HMCS *Orillia* (T/Lt Cdr W.E.S. Briggs).

Trehata (Captain J. Lawrie). Commodore ship. By U.176. Thirty-one died. Twenty-five picked up by the *Inger Lise* (Nor.) and landed at Preston.

U.210. (Krvkpt. Rudolf Lemcke). Rammed and sunk by HMCS *Assiniboine* (Lt Cdr H.H. Stubbs). Six died. Ten picked up by HMCS *Assiniboine*, 28 by HMS *Dianthus*, and all landed at Liverpool.

U.379 (Kptlt Paul-Hugo Kettner). Depth-charged, rammed and sunk by HMS *Dianthus*. Five picked up by HMS *Dianthus*. Thirty-seven died.

KIOTO (Captain A.L. Beckett). Sailed independently from Diego Suarez (Madagascar) for Baltimore via Cape Town and Trinidad. Torpedoed twice by U.514 (Kptlt Hans-Jürgen Auffermann) at about 3.20pm on 15 September 1942 and drifted ashore at Columbus Point, Tobago. Shelled by the U-boat at about 1.20 the next morning and destroyed by fire. Twenty died. Fifty-four were picked up by the *Trinidad* and landed at Scarborough, Tobago.

KYNO (Captain W.A. Thompson). Bound for Hull from New York, sailing in Convoy HX.66 which left on 16 August 1940. Torpedoed and sunk by U.28 (Kptlt Günter Kuhnke) at 8.57pm on the 28th in position, 58°06′N 13°26′W. Five died. Thirty-two were picked up by the *Queen Maud* and landed at Methil.

OTHER SHIPS SUNK IN CONVOY HX.66 – ALL BY U.32 (OBLT HANS JENISCH)

Chelsea (Captain R. Harrison). Twenty-four died. Eleven picked up by the armed trawler HMS *Lord Cecil* and landed at Scrabster, Caithness.

Mill Hill (Captain R.D. Buisson). All 34 died.

Norne (Captain Leif Hauge). Seventeen died. Eleven picked up by the corvette HMS *Hibiscus* (Lt Cdr R. Phillips) and landed in Scotland on the 31st.

LEO. In Convoy CW.8 (Channel Westward) when it was attacked on the morning of 25 July 1940 by a wave of Junkers 87 'Stukas', 50 Bf 109s, and E-boats, in the Dover Strait; also fired upon from the French shore. Bombed and sunk; seven died. Ten RAF Spitfires engaged the Bf 109s and 3 RAF pilots died. At 2.30pm, 40 more Junkers 88s and over 50 Bf 109s resumed the attack which was met by 20 Spitfires and a flight of Hurricanes. Six more RAF pilots died and 11 coal ships were sunk, including the *Leo*.

LESBIAN. Seized by the Vichy French in Beirut in 1940 and later scuttled. None died, but no further details.

LISBON. Wrecked off Rattray Head at about 6.50am on 30 October 1940. All 30 rescued by the Peterhead lifeboat *Julia Park Barry* which, owing to the atrocious weather, landed them at Fraserburgh. That same day, the lifeboat also rescued survivors of the *Simonburn*, *Alcora* and *Baron Minto*. (See under HOGARTH, H., & CO./BARON LINE.)

MARDINIAN (Captain J. Every, ex-*Palmella*). Bound for Methil from Trinidad, sailing in Convoy SC.2 which left Sydney, Cape Breton, on 25 August 1940. Torpedoed and sunk by U.28 (Kptlt Günter Kuhnke) at 4.47am on 9 September in position 56°37′N 09°00′W. Six died. Twenty-one were picked up by the ASW trawler HMS *St Apollo* and landed at Belfast. Ten landed from a lifeboat at Leverburgh, South Uist, and one rescued by the Armed Merchant Cruiser HMS *Aurania* (A/Captain I.W. Whitehorn). (See under *Serbino* below.)

OTHER SHIPS SUNK IN CONVOY SC.2 – ALL BY U.37 (KPTLT GÜNTHER PRIEN)

Gro (Nor.) (Captain Paul Brun). Eleven died, including 8 in the engine room and 2 found tied to a drifting raft by the corvette HMS *Periwinkle* (Lt Cdr H. Row) on

27 September. Twenty-one were picked up by the *Burdwan* during the evening of the 10th, transferred to the corvette HMS *Arabis* and landed at Liverpool on the 13th.

José de Larrinaga (Captain A.T. Gass). All 40 died.

Neptunian (Captain A.T. Campbell). All 36 died.

MALVERNIAN. Requisitioned by the Royal Navy. Commissioned as an ocean boarding vessel on 1 January 1941 and became HMS *Malvernian* (Cdr J.M.S. Robertson). Bombed by a Focke-Wulf 200 Condor on 1 July 1941 and 26 died. Bombed and set on fire by a Focke-Wulf 200 Condor on 11 July 1941 in position 47°37′N 19°07′W. Abandoned and sank about 8 days later. Thirty-two landed at Corunna on the 19th. Twenty-one landed at Vigo on the 22nd. Some rescued, perhaps by a Spanish fishing vessel, after 3 weeks on a raft, and the remainder (about 107) picked up by German minesweepers when their lifeboats were nearing land. Number of dead unknown.

OPORTO (Captain F. Bird, ex-*Estrellano*). Bound for Seville from London and in Convoy OS.44 (Outward Southend, Liverpool to Freetown) which left on 6 March 1943. Torpedoed and sunk by U.107 (Kptlt Harald Gelhaus) at 5.30am on the 13th in position 42°45′N 13°31′W. Forty-three died, including Captain Bird. Four were picked up by the corvette HMS *Spiraea* (Lt A.H. Pierce), transferred to the corvette HMS *Gentian* (T/A/Lt Cdr E.W.C. Dempster) and landed at Gibraltar.

OTHER SHIPS SUNK IN CONVOY OS.44 – ALL BY U.107

Clan Alpine. See under CLAN LINE.

Djambi (Du.). In collision with the *Silver Beech* on the 13th and sank. All picked up by the sloop HMS *Fleetwood*. (Cdr W.B. Piggott).

Marcella (Captain R. Downie). All 44 died.

Sembilangan (Du.) (Captain P.M. Leguit). Cargo of ammunition exploded. Eight-six died. 4th Engineer blown overboard and picked up by HMS *Spiraea*.

PALMELLA (Captain J. Every). Independently bound for Oporto from London when torpedoed and sunk by U.37 (Oblt Asmus Nicolai Clausen) at 8.22pm on 1 December 1940 in position 40°30′N 13°30′W. One died. Twenty-eight were picked up by the Spanish trawler *Navemar* and landed at Lisbon.

POLO. In Bougie, Algeria, on 17 January 1943 when there was a cargo fire and an explosion. Scuttled off the port on the 19th. Two died.

RUNO (Captain C.H. Tully). Bound for Alexandria from Benghazi and in the company of 3 other merchant ships and 3 escorts when torpedoed and sunk by U.593 (Kptlt Gerd Kelbling) at about 0020 hours on 11 April 1943 in position 32°15′N 23°55′E. Sixteen died. Twenty-one rescued and landed at Alexandria on the 13th.

SALMO. Seized in Morocco by the Vichy French on 3 July 1940 and renamed *St Emile*. None died.

SERBINO (Captain L.E. Brooks). Bound for Liverpool from Mombasa, sailing in Convoy SL.89 which left Freetown on 5 October 1941. Torpedoed and sunk by U.82 (Oblt Siegfried Rollman) at 10.03pm on the 21st in position 51°10′N 19°20′W. Fourteen died. Fifty-one were picked up by the corvette HMS *Asphodel* (Lt Cdr K.W. Stewart) and landed at Gourock.

OTHER SHIPS SUNK AND DAMAGED IN CONVOY SL.89

HMS *Aurania* (A/Captain I.W. Whitehorn). Damaged by U.123 (Kptlt Reinhard Hardegen). At least 3 died. Repaired and returned to service in 1944 as the repair ship HMS *Artifex*.

Treverbyn (Captain H.E. Edwards). Sunk by U.82. All 46 died.

SILVIO. Severely damaged in Alexandra Dock during an air raid on Liverpool during the night of 20/21 December 1940. Scrapped. One died. What became known as the Christmas Blitz extended over the nights 20 to 22 December and many civilians died.

TASSO (Captain A. Herbert). Bound for Oban from Demerara, sailing in Convoy HX.90 which left Halifax on 21 November 1940. Torpedoed and sunk by U.52 (Kptlt Otto Salman) at 7.23am on 2 December in position 55°03′N 18°04′W. Five died. Twenty-seven were picked up by the destroyer HMS *Viscount* (Lt Cdr M.S. Townsend) and landed at Liverpool.

OTHER SHIPS SUNK AND DAMAGED IN CONVOY HX.90

Appalachee (Captain W. Armstrong). By U.101 (Kptlt Ernst Mengersen). Seven died. Thirty-two picked up by the corvette HMS *Heliotrope* (Lt Cdr J. Jackson) and landed at Londonderry.

Conch. See under SHELL GROUP.

Dunsley. Straggling when damaged by U.47.

Goodleigh (Captain W.W. Quaitre). By U.52. One died. Thirty-six picked up by HMS *Viscount*.

HMS *Forfar*. See under *Montrose*, CANADIAN PACIFIC.

Kavak (Captain J. Napier). By U.101. Twenty-five died. Sixteen picked up by HMS *Viscount*.

Loch Ranza. Damaged by U.101, but continued at 6 knots. None died.

Lady Glanely (Captain A. Hughson). By U.101. All 32 died.

Stirlingshire. See under CLAN LINE.

Victoria City (Captain A. Longstaff). Straggling when torpedoed by U.104 (Oblt Hans-Peter Hinsch). All 43 died.

Ville d'Arlon (Belg.) (Captain A. Wilding). By U.47 (Kptlt Günther Prien). All 56 died.

W. Hendrik. Bombed by a Focke-Wulf 200 Condor at 11am on 3 December; there was an explosion and she was set ablaze. Five died.

Wilhelmina (Captain J.B. Rue). By U.94. Thirty-four picked up by the corvette HMS *Gentian* (Lt Cdr R.O. Yeomans) and landed at Gourock.

TEANO. Sunk in a collision with the *Chyebassa* in the River Humber in position 53°35′N 00°02′E. One died.

THURSO (Captain W. Walker). Bound for Liverpool from Lisbon, sailing in Convoy HG.84 and sunk by U.552 at the same time as the *City of Oxford* (see above). Thirteen died. Twenty-nine were picked up by HMS *Marigold* and landed at Greenock.

TRENTINO. Scrapped after being damaged in the Liverpool Blitz of 3 and 4 May 1941. None died. (See under *Domino* above.)

TRURO (Captain J.C. Egner). Bound independently for Trondheim from Hull when stopped by U.36 (Kptlt Wilhelm Fröhlich) at 7.05pm on 15 September 1939. Crew ordered to take to the lifeboats before the ship was torpedoed and sunk in position 58°20′N 02°00′E. All 20 were picked up by the Belgian trawlers *Nautilus* and *Edwaard Van Flaareren* and landed from one of the latter at Aberdeen on the 17th.

VOLO (Captain G.R. Whitefield). Bound for Alexandria from Tobruk, joined Convoy ME.8 (Malta East) which left Malta on 26 December 1941. Torpedoed and sunk by U.75 (Kptlt Helmuth Ringelmann) in the early hours of the 28th in position 31°45′N 26°48′E. Twenty-four died; 14 were picked up by the landing craft HMS LCT-11 and landed at Alexandria.

VOLTURNO. Bound for the UK, sailing from Lisbon with the *Shetland* and 2 neutral ships on 23 June 1943. Escorted by the corvette FFS *Renoncule* and the ASW trawler HMS *Sapper* (T/Lt R.C. Lees); they were to join Convoy MKS.15 which was to become part of Convoy SL.131 the following day. The ex-Lisbon group was attacked by 3 Focke-Wulf 200 Condors shortly after sailing. Both the *Volturno* and *Shetland* were sunk west north-west of Cape St Vincent. Four died on the *Volturno* and 3 on the *Shetland*.

Managed for Ministry of War Transport

BELLONA (Captain T. Nielsen) (ex-Danish). Bound for Reykjavik from Hull when bombed by a German plane and set on fire 4 miles east of Gourdon, Kincardineshire, on 8 October 1940. Drifted ashore at Strathlethan Bay, south of Stonehaven, on the 9th and wrecked. Six crew and 3 fish cargo workers died. Sixteen crew and 4 fish cargo workers survived.

CAP PADARAN (Captain E. Garner) (ex-Vichy French). Bound for Taranto in Convoy HA.11 (Heel of Italy to Augusta) when torpedoed by U.596 (Oblt Victor-Wilhelm Nonn) at 1.17pm on 9 December 1943. Taken in tow, but broke her back and sank in position 39°15′N 17°30′E. Five died. One hundred and ninety-two were picked up by the armed trawler HMS *Sheppey* (Sub Lt B.F. Wimbush) and landed at Augusta.

CELTE. Bound for Hull from Reykjavik when bombed and sunk off the Faroes by a Focke-Wulf 200 Condor on 27 April 1941. None died.

D'ENTRECASTEAUX (Captain W. Jones) (ex-Vichy French). Bound for the UK from Beira via Table Bay, Pernambuco and St Thomas, Virgin Islands, sailing independently from Pernambuco on 30 October 1942. Torpedoed and sunk by U.154 (Kptlt Heinrich Schuch) on 8 November in position 15°30′N 57°00′W. Three died. Sixty-three landed on the island Dominica on the 14th.

DIANA. Bound for Hull from Reykjavik when bombed and sunk by a German plane on 9 June 1941. One died.

EBRO. Bound for Hull (perhaps from Reykjavik) when wrecked off Rattray Head, Aberdeenshire, on 18 March 1942. None died.

EGHOLM (Captain K.S. Kristensen) (ex-Danish). Bound for London from Leith and in Convoy FS.1739 when torpedoed and sunk by U.2322 (Oblt Fridtjof Heckel) on 25 February 1945 in position 55°50′N 01°32′W. Five died. Twenty-one landed at the Tyne.

FLORA II (Captain P.K.J. Nielsen) (ex-Danish). Bound for Hull via Scrabster, sailing from Reykjavik on 2 August 1942. Torpedoed and sunk by U.254 (Kptlt Hans Gilardone) at 9.27am on the 2nd in position 62°45′N 19°07′W. All 30 were picked up from 2 lifeboats by the Icelandic trawler *Juni* and landed at Reykjavik.

LWOW (ex-Polish). Sunk during the disastrous air raid on Bari which began at 7.25pm on 2 December 1943. Two died. (For details of the Bari raid, see under *Testbank*, WEIR, ANDREW, & CO./BANK LINE.)

Federal Steam Navigation Co.

CAMBRIDGE (Captain Paddy Angell). Bound for Sydney and Brisbane from Melbourne when she struck a mine off Wilson Promontory in the Bass Strait and the southernmost part of Australia at 11pm on 7 November 1942 and sank. Sole casualty was the Carpenter, John Kinnear, who returned to his cabin to retrieve money. Fifty-five were picked up from 3 lifeboats the next morning by the auxiliary minesweeper HMAS *Orara* and landed at Port Welshpool. It was estimated that about 60 mines were laid by the German ships *Pinquin* and *Passat*. Following the sinking of the *Cambridge*, the Bass Strait was swept and 43 mines disposed of.

CUMBERLAND (Captain E.A.J. Williams). Bound for Port Chalmers, New Zealand, from Glasgow, sailing in Convoy OB.202 which left Liverpool on 22 August 1940 and dispersed on the 26th. Torpedoed by U.57 (Oblt Erich Topp) at 0048 hours on the 24th in position 55°44′N 07°32′W. Tried to reach port, but sank 8 miles from Inishtrahull. Four died and 54 landed at Moville, Co. Donegal.

DORSET (Captain J.C. Tuckett). Bound for Malta in Convoy WS.21S (Operation Pedestal) which sailed from Gibraltar on 10 August 1942. On the 13th, having been hit by two bombs delivered in separate attacks by German dive bombers, her cargo of high octane fuel caught fire, her engine room flooded and she was abandoned. All crew were picked up by HMS *Bramham* (Lt E.F. Baines) and some hours later the *Dorset* sank. (For details of Convoy

WS.21S, see under *Waimarama* and *Empire Hope*, SHAW SAVILL & ALBION, *Clan Ferguson*, CLAN LINE, *Deucalion* and *Glenorchy*, HOLT, ALFRED, & CO., and *Ohio*, SHELL GROUP.)

HERTFORD (Captain J.C. Tuckett). Bound independently for the UK from Australia and New Zealand via the Panama Canal when torpedoed twice by U.571 (Kptlt Helmut Möhlmann) at about 9pm on 29 March 1942. Torpedoed again about half an hour later and sank in position 40°50′N 63°31′W. Four died. Captain Tuckett and 18 others landed at Liverpool, Nova Scotia. Twenty-one were picked up by the *Glenstrae* and 18 by the *Fort Townsend*.

HUNTINGDON (Captain Styrin). In Convoy OB.288 which left Liverpool on 18 February 1941 and dispersed on the 22nd. Torpedoed by the Italian submarine *Bianchi* (C.C. Adalberto Giovannini) at 2.35am on the 24th and abandoned. Torpedoed again at 3.12am and sank in position 58°25′N 20°23′W. Bitterly cold and snowing when all 67 were picked up from lifeboats by the *Papalemos* (Gr.) whose Master risked his own ship by stopping. (For other ships sunk after the dispersal of Convoy OB.288, see under *Sirikishna*, SALVESEN, CHRISTIAN.)

MIDDLESEX. Sunk by a mine near the island of Flat Holm in the Bristol Channel on 10 January 1941. All rescued.

NORFOLK (Captain F. Lougheed). Sailed independently on 15 June 1941 for New York and New Zealand from Newport, Monmouthshire. Torpedoed by U.552 (Oblt Erich Topp) at 1.30am on the 18th. At 2am the now surfaced U-boat was seen heading for the ship, but crash-dived when the *Norfolk*'s stern gun opened fire on her. At 2.30am the ship was stopped and abandoned, and the lifeboats were clear of the ship when a second torpedo went into her. At 3am she was hit by a third torpedo and sank an hour later in position 57°17′N 11°14′W. One died. Seventy were picked up by the destroyer HMS *Skate* (Lt F.P. Baker) which detached from Convoy HG.64 and landed at Londonderry.

NOTTINGHAM (Captain F.C. Pretty). On her maiden voyage and bound independently for New York from Glasgow when torpedoed by U.74 (Kptlt Eitel-Friedrich Kentrat) at 10.34pm on 7 November 1941. Torpedoed again at 11pm and sank in position 53°24′N 31°51′W. The crew were seen to abandon the ship in lifeboats, but were never seen again. All 62 died, including Mr H.K. Cockerill, who had been 1st Mate of the *Norfolk*.

ROTORUA (Captain E.R.H. Kemp). Bound for Avonmouth from Lyttleton, commodore ship of Convoy HX.92 which left Halifax on 29 November 1940. Torpedoed by U.96 (Kptlt Heinrich Lehmann-Willenbrock) at 3.12pm on 11 December and sank in position 58°56′N 11°20′W. Twenty-two died. Two taken prisoner by the U-boat and landed at Lorient on the 29th. One hundred and eight were picked up by the trawlers HMS *Varanga* (T/Lt G.C. Crowley), HMS *Alsey* (Lt H.A. Inglis) and HMS *Ebor Wyke* (T/A/Skipper T.E. Olgeirsson).

OTHER SHIPS SUNK IN CONVOY HX.92 – ALL BY U.96

Macedonier (Belg.) Four died. Thirty-seven picked up by the *Súlan* (Ice.) and landed at Fleetwood.

Stureholm (Swed.) (Captain Sven Olander). This ship was in Convoy HX.84 and had returned to Halifax. See under *Maidan*, BROCKLEBANK LINE. The crew were seen abandoning ship in 4 lifeboats but were never seen again. All 32 died.

Towa (Du.) (Captain W. Smit). Eighteen died. Nineteen picked up by the destroyer HMS *Matabele* (Cdr R.StV. Sherbrooke) and landed at Scapa Flow on 16 December.

SAINT DUNSTAN (Captain T.G. Cookes). Torpedoed by U.57 at the same time as the *Cumberland* and sank while under tow on the 27th. Fourteen died. Forty-nine were picked up by the rescue ship *Copeland* (Captain J. McKellar) but transferred first to the destroyer HMS *Witch* (Lt Cdr J.R. Barnes) and then to the destroyer HMS *Wanderer* (Cdr J.H. Ruck-Keene) which landed them at Belfast on the 25th. The *Havildar* was damaged by U.57, but reached port under tow.

SOMERSET. Bound for the UK in Convoy SL.72 which left Freetown on 17 April 1941. At 7am on 11 May the convoy was attacked by Focke-Wulfs and she suffered a direct hit and a near miss and broke in two. The stern section sank, but the forward section was sunk by the corvette HMS *Alisma* in position 54°54′N 16°20′W. None died.

SURREY (Captain F. Lougheed, ex-*Norfolk*). Bound for Sydney, Australia, from New York, sailing from Hampton Roads on 29 May 1942. Torpedoed twice by U.68 (Krvkpt. Karl Friedrich Merten) at 6.17am on 10 June, but did not sink until torpedoed again at 7.22am in position 12°45′N 80°20′W.

The *Ardenvohr* (Captain P.E. Crickmer) was sunk by U.68 at the same time and the survivors of both ships were questioned by the Germans. When a crew member of the *Surrey* was seen clinging to a buoy they took him on board before diving. Shortly afterwards, however, an underwater explosion damaged the U-boat and when she resurfaced the man was placed in one of the *Ardenvohr*'s lifeboats. Twelve died on the *Surrey* and one on the *Ardenvohr*. The latter ship had picked up 17 survivors of the *Velma Lykes* (US) (Captain Hans G. Beck) sunk by U.158 (Kptlt Erwin Rostin) on 5 June, and all survived their second sinking. Thirty-five crew of the *Surrey* were picked up by the Colombian sailing ship *Resolute* but transferred to the destroyer USS *Edison* (Cdr W.R. Headden). A further 20 were picked up by the *Flora* (Du.) (Captain A. de Haan) and the *Potomac* (Pan.) and all were landed at Colon and Cristobal. (The *Flora* and the *Resolute* were themselves sunk on 18 and 23 June respectively.)

WESTMORELAND (Captain E.A. Burton). Bound independently for Liverpool from Wellington, New Zealand, sailing from Colon on 25 May 1942. Torpedoed by U.566 (Kptlt Dietrich Borchert) at 8.46am and again at 9.32am, on 1 June 1942. From 10.20am, shelled by the U-boat until she sank at 1.08pm in position 35°55′N 63°35′W. Three died. Forty-five were picked up by the *Cathcart* (Can.) and landed at Halifax. Twenty picked up by the *Henry R. Mallory* (US) were landed at New York.

Furness, Withy Group

FURNESS, WITHY & CO. LTD

MANAQUI (Captain C.E. Wordingham). Bound for Kingston, Jamaica, sailing from Cardiff on 19 February 1942 and in Convoy OS.20 which left Belfast Lough on the 23rd. Detached from the convoy and due to arrive about 20 March, but went missing and all 41 lost. It is believed that she was sunk by the Italian submarine *Morosini* (C.C. Athos Fraternale) on 12 March, although Fraternale thought he had sunk the *Stangarth*, subsequently sunk by U.504 on the 16th. The *Charles Racine* (Nor.) (Captain A. Svendsen) also detached from Convoy OS.20 and was torpedoed and sunk by the Italian submarine *Giuseppe Finzi* (C.C. Ugo Guidice) on 9 March. All 41 were picked up from 4 lifeboats.

PACIFIC GROVE (Captain E.W. Pritchard). Bound for Glasgow, sailing in Convoy HX.232 which left New York on 1 April 1943. Torpedoed and sunk by U.563 (Kptlt Götz von Hartmann) at approximately 4.40am on the 12th when in position 54°10′N 30°00′W. Eleven died. Fifty-six were picked up by the corvette HMS *Azalea* (Lt G.C. Geddes) and landed at Gourock. (For details of other ships sunk in Convoy HX.232, see under *Fresno City (II)*, REARDON SMITH LINE.)

PACIFIC PIONEER (Captain Hugh Campbell). Bound for New York from Belfast, sailing in Convoy ON.113 which left Liverpool on 17 July 1942. Torpedoed and sunk by U.132 (Kptlt Ernst Vogelsang) at 1.10am on the 30th in position 43°30′N 60°35′W. All 71 were picked up by the corvette HMCS *Calgary* (Lt G. Lancaster) and landed at Halifax. (For details of other ships sunk in Convoy ON.113, see under *Empire Rainbow*, ROPNER SHIPPING CO.)

PACIFIC PRESIDENT (Captain J.S. Stuart). Bound for New York from Leith, sailing in Convoy OB.251 which left Liverpool on 28 November 1940 and dispersed on 1 December when it reached 17°20′W. Torpedoed twice and sunk by U.43 (Oblt Wolfgang Lüth) at 9am on the 2nd in position 56°04′N 18°45′W. All 52 died.

> **OTHER SHIPS SUNK AFTER DISPERSAL OF CONVOY OB.251 – ALSO ON THE 2ND**
>
> *Samnanger* (Nor.) (Captain Andreas Hansen). By U.99 (Kptlt Otto Kretschmer). All 30 died.
>
> *Victor Ross* (Captain E.B. Case). By U.43. All 44 died.

PACIFIC RANGER (Captain W. Evans). Bound for Manchester from Vancouver, via Seattle, Panama and Bermuda, sailing in Convoy HX.77 which left Halifax, Nova Scotia, on 30 September 1940. Torpedoed and sunk by U.59 (Kptlt Joachim Matz) at 6.03pm on 12 October in position 56°20′N 11°43′W. Nineteen were picked up by an escort ship. Thirteen picked up by the Icelandic trawler *Þormóður* were landed at Reykjavik on the 21st.

Twenty-three in a lifeboat reached Glencolumbkille near Killybegs, Co. Donegal. None died. (For details of other ships sunk in Convoy HX.77, see under *Port Gisborne*, PORT LINE.)

PACIFIC RELIANCE (Captain E.O. Evan). Bound for the UK from New Westminster and Los Angeles, commodore ship of Convoy HX.19 which sailed from Halifax on 7 February 1940. Dispersed from the convoy when torpedoed by U.29 (Kptlt Otto Schuhart) shortly after midday on 4 March and sank about 40 minutes later in position 50°23′N 05°49′W. All 53 were picked up by the *Macville* and landed at Newlyn, Cornwall. The *Loch Maddy* (Captain W.J. Park), also in Convoy HX.19, was torpedoed and damaged by U.57 (Kptlt Claus Korth) shortly after 6pm on the 21st and abandoned. Four died. Thirty-five were picked up by the destroyer HMS *Diana* (Lt Cdr E.G. Le Geyt) and landed at Scapa Flow. Torpedoed by U.23 (Kptlt Otto Kretschmer) at 1.07am the next day, but as the stern section stayed afloat it was taken in tow by the tug HMS *St Mellons* (Lt H. King) and beached at Inganess Bay, Orkney, where the cargo was salvaged.

BERMUDA & WEST INDIES SS CO. LTD

CASTLE HARBOUR (Captain F. Theaker). Bound for Pernambuco in Convoy TRIN.19 which left Trinidad on 16 October 1942. Torpedoed by U.160 (Kptlt Georg Lassen) at 9.20pm that same day and sank in a matter of seconds in position 11°00′N 61°10′W. Nine died. Fourteen, including the seriously injured Captain and two others, were picked up by the US submarine chaser USS SC-53 and landed at Port of Spain. The *Winona* (US) (Captain J.B. Rynbergen), also in Convoy TRIN.19, was torpedoed and damaged by U.160 at the same time as the *Castle Harbour*. Reached Port of Spain under her own power. None died.

NERISSA (Captain G.R. Watson). Bound for Liverpool in Convoy HX.121 which sailed from Halifax, Nova Scotia, on 16 April 1941. Straggling when torpedoed and sunk by U.552 (Oblt Erich Topp) at about midnight on the 30th in position 55°57′N 10°08′W. Eight-three crew and 124 passengers died. Eight-three, including three stowaways, picked up by the destroyer HMS *Veteran* (Cdr W.T. Couchman) were subsequently transferred to the corvette HMS *Kingcup* (Lt R.A.D. Cambridge) and landed at Londonderry. (For details of other ships sunk in Convoy HX.121, see under *Port Hardy*, PORT LINE.)

JOHNSTON-WARREN LINE

AVIEMORE (Captain M. Forsythe). Bound independently for Montevideo and Buenos Aires from Swansea when torpedoed and sunk by U.31 (Kptlt Johannes Habekost) at 8.15am on 16 September 1939 in position 49°11′N 13°38′W. Twenty-three died. Eleven were picked up by the destroyer HMS *Warwick* (Lt Cdr M.A.G. Child) and landed at Liverpool on the 18th.

INCEMORE. Bound for Montreal from Manchester, sailing in Convoy OB.209 which left Liverpool on 5 September 1940 and dispersed on the 9th. Ran aground on the 16th on the Anticosti Reef, where the St Lawrence River enters the Gulf. Under precipitous cliffs and pounded by high seas 2 lifeboats were launched, but although smashed to pieces, no lives were lost. Other crew members were taken aboard the salvage tug *Foundation Aranmore* by breeches buoy.

JESSMORE. In Convoy OG.53 which sailed from Liverpool on 15 February 1941 bound for Gibraltar. Collided with the *Baron Haig* on the 19th. Taken in tow by the destroyer HMS *Scimitar* but sank on the 21st. No information as to whether or not there were casualties.

NEWFOUNDLAND (Captain J.E. Wilson). Hospital ship lying twenty miles off Salerno on 12 September 1943 when subjected to 2 air attacks by German planes. Undamaged, but moved a further 20 miles from the port to what Captain Wilson believed would be a safer position. Another three hospital ships, similarly fully illuminated, took the same precaution, but at about 5am on the 13th a single aircraft released a glider bomb which struck the boat deck, put her wireless room out of action, destroyed her fire-fighting equipment and set her on fire. When another explosion occurred, the order was given to abandon ship. Captain Wilson and 17 crew remained on board and, together with men from the destroyer USS *Plunkett*, fought for 36 hours to extinguish the fire. When this proved impossible, the ship was scuttled and sunk by the *Plunkett*. Four crew, 5 doctors, 6 nurses and 6 Army medical staff died. All 103 US nurses, who were to be landed at Salerno, were rescued as were the only two patients on board. The destroyer USS *Mayo* and HMHS *Andrew* assisted in the rescue.

NOVA SCOTIA (Captain A. Hender). Troopship bound independently for Durban from Port Tewfik and Aden when torpedoed 3 times by U.177 (Kptlt Robert Gysae) at 7.15am on 28 November 1942 and sank within 10 minutes in position 28°30′S 33°00′E. Until she surrendered to the Allies on 8 September 1943, Italy was Germany's ally, and when Gysae discovered that Italians were among the survivors he was horrified and repeatedly shouted in English, 'I am sorry … I am terribly sorry … I will radio Berlin … Help will come … Be brave.' But when BdU (Befehlshaber der U-boote – U-boat Command) responded with, 'Continue operating. Waging war comes first. No rescue attempts', he notified the Portuguese authorities. Dispatched from Lourenço Marques, the frigate *Alfonso de Albuquerque* subsequently arrived and rescued 194 from rafts and from the water. Eight hundred and fifty-eight died (many from sharks), including 650 out of the 780 civilian Italian internees being carried. (The reason for BdU's seemingly heartless response is perhaps explained under *Laconia*, CUNARD WHITE STAR LTD.)

PRINCE LINE

CYPRIAN PRINCE. In Piraeus on 6 April 1941, the day the Germans invaded Greece and shortly after 9pm bombed shipping in the harbour. Struck by a parachute mine and beached near Salamis. Four died and 32 survived. (See under *Clan Fraser*, CLAN LINE.)

INDIAN PRINCE. Bound for Colombo, Bombay and Karachi, sailing in Convoy OS.57 which left Liverpool on 27 October 1943. Joined Convoy KMS.31 at Gibraltar on 10 November. A German air attack began at 6.20pm the next day when the convoy was north-east of Oran. Struck by an aerial torpedo and taken in tow, but sank in position 36°10′N 00°06′W. DEMS Gunner S.F. Turner, P/JX 289636, died in the attack and Mr W.A. White, the 2nd Engineer, died of his injuries in January 1945. Sixty survived. (For details of other ships sunk and damaged in Convoy KMS.31, see under *Birchbank*, WEIR, ANDREW, & CO./BANK LINE.)

LANCASTRIAN PRINCE (Captain F.R. Elliott). Bound for Boston, Massachusetts, sailing in Convoy ON.176 which left Liverpool on 31 March 1943. Torpedoed and sunk by U.404

(Kptlt Otto von Bülow) shortly before 2am on the 12th in position 5018N 4248W. All 45 died.

(The destroyer HMS *Beverley* (Lt Cdr R.A. Price) was seriously damaged when she collided with the *Cairnvalona* on 9 April 1943. She was torpedoed and sunk by U.188 (Kptlt Siegfried Lüdden) on the 11th. One hundred and fifty-one died and 4 survived.)

NORMAN PRINCE (Captain W.R. Harries). Bound independently for St Lucia, sailing from Barranquilla in Colombia on 24 May 1942. Torpedoed by U.156 (Kptlt Werner Hartenstein) at 1.03am and at 1.37am on the 29th and sank in position 14°40′N 62°15′W. Sixteen died. Thirty-two were picked up by the *Angouleme* (Fr.), landed at Martinique and interned by the Vichy French. Radio Officer H.J. Tanner was rescued after two and a half days by USCGC *Unalga*.

NORTHERN PRINCE. With a cargo of ammunition, sailing in Convoy ANF.24 which left Alexandria on 1 April 1941 bound for Piraeus. Sunk by German planes in Antikythera Strait on the 3rd in position 35°34′N 23°23′E. All survived.

SIAMESE PRINCE (Captain E. Litchfield). Bound independently for Liverpool from New York when torpedoed 3 times by U.69 (Kptlt Jost Metzler) between 9.19pm and 10.12pm on 17 February 1941, sinking in position 59°53′N 12°12′W. The U-boat witnessed the crew abandoning the ship in lifeboats, but the crew were never seen again. All 57 died.

WELSH PRINCE (Captain H.M. Butlin). Bound for New York from London, sailing in Convoy FN.71 which left Southend at 8.55am on 6 December 1941. Struck a mine when off Spurn Head, broke in two and sank in position 53°23′N 00°58′E. All survived.

WESTERN PRINCE (Captain J. Reid). Sailed independently from New York on 6 November 1940 and from Halifax, Nova Scotia, on 29 November bound for Liverpool. Torpedoed by U.96 (Kptlt Heinrich Lehmann-Willenbrock) at 8.55am on 14 December. The U-boat waited for her to be abandoned before putting a second torpedo into her at 10.21am and she sank in position 59°32′N 17°47′W. Fifteen died. One hundred and fifty-three were picked up by the *Baron Kinnaird*. One was picked up by the destroyer HMS *Active* (Cdr E.C.L. Turner) and landed at Gourock.

RIO-CAPE LINE

BRITISH PRINCE. Bound for London from New York, commodore ship of Convoy SC.43 which left Sydney, Cape Breton, on 5 September 1941. Bombed and sunk by German planes when in position 53°52′N 00°25′E, north of Spurn Head, on the 26th. All rescued.

CHINESE PRINCE (Captain W. Finch). Bound independently for Liverpool from Port Said and Cape Town when torpedoed and sunk by U.552 (Kptlt Erich Topp) at 4.14am on 12 June 1941 in position 56°12′N 14°18′W. Forty-five died. Nineteen were picked up by corvettes HMS *Arbutus* (T/Lt A.L.W. Warren) and HMS *Pimpernel* (Lt F.H. Thornton) and landed at Londonderry.

CINGALESE PRINCE (Captain J. Smith). Bound for Liverpool from Bombay, Cape Town and Trinidad, sailing independently when torpedoed and sunk by U.111 (Kptlt Wilhelm Kleinschmidt) on 20 September 1941 in position 02°00′S 25°30′W. Fifty-seven died. Eighteen were picked up by the *Castillo Montjuich* (Sp.) and landed at St Vincent, Cape

Verde Islands. One was picked up by the sloop HMS *Weston* (Cdr J.G. Sutton), another by the sloop HMS *Londonderry* (Cdr J.S. Dalison) and landed at Londonderry on 3 November. **JAVANESE PRINCE** (Captain G. Gillanders). Bound for New York, sailing from Cardiff on 14 May 1941 and from Milford Haven on the 17th. Torpedoed and sunk by U.138 (Oblt Franz Gramitzky) at 9.24pm on the 20th when in position 59°46′N 10°45′W. One died. Fifty eight were picked up by the destroyers HMS *Faulknor* (Capt. A.S. de Salis) and HMS *Lincoln* (Lt R.J. Hanson) and by the rescue tug HMS *Assurance* (Sub Lt E.E. Litts). All survivors were then transferred to the *Toward* (Capt. A.J. Knell) and landed at Gourock on the 28th. **SARDINIAN PRINCE**. Bound for Philadelphia from Manchester, sailing in Convoy OB.294 which left Liverpool on 5 March 1941 and dispersed in position 51°29′N 20°30′W on the 9th. Intercepted by the *Scharnhorst* on 16 March 1941 when in position 43°46′N 44°00′W and all 44 taken prisoner before she was sunk. (For details of other ships sunk by the *Scharnhorst* and *Gneisenau*, see under *British Strength*, BRITISH TANKER CO. LTD.) **SCOTTISH PRINCE** (Captain W.R.M. Hill). Bound for the UK from Calcutta and Cape Town. Sailing independently when torpedoed, shelled and sunk by U.68 (Krvkpt. Karl Friedrich Merten) at about 1.30pm on 17 March 1942 in position 04°10′N 08°00′W. One died. Thirty-eight were landed at Cape Palmas, Ivory Coast, and taken to Freetown by the corvette HMCS *Weyburn* (Lt T.M.W. Golby).

Managed for Ministry of War Transport

EMPIRE COMMERCE. Off Margate on 9 June 1940 when severely damaged by a mine and beached. Refloated on the 11th, but beached again the next day and declared a total loss. Two died. **EMPIRE STANLEY** (Captain A.J. Pilditch). Bound for Beirut from Lourenço Marques, sailing independently from Durban on 13 August 1943. Torpedoed and sunk by U.197 (Krvkpt. Robert Bartels) at 3.50pm on the 17th when in position 27°08′S 48°15′E. Twenty were picked up by the *Socotra* and landed at Bombay on the 27th. Nine picked up by the corvette HMS *Thyme* (Lt H. Roach) were landed at Durban on the 29th. **FRED W. GREEN** (Captain A.G. Sampson). Bound for Freetown, sailing from New York on 15 May 1942 and from Bermuda on the 29th. Shelled and machine-gunned by U.506 (Kptlt Erich Würdemann) between 2.50am and 5.42am on the 31st and sank in position 30°20′N 62°00′W. Würdemann asked the occupants of one of the 2 lifeboats if there was anything he could do for them (an offer which they refused) and apologised for having to sink their ship. Five died. Thirty-eight, including six wounded, were picked up by the destroyer USS *Ludlow* (Lt Cdr C.H. Bennett) on 1 June and landed at Bermuda on the 17th. **SAMPA** (Captain H.N. Sherwell). In a convoy off North Foreland at 5.12pm on 27 February 1945 when she struck a mine and, with her back broken, sank within 15 minutes. Twelve were killed by the explosion and 4, who died later, were taken to Sheerness by the destroyer HMS *Middleton*. Captain Sherwell, who was blown off the bridge into the sea, was picked up and landed at Southend. The *Sampa*, a Liberty ship, had a crew of 53 and 9 passengers. (Captain Sherwell was the Master of the *Samtampa* when she was lost with all hands on the rocks at Sker Point, near Porthcawl, Glamorgan, in 1947.)

Harrison Line

ASTRONOMER. Bound for Scapa Flow from Rosyth when torpedoed by U.58 (Kptlt Herbert Kuppisch) shortly before midnight on 1 June 1940. Two more torpedoes were put into her between 3am and 5am the next day and she sank in position 58°02′N 02°07′30W. Four members of her crew died. One hundred and nine survivors, including naval personnel, were picked up by ASW trawlers HMS *Stoke City* (Lt Cdr N.C.H. Scallan) and HMS *Leicester City* (Lt A.R. Cornish) and landed at Rosyth.

AUDITOR (Captain E. Bennett). Bound for Beira via Cape Town, sailing from the UK on 20 June 1941 in Convoy OB.337. After the convoy had dispersed, sailing independently at 3.55am on Friday 4 July when torpedoed and sunk by U.123 (Kptlt Reinhard Hardegen) in position 25°53′N 28°23′W. The crew got away in 3 lifeboats and, as an SSSS message had been transmitted, they remained together at sea anchors until the Sunday when it seemed evident that no help was arriving. The boats then made independently for the Cape Verde Islands. Boat No 3, with the 2nd Mate, Mr D.O. Percy, in charge, landed on the island of Sao Antao on the 14th and its occupants were taken to the island of St Vincent the next day by the Portuguese sloop *Bartolomeu Dias*. No 2 boat, with the 1st Mate, Mr H.T. Wells, in charge, was approaching St Vincent on the 16th when they were picked up by a Portuguese schooner and taken to Porto Grande. No 1 boat, with Captain Bennett in charge, reached Sao Antao on the 16th. Two died and 69 survived. One of those rescued was Senior 3rd Mate Mr J.F. Booth who had previously survived the sinking of the *Planter* and was destined to survive the sinking of the *Merchant* and the *Empire Explorer*.

The survivors were repatriated in different ways. Captain Bennett went by Cape Town where he was given command of the Free French ship *Commandant Dorise* which reached England in June 1942. Mr G. Monk, the 2nd Radio Officer, and Mr R. Doyle, the Chief Steward, were taken to Lisbon on the Portuguese ship *Serpa Pinto* where Mr Monk joined the Danish ship *Ebro* and Mr Doyle sailed as a passenger on the *Cortes* (Captain D.R. McRae). At Gibraltar on 15 September both ships joined Convoy HG.73 bound for the UK. But of the 25 ships which sailed in the convoy, 10 were sunk and all 42 on the *Cortes* were lost. (See under *Springbank*, WEIR, ANDREW, & CO./BANK LINE.) The *Robert L. Holt* (Captain J.H. Kendall), owned by John Holt & Co. and also sailing independently after the dispersal of Convoy OB.337, was sunk by U.69 (Kptlt Jost Metzler) the day before the *Auditor*. All 49 died.

BARRISTER (Captain H. Collins). In ballast from Algiers, joined Convoy MKS.4 which had sailed from Bône on 22 December 1942 bound for the UK. On 3 January 1943 the convoy split into 2 sections and the *Barrister*, bound for the Clyde, proceeded in the section routed round the north of Ireland. In bad weather and with visibility poor, she became separated from the other ships and, at about 8am on the 4th, when it was suddenly realised they were heading for a large rocky crag, the 3rd Mate, Mr J. Bean, ordered 'Hard-a-port' to avoid it. But there were rocky shoals all round them and the ship ran aground with some force on what they later learned was Inishshark, in Co. Galway. A loud crack below the bridge was heard, together with the sound of rivets bursting, so Captain Collins rang 'Stop engines' and ordered 'Abandon ship'. Because the ship was on UK Double Summer Time it was only then becoming light.

Presumably because flares and rockets had been set off, the corvette HMCS *Kitchener* (Cdr Bill Evans) arrived to assist. The men in the first three lifeboats to be launched were picked up by her and subsequently landed at Londonderry. The fourth boat, with Captain Collins, 6 officers and a few seamen, was picked up by the corvette HMS *Landguard* whose commander, on learning that there were secret documents in the ship's safe, insisted that the 2nd Mate, Mr H. Skelly, go back for them, which he did after the sea had gone down the next morning. Then, in order to provide the information that would be required by the Receiver of Wrecks, the naval commander had Mr Skelly, Mr Bean and Cadet E. Parry carried to the island of Inishbolin by a fishing boat. There they remained in a large damp house until the officials arrived, after which they were taken home via Dublin. Those who remained on the *Landguard* were landed at Liverpool. All 74 survived.

CHANCELLOR (Captain W.B. Wilford). Bound for Liverpool from Belize and New Orleans, in Convoy HXF.11 which sailed from Halifax, Nova Scotia, at 10am on 2 December 1939. When the convoy was in dense fog she collided with the tanker *Athelchief* at about 8.45pm, was severely damaged and abandoned in position 44°30′N 61°51′W. All 42 were picked up from 3 lifeboats by the rescue ship *Oropesa* (Captain Dunn) which, while trying to catch up with the convoy, collided with the unescorted *Manchester Regiment* at about 3am on the 4th. The *Manchester Regiment*, which had been in Convoy OB.41 until it dispersed on 27 November, sank in a short space of time. Nine of her men were lost when their lifeboat overturned, the remaining 61 being rescued by the damaged *Oropesa*, a remarkable feat in such atrocious weather. The *Oropesa* returned to Halifax, as the *Athelchief* had done 2 days earlier. The *Chancellor* sank on the 3rd when the tug *Foundation Franklin* was attempting to tow her to Halifax. (See also under *Manchester Regiment*, MANCHESTER LINERS.)

COLONIAL (Captain J.J. Devereaux). Bound for Cape Town via Freetown, commodore ship of Convoy OB.318 which left Liverpool on 2 May 1941 and dispersed on the 10th. At about 8.20pm on the 26th she was shelled by U.107 (Kptlt Günther Hessler) and struck by 2 torpedoes about 40 minutes later. But it was not until 1am the next day that a third torpedo sank her in position 09°13′N 15°09′W. As the authorities had been alerted by an SSSS message from the *Colonial*, the entire crew of 83 were picked up by the battleship HMS *Centurion* (Lt Cdr R.W. Wainwright) during the early evening of the 27th and landed at Freetown. (For details of other ships lost in Convoy OB.318, see under *Ixion*, HOLT, ALFRED, & CO.)

CONTRACTOR (Captain A. Brims). Bound for Bombay from Glasgow and in Convoy GTX.6, from Gibraltar to Port Said, when torpedoed and sunk by U.371 (Kptlt Waldemar Mehl) shortly before 4pm on 7 August 1943 in position 37°15′N 07°21′E. Seventy-five, including several who were injured when a depth charge exploded near them, were picked up by the minesweepers HMS *BYMS-2011* (J811) (Lt L. Hutchinson), HMS *BYMS-2014* (J814) (Sub Lt R.R. Macintosh), HMS *BYMS-2024* (J824) (Skipper J. Hunt) and HMS *BYMS-2209* (J1009) (Lt J.G. Reeve) and landed at Malta. Seven died and 74 survived.

COUNSELLOR (Captain A. de Legh). Commodore ship of Convoy HX.22 which sailed from Halifax on 22 February 1940. Approaching Liverpool Bar Light in position 53°38'N 3°23'W on 8 March when struck by a magnetic mine. All 67, including 9 injured, landed at Princes Landing Stage.

CRAFTSMAN (Captain W.E. Halloway). Bound for Cape Town from Rosyth and sailing independently when she was intercepted on the morning of 9 April 1941 by the German raider *Kormoran* (Captain Theodor Detmers) in position 00°32'N 23°37'W. As her Radio Officers were transmitting a QQQQ message, and gunners were running aft to man her gun, the *Kormoran* opened fire, killing 5 men, badly damaging her and setting her on fire amidships. Ten minutes later, her engines were stopped and 43 men, including the severely wounded Master, were taken on board the raider to eventually become PoWs in Germany. After a failed attempt by a boarding party to scuttle her, due to the floats attached to an anti-submarine net in her otherwise ballast cargo, she was sunk by a torpedo. The wounded were later transferred to the tanker *Nordmark* which had a well-equipped hospital and made a safe passage through the Strait of Dover to Cuxhaven. The others were transferred to the supply tanker *Dresden* and landed at Saint-Jean-de-Luz in SW France on 20 May. Six died and 42 survived.

DALESMAN (Captain E.G. Horne). Sailed in a small convoy from Alexandria on 10 May 1941 and, together with the *Logician,* arrived in Suda Bay on the north coast of Crete at about 2am on the 13th. Crete was under heavy siege by the Germans and the *Dalesman* was bombed and sunk on the day after her arrival. One died from his injuries, 32 became PoWs and 24 escaped, including the Master.

Cadet John Dobson, making his first trip to sea, was taken prisoner but snatched a rifle from one of the guards and escaped. After serving for several days with gunners of a New Zealand battery, he and his new comrades journeyed to Sfakia, on the south coast, where they boarded an LCT in which to escape from the island. It was then found that John Dobson was the only one who could navigate and, under his command, the LCT reached the coast of Egypt, somewhere east of Sollum and occupied by the British Army. John Dobson was awarded the BEM, but had to give up the sea because he suffered from shell shock.

The *Dalesman* was raised by the Germans, renamed *Pluto* and employed in the Mediterranean. In 1944, she was bombed and sunk by the RAF when in Trieste, but raised after the war and returned to service.

DAVISIAN (Captain E.B. Pearce). Bound independently from Cardiff to the West Indies when intercepted by the German raider *Widder* (Captain Helmuth von Ruckteschell) on 10 July 1940 in position 18°09'N 54°40'W. No warning was given before the raider opened fire; bringing down her main aerial so that a QQQQ message could not be transmitted, setting her on fire and killing a man. Even when Captain Pearce signalled that the ship was being abandoned, the guns kept firing for a further 8 minutes. After a boarding party had tried to scuttle the *Davisian* without success she was sunk by a torpedo. The surviving members of the crew, including 6 wounded, were taken on board the *Widder* where they joined 45 survivors from the *British Petrol*, sunk on 13 June, and those from the Norwegian tanker *Krossfonn*, taken as a prize on 26 June without loss of life.

When the *King John* (Captain G.F. Smith) was sunk on 13 July, von Ruckteschell learned that there were 59 men in her lifeboats, including 21 from the Panamanian ship *Santa Marquerita* whom the *King John* had picked up when she was sunk by U.29 (Kptlt Otto Schuhart) on 2 July. The now large number of prisoners presented a problem and von Ruckteschell solved it by taking on board only the Master and Chief Engineer of the *King John*. The others were left in the boats, the largest of his own boats was added to their number and 41 men from the *Davisian*, excluding Captain Pearce, were ordered into them. After being provided with water, supplies, sails and compasses, they were advised to make for the Lesser Antilles. Some landed on the island of Anguilla on 17 and 18 July, while one, with 25 survivors from the *Davisian*, was picked up by the Norwegian ship *Leif* (Captain Lars K. Holm Brynildsen). Because von Ruckteschell continued to fire on ships after they had surrendered, he was tried as a war criminal and sentenced to 10 years in prison. This was commuted to 7 years, but he died in 1948; shortly after being told he was to be released due to a heart condition. (See also under *British Petrol*, BRITISH TANKER CO. LTD.)

DAYTONIAN (Captain J.J. Egerton). Bound for Halifax from Mobile, and sailing independently when struck by 2 torpedoes fired by the Italian submarine *Enrico Tazzoli* (C.C. Carlo Fecia di Cossato) on 13 March 1942 in position 26°33′N 74°43′W. The submarine then surfaced and shelled the ship before sinking her with a third torpedo. Prior to departing, the submarine's commander asked if they were all right and if there was anything they required. One died and the other 57 were picked up from the lifeboats the next day by the Dutch tanker *Rotterdam* and landed at Nassau on the 15th.

DESIGNER (Captain D.A. McCallum). Bound for Cape Town from Ellesmere Port, sailing in Convoy OB.341 which left Liverpool on 30 June 1941 and dispersed in position 48°30′N 26°30′W on 6 July. Sailing independently when torpedoed by U.98 (Kptlt Robert Gysae) shortly before 2am on the 9th, she sank in 6 minutes in position 42°59′N 31°40′W. Sixty-seven died. Several days later, 10 Lascars and a Royal Marine gunner who had gone out of his mind and never recovered were picked up from floating cargo by the Portuguese sailing ship *Souta Princesca* and landed at Leixões. The *Inverness* (Captain J.M. Henderson), also dispersed from the convoy, was sunk by U.98 about two and a half hours later that day. Six died and 37 succeeded in reaching Corvo Island in the Azores.

DIPLOMAT (Captain W.A. Hansen). Bound for Liverpool from New Orleans via Bermuda, sailing in Convoy HX.88 which left Halifax on 14 November 1940. On the 27th she was straggling from the convoy when torpedoed and sunk by U.104 (Kptlt Harald Jürst) in position 55°42′N 11°37′W. Fourteen died and 43 were picked up by the destroyer HMS *Active* (Cdr E.C.L. Turner) which landed them at Greenock.

DIRECTOR (Captain W. Weatherall). Bound for Beira from Durban and sailing independently on 15 July 1944 when torpedoed and sunk at 1am by U.198 (Oblt Burkhard Heusinger von Waldegg) in position 24°30′S 35°44′E. When the U-boat surfaced and its commander asked for the Master he was told that he had gone down with the ship, but when he went on to ask if there was anything he could do, the incognito Captain Weatherall facetiously asked for a tow. The 29 men in No 1 lifeboat were picked up by the Portuguese sloop *Gonçalves Zarco* (Captain Zola da Silva) at about 9pm on the 18th. The sloop then made a search for No 2 boat, containing 28 men, but was unable to find it and it landed near the entrance of the Kosi River on the 20th. The survivors from No 1 boat were landed at Lourenço Marques from where they went on to Durban by rail. Those from No 2 boat were airlifted to Durban. One drowned. Fifty-seven survived.

HUNTSMAN (Captain A.H. Brown). Bound for London from Calcutta when intercepted by the German pocket battleship *Admiral Graf Spee* (Captain Hans Langsdorff) during the evening of 10 October 1939. As Langsdorff threatened to open fire if the radio were used, Captain Brown complied. The crew of 82 were then taken on board the battleship and a prize crew boarded the *Huntsman*. The intention was to sail the ship to Germany, but after considering that this would be extremely difficult due the Royal Navy's blockade, she was scuttled. With the exception of 4 senior officers, all from the *Huntsman* were transferred to the *Altmark* (Captain Dahl) and were among the 299 prisoners released when she was intercepted by HMS *Cossack* (Captain P. Vian) in Norwegian territorial waters on 16 February 1940.

Following the Battle of the River Plate, on 13 December 1939, all 61 prisoners on the *Graf Spee*, including the 4 officers from the *Huntsman*, were released after she anchored in Montevideo harbour the next day. Langsdorff, who treated his prisoners well, unlike Captain Dahl of the *Altmark*, had the *Graf Spee* scuttled at 8pm on 17 December. He and the surviving members of his crew were taken to Buenos Aires, but due to having lost his ship and not relishing returning to face a hostile reception in Nazi Germany, he shot himself.

INANDA and **INKOSI**. Bombed and sunk in London docks on the same night in September 1940. The MOWT subsequently salvaged and rebuilt both vessels, renaming them *Empire Explorer* and *Empire Chivalry* respectively. Five were killed and 37 survived on the *Inanda*. All 27 survived on the *Inkosi*.

LOGICIAN (Captain W. Jones). Sailed in a small convoy from Alexandria on 10 May 1941 and, together with the *Dalesman*, arrived in Suda Bay, on the north coast of Crete, at about 2am on the 13th. On the 15th she was hit by 3 bombs but succeeded in discharging her cargo before being sunk by further bombing on the 25th; 5 days after the start of the German invasion of the island. Six died, 20 became PoWs, and 27 escaped on ships to Alexandria.

MAGICIAN (Captain G.H. Howard). Bound for London from Trinidad, ran ashore in thick fog on Craig Ewen Point, 2 miles north of Peterhead on 14 April 1944. Attempts to salvage her failed. All 80 survived.

MERCHANT. Bound for Trinidad and Demerara from London on Christmas Eve 1941 when she struck a mine 10 miles east of Yarmouth. She was abandoned the following day and sank in approximate position 52°40′N 02°04′E. One died and 44 landed at Grimsby.

OBSERVER (Captain J. Davidson). Bound for Baltimore via Trinidad, sailing independently from Cape Town on 29 November 1942. Struck by 2 torpedoes fired by U.176 (Kptlt Reiner Dierksen) at about 6.30pm on 16 December and, with a cargo consisting mainly of chrome ore, sank within half a minute in position 05°30′S 31°00′W. The U-boat surfaced and after Dierksen had questioned men on a raft regarding details of the ship, and ignored their request for food and water, it made off into the darkness. By the next day, the 15 survivors were on two rafts with Quartermaster W.J. Smith in charge. They kept together to begin with, but when 7 of the Lascars refused to accept his strict regime, Mr Smith put them on one raft and the rafts separated on the 18th.

At 11am on the 20th, the 8 men on Mr Smith's raft thought that help would arrive when a Catalina flying boat circled overhead. But no help came and at midnight on the 22nd a fully illuminated neutral failed to come to their assistance. At 10am on Christmas Eve, however, they sighted Brazilian fishing boats. The fisherman provided them with food and water and landed them at Fortaleza at 9pm. A search for the other raft was made the next day and the 7 recalcitrant Lascars were rescued. Sixty-six died and 15 survived.

PLANTER (Captain D.H. Bryant). Bound for Manchester from Suez via the Cape, in Convoy SL.53 which sailed from Freetown on 27 October 1940. Straggling from the convoy when torpedoed by the surfaced U.137 (Kptlt Herbert Wohlfarth) at 7.15pm on 16 November and sank in position 55°38′N 08°28′W. The crew of 72 got away in 4 lifeboats, but although they attempted to keep together one drifted away and the 13 men in it were never seen again. Thirteen died. Sixty were picked up by the destroyer HMS *Clare* (Lt Cdr C. Gwinner) on the 17th and landed at Londonderry the next day. Forty-three of the survivors were Lascars who, wishing to be repatriated to Calcutta, embarked on the *Jumna* which sailed from Liverpool in Convoy OB.260 – see under NOURSE LINE. (For details of other ships sunk in Convoy SL.53, see under *Apapa*, ELDER DEMPSTER LINE.)

POLITICIAN (Captain Beaconsfield Worthington). Bound for Kingston, Jamaica, and New Orleans and routed by way of the Minch, sailing independently from Liverpool on 3 February 1941. Owing to foul weather, ran onto a rock about half a mile south-east of the island of Calvay at about 7.45am on the 5th. But as Captain Worthington did not know the position of his ship his first distress message indicated only that the engine room was flooded and that they were abandoning her. His second message confused the issue because he then thought that they were south of Barra, so that the corvette sent to assist, HMS *Abelia*, could not locate her. Her position was eventually made known to the authorities by people standing on Rosinish Point on Eriskay. They saw a port lifeboat, which contained 26 non-essential crew, being lowered by the ship as Captain Worthington feared that she might break up, and the boat being swept along in the rough sea until the men were flung out of it onto the shore. At 4.45pm the Barra lifeboat arrived and took off the rest of the crew. All 52 survived. Compton Mackenzie's book *Whisky Galore* is based on, and romanticises, the story of the *Politician*, which he calls *Cabinet Minister*, while the true version is given in *Polly* by Roger Hutchinson.

SCHOLAR (Captain W.R. Mackenzie). Bound for Manchester from Galveston, sailing in Convoy HX.72 which left Halifax on 9 September 1940. Torpedoed by U.100 (Kptlt Joachim Schepke) shortly before 1am on the 22nd in position 55°11′N 17°58′W. After a failed attempt the next day to tow her by the tug HMS *Marauder* (Lt W.J. Hammond) she was scuttled by the destroyer HMS *Skate* (Lt F.P. Baker). All 45 were rescued by the *Skate* and landed at Londonderry on the 23rd.

OTHER SHIPS SUNK IN CONVOY HX.72

Baron Blythswood. See under HOGARTH,H., & CO./BARON LINE.

Blairangus (Captain H. Mackinnon). Sunk by U.48 (Kptlt Heinrich Bleichrodt). Seven died and 27 picked up by the *Pikepool*.

Canonesa (Captain F. Stephenson). Sunk by U.100. One died. Sixty-two picked up by the corvette HMS *La Malouine* (Lt Cdr R.W. Keymer) and landed at Greenock.

Dalcairn (Captain E. Brusby). Sunk by U.100. All 48 picked up by HMS *La Malouine*.

Elmbank (Captain H.T. Phillips). See under WEIR, ANDREW, & CO./BANK LINE.

Empire Airman (Captain J.B. Raine). Damaged by U.100. Taken in tow, but sank. Thirty-three died. Four picked up by HMS *La Malouine*.

Frederick S Fales (Captain F. Ramsay). Sunk by U.100. Eleven died and 32 picked up by HMS *La Malouine*.

Invershannon. See under WEIR, ANDREW, & CO./BANK LINE.

Simla (Nor.) (Captain Hans von Krogh). Sunk by U.100. Cargo of scrap metal and steel. Sank so fast that there was no time to launch the lifeboats. Five died. Thirty-one picked up by the corvette HMS *Heartsease* (Lt Cdr E.J.R. North).

Torinia (Captain H. Jackson). Damaged by U.100. Sunk by the destroyer HMS *Skate* (Lt F.B. Baker). All 55 picked up by the *Skate* and landed at Londonderry.

(*Broompark*. Damaged by U.48. One died.)

(*Collegian*. A straggler. Damaged by U.32 (Oblt Hans Jenisch). Escorted to Belfast by HMS *Heartsease* and the sloop HMS *Lowestoft* (Cdr A.M. Knapp).)

SCIENTIST (Captain G.R. Windsor). Bound for the UK, sailing independently from Durban to join a convoy at Freetown. Intercepted by the German raider *Atlantis* (KptzS. Bernhard Rogge) in position 19°20′S 04°15′E during the afternoon of 3 May 1940 and transmitted a QQQQ message, heard only by the raider. Shelled until the transmissions ceased, and when she was abandoned and her boats were alongside the *Atlantis*, German sailors jumped into them and took charge of the wounded. Further shelling failed to sink the blazing *Scientist* so that a torpedo was put into her to finish the job.

After the Norwegian ship *Tirranna* (Captain E.H. Gundersen) was captured, looted and a prize crew put on board, the *Atlantis* parted company with her and went on to capture two more ships before meeting up with her again 6 weeks later. Many of the prisoners, including the sick and wounded, were transferred to her and she set sail for St Nazaire on 4 August. During the passage, however, her prize captain Lt Waldeman decided it was safer to make for somewhere in unoccupied France, but when they anchored off Cape Ferrat on 22 September the unhelpful Vichy authorities advised him to proceed to Bordeaux. While waiting for an escort in the Gironde estuary she was torpedoed by the submarine HMS *Tuna* (Captain Cavanagh-Mainwaring) at midday on the 23rd. Out of the 292 on board, 87 died, including 71 Indians (in the tweendecks) and Obermaschinenmaat

Karl Seeger, one of the prize crew, who lost his life by trying to save a terrified woman passenger who would not leave the ship. After spending 3 hours clinging to wreckage, the survivors were rescued by German ships.

The *Atlantis* went on to sink 4 more ships in the Indian Ocean and when the Yugoslav ship *Durmitor* was captured on 22 October and a prize crew installed, 260 prisoners, including those from the *Scientist*, were transferred to her on the 26th. One died when the *Scientist* was shelled, 2 died when the *Tirranna* was sunk, 22 became prisoners in Germany, and 47 were released at Merca on 25 February 1941. (See *Durmitor* under *Athelking*, ATHEL LINE.)

STATESMAN (Captain D.A McCallum). Sailed independently from New Orleans and when 200 miles west of Inishtrahull, Co. Donegal, was attacked by a Focke-Wulf 200 Condor at first light on 17 May 1941. Struck by 2 bombs, machine-gunned, abandoned and sank at 8.45am in position 56°44′N 13°45′W. The 2nd Mate was killed and the remaining 50 were rescued from the lifeboats by the *Trojan Star* at 5pm but transferred to the corvette HMCS *Hepatica* at about 11pm and landed at Londonderry the following evening.

TRAVELLER (Captain H.M. Fitzsimmons). On passage from New Orleans to Halifax, Nova Scotia, to join a convoy to the UK when struck by 2 torpedoes fired by U.106 (Oblt Hermann Rasch) at 8.42am on 26 January 1942 in position 40°00′N 61°45′W. Sank within minutes and all 52 died.

TRIBESMAN (Captain H.W.G. Philpott). Bound for Calcutta from Liverpool and sailing independently when intercepted and shelled by the German battleship *Admiral Scheer* (Captain Theodor Krancke) in position 15°00′N 35°00′W at 9pm on 1 December 1940. Set on fire and abandoned, some by the lifeboats and others by jumping into the sea. Seventy-six were picked up by the *Scheer*, but 2 boats with 59 in them escaped in the darkness and were never seen again. The *Tribesman* had a complement of 135, including 54 Lascars who were being repatriated after serving on the *Explorer*. Fifty-nine died and 76 became PoWs.

After the Norwegian tanker *Sandefjord* (Captain Torger S. Torgersen) was captured on 18 January 1941 over 200 prisoners were transferred to her. *Sandefjord* reached Bordeaux on 27 February. The *Scheer* reached Bergen on 30 March and docked at Kiel on 1 June. On her patrol, she had sunk 14 cargo ships, captured 2 tankers and sunk the AMC *Jervis Bay*.

WAYFARER (Captain J. Wales). Bound for the UK via Aden, sailing independently from Beira on 16 August 1944. Torpedoed and sunk at 9.30pm on the 19th by U.862 (Krvkpt. Heinrich Timm) in the estimated position 14°30′S 42°20′E. Ten men on a raft reached an uninhabited island in the Mozambique Channel on the 30th and were subsequently rescued by local fishermen and landed at the village of Orlumbo in the extreme north of Mozambique, on 2 September. They were eventually taken to Mombasa where they boarded a troopship for home. Fifty-one died and 10 survived.

Managed for Ministry of War Transport

ARICA (Captain Beaconsfield Worthington, ex-*Politician*). (The captured Vichy French ship *Zenon*.) Bound for Trinidad and Demerara from London and in Convoy T.24 which sailed from Port of Spain for Demerara at 6am on 6 November 1942. Torpedoed at 4.20pm by U.160 (Kptlt Georg Lassen) in position 10°58′N 60°52′W and broke in two. As the lifeboats could not be lowered and the rafts had jammed, the crew jumped into the water. The after part of the ship, where the ratings were accommodated, sank in about 5 minutes, and the fore part followed it some 3 hours later. Twelve died. Fifty-five were picked up by the trawler HMS *Lady Elsa* (Lt S.G. Phillips) shortly before 7pm and landed at Port of Spain.

EMPIRE EXPLORER (Captain E.B. Stephens) (Previously called the *Inanda*). Bound for the UK from the West Indies and sailing independently when torpedoed by U.575 (Kptlt Günther Heydemann) shortly before midnight on 8 July 1942. Abandoned when a second torpedo struck. Yet another torpedo was put into her, and shelled and set on fire before she sank at about 4am on the 9th in position 11°40′N 60°55′W. Three died and 68 were picked up by MTB337 which landed them at Tobago.

Henderson Line

HENZADA (Captain W.I. McIntosh). Bound for Santos from Ellesmere Port and sailing independently when torpedoed and sunk by U.199 (Kptlt Hans-Werner Kraus) at 9.30am on 24 July 1943 in position 25°30′S 44°00′W. Two men in the stokehold died and the remaining 62 were picked up 7 hours later by the Panamanian tanker *Baltic*, and landed at Montevideo. A week later, U.199 was depth-charged and sunk by a US Navy ship and two Brazilian planes. Forty-nine died and 2 survived.

KALEWA. Bound for Cape Town from Glasgow when in collision with the ex-Danish ship *Boringia* on 1 August 1942 and sank in position 30°16′S 13°38′E. All rescued by the *Boringia* (Captain S.H.K. Kolls) and landed at Cape Town.

After being repaired, the *Boringia* was bound independently for Hampton Roads when she was torpedoed by U.159 (Kptlt Helmut Witte) at 11.55pm on 7 October. Torpedoed again about 10 minutes later, she sank in position 35°09′S 16°32′E. Abandoned when the second torpedo struck, killing most of the occupants of the 2 lifeboats lying alongside and the 1st Mate, who was standing on the deck above them, and severely wounding his wife who was signed on as a stewardess. Twenty-five died. Captain Kolls and 34 others, in 2 lifeboats, set sail for Cape Town but were picked up some hours later by the *Clan MacTavish* (Captain E.E. Arthur). At 9.07am on the 8th, however, the *Clan MacTavish* was herself torpedoed by U.159 and sank within 2 minutes. Captain Arthur, 53 crew and 7 survivors from the *Boringia*, including the injured stewardess, died. An aircraft directed the *Matheran* to the scene. She picked up 39 of the *Clan Mactavish*'s crew and 28 from the *Boringia*, and landed at Cape Town the next day. (See also under *Clan Mactavish*, CLAN LINE.)

KANBE (Captain J.F.T. Burke). Homeward bound from Alexandria via Takoradi and Freetown, straggling from Convoy TS.38 when torpedoed and sunk by U.123 (Oblt Horst von Schroeter) at about 1am on 9 May 1943 in approximate position 05°10′N 11°10′W. Sixty-one died. Five Lascars were picked up by the *Rio Francoli* (Sp.) and landed at Santa Isabel, Fernando Po.

KATHA (Captain S. Thomson). Bound for Calcutta via Durban and Colombo, in Convoy OS.45 which sailed from Liverpool on 24 March 1943. Torpedoed and sunk shortly before 7pm on 2 April by U.124 (Kvkpt. Johann Mohr) in position 41°02′N 15°39′W. Just before dawn the next day, the rescue ship *Danby* (Captain Riding) arrived and spent 4 hours picking up survivors, some from a raft and others from the water; the latter were located by the red lights attached to their lifejackets. Together with others rescued by the corvette HMS *La Malouine* (Lt V.D.H. Bidwell) they were transferred to the Canadian ship *New Northland* and landed at Freetown. After only one night in Freetown they boarded the *Queen Mary* which transported them to the Clyde. Six died: 5 trapped in the engine room and one crushed when abandoning ship. Fifty-eight survived. The *Gogra*, immediately ahead of the *Katha*, was also sunk by U.124. (See under BRITISH INDIA STEAM NAVIGATION CO.) About an hour after sinking the two ships, U.124 was depth-charged and sunk by the sloop HMS *Black Swan* (Lt Cdr R.C.V. Thomson) and the corvette HMS *Stonecrop* (Lt Cdr J.P. Smythe) and all 54 died.

KEMMENDINE (Captain R.B. Reid). Outward bound from the UK via the Cape when intercepted and shelled by the raider *Atlantis* (KptzS. Bernhard Rogge) in position 04°12′S 81°47′E at about 10am on 13 July 1940. No one was killed and the 112 crew and 35 passengers, including 5 women and 2 children, were transferred to the raider, with the latter hoisted on board in coal buckets due to the pitching of the lifeboats. A boarding party went on board the *Kemmendine*, but with the ship on fire they were unable to place demolition charges and it required two torpedoes to sink her.

Three days previously, the *Atlantis* had captured the Norwegian ship *Tirranna* (Captain E.H. Gundersen) and on 4 August the Doctor, Chief Engineer, the Junior Cadet and most of the Lascar crew of the *Kemmendine*, together with prisoners from other sunken ships, were transferred to her for the passage to Bordeaux under a prize crew commanded by Lt Waldemann. Rogge had radioed to alert the authorities of the prison ship's arrival, but they tried to contact her on the wrong frequency and while awaiting an escort in the Gironde estuary at midday on 23 September she was torpedoed by the submarine HMS *Tuna* (Captain Cavanagh-Mainwaring). (See under *Scientist*, HARRISON LINE.)

PEGU. From Glasgow and entering the Mersey on the night of 24 December 1949 to load for Rangoon when she went aground near the Beta Buoy. Refloated on the 26th, but hit the revetment and broke her back. All 103 rescued by the New Brighton lifeboat. The wreck is still in situ.

SAGAING (Captain S.S. Duncan). At anchor in Trincomalee during a Japanese air raid on 9 April 1942. Hit by 2 bombs and abandoned when it became impossible to control the fire. Deliberately sunk by gunfire after part of her cargo had been salvaged. No details of casualties.

YOMA (Captain G. Patterson). Troopship bound for Alexandria and Port Said and in Convoy GTX.2 which left Tripoli on 16 June 1943. She had a crew of 168 and carried 1,128 British troops and 665 men of the Free French Navy, a total of 1,961. Torpedoed at about 7.30am the next day by U.81 (Oblt Johann-Otto Krieg) in position 33°03′N 22°04′E and sank within minutes. The minesweepers HMAS *Lismore* (Lt L.C.G. Lever), HMAS *Gawler* (Lt Cdr W.J. Seymour), HMS *MMS-102* (Sub Lt R.L. Simpson, RNZNVR) and HMS *MMS-105* (Lt W. Henderson), and the *Fort Maurepas* took part in the rescue work. Thirty-three crew and 484 military personnel died. One thousand four hundred and seventy-seven were rescued and landed at Derna, in Libya.

Managed for Ministry of War Transport

BOTWEY (Captain E. Gordon). Ex-*Manchester Producer* and destined for the scrap yard when requisitioned by the MOWT at a time when everything that could float was needed. The same could be said of Captain Gordon, who returned to the sea at the age of 65. Bound for Port Sulphur in Louisiana from Ellesmere Port in Convoy OS.1 which sailed from Liverpool on 24 July 1941 when torpedoed and sunk by U.141 (Kptlt Philipp Schüler) at about 3.30am on the 26th in position 55°42′N 09°53′W. All 53 were picked up by the rescue ship *Copeland* (Captain W.J. Hartley) and landed at Greenock on the 28th.

OTHER SHIPS SUNK AND DAMAGED IN CONVOY OS.1

Atlantic City. Damaged by U.141 and abandoned. Reboarded and reached the Clyde.

Shahristan. See under STRICK LINE.

Sitoebondo (Du.) Dispersed from the convoy when torpedoed and sunk by U.371. All 77 abandoned the ship in 3 lifeboats. One boat, containing 19, was never found. Those in the other 2 boats picked up by the *Campeche* the next day. Two picked up from a raft by the *Campero* (Sp.) after being adrift for about 6 days.

EMPIRE CITIZEN (Captain E.C. Hughes). The ex-German ship *Wahehe,* captured by the Royal Navy on 21 February 1940. Bound for Rangoon, sailing from Liverpool in Convoy OB.279 on 28 January 1941. As the convoy dispersed on 2 February the *Empire Citizen* was proceeding independently when torpedoed and sunk by U.107 (Kptlt Günther Hessler) at 1.45am on the 3rd in position 58°12′N 23°22′W. All cleared the ship in the 2 port lifeboats and on a raft, but the boats were not seen again. There were originally 10 men on the raft, but in the bitter cold, snow storms, and with high seas running, only 6 remained when they were seen and picked up 2½ days later by the corvette HMS *Clarkia* (Lt Cdr F.J.G. Jones). Sixty-six crew and 12 passengers died, including one from the raft after being rescued. Among the survivors landed by the *Clarkia* at Londonderry was Cadet David Peebles, who was destined to lose his life 3 years later on the *Kanbe*.

NEVADA II (Captain Perinnes). Formerly a French ship and still manned by a French crew and Senegalese. Bound for West Africa and sailing to join a convoy at Oban on 20 July 1942 when she ran aground in fog on the rocky coast of the Isle of Coll. All brought safely ashore by bosun's chair, but the same means allowed locals to board and plunder the NAAFI stores she was carrying. The ship's cat was left behind but rescued 2 months later. (For an amusing description of the plundering of the *Nevada II*, see the article by Robert Sturgeon in *The Coll Magazine* of 1985, available on the web.) Parts of the wreck can still be seen.

SAMBUT (Captain M. Willis). With 580 troops, armoured cars, weapons, ammunition and cans of petrol on the foredeck, sailed from Southend anchorage at 6am on D-Day, 6 June

1944, to take part in the invasion of Normandy. When in the Strait of Dover about noon she was hit by 2 shells fired by a German shore battery at Calais and as the pumping gear was damaged, the ensuing fires could not be tackled. Towards 1pm, when the order was given to abandon ship, only the undamaged starboard lifeboats could be launched. The wounded were taken off and the surviving troops went over the side where they were picked up, mostly by small boats. Six crew died and Cadet Kenneth Campbell had to have an arm amputated. One hundred and thirty troops died. The *Sambut*, a Liberty ship, drifted onto the Goodwins and was eventually sunk by the Royal Navy in position 51°08′N 01°33′E.

Hogarth, H., & Co./Baron Line

BARON AILSA (Captain G.R. Logan). Bound for the Tyne, sailing in Convoy FN.96 which left Southend-on-Sea on 16 February 1940. Sank when she struck a mine on the 17th in position 53°17′N 01°12′E. Two died, including Captain Logan; the others were picked up by the ASW trawler HMS *Beech*.

BARON ARDROSSAN (Captain McPhail). Bound for Hull from Calcutta when at 1am on 30 December 1940 she ran onto rocks off the SE tip of Sandray Island in the Outer Hebrides in approximate position 56°52′N 07°29′W and broke her back. All 54 survived.

BARON BLYTHSWOOD (Captain J.M.R. Davies). Bound for Port Talbot from Wabana, Newfoundland, sailing in Convoy HX.72 which left Halifax, Nova Scotia, on 9 September 1940. Torpedoed by U.99 (Kptlt Otto Kretschmer) at 4.19am on the 21st and, carrying iron ore, sank within a minute in position 56°N 23°W. All 34 died. (For details of other ships sunk and damaged in Convoy HX.72, see under *Scholar*, HARRISON LINE.)

BARON CARNEGIE (Captain G.S. Cumming). Bound for Takoradi from Swansea, sailing in Convoy OB.334 which left Liverpool on 11 June 1941. Bombed and damaged by German planes that day and taken in tow by the tug *Seine*, but sank in position 52°04′N 05°30′W. Twenty-five died.

BARON COCHRANE (Captain L. Anderson). Bound for Pernambuco and Rio de Janeiro, sailing in Convoy ON.154 which left Liverpool on 18 December 1942 and Lough Foyle the next day. Torpedoed and damaged by U.406 (Kptlt Horst Dieterichs) at 11.17pm on the 28th. Torpedoed and sunk by U.123 (Oblt Horst von Schroeter) at 0053 hours the next day and sank in position 43°23′N 27°14′W. Two died. Forty-two were picked up by the destroyer HMS *Milne* (Capt. I.M.R. Campbell) and landed at Ponta Delgada in the Azores.

> **OTHER SHIPS SUNK IN CONVOY ON.154**
>
> *27 December*:
>
> *Empire Union* (Captain H.A. MacCallum). By U.356 (Oblt Günther Ruppelt). Six died. Sixty-three picked up by the rescue tug *Toward* (Captain G.K. Hudson) and landed at Halifax on 9 January 1943.

King Edward (Captain J.H. Ewens). By U.356. Twenty-three died. Twenty picked up by the *Toward*. Five picked up by HMCS *Napanee* (Lt F. Henderson) and landed at St John's, Newfoundland.

Melrose Abbey (Captain F.J. Ormod). By U.356. Seven died. Twenty-seven picked up by the *Toward* but transferred to the corvette HMCS *Shediac* (Lt J.E. Clayton) and landed at Ponta Delgada.

Soekaboemi (Du.) (Captain H.A. van der Schoor de Boer). Damaged by U.356 and abandoned. Sunk by U.441 (Kptlt Klaus Hartmann). One died. Sixty-nine picked up by the *Toward* and HMCS *Napanee*.

28 December:

Empire Wagtail (Captain G. Almond). By U.260 (Kptlt Hubertus Purkhold). All 43 died.

Melmore Head (Captain W.J. Leinster). By U.225 (Oblt Wolfgang Leimkühler). Fourteen died and 35 picked up by HMCS *Shediac*.

Zarian. See under UNITED AFRICA CO. LTD.

29 December:

Empire Shackleton (Captain H.E. Jones). Commodore ship damaged by U.225 on the 28th. Sunk by U.435 (Kptlt Siegfried Strelow). All 69 survived: 45 picked up the next day by the special service vessel HMS *Fidelity*, 7 by HMCS *Shediac*, 17 by the *Calgary* which landed them at Freetown. (See HMS *Fidelity* below).

Lynton Grange (Captain R.S. Grigg). Damaged by U.406 on the 28th. Sunk by U.628 (Oblt Heinrich Hasenschar). All 52 picked up by HMS *Milne*.

Norse King (Nor.) (Captain Lorentz Tvedt). Damaged by U.591 (Kptlt Hans-Jürgen Zetzsche) on the 28th. Sunk by U.435. All 35 died.

President Francqui (Belg.) (Captain G. Bayot). Damaged by U.225. Sunk by U.336 (Kptlt Hans Hunger). Captain Bayot taken prisoner by U.225. Five died. Fifty-two picked up by the corvettes HMCS *Prescott* (Lt W. McIsaac) and HMCS *Shediac* and landed at Ponta Delgada.

I quote from an article written by Ted Paxton who served on HMCS *Shediac*:

> In Ponta del Grada the *Shediac* tied up astern of a U-boat. It was December 31st, New Year's Eve. In a neutral port you are not allowed to go ashore. However, the native people were swarming on the jetty and handing bottles of wine to the Germans. When *Shediac* and *Battleford* tied up they did the same for the Canadians. Some of the U-boat crew went ashore and the *Shediac* crew followed. By this time, most of both crews were under the influence. We got into a pub-type restaurant with Germans and Canadians at adjoining tables, approximately 30 German sailors and 40 Canadians. The German sailors sent over a round of beer and wine; we did the same and soon we were sitting at each other's tables. There was not a nasty word said. The place closed at 1.00am and we walked back to our vessels together. *Shediac* and *Battleford* left at 8.00am on New Year's Day but the U-boat was not allowed to leave until eight hours later. *Shediac* and *Battleford* both arrived at St John's, Newfoundland, on January 8th, 1943.

Ville de Rouen (Captain H.C. Skinns). Damaged by U.225 on the 28th. Sunk by U.662 (Krvkpt. Wolfgang Hermann). All 71 picked up by HMCS *Shediac*.

30 December:

HMS *Fidelity* (Lt C.A.M. Costa). Developed engine trouble and heading independently for the Azores when sunk by U.435. Three hundred and sixty-nine died, including the survivors of the *Empire Shackleton*. The ship's MTB and the Kingfisher seaplane, for anti-submarine control, had been launched on the 28th and it was the latter which spotted the lifeboats containing the survivors of the *Empire Shackleton*. The MTB broke down and its 8 crew subsequently picked up by the corvette HMCS *Woodstock* (T/A/Cdr G.H. Griffiths). The 2 men from the seaplane were rescued by the destroyer HMCS *St Laurent* (A/Cdr G.S. Windeyer). Several U-boats were damaged and U.356 was depth-charged and sunk with the loss of all her 46 crew.

(On 27 December, the escort refuelling tanker *Scottish Heather* was damaged by U.225 and abandoned, but the 2nd Mate and other crew members reboarded and got her going again. They then searched for those in the lifeboats and, after picking them up, sailed the ship to the Clyde. All 54 survived.)

BARON DECHMONT (Captain D. MacCallum). Bound for Pernambuco from Barry and sailing independently when torpedoed and sunk by U.507 (Krvkpt. Harro Schacht) at 6pm on 3 January 1943 in position 03°11′S 38°41′W. Captain MacCallum was taken prisoner by the U-boat and was on her when sunk by a US Navy Catalina flying boat on the 13th and all 54 on board died. Eight of the *Baron Dechmont*'s crew died, including the Captain. Thirty-six landed from a lifeboat at Fortaleza in Brazil.

BARON ERSKINE (Captain G.S. Cumming, ex-*Baron Carnegie*). Bound for Garston, sailing from Tampa, Florida, on 9 December 1941. Joined Convoy SC.62 which left Sydney, Cape Breton, on the 27th. Owing to bad coal, fell out of the convoy on 1 January 1942 and was torpedoed and sunk by U.701 (Kptlt Horst Degen) at 4.27pm on the 6th in position 59°15′N 18°30′W. All 40 died.

BARON JEDBURGH (Captain E.A. Brown). Unescorted and bound for Durban from New York via Trinidad and Cape Town when torpedoed and sunk by U.532 (Frgkpt. Ottoheinrich Junker) on 10 March 1945 in position 10°02′S 25°00′W. One died. Thirty-three landed at Cabedello in Brazil on the 22nd. Twenty-five were picked up by the *Sandown Castle* on the 16th and landed at Montevideo on the 26th.

BARON KELVIN (Captain W.L. Ewing). Sailing independently and bound for Melilla from Lisbon when torpedoed and sunk near Gibraltar by U.206 (Kptlt Herbert Opitz) at 6.14am on 19 October 1941. Twenty-six died. Fifteen were picked up by the *Urola* (Sp.) and landed at Gibraltar. One picked up by the destroyer HMS *Duncan* (Lt Cdr A.N. Rowell) was landed at Gibraltar.

BARON KINNAIRD (Captain L. Anderson, ex-*Baron Cochrane*). Bound for Macorís in the Dominican Republic from Middlesbrough, sailing in Convoy ON.169 which left Liverpool on 22 February 1943. Began straggling from the convoy on 6 March and was torpedoed and sunk by U.621 (Kptlt Max Kruschka) at 7.17pm on the 11th in position 53°N 40°W. All 41 died.

BARON LOUDOUN (Captain J.H. Johnson). Bound for Barry from Bône and in Convoy HGF.34 which sailed from Gibraltar on 13 June 1940. Torpedoed and sunk by U.48

(Krvkpt. Hans Rudolf Rösing) at about 3am on the 19th in position 45°00'N 11°21'W. Three died. Thirty were picked up by the sloop HMS *Scarborough* (Cdr C.T. Addis) and landed at Liverpool. (For details of other ships sunk in Convoy HGF.34, see under see under *British Monarch*, BRITISH TANKER CO. LTD.)

BARON LOVAT. Bound for Huelva from the Tyne, sailing in Convoy OG.63 which left Liverpool on 25 May 1941. Torpedoed and sunk by the Italian submarine *Guglielmo Marconi* (C.C. Mario Paolo Pollina) on 6 June in position 35°30′ N 11°30'W. All 35 survived.

OTHER SHIPS SUNK IN CONVOY OG.63

Glen Head. By aircraft. Twenty-seven died.

Taberg (Swed.). By the *Marconi*. Sixteen died. Six picked up by an RN ship and landed at Gibraltar.

BARON MINTO. Bound for Hull from Texas City, sailing in Convoy HX.80 which left Halifax, Nova Scotia, on 12 October 1940. Wrecked near Rattray Head, Aberdeenshire, on the 30th. Further damaged by aircraft on 14 February 1941 and became a total loss. Survivors rescued by the Peterhead lifeboat *Julia Park Barry* which, due to the atrocious weather, landed them at Fraserburgh.

BARON NAIRN (Captain J. Kerr). Bound for Nuevitas in Cuba, sailing in Convoy OB.328 which left Liverpool on 29 May 1941 and dispersed on 2 June. Torpedoed and sunk by U.108 (Kptlt Klaus Scholtz) at 0006 hours on the 8th in position 47°35'N 39°02'W. One died. Eighteen were picked up by the corvette HMCS *Chambly* (Cdr J.D. Prentice) and landed at St John's. Twenty-one reached Galway in a lifeboat on the 27th.

OTHER SHIPS SUNK AFTER DISPERSAL OF CONVOY OB.328

Wellfield (Captain J.E. Smith). By U.48 (Kptlt Herbert Schultze) on 5 June. Eight died. Nineteen picked up by the *British Ardour* and landed at New York. Fifteen picked up from a lifeboat by the *Heina* (Nor.) and landed at Halifax.

Yselhaven. See below.

BARON NEWLANDS (Captain W.L. Ewing, ex-*Baron Kelvin*). Bound independently for Freetown from Takoradi when torpedoed and sunk by U.68 (Krvkpt. Karl-Friedrich Merten) at 11.17pm on 16 March 1942 in position 04°35'N 08°32'W. Eighteen died. Twenty, including Captain Ewing, landed near Cape Palmas in Liberia and made their way on foot to Freetown.

BARON OGILVY (Captain H. Steven). Bound for Cape Town, sailing independently from Rio de Janeiro on 18 September 1942. Torpedoed and sunk by U.125 (Kptlt Ulrich Folkers) at about 1pm on the 29th in position 02°30′N 14°30′W. Eight died and 3 wounded. Thirty-three were picked up by the *Mouzinho* (Port.) and landed at Cape Town.

BARON PENTLAND (Captain A.B. Campbell). Bound for Hartlepool, sailing in Convoy SC.42 which left Sydney, Cape Breton, on 30 August 1941. Straggling when torpedoed and damaged by U.652 (Oblt Georg-Werner Fraatz) on 10 September and sunk by U.372 (Kptlt Heinz-Joachim Neumann) on the 19th in position 61°15′N 41°05′W. Two died. Thirty-nine were picked up by the corvette HMCS *Orillia* (Lt Cdr W.E.S. Briggs) and landed at Reykjavik. (For details of other ships sunk in Convoy SC.42, see under *Stonepool*, ROPNER SHIPPING CO.)

BARON SALTOUN. Bound for Cherbourg from Hull when sunk by a mine in Cherbourg Roads on 12 June 1940. One died. No further details.

BARON SEMPLE (Captain P.J. Carnie). Bound for Freetown and the UK from Rio de Janeiro and sailing independently when torpedoed and sunk by U.848 (Frgkpt. Wilhelm Rollmann) on 2 November 1943 in position 05°00′S 21°00′W. All 62 died. See also under *Peisander*, HOLT, ALFRED, & CO.

BARON VERNON (Captain P. Liston). Bound for Port Talbot from Pepel, sailing in Convoy SL.125 which left Freetown on 16 October 1942. Torpedoed and sunk by U.604 (Kptlt Horst Höltring) at about 11pm on the 30th in position 36°06′N 16°59′W. All 49 were picked up by the *Baron Elgin* and landed at Madeira. (For details of other ships sunk in Convoy SL.125, see under *Nagpore*, P&O.)

Managed for Ministry of War Transport

ANADYR (Captain J. Bouteiller). Dispersed from Convoy TJ.30 and bound for Cape Town from New York and Trinidad when torpedoed and sunk by U.129 (Oblt Richard von Harpe) on 6 May 1944 in position 10°55′S 27°30′W. Six died. Eight landed at Porto de Galhinas and 39 landed 20 miles south of Pernambuco.

EMPIRE CONVEYOR (Captain F.B. MacIntyre). Bound for Manchester from Montreal and sailing independently when torpedoed and sunk by U.122 (Krvkpt. Hans-Günther Looff) on 20 June 1940 in position 56°16′N 08°10′W. Three died. Thirty-eight were picked up by the destroyer HMS *Campbell* (Lt Cdr R.M. Aubrey) and landed at Liverpool on the 21st.

EMPIRE MALLARD. Bound for Liverpool from New York, sailing in Convoy SC.46 which left Sydney, Cape Breton, on 24 September 1941. In fog collided with the *Empire Moon* on the 26th and sank just south-west of Point Amour in the Strait of Belle Isle. None died and the *Empire Moon* was only slightly damaged.

EMPIRE PROGRESS (Captain T.S. Hewitt). Bound for Tampa from Glasgow, sailing in Convoy ON.80 which left Liverpool on 27 March 1942. Dispersed from convoy when torpedoed and sunk at 0024 hours on 14 April by U.402 (Kptlt Freiherr Siegfried von Forstner) in position 40°29′N 52°35′W. Twelve died. Thirty-eight were picked up by the *Olaf Fostenes* (Nor.) and landed at Halifax.

FORT CHILCOTIN (Captain J. Kerr). Dispersed from Convoy JT.2 and bound for Freetown and the UK from Rio de Janeiro when torpedoed and sunk by U.172 (Kptlt Carl Emmermann) at 9pm on 24 July 1943 in position 15°03′S 32°36′W. Four died. Fifty-three were picked up by the tanker *Tacito* (Arg.) on the 29th and landed at Rio de Janeiro on 1 August.

HAULERWIJK. Bound for Tampa from Milford Haven when torpedoed and sunk by gunfire by U.32 (Kptlt Hans Jenisch) on 30 September 1941 in position 53°34′N 27°28′W. Four died and 27 survived. No further details.

OCEAN VANQUISHER. In Algiers on 12 December 1942 when sunk by a limpet mine placed by frogmen from the Italian submarine *Ambra* (T.V. Mario Arillo). Two died. Raised, sold and repaired after the war and owned by Italian companies until broken up in Hirao, Japan, in 1963. Ships damaged by the frogmen were the *Empire Centaur*, *Berto* (Nor.) and *Harmattan*.

OCEAN VOYAGER (Captain D. MacKellar). In Tripoli harbour on the night of 19 March 1943, loaded with aviation spirit, high explosives and military stores brought from Alexandria. Struck by 3 bombs during an air attack and set on fire. With the Master dead, the 1st Mate, Mr G.P. Stronach, assumed command and many were saved due to his efforts and those of the 2nd Engineer, Mr H. Hotham. Five died and 10 wounded. The ship blew up the following day.

OMBILIN (Captain Ellens). Bound for Cape Town from Trinidad when torpedoed and sunk by the Italian submarine *Enrico Tazzoli* (C.C. Carlo Fecia di Cossato) on 12 December 1942 in position 07°25′N 39°19′W. The Master and Mr Geenemans, the Chief Engineer, were taken prisoner by the submarine and 79 rescued. The *Enrico Tazzoli* sank the *Empire Hawk* the same day.

SUPETAR. Formerly a Yugoslavian ship, she was torpedoed and sunk by the Japanese submarine I-16 on 13 June 1942 in position 21°49′S 35°50′E. No further details.

TYSA. Bound for Baltimore from Cape Town when torpedoed by the Italian submarine *Morosini* (T.V. Francesco D'Allessandro) on 30 June 1942 in position 25°33′N 57°33′W. All 43 were rescued and the ship was sunk by escorting warships.

WESTERN CHIEF. Bound for Newport, Monmouthshire, sailing in Convoy SC.24 which left Halifax on 28 February 1941. Straggling when torpedoed and sunk by Italian submarine *Emo* (T.V. Giuseppe Roselli Lorenzini) shortly after 1pm on 14 March in position 58°52′N 21°13′W. Twenty-four died and 19 survived.

YSELHAVEN (Du.) (Captain M.P. de Waard). Bound for the St Lawrence River, dispersed from Convoy OB.328 when torpedoed and sunk by U.43 (Kptlt Wolfgang Lüth) at 8.24pm on 6 June 1941 in position 49°25′N 40°54′W. Twenty-four died. Survivors abandoned the ship in 2 lifeboats. Fifteen men in one boat were never seen again, while 10 in the other were picked up by the *Hammarland* (Finn.) on the 15th and landed at Norfolk, Virginia. (See *Baron Nairn* above.)

Holt, Alfred, & Co.

(BLUE FUNNEL LINE, GLEN LINE & NSMO)

AENEAS (Captain D.L.C. Evans). Bound for Glasgow from London in Convoy OA.177G when bombed and sunk off Start Point in Devon during the late afternoon of 2 July

1940. Eighteen died out of her crew of 120. Survivors were picked up by the destroyer HMS *Witherington* but one died later in hospital.

AGAPENOR (Captain P.W. Savery, ex-*Helenus*). Bound for London from Karachi and sailing unescorted when she picked up 36 survivors of the *Glendene*, sunk on 8 October 1942, south-west of Freetown. Between approximately 2am and 2.20am on the 11th she herself was struck by 2 torpedoes fired by U.87 (Kptlt Joachim Berger) and sank in position 06°53′N 15°23′W. Six died out of her complement of 131. The survivors, plus the 36 from the *Glendene*, were taken to Freetown by the corvette HMS *Petunia* (Lt Cdr J.M. Rayner) and brought home on the *Carnarvon Castle*.

ANCHISES (Captain D.W. James). Bound for Liverpool from Australia and about 120 miles north-west of Bloody Foreland on the NW coast of Ireland in the early afternoon of 27 February 1941 when bombed by a Focke-Wulf 200 Condor and severely damaged by several near misses. One hundred and thirty-four people, including 5 women and 2 children, left the ship in 6 lifeboats, while 34 remained on board in the belief that she might be towed. By 5am the next day, however, the situation had become so serious that Captain James decided to abandon ship. Flares were burned and rockets fired before the crew began taking to the only remaining lifeboat which, due to the high sea running, had its propeller and most of its oars smashed during launching. The corvette HMS *Kingcup*, having seen a rocket, came to the rescue but in manoeuvring alongside wrecked the lifeboat so that 20 of its occupants were thrown into the water. Captain James and a quartermaster lost their lives in this incident, but the others were saved. The *Kingcup* then began looking for the other boats and succeeded in finding 5 of them before it became dark. Those in the sixth boat were picked up by the Canadian destroyer HMCS *Assiniboine*. According to Admiralty records the *Anchises* sank after being bombed again on the 28th.

AUTOLYCUS (Captain R.C. Neville). In Calcutta, and only partly loaded when ordered to sail, as the authorities were anxious for ships to clear the port due to the false Japanese threat of air raids. Sailed for the UK via the Cape on 5 April 1942 in an unescorted convoy of 6 ships. Shelled and sunk by the Japanese cruisers *Kumano* and *Suzuya*, and the destroyer *Shirakum* on the 6th when in position 19°40′N 86°50′E. Two lifeboats got away. Survivors from one boat were picked up by the *Indora* which, with survivors from the *Malda* also on board, was herself sunk that same day. The other boat, commanded by Captain Neville, succeeded in reaching the coast of Orissa on the 8th. Four Europeans and 12 Chinese died.

AUTOMEDON (Captain William B. Ewan). Bound independently for Penang and about 250 miles from the NW tip of Sumatra when intercepted by the German raider *Atlantis* (KptzS. Bernhard Rogge) at about 7am on 11 November 1940. The latter ordered the *Automedon* not to transmit, and shelled her when the order was ignored, killing the Master, severely wounding the Mate, killing the other deck officers and slightly wounding Mr Donald Stewart, the 2nd Mate. After the surviving crew and passengers had been transferred to the *Atlantis*, the *Automedon* was scuttled and sank shortly after 3pm.

The capture of the ship was particularly fortuitous for the Germans (and the Japanese) as, due to the killing of the deck officers, not only did the secret code books fall into their hands but they also acquired top-secret mail addressed to the Far East High Command,

Intelligence Service papers and information regarding minefields. Together with others prisoners on board the *Atlantis*, those from the *Automedon* were transferred to the captured Norwegian tanker *Storstad* on 9 December and landed at Bordeaux on 5 February 1941. Along with 3 engineers from other ships, the 4th Engineer Mr Samuel E. Harper jumped from the train conveying them to Germany some 5 weeks later. They succeeded in reaching Marseille in unoccupied France where the Rev. Donald Caskie organised their crossing into Spain. Mr Harper arrived home from Gibraltar on 27 June 1941. Six died when the ship was shelled, 2 died from their wounds and approximately 97 became PoWs. (See also under *Nowshera*, BRITISH INDIA STEAM NAVIGATION CO.)

BRECONSHIRE. Requisitioned by the Admiralty and became HMS *Breconshire* (Captain C.A.G. Hutchinson). With army and RAF passengers on board, sailed from Alexandria on 20 March 1942 in Convoy MW.10 which consisted of only 3 other ships – the *Clan Campbell*, *Pampas* and the Norwegian *Talabot* – loaded with ammunition. Bound for Malta, the small convoy was heavily escorted. On the 22nd, the convoy came through an air attack relatively unscathed and in the evening the ships were ordered to proceed independently, each ship accompanied by a destroyer. *Clan Campbell* was bombed and sunk the next day, and the *Breconshire* was hit and disabled within 8 miles of Grand Harbour on the 24th. Ships of the Royal Navy made an unsuccessful attempt to tow her, but on the 27th she again came under heavy air attack and was sunk.

The crew were being carried to Gibraltar on the destroyer HMS *Havock* when she ran aground on Cape Bon on 6 April and became a total loss. They subsequently suffered internment under the Vichy French until the Allies invaded North Africa in November. The *Pampas* and the *Talabot* succeeded in reaching Grand Harbour, but both were lost during air raids involving in the region of 300 'Stukas'. The ordeal of Convoy MW.10 is known as the 2nd Battle of Sirte, and HMS *Breconshire*, which was also in the first battle of that name in December 1941, made more trips to beleaguered Malta than any other merchantman. In April 1954, she was raised and towed upside down to Trieste for breaking up.

CALCHAS (Captain W.R.F. Holden). Unescorted and bound for Liverpool from Sydney, Australia, when torpedoed by U.107 (Kptlt Günther Hessler) at 10.25am on 21 April 1941. All passengers and crew not required to try to save the ship took to 5 lifeboats which stood off at some distance from her. One boat had been wrecked and the other, a motorboat, was retained to take off the remaining crew. About three-quarters of an hour later, however, a second torpedo struck, killing most of those still on board, including all the deck officers. When the ship went down in position 23°50′N 27°00′W the undamaged but unprovisioned motorboat floated clear.

As an SSSS message had been transmitted and acknowledged, the lifeboats remained in the same position until the 22nd before it was decided to make for the Cape Verde Islands. The boats tried to keep together but, on the 23rd, boats 3, 4 and 5 sailed out of sight of the others. The mast of No 4 was torn out of its seating the following day and, as it was in danger of being swamped, its occupants transferred into No 5. On the 24th, the more heavily laden No 3 boat also became in danger of being swamped so that it was taken in tow by No 5, but when the sea moderated on the 27th it was decided to abandon it, its occupants also transferring to No 5. Early on the morning of the 29th, No 5 boat held 16 Europeans, 17 Chinese crew and 4 passengers when a ship, thought to be French or neutral, was sighted. But although she also sighted them, she sheered off and left them to their fate. During the ensuing ordeal, the 2nd Radio Officer, with his mind unhinged, jumped overboard and the Chinese gave trouble, one of whom and a passenger died. At 3am on 6 May the boat ran aground near St Louis in Senegal, but 3 more died after they landed. Boats No 6 and 8 remained together until 29 April.

On the afternoon of 4 May, No 6 landed on the island of Sal in the Cape Verde Islands while No 8, with 11 Europeans, including a woman passenger, and 7 Chinese, landed at about the same time on the adjacent island of Boa Vista. On 5 May, the remaining lifeboat, called the 'Spare', with 9 Europeans and 7 Chinese on board, landed on the opposite side of Sal to that on which No 6 had landed the previous day. A Chinese died shortly after they landed and, together with those of the latter boat, they were taken to St Vincent and then to Sierra Leone for repatriation home. Twenty-four died and 89 survived. (After the war, Hessler, the son-in-law of Admiral Dönitz, worked on the campaign records of the U-boats for the British Admiralty.)

CENTAUR (Captain G.A. Murray). An Australian hospital ship engaged in carrying wounded to Australia from Port Moresby in New Guinea. When fully illuminated according to the Geneva Convention and fortunately on her outward run so that she carried no wounded, at 4.15am on 14 May 1943 she was torpedoed by the Japanese submarine I-177 (Lt Cdr Hajime Nakagawa) some 50 miles east of Brisbane. As she sank within 3 minutes, lifeboats could not be launched nor a distress signal sent to alert the authorities. The survivors, clinging to wreckage and an upturned lifeboat and existing on the small amount of food stowed in 2 rafts, were not spotted until an RAAF Avro Anson flew over them at 2pm on the 15th. The destroyer USS *Mugford* was then directed to the scene and succeeded in picking up only 1 nurse and 63 others. Captain Murray, 44 crew, the ship's padre, 18 doctors, 11 nurses and 193 other medical personnel of the 2/12th Field Ambulance Unit lost their lives. The surviving nurse, Sister Ellen Savage, was awarded the George Medal as, although injured, she greatly assisted the other survivors. After the war, Nakagawa was tried as a war criminal, but surprisingly not for the sinking of the *Centaur*. He was found guilty of machine-gunning the survivors of the *British Chivalry*, *Sutlej* and *Ascot* when they were in lifeboats and on rafts, after he had sunk their ships when in command of I-37 in February 1944. He served only 6 years of his sentence of 8 years' hard labour, was released in 1954 and died at the age of 84. (See under *British Chivalry*, BRITISH TANKER CO. LTD, and *Sutlej*, NOURSE LINE.)

CHILEAN REEFER (Captain T. Bell). A 1,739-ton ex-Danish ship managed for the MOWT, bound independently for Halifax and sailing from Loch Ewe on 9 March 1941 with a crew consisting of 18 British, 12 Danish and 6 Chinese. Intercepted by the German battle cruiser *Gneisenau* (KptzS. Otto Fein) during the early evening of the 15th and transmitted an RRRR message, giving her position as 46°11′N 44°51′W. Shelled, hit, stopped and abandoned, but the starboard lifeboat up-ended when the slip-hook was released by a naval gunner and its occupants were tipped into the sea.

While still shelling the burning ship, the *Gneisenau* ordered all the boats to come alongside her, but from his boat Captain Bell replied that his rescue work was incomplete and continued to pick up men from the water. When darkness prevented further search, he steered his boat to the lee side of the *Gneisenau*; this almost resulted in tragedy as, when the boat was passing under her stern, she moved forward on her engines. It was only with great difficulty that they got clear, but the tiller was destroyed by the contact.

Second Mate Mr C.T. Collett, 4th Engineer Mr G. Jones and Ordinary Seaman H. Jensen were the only occupants of another lifeboat, and when they approached the *Gneisenau* they were ordered to climb on board. Mr Collett was then asked to admit that the *Chilean Reefer* was a decoy, acting in collusion with a British warship which was known to be in the vicinity. When he refused, he was thrown into a bare cell and kept in isolation for 2 days with very little food. He was then interrogated again and when the Germans were satisfied of his ship's innocence, he and his companions were allowed to join the ship's other prisoners. Contrary to International Law, the *Gneisenau* made no attempt to save survivors and when she docked in Brest the prisoners were paraded through the streets before being taken to Germany in cattle trucks.

The *Chilean Reefer* was still afloat and burning, and the weather deteriorating, when those in Captain Bell's lifeboat saw a searchlight stab the darkness. They thought it was the *Gneisenau* returning and fired a red flare, but it turned out to be the battleship HMS *Rodney* which had heard the RRRR message while escorting Convoy HX.114. Four men were lost with the ship, and the Chief Engineer, 1st Radio Officer G. Williams and DEMS gunner John Erskine, RFR, P/J 12656, died on the *Rodney*. (For details of the many ships sunk and captured by the *Scharnhorst* and the *Gneisenau*, see under *British Strength*, BRITISH TANKER CO. LTD.)

CLYTONEUS (Captain S.G. Goffey). Returning from the Dutch East Indies and in position 56°23′N 15°28′W, about 280 miles north-west of Bloody Foreland, when at 8am on 8 January 1941 she was bombed, machine-gunned and set on fire by a single Focke-Wulf 200 Condor. The crew abandoned her in 3 lifeboats, 2 of which were picked up by the destroyer HMS *Wild Swan* and the other by the AMC *Esperance Bay*. One AB wounded and no lives lost.

CYCLOPS (Captain L.W. Kersley). On unescorted passage from Hong Kong to Liverpool via Auckland, the Panama Canal and Halifax when at about 7.45pm on 11 January 1942 she was torpedoed by U.123 (Kptlt Reinhard Hardegen) in position 41°51′N 63°48′W. The lifeboats were launched, but most of the crew were still on board when a second torpedo struck and they had to jump into the freezing water. As an SSSS message had been transmitted, the survivors were picked up by HMCS *Red Deer* (Lt A. Moorhouse) and taken to Halifax. Eighty-seven died and 95 survived. (The reason for the large complement was that the *Cyclops* was carrying 78 Chinese seamen to Halifax to join other ships.)

DARDANUS (Captain A. English). In Calcutta when ordered to sail, as the authorities were anxious for ships to clear the port due to the false Japanese threat of air raids. Accompanied by 2 other merchant ships (Greek and Norwegian) but without an escort, she sailed on 2 April 1942 bound for Colombo. On the evening of the 4th, the ships parted company and early the next morning the *Dardanus* was bombed by 2 planes from the Japanese aircraft carrier *Ryujo*. One bomb hit a forward hold and another disabled her engine room, causing her to be abandoned.

After the planes had gone and it was evident that the ship was not sinking, the crew returned on board. As the British India Company's *Gandara* had now come upon the scene, a line was attached and she began towing the *Dardanus* to Madras. At 7.30pm on the 6th, however, a high-level plane bombed the ships and shortly afterwards Japanese warships approached and began shelling from a distance of about 3 miles. The *Gandara* slipped the tow, but when shells from the cruisers *Mogami* and *Mikuma* repeatedly hit both ships they were abandoned. The warships then closed to finish off the ships, but the *Dardanus* did not sink until torpedoed later by the destroyer *Amagiri* in approximate position 16°00′N 82°20′E. All 4 of the *Dardanus*'s lifeboats reached the coast of Orissa on the 7th and there were no casualties. Nine of the *Gandara*'s crew died. (Other ships sunk by the Japanese warships within a matter of days were *Silksworth*, *Shinkuang*, *Ganges*, *Taksang*, *Sinkiang*, *Exmoor* (US), *Bienville* (US), *Selma City* (US), *Banjoewangi* (Du.), *Batavia* (Du.), *Van der Capellen* (Du.) and those listed under *Autolycus*.)

DEUCALION (Captain Ramsay Brown). In Convoy WS.21S (Operation Pedestal) which consisted of 14 ships and sailed from Gibraltar on 10 August 1942 bound for Malta. The first attack on the convoy was made during the afternoon of the next day when the aircraft carrier HMS *Eagle* was torpedoed and sunk by U.73 (Kptlt Helmut Rosenbaum). The air attacks began at 8am on the 12th and in the afternoon the *Deucalion* was struck by 2 bombs. The engines were stopped so that the situation could be assessed and the ship, accompanied by HMS *Bramham*, proceeded along the Tunisian coast when it was found that only Nos 1 and 5 holds were flooded. At 7.45pm, 2 planes dropped bombs which narrowly missed the ship, but when she was off Cani Rocks lighthouse about an hour and a half later, a torpedo bomber scored a hit on the aviation spirit and kerosene in No 6 hold and set the after end of the ship ablaze. The crew then took to the lifeboats and rowed to the *Bramham*, from which some of them later transferred to assist the exhausted crew of the disabled tanker *Ohio*. The *Deucalion* sank after being abandoned; none of her crew died but a DEMS gunner was seriously injured. Only 5 of the merchant ships reached Malta. (See also under *Glenorchy* and, for further details, under *Waimarama* and *Empire Hope*, SHAW SAVILL & ALBION, *Clan Ferguson*, CLAN LINE, *Dorset*, FEDERAL STEAM NAVIGATION CO. and *Ohio*, SHELL GROUP.)

DOLIUS (Captain G.R. Cheetham). Bound for New York and in Convoy ONS.5 which sailed from Liverpool on 21 April 1943. Torpedoed and sunk by U.638 (Kptlt Oskar Staudinger) at 2pm on 5 May in position 54°00′N 43°35′W. Four died and 66 were picked up by the corvette HMS *Sunflower* (Lt J. Plomer, RCNVR) which landed them at St John's, Newfoundland. The *Sunflower* subsequently destroyed the U-boat, when all 44 on board died.

From 29 April until 6 May the convoy suffered attacks from over 30 U-boats when, unfortunately, Bletchley Park was unable to decode messages exchanged between the U-boats and the BdU (U-boat Command) due to changes made by the Germans in the Enigma machine settings.

OTHER SHIPS SUNK IN CONVOY ONS.5

Bonde (Nor.) (Captain Finn Abrahamsen). Sunk by U.266. Fourteen died. Twelve picked up by HMS *Tay*.

Bristol City. See under BRISTOL CITY LINE.

Gharinda (Captain R.E. Stone). Sunk by U.266. All 92 picked up by HMS *Tay*.

Harbury (Captain W.E. Cook). Sunk by U.629 (Kptlt Heinrich Hasenschar). Seven died. Forty-two picked up by HMS *Northern Spray*.

Harperley (Captain J.E. Turgoose). Sunk by U.264. Ten died. Thirty-nine picked up by HMS *Northern Spray*.

Lorient (Captain W.J. Manley). A straggler. Sunk by U.125 (Kptlt Ulrich Folkers). All 40 died.

McKeesport (US) (Captain O.J. Lohr). Sunk by U.258 (Kptlt Wilhelm von Mässenhausen). One died. Sixty-seven survivors picked up by the rescue trawler HMS *Northern Gem* (Skipper Lt J.V. Mullender) and landed at St John's, Newfoundland, on 8 May.

North Britain (Captain J.L. Bright). A straggler. Sunk by U.707 (Oblt Günter Gretschel). Thirty-five died. Eleven survivors picked up by the rescue trawler HMS *Northern Spray* (Lt F.A.J. Downer) and landed at St John's on the 8th.

Selvistan. See under STRICK LINE.

Wentworth (Captain R.G. Phillips). Torpedoed by U.358 and scuttled by HMS *Loosestrife*. Five died. Forty-two picked up by the *Loosestrife*.

West Madaket (US) (Captain Hans Schroeder). A straggler. Torpedoed by U.584 (Kptlt Joachim Deecke) and scuttled by the corvette HMS *Pink* (Lt R. Atkinson). All 61 on board picked up by the *Pink* and landed at St John's on the 9th.

West Maximus (US) (Captain E.E. Brooks). Sunk by U.264 (Kptlt Hartwig Looks). Six died. Fifty-six picked up by HMS *Northern Spray*.

Escort EG.B7, commanded by Cdr Peter Gretton, sank U.125, U.192, U.438, U.531, U.630 and U.638 during the battle, and U.209, having been damaged by a Catalina on 5 May, sank on her way back to base.

EUMAEUS (Captain J.E. Watson). Bound for Singapore via Freetown, the Cape and Colombo, sailing independently when shelled by the Italian submarine *Commandante Cappellini* (C.C. Salvatore Todaro) in position 8°55′N 15°03′W at 6am on 14 January 1941. Fought a running battle with the submarine, but had to be abandoned before sunk by a torpedo. With all the boats, except a small dinghy, destroyed, the survivors clung to wreckage until rescued by anti-submarine trawlers HMS *Bengali* and HMS *Spaniard* and landed at Freetown. Eight of her crew of 91 died, as did 15 of the 400 service personnel she was carrying. The submarine, damaged by gunfire from the ship and by bombs dropped by a Walrus from HMS *Albatross*, had to put into Las Palmas for repairs.

EURYLOCHUS (Captain A.M. Caird). Bound for Takoradi and sailing independently when shelled by the raider *Kormoran* (Captain Theodor Detmers) at about 6.30pm on

29 January 1941 in position 8°15′N 25°04′W. With his steering gear destroyed, Captain Caird signalled to the raider that he was abandoning ship, but although an acknowledgement was received, the shelling continued and the bridge was sprayed with machine-gun fire. After the ship had been abandoned, a party from the *Kormoran* placed time bombs on board, but when they failed to sink her a torpedo did the job, at the same time killing the occupants of one of the 3 lifeboats which had been launched. Those in the other boats, 3 Europeans and 39 Chinese, were picked up by the *Kormoran*. The raider, however, failed to spot the 2 crowded rafts containing Captain Caird and 27 others. At about 11am on the 30th, the latter were picked up by the Spanish ship *Monte Teide* (Captain Policarpo Munecas) which met the AMC HMS *Bulolo* the next morning. Only the wounded and 8 Europeans were transferred to the *Bulolo* while Captain Caird and Mr Creech, the Chief Engineer, chose to remain with the Chinese until the *Monte Teide* landed them at Buenos Aires. On 7 February, the *Kormoran* rendezvoused with the supply ship *Normark* and 170 prisoners were transferred to her, but 3 Chinese from the *Eurylochus* were still on board the *Kormoran* when she was sunk in November. A QQQQ message was transmitted when the attack began on the *Eurylochus*, and Detmers justified his continued gunfire, after abandoning had been intimated, on the grounds that he was told that the Radio Officers were still transmitting. Two Europeans and 9 Chinese died.

EURYMEDON (Captain J.F. Webster). Bound for Java via the Cape, sailing from Liverpool in Convoy OB.217 on 21 September 1940. Four U-boats attacked shortly after the convoy dispersed at noon on the 25th and at about 2pm when in position 53°34′N 20°23′W a torpedo fired by U.29 (Kptlt Otto Schuhart) struck the engine room, killing everyone in it and destroying 2 of the lifeboats. Other lifeboats were then launched, but the 2 starboard ones were loaded and still hung in their davits when a second struck, killing the passengers and crew who occupied them. In response to the SSSS message which had been transmitted, the Canadian destroyer HMCS *Ottawa* (Cdr E.R. Mainguy) arrived at 4pm and picked up those in the boats, but having assessed the damage, Captain Webster and Mr Stanger, the 1st Mate, remained on board in the hope that the ship might be saved. In the evening, 4 lifeboats from the torpedoed *Sulairia* arrived alongside the *Eurymedon* and her Master joined the two officers on the *Eurymedon*. But the next morning, when it was evident the ship was sinking, they took to one of the *Sulairia*'s lifeboats. The *Ottawa* had departed the previous day, but when she returned, all boarded her and were landed at Gourock on the 27th. Ten Europeans, 10 Chinese and 9 passengers were lost on the *Eurymedon*.

OTHER SHIPS SUNK AFTER THE DISPERSAL OF CONVOY OB.217

Corrientes. See under DONALDSON LINE.

Darcoila (Captain W. Anderson). Sunk by U.32. All 31 died.

Sulairia. See under DONALDSON LINE.

Tancred (Nor.) (Captain Einar Hansen). Sunk by U.32 (Oblt Hans Jenisch). All 39 picked up by the *Tricolor* (Nor.) the next day and landed at New York.

GLENORCHY (Captain G. Leslie). In Convoy WS.21S (Operation Pedestal). Torpedoed at about 2am on 13 August 1942 by one of the 19 Italian MTBs which lay in wait between Cape Bon and Pantellaria. Mr R.A. Hanney, the 1st Mate, and 8 others on a raft were captured by an MTB and became PoWs for the duration. Two lifeboats landed on a beach near Kelibia, on Cape Bon in Tunisia, from where their 108 occupants witnessed a violent explosion on the *Glenorchy* which had tins of aviation spirit in her cargo. In spite of the pleas of his officers, Captain Leslie chose to remain on board and went down with his ship. Those who landed in Tunisia eventually reached Algeria where they were interned by the Vichy French until the Allied invasion of North Africa in November and brought home on the *Orontes*. Only men in the engine room lost their lives – 5 engineers, including Mr J. Threlfall, the Chief, and 2 greasers. The *Glenorchy*'s complement consisted of 99 crew plus 25 naval staff and passengers. (See also under *Deucalion*.)

GLENSHIEL (Captain Ramsay Brown). Bound for Australia from Bombay when torpedoed by the Japanese submarine I-7 (Cdr Ankyu) in position 01°00′S 78°11′E at 2.30am on 3 April 1942. With the engines stopped and the ship settling by the stern, Captain Brown decided to abandon ship and the boats were just clear when a second torpedo struck and sank her. An SSSS message had been sent and acknowledged by Colombo and at 5.30pm the destroyer HMS *Fortune* arrived to pick them up. All 100 crew and passengers saved.

HECTOR. Requisitioned as an AMC in 1940 and being decommissioned in Colombo when the port was attacked by Japanese carrier aircraft on 5 April 1942. She was struck by several bombs and sank. Raised and beached in 1946 and sold for scrap. Had a reduced crew on board. There were casualties, but no details. The destroyer HMS *Tenedos* (Lt Richard Dyer) was also sunk in the attack with great loss of life.

HELENUS (Captain P.W. Savery). Unescorted and bound for Liverpool from Penang when torpedoed and sunk by U.68 (Krvkpt. Karl Friedrich Merten) at about 2.30pm on 3 March 1942 in position 06°01′N 12°02′W. Five died. The remaining 76 crew and 10 passengers were picked up by lifeboats from the *Beaconsfield* at 10.30pm and landed at Freetown on the 5th.

IXION (Captain W.F. Dark). Bound for New York from Glasgow and in Convoy OB.318 which sailed from Liverpool on 2 May 1941. Torpedoed by U.94 (Kptlt Herbert Kuppisch) at 9.15pm in position 61°29′N 22°40′W on the 7th and abandoned, but did not sink until early the following morning. No lives lost. Eight-six were picked up by the *Nailsea Manor* and landed at Sydney, Cape Breton. Nineteen picked up by the corvette HMS *Marigold* (Lt W.S. Macdonald) were landed at Greenock.

OTHER SHIPS SUNK IN CONVOY OB.318

7 May:

Eastern Star (Nor.) (Captain Olav Østervold). Sunk by U.94. All 40 picked up by anti-submarine trawler *Daneman* (Lt A.H. Ballard, RNR) and landed in Reykjavik on the 12th.

9 May:

Aelybryn. Damaged by U.556 (Kptlt Herbert Wohlfarth) on the 10th.

Bengore Head (Captain W.J. McCabe). Sunk by U.110 (Kptlt Fritz-Julius Lemp). One died. Sixteen picked up by the *Borgfred* (Nor.) and landed at Sydney, Cape Breton, on the 18th. Twenty-four picked up by the corvette HMS *Aubretia* (Lt Cdr V.F. Smith) and landed at Reykjavik.

Empire Cloud. Badly damaged by U.201 (Kptlt Adalbert Schnee).

Esmond. See under DONALDSON LINE.

Gregalia. See under DONALDSON LINE.

U.110 (Kptlt Fritz-Julius Lemp). Captured after being depth-charged by the escort, and an Enigma machine and code books taken before she was allowed to sink. Fifteen, including Lemp, died and 32 survived. Sunk after the convoy dispersed in position 60°12′N 34°30′W.

10 May:

Empire Caribou. See under REARDON SMITH LINE.

Gand (Belg.) (Captain Michel Hostens). Sunk by U.556. One died. Forty-three rescued.

23 May:

Berhala (Du.) (Captain L.J. Tymons). Sunk by U.38 (Kptlt Heinrich Liebe). Three died. Fifty-nine picked up by a British warship and landed at Freetown.

24 May:

Vulcain (Captain J.R. Lewis). Sunk by U.38. Seven died. Thirty-four reached Boffa, Guinea, by lifeboat and interned by the Vichy French.

27 May:

Colonial. See under HARRISON LINE.

MARON (Captain D. Hey). Took part in the invasion of North Africa (Operation Torch) and, having discharged most of her cargo in Algiers, sailed from the port in a 4-ship convoy on the evening of 12 November 1942. Torpedoed at 3pm the next day by U.81 (Kptlt Friedrich Guggenberger) and sank within 15 minutes in position 36°27′N 00°55′W. The boats were already swung out and all 81 got away. They were picked up by the corvette HMS *Marigold* (Lt J.A.S. Halcrew) and taken to Gibraltar, from where they were repatriated to the UK on the *Mooltan*.

MEDON (Captain S.R. Evans). Bound for Trinidad from Mauritius and sailing independently when torpedoed by the Italian submarine *Reginaldo Giuliani* (C.F. Giovanni Bruno) at about 4am on 10 August 1942 in position 9°26′N 38°28′W. An SSSS message was transmitted and everyone got away in 4 lifeboats, but when men returned to make a more thorough assessment of the damage, collect stores and send another SSSS, shells began to fall close to the ship so that they hurriedly left. At 8am a second torpedo sank the ship.

It was decided to make for British Guiana (now Guyana), but the boats became separated. The 20 people in No 4 boat (Mr E.G. Painter, 3rd Mate) were picked up by the *Tamerlane* (Nor.) (Captain Krafft) on the 17th. The 14 in No 1 boat (Captain Evans) were picked up by the *Rosemount* (Pan.) on the 18th. The 16 in No 3 boat (Mr J.F. Fuller, 2nd Mate) were picked up by the *Reedpool* (Captain W.J. Downs) on 13 September. The 14 in No 2 boat (Mr G. Edge, 1st Mate) were picked up by *Luso* (Port.) (Captain Botto) on 14 September. On 20 September, the *Reedpool* was torpedoed and sunk by U.515 (Kptlt Werner Henke) in position 08°58′N 57°34′W. Six of the *Reedpool*'s crew died. Captain Downs was taken prisoner and the remaining 34, plus the 16 survivors of the *Medon*, were picked up the next day by the British schooner *Millie M Masher* (Captain F. Barnes) and landed in Georgetown, British Guiana, on the 24th. No lives were lost on the *Medon*. (See also under *Reedpool*, ROPNER SHIPPING CO.)

MEMNON (Captain J.P. Williams). Bound for Avonmouth from Australia via Freetown and sailing independently when torpedoed and sunk by U.106 (Kptlt Jürgen Oesten) at 2pm on 11 March 1941 in position 20°41′N 21°00′W. As an SSSS message had been transmitted, and acknowledged by a Spanish ship, the 2 lifeboats which got away remained close to where the ship sank in the hope that help would arrive. But when none had arrived by the 13th, they decided to make for Bathurst in Gambia, as this was British territory. The boats sailed together until the following evening when they thought it best to proceed independently, as Captain Williams' boat was making better progress than that of Mr McCarthy, the 1st Mate.

On the morning of the 19th, those in Captain Williams' boat sighted land which they recognised as being about 100 miles north of Dakar and on the same day a French ship passed within 6 cables' length but ignored their signals. At midday on the 21st they landed at the fishing village of Yoff, near Dakar in Senegal, French West Africa, and in the evening were taken to a military hospital where they were fed and rested. When 2 men from the Mate's boat were admitted on the 23rd they learned that the latter had received food and water from a ship outside the harbour before sailing on to Bathurst.

When those in Mr McCarthy's boat had arrived off St Louis on the 21st they met the French ship *Kilissi*. Food and water were supplied by the *Kilissi* and she took on board the two men referred to above. The lifeboat arrived at Bathurst on the 24th and all were admitted to the hospital.

Captain Williams and the older members of his crew were released by the Vichy French as soon as they were fit to travel, but the younger men were interned in an unpleasant camp in the interior until their exchange was negotiated. According to Captain S.W. Roskill in *A Merchant Fleet in War*, 4 men died when the *Memnon* was torpedoed, 1 died in the Mate's boat and the remaining 69 landed safely. However, on the U-boat website it states that 'one of these lifeboats with 24 survivors had been found by the German battleship *Gneisenau*, which took three passengers and one gunner as prisoners on board'.

There were many Distressed British Seamen awaiting repatriation from British West Africa and when the former Vichy French ship *Criton*, captured by HMS *Cilicia*, required a volunteer crew to take her to the UK, G.A. Whalley and Peter leQ. Johnson signed on as her 2nd and 3rd Radio Officers, the positions they had held on the *Memnon*. The *Criton* (Captain Gerald

Dobeson, ex-*Wray Castle*), however, was sunk by the Vichy French ship *Air France IV* on 21 June 1941. Four died. The remainder suffered the worst treatment meted out to British merchant seamen by the Vichy French, serving the longest period of internment in French West Africa and not arriving home until 15 January 1943.

MENTOR (Captain A. Pope). Bound independently for Cape Town and Bombay from New Orleans when torpedoed in the engine room by U.106 (Kptlt Hermann Rasch) shortly after 2am on 28 May 1942 in position 24°11′N 87°02′W. Four lifeboats had left the ship when a second torpedo struck and sank her. The survivors were picked up by the *Antilochus* on the 31st and landed at Key West, Florida. The 4th Engineer and three Chinese firemen were killed when the first torpedo struck but the remaining 82 survived.

MERIONES (Captain W.J. Peard). Bound for Australia via Hull and in Convoy FN.389 which sailed from Southend on 21 January 1941. Grounded on the South Haisborough sandbank near Cromer and all attempts to free her failed. Bombed on the 24th and became a total loss. No lives lost.

MYRMIDON (Captain A.M. Caird). Bound for Cape Town from Freetown and in a 3-ship convoy when torpedoed and sunk at about 2.30am on 5 September 1942 by U.506 (Kptlt Erich Würdemann) in position 00°45′N 06°27′W. All 116 crew and 129 passengers were picked up from 10 lifeboats by the destroyer HMS *Brilliant* (Lt Cdr A.G. Poe) and landed at Pointe Noire, French Equatorial Africa. No lives lost.

PATROCLUS. Requisitioned by the Admiralty in September 1939 and converted into an AMC, HMS *Patroclus* (Captain G.C. Wynter). Together with the AMC HMS *Laurentic* (Captain E.P. Vivian), went to the aid of the unescorted *Casanare* (Captain J.A. Moore) when, with a cargo of bananas, she transmitted an SSSS message after being torpedoed by U.99 (Kptlt Otto Kretschmer) at 9.40pm on 3 November 1940 and subsequently sank in position 53°58′N 14°13′W. Both AMCs were then sunk by U.99 in the early hours of the 4th. Nine died on the *Casanare* and 54 were picked up by the destroyer HMS *Beagle* (Lt R.H. Wright) and landed at Greenock. Fifty-six died on HMS *Patroclus* and 263 were picked up by HMS *Beagle*. Fifty-one died on the *Laurentic* and 368 picked up by the destroyer HMS *Hesperus* (Lt Cdr D.G.F.W. McIntyre) were landed at Greenock.

PEISANDER (Captain A. Shaw). Bound independently for Liverpool from Australia via the Panama Canal when torpedoed by U.653 (Kptlt Gerhard Feiler) at 12.50pm on 17 May 1942 in position 37°24′N 65°38′W. All 3 starboard lifeboats were destroyed, but the 3 port ones were clear of the ship when a second torpedo sank her. As the wireless room was also destroyed, no SSSS was transmitted.

On the 21st a ship approached No 2 boat, but then hurriedly departed. On the 24th a US plane spotted them and dropped supplies. On the 25th they were picked up by the USCGC *General Green* and landed at Newport, Rhode Island. After 3 days' sailing, the other 2 boats were approached by the *Baron Semple* but refused the offer to be taken on board when they learned that she was bound for South Africa, and subsequently landed at Nantucket Island on the 24th. All 65 survived, including 4 passengers.

PERSEUS (Captain G.G. Rundle). Sailed independently from Trincomalee on 15 January 1944 bound for Calcutta. Struck by a torpedo fired by the Japanese submarine I-165

(Lt Cdr Tsuruzo Shimizu) at 11.45am on the 16th in position 12°00′N 80°14′E and abandoned when a second one struck her about 10 minutes later. Two of the lifeboats were damaged but the crew took to the other 4 boats, 2 of which were motorised. Yet another torpedo hit the ship when the boats were clear of her. As an SSSS message had been transmitted and acknowledged by Madras, an Indian corvette and 4 MTBs arrived at 5pm and all were rescued. None died, but one man was seriously injured.

PHEMIUS (Captain T.A. Kent). Sailed independently from Takoradi on the Gold Coast on 19 December 1943 bound for Lagos. Intercepted by a plane that same evening and ordered to return to Takoradi. Torpedoed when in position 05°01′N 00°47′E at 11pm by U.515 (Kptlt Werner Henke). Another torpedo struck her as the boats were being lowered and, when 4 were clear of the ship, the U-boat surfaced and approached No 6, asking for the Master and the name of the ship. Unable to find Captain Kent, who was in No 4, the 1st Radio Officer Mr D.B.L. Grew was taken prisoner. When the U-boat had gone, the boats searched for people in the water and picked up about 30. At daylight the next morning the Free French corvette *Commandant Drague* rescued 78 crew and 14 passengers and landed them at Takoradi that same day. Four crew and 19 passengers died. (This was the same *Phemius* which lost her funnel in the hurricane in the Caribbean in November 1932.)

PROTESILAUS (Captain A.H.D. Shand). Struck a mine when off the Mumbles Lighthouse at about 9.30am on 21 January 1940. Taken in tow, but grounded and became a total loss. Crew taken to Swansea. No casualties.

PYRRHUS (Captain W.T. Spencer). Bound for the Far East, she joined Convoy OG.18 which formed at sea on 15 February 1940. Torpedoed by U.37 (Krvkpt. Werner Hartmann) at about 4pm on the 17th and broke in two in position 44°02′N 10°18′W. With the mainmast, and consequently the wireless aerials, brought down, it was impossible for an SSSS message to be transmitted. The survivors got away in the lifeboats and were picked up by the *Uskside* and the *Sinnington Court* which landed them at Gibraltar on the 22nd. Eight Chinese engine room staff died. Seventy-seven survived, including the Vice-Commodore and his staff. The fore section of the ship remained afloat for 2 days.

RHEXENOR (Captain Leonard Eccles). Bound independently for Saint John, New Brunswick, from Freetown when torpedoed by U.217 (Kptlt Kurt Reichenbach-Klinke) at 6.45am on 3 February 1943 in position 24°59′N 43°37′W. The U-boat surfaced when the lifeboats were being lowered and the last one was just clear of the ship when it was sunk by gunfire. When the U-boat then approached No 5 boat and asked for the Master Mr G.W. Allen, the 4th Mate replied that he must have gone down with the ship. But not convinced of this, Reichenbach-Klinke took Mr Allen into the conning tower where he was told that he would be allowed to return to the lifeboat only if he identified the Master. After they had gone round the lifeboats and Mr Allen 'failed to see' Captain Eccles who had taken the precaution of donning a raincoat and soft hat, he was carried off in the U-boat which was subjected to depth-charging before reaching Brest on the 23rd.

On Captain Eccles' recommendation it was decided that the 4 lifeboats, which were well-provisioned and contained a chart and the February data from a Nautical Almanac, should set a course for Antigua in the Leeward Islands, about 1,200 miles away. But although they attempted to keep together, this proved impossible. No 1 boat (Captain Eccles), in which the 2nd Cook died on the 14th day, landed at Guadeloupe on the 20th. From there they were taken to Martinique and eventually to New York for a passage home. No 4 boat (Mr M.J. Case, 1st Mate) landed at St John's, Antigua, on the 21st. No 3 boat (Mr W.M. Thomas, 2nd Mate) was sighted on the 23rd by two planes, which dropped canisters of water and cigarettes, and indicated that help was on its way. At 9.30pm they were picked up by the American ship *Conqueror* and taken to the island of St Thomas from where they went on to New York. No 5 boat (Mr S.A.G. Covell, 3rd Mate), in which the officer successfully operated on a fireman's septic hand with a razor, and an AB died on the eleventh day, landed at the island of Jost van Dyke in the Tobago group on the 23rd. (Mr Thomas did only one more voyage, as 1st Mate of the Liberty ship *Samite*, managed by Holts, with Captain Eccles again as the Master. During that eventful voyage he suffered pain from frostbite in his feet; when I saw him in the Liverpool Office after the war, he leaned heavily on two sticks and walked with great difficulty.)

STENTOR (Captain William Williams). Bound for Liverpool from Freetown in Convoy SL.125 when torpedoed and sunk by U.509 (Krvkpt. Werner Witte) at 7.30pm on 27 October 1942 in position 29°13′N 20°53′W. The explosion caused the bridge area to be showered by burning palm oil. Captain Williams suffered severe burns, the Vice-Commodore Captain R. Garstin was blinded and the ship's surgeon, Dr W. Chisholm, sacrificed his life by continuing to administer to the many who were burned. Although the ship sank within 10 minutes, 4 or 5 lifeboats got away but the remainder of the crew had to jump into the water. The corvette HMS *Woodruff* (Lt Cdr F.H. Gray) arrived to pick up survivors, but broke off to hunt a U-boat contact before returning to pick up the others. One hundred, transferred to the destroyer HMS *Ramsey* (Lt Cdr R.B. Stannard), were landed at Liverpool, while those remaining on the *Woodruff* were landed at Milford Haven. Forty-five lost their lives, including Captain Williams, Vice-Commodore Garstin and 23 passengers. Two hundred and two survived. (For details of other ships lost and observations on Convoy SL.125, see under *Nagpore*, P&O.)

TALTHYBIUS (Captain T.A. Kent). Arrived in Singapore from Bombay on 26 January 1942 when the city was being subjected to Japanese air raids. Her military cargo was almost completely discharged at the wharf when on the 7th she was straddled by bombs. One or two struck home, while near misses punctured holes along her starboard side. She was then moved into a dock where she sank to the bottom. The Chinese crew had deserted and on the 11th the Admiral of the port ordered the European crew to leave the ship. They sailed from Singapore on the small and crowded naval auxiliary HMS *Ping Wo* on the 12th and landed at Batavia on the 15th. There is no information regarding casualties or how the crew were brought home, but Captain Kent was Master of the *Phemius* (see above). The *Talthybius* was raised by the Japanese and renamed the *Taruyasu Maru*. She struck a mine near Sado Island on 30 June 1945 and was found submerged in Maizura harbour on the W coast of Honshu after hostilities had ceased. Again raised, she was brought home via Singapore to load scrap iron and arrived at Briton Ferry on 7 September 1949 to be scrapped.

TANTALUS (Captain R.O. Morris). With her engine room machinery dismantled, she left Hong Kong under tow by the tug *Keswick* on 5 December 1941 bound for Singapore. The Japanese attack on Pearl Harbor took place on the 7th and when Japan declared war on Britain as from 6am on the 8th, all British ships in the area were instructed to find refuge where they could. Captain Morris decided that as the speed of the tow was only 5 knots, his best bet was Manila, where they arrived on the evening of the 11th. As the port was continually being bombed by Japanese planes, Captain Morris thought it safer to move the ship to nearby Bataan, but although she had not been hit he realised the situation was hopeless and took all his crew ashore early on the 26th. It was all well that he did so, as from the beach that day they saw the *Tantalus* capsize and sink after receiving direct hits. When Manila fell to the Japanese on 3 January 1942 all were taken prisoner. T.H. Fletcher, the 3rd Mate, and H.E. Weekes, an AB, were later executed because they were caught trying to escape. No details of how the others survivors fared.

TEIRESIAS (Captain J.R. Davies). Arrived off St Nazaire on 17 June 1940 to assist in the evacuation of military personnel from France. Straddled by bombs from Junkers 88s and although receiving no actual hits, near misses damaged her so that she eventually sank. Two lifeboats, sent away at the outset, reached the French coast. A fishing boat then took them to St Nazaire from where they were carried to Plymouth by the small naval auxiliary vessel HMS *Oracle*. The remainder of the crew were picked up by the *Holmside* and landed at Falmouth. One man died.

TITAN (Captain W.F. Dark). Bound for Sydney, Australia, from London, in ballast, and joined Convoy OA.207 after bunkering at Methil on 31 August 1940. Torpedoed and sunk by U.47 (Kptlt Günther Prien) at 0040 hours on 4 September when in position 58°14′N 15°50′W. Six died. Twenty-four Europeans and 66 Chinese were picked up from 2 lifeboats by the corvette HMS *Godetia* (Lt Cdr G.V. Legassick) and the Canadian destroyer HMCS *St Laurent* (Cdr H.G. DeWolf).

TROILUS (Captain Evan Williams). Sailing independently and bound for Liverpool from Colombo via Aden when torpedoed at about 2.30am on 1 September 1944 by U.859 (Kptlt Johann Jebsen) in position 14°10′N 61°04′E. Using the emergency aerial, an SSSS message was transmitted but not acknowledged, and 2 more torpedoes struck when the boats were being lowered. Five boats got away, but Captain Williams had to jump into the sea. The boats stayed in the position until the 3rd, when it was decided to make for the India. The tanker *Cornwallis* hove into sight that evening, but believing she had seen a U-boat, sheered off. An RAF Catalina spotted them on the 5th. They were picked up about 10pm by the frigates HMS *Taff* (Cdr G.A.G. Ormsby) and HMS *Nadder* (Lt Cdr P.E. Kitto) and landed at Aden on the 10th. Four crew and 2 female passengers died. Seventy-nine crew and 16 passengers survived.

ULYSSES (Captain J.A. Russell). Sailing independently and bound for Liverpool from Australia via the Panama Canal and Halifax when she collided with the Panamanian tanker *Gold Heels* during the early hours of 8 April 1942. As the ship's bow was badly damaged so that she was able to proceed only at reduced speed, Captain Russell decided to make for Newport News. The next morning they met a small US patrol boat and asked that their plight be made known to the authorities. No assistance came, however, and on the afternoon of the 11th the *Ulysses* was torpedoed by U.160 (Kptlt Georg Lassen) when in position 34°23′N 75°35′W. The engines were stopped and all 10 boats had barely cleared the ship when a second torpedo struck. Captain Russell, most of the officers and the DEMS gunners had remained on board, but all were now ordered off apart from the deck officers. The latter, however, soon left on a raft when it became evident that the ship was going down, and minutes later a third torpedo finished her off. At dusk the destroyer USS *Manley* picked up the entire 290 crew and passengers and landed them at Charleston, South Carolina, the following day.

DUTCH BLUE FUNNEL

Alfred Holt & Co. also owned the Nederlandsche Stoomvaart Maatschappij Oceaan (NSMO), known in maritime circles as Dutch Blue Funnel. The Masters were always Dutch, but British officers and men of the parent company also served on them.

LAERTES (Captain G.J. van Heel). In April 1942 in New York where she loaded 5,230 tons of war material, including 3 aircraft, 17 tanks and 20 trucks, for Bombay. Her route was via the Cape, but the initial part of her passage was southwards along the coast where, due to the lack of a convoy system, it was the practice to proceed in short hops. From New York to the Delaware she was escorted by an American destroyer, but from then on she was on her own. Ships anchored at night, as the U-boats came closer in to the shore then. The *Laertes* spent the night of 29/30 April in the Delaware and the following night in the Chesapeake before continuing farther south.

In mid-January 1942, shortly after the United States entered the war, U-boats began to operate off the east coast. The Operation was called Paukenschlag (Drum Roll) and, by May, 30 boats were taking part with 'milch cows' (U-boat tankers) in attendance to allow them to remain longer at sea. As a coastal convoy system was not introduced until May, and not fully implemented until August, many ships were disposed of and at that time the U-boat men referred to the eastern seaboard as the 'Golden West'. Indeed their task was made easy because there were no blackout restrictions in the coastal towns and because ships could use their radios and sail fully illuminated.

On the night of 2/3 May, the *Laertes* was in approximate position 28°21′N 80°23′W near Cape Canaveral in Florida when at about 4am a torpedo struck her on the port side of No 6 hold, disabling her steering gear and breaking her main shaft. Captain van Heel immediately ordered the lifeboats to be launched, but while this was being done a second torpedo hit the ship beneath No 3 boat and the 17 men in it were killed. The 1st Mate and a British seaman were blown overboard from the boat deck. The former drowned, but the seaman was later rescued by a US Navy flying boat.

In response to the SSSS which had been transmitted, a plane arrived at daylight and signalled to the boats to head for the coast. They landed on Cocoa Beach 6 hours later and when a kindly lady bystander handed a white garment to a young British seaman to wipe the oil from his face, he responded by giving her the lamp from his lifejacket. The *Laertes* was sunk by U.109 (Kptlt Heinrich Bleichrodt).

POLYDORUS (Captain H. Brouwer). On 8 November 1942 she sailed from the UK in Convoy ON.145 and a week later left the convoy to make independently for Freetown. On hearing an explosion in the afternoon of the 25th, the Master ordered the crew to action stations and when darkness fell took an easterly course to try to shake off the enemy. At about 9pm, however, a U-boat on the surface opened fire with machine guns and other heavier weapons. The *Polydorus* returned the fire, dropped smoke floats and made off at full speed. Thus began what is believed to be the longest single-ship chase by a U-boat during the war. It is a long story, but a condensed version is contained in Queen Juliana's tribute to the *Polydorus* which she made five years after the war ended:

> We Juliana, by the Grace of God, Queen of the Netherlands, Princess of Orange-Nassau etc. etc., do hereby decree to grant the 'Royal Mention in the Orders of the Day' to the lost steamship *Polydorus*, owned by the Nederlandsche Stoomvaart Maatschappij Oceaan N.V. of Amsterdam, on the following grounds:
>
> On November 25th 1942 S.S. *Polydorus* was on passage without escort from England to Freetown, when she was attacked by a German submarine firing three torpedoes, which missed their target. The same evening the ship was assailed by artillery fire. The attack was answered by means of the 10cm gun and the Oerlikon machine guns, while at the same time a smoke screen was laid. The fight, in which S.S. *Polydorus* was damaged, was broken off.
>
> On November 26th at dawn the submarine again fired three torpedoes, which were successfully avoided. Once more a fight ensued, during which the attacker sustained hits.*
>
> When the submarine endeavoured to attack from the direction of the low sun, this was frustrated by steaming at full speed, while once more a smoke screen was laid.
>
> On November 27th at about 4 o'clock in the morning the ship was finally hit by two torpedoes and sank an hour later.
>
> The whole crew of 79 men,** with the exception of one man,† took to the boats and were picked up two days later by a Spanish vessel. Throughout the engagement the crew, from high to low, showed excellent moral strength and discipline.
>
> Soestdijk, September 14 1950
>
> (signed) JULIANA

*   *This is incorrect, as no hits were scored.*
** *It was 81.*
†   *A Chinese fireman who died in a lifeboat from injuries he had received on board.*
   After abandoning ship, Captain Brouwer had all the stores transferred from the rafts and damaged lifeboats to the 3 good boats. The following morning the latter set off together on a south-easterly course and when they saw the lights of a ship at about 3am on the 29th they signalled to her and she came alongside to pick them up. She was the Spanish ship Eolo. *Everything was done to make the survivors as comfortable as possible and they were landed at Las Palmas in the Canary Islands on 5 December. The U-boat which pursued and sank the* Polydorus *was U.176, commanded by Krvkpt. Reiner Dierksen, who reported the position as 09°01´N 25°38´W.*

POLYPHEMUS (Captain C. Koningstein). Sailed from Sydney, Australia, for Liverpool on 16 April 1942. Her route was via the Panama Canal and Halifax, Nova Scotia; when she was near Bermuda on 25 May a lifeboat was spotted and she picked up 14 survivors from the Norwegian tanker *Norland*, the latter having been torpedoed by U.108 (Krvkpt. Klaus Scholtz) on the 20th in approximate position 31°29′N 55°37′W. At about 6.15pm the following day, 2 torpedoes struck the after end of the *Polyphemus*, putting her engine room out of action and killing 15 Chinese who were in their fo'c'sle at the stern. Captain Koningstein immediately ordered the lifeboats to be launched and then gave the order to abandon ship.

When the 5 lifeboats containing the survivors lay off the ship, U.578 (Krvkpt. Ernst-August Rehwinkel) surfaced beside them and Rehwinkel asked the usual questions concerning cargo, destination, etc.* He then enquired if anyone was injured and if they needed supplies; when he received negative answers to both questions, he passed over a carton of cigarettes and gave them the course and distance to New York. His solicitous behaviour, however, was treated with suspicion as several of the U-boat's crew were photographing the proceedings – perhaps for propaganda purposes. At 7pm the *Polyphemus* sank stern first and the U-boat departed.

The 60 survivors in the lifeboats were 370 miles north of Bermuda in position 38°12′N 63°22′W when they began their journeys. Three of the boats reached Nantucket Island, Massachusetts, and those in the other 2 were picked up by the *D/S Maria Amelia* (Port.) which took them to New York. All 14 from the *Norland* survived their second ordeal. Earlier on 29 May, the same day that they were rescued by the Portuguese vessel, No 4 lifeboat, commanded by the 1st Mate Mr Brandenburg, was spotted by U.566 (Kptlt Dietrich Borchert). Borchert brought his boat alongside and, after making enquiries about their ship, informed them of their actual position, provided them with water and wished them a safe passage.

The cargo was obvious as bags of wheat and wool were floating on the sea, but they refused to give their destination.)

Jardine, Matheson & Co.

CHAKSANG. Sailing unescorted and bound for Rangoon from Madras, in ballast, when torpedoed and sunk by gunfire by the Japanese submarine I-66 (Lt Cdr Zennosuke Yoshitome) on 22 January 1942 in position 15°42′N 95°02′E. Five died and 61 survived. No further details.

FAUSANG. Scuttled at Hong Kong in December 1941 to avoid capture by the Japanese. Salvaged by them and sailed as the *Fusei Maru* until shelled and sunk by the submarine USS *Seawolf* (Lt Cdr R.L. Gross) on 22 September 1943 in position 31°28′N 127°24′E.

FUH WO. Requisitioned by the Admiralty in 1940 and employed as a minesweeper until destroyed at Singapore in 1942, either by bombing or to avoid capture by the Japanese.

HAN WO. Tug, requisitioned by the Admiralty in 1940. Scuttled in Hong Kong in December 1941 to avoid capture by the Japanese.

HINSANG. Scuttled at Hong Kong on Christmas Day 1941 to avoid capture. Raised by the Japanese in 1943 and sailed as the *Kensei Maru* until bombed and sunk by US Navy carrier-based aircraft of Task Force 38, 25 miles south-east of Phanrang, Vietnam, on 12 January 1945 in position 11°10′N 108°55′E.

HOSANG. Aground when captured by the Japanese at Palembang on 13 February 1942. Salvaged and renamed *Gyozan Maru*. On 21 November 1944 she was torpedoed and damaged by the submarine USS *Flounder* (Cdr J.E. Stevens) in position 10°36′N 115°08′E and sunk by the submarine USS *Guavina* (Lt Cdr C. Tiedeman).

HSIN CHANG WO. Captured by the Japanese at Ichang in 1941. No further information.

KIA WO. Captured by the Japanese in 1941 and renamed *Matsushima Maru*. In Hong Kong on 16 January 1945 when the port was attacked by planes from US Task Force 38. Struck by a bomb and set on fire, but eventually returned to owners.

KIANG WO. Captured by the Japanese at Ichang on 8 December 1941 and crew taken prisoner. Renamed *Rozan Maru*. Bombed and sunk by carrier-based planes of US Task Force 38 on 21 September 1944 in position 14°35′N 120°55′E.

KUM SANG (Captain W.J. Lawrence). Unescorted and bound for the UK from Colombo when torpedoed and sunk by U.125 (Kptlt Ulrich Folkers) at 6.20am on 30 September 1942 in position 04°07′N 13°40′W. Four died. One hundred and ten landed from lifeboats at Cape Mount, Liberia, and taken to Freetown by British motor launches.

KUNG WO. Requisitioned by the Admiralty in 1941. Laden with refugees, she sailed from Singapore at midnight on 12 February 1942 in an attempt to escape the Japanese. Sunk by Japanese fighter-bombers on the 14th. Survivors reached Banka Island in lifeboats, where they remained for a week before taken to Dabo on Sinkep Island, south of Sumatra, on the Sultan of Johore's yacht, from where they went on to Sumatra on river boats. They then went by train to Padang where most became stranded and were taken prisoner early in March.

KUT WO. Captured by the Japanese in the China Sea in 1941 and renamed *Renzan Maru*. Torpedoed and sunk by the submarine USS *Porpoise* (Lt Cdr J.R. McKnight) near Yap Island on 1 January 1943.

LI WO (T/Lt T. Wilkinson). Requisitioned by the Admiralty in 1940 and used as a patrol vessel. Manned by a scratch crew consisting mostly of survivors of HM ships but also of members of army and RAF units and one civilian, sailing from Singapore on 13 February 1942 bound for Tanjung Priok. Bombed and badly damaged the next day, but attacked a heavily escorted Japanese convoy and set a Japanese transport on fire before she herself was sinking and Lt Wilkinson gave the order to abandon ship. Of her crew of 84, only about 10 survived to become PoWs. Lt Wilkinson, who remained on his ship and went down with her, was posthumously awarded the Victoria Cross.

LOONG WO. Captured by the Japanese in the China Sea in 1941. Renamed *Kosan Maru*, sunk by a mine in the River Yangtze on 19 March 1945.

MIN WO. Tug, captured by the Japanese in 1941. Presumed war loss.

MING SANG. Scuttled at Hong Kong in December 1941 to avoid capture. Salvaged by the Japanese and renamed *Bisan Maru*. Sunk by the submarine USS *Bowfin* (Cdr J. Corbus) about 90 miles north-west of Palau on 14 May 1944.

PAO WO. Captured by the Japanese in the China Sea in 1941 and renamed *Rasan Maru*. Returned to owners after the war.

SHUN WO. Tug, scuttled at Hong Kong in December 1941 to avoid capture by the Japanese.

SIANG WO. Requisitioned by the Admiralty as an anti-submarine ship in 1940. Bombed by Japanese planes on 13 February 1942 while carrying refugees from Singapore. Run aground on Banka Island from where 2 survivors were taken to Tanjung Priok on the 10-ton motor yacht *Carimon*. Several died; at least 1 as a PoW.

SUI SANG. Went on fire in Abadan in 1942. Drifted ashore and declared a total loss.

SUI WO. Requisitioned by the Admiralty as an accommodation ship. Lost or scuttled at Singapore on 13 February 1942 to prevent capture by the Japanese.

TAI SANG. Sunk by a British mine off Singapore on 24 January 1942.

TAK SANG. Bound for Colombo from Calcutta, commodore ship of a small convoy which sailed from Diamond Harbour on the Hooghly River at dawn on 5 April 1942 but dispersed at sunset due to the *Harpasa*, 40 miles astern, being bombed by Japanese carrier-based planes. Sunk by the latter the following day.

TUNG WO. Requisitioned by the Admiralty as an Armed Boarding ship in 1940. Bombed and sunk at Penang on 13 December 1941. An unconfirmed report claims that she was salvaged by the Japanese and renamed *Dowa Maru*, sunk by the submarine USS *Guavina* (Lt Cdr C. Tiedeman) on 22 November 1944 in position 10°23′N 114°21′E.

YAT SHING (Captain A.M. Jewell). Scuttled at Hong Kong in December 1941. Salvaged by the Japanese and renamed *Nissho Maru*. There are three conflicting reports regarding her demise: 1. Sunk by gunfire by submarine USS *Narwhal* (Lt Cdr C.W. Wilkins) on 24 July 1942 in position 45°09′N 147°31′E; 2. Torpedoed by the submarine USS *Hoe* (Lt Cdr V.B McCrea) on 25 February 1944 in position 05°50′N 126°00′E; 3. Mined off Yawata, Kyoto, Japan, on 23 July 1945. Captain Jewell was among those who died in Hong Kong.

YU SANG. Requisitioned by US Navy. Bombed and sunk in Manila Bay on 4 September 1942.

Note: Hong Kong, then British, but restored to China in 1997, was invaded by the Japanese on 1 December 1941 and surrendered on Christmas Day. Malaya, then British, but now part of independent Malaysia, was invaded by the Japanese, at Kota Bharu, at about 0030 hours on 8 December 1941 and surrendered at Singapore on 15 February 1942. On 15 August 1945, the Japanese surrendered unconditionally to the Allies, bringing an end to the Second World War.

Lamport & Holt Line

BALZAC. Bound independently for Liverpool from Rangoon when intercepted by the German raider *Atlantis* (KptzS. Bernhard Rogge) on 22 June 1941 and sunk by gunfire in position 15°16′S 27°43′W. Four died. Forty-three, taken on board the *Atlantis*, were subsequently transferred to another ship, most likely to have been the *Tannenfels* and became PoWs in Germany.

BIELA (Captain D. Anderson). Bound for Buenos Aires, sailing in Convoy ON.62 which left Liverpool on 1 February 1942. Dispersed from the convoy when at about midnight on the 14th she was torpedoed by U.68 (Kptlt Robert Gysae) in position 42°55N 45°40W. All 49 died.

BONHEUR (Captain L.O. Everett). Bound for Rosario, sailing from Liverpool in Convoy OB.228 on 13 October 1940 and torpedoed by U.138 (Oblt Wolfgang Lüth) in position 57°10′N 08°36′W, north-west of Cape Wrath, on the 15th. All 39 were picked up by the trawler HMS *Sphene* (Skipper W.J.J. Tucker) and landed at Belfast. The convoy dispersed on the 17th and the *Uskbridge* (Captain W.B. Smith) and *Dokka* (Nor.) (Captain A.J. Pedersen) were sunk that day by U.93 (Kptlt Claus Korth). The *Uskbridge* lost 2 of its 29 crew, while the *Dokka* lost 10 out of its crew of 17.

BRONTE (Captain S. Connelly). Sailed from Liverpool in Convoy OB.25 on 26 October 1939 with the destroyers HMS *Walpole* (Lt Cdr A.F. Burnell-Nugent) and HMS *Whirlpool* (Lt Cdr M.B. Ewart-Wentworth) as the escort. At 7.30pm the next day, when the convoy was 180 miles west of Land's End, the *Bronte* was torpedoed by U.34 (Kptlt Wilhelm Rollmann). After an attempt had been made to tow her, she was sunk by gunfire from both destroyers when in position 50°07′N 10°36′W on the 30th; the same day that the convoy dispersed. All 42 crew were picked up by the *Walpole* which returned to Liverpool on the 31st. The convoy suffered no other casualties.

BROWNING (Captain I. Sweeney). In Convoy KMS.2 (UK to Mediterranean Slow) and under sealed orders, sailing from Liverpool at the end of October 1942 to take part in Operation Torch. When the convoy was 60 miles north of Oran, the Oran section detached from it and, with Captain Sweeney as Commodore, was heading for the port when a destroyer hailed the *Browning* with revised instructions. It appeared that Oran had not yet been cleared to receive them and they were redirected to nearby Arzew Bay where they anchored for the night. At 11am on 12 November the 6 ships resumed their passage to Oran and at 1pm were about 12 miles from the port when the *Browning* was torpedoed by U.593 (Kptlt Gerd Kelbling) in position 35°53′N 00°33′W. As it was evident that the ship was sinking and there was a danger of the high explosives in her cargo exploding, the crew took to the lifeboats. Three explosions then blew the *Browning* to pieces. All but one of the 62 on board survived; the casualty being 15-year-old Deck Boy Ronald White who was blown over the side when the torpedo hit. The MS trawler HMS *Fluellen* (Lt H.N. Rogers) took the survivors to Oran from where they were repatriated to the UK on the *Empress of Scotland*.

BRUYÈRE (Captain T. Major). On passage from Buenos Aires to the UK and sailing independently when torpedoed and sunk by U.125 (Kptlt Ulrich Folkers) just before midnight on 23 September 1942 in position 04°55′N 17°16′W. All 51 were rescued by the corvette HMS *Petunia* (Lt Cdr J.M. Rayner) and the armed trawler HMS *St Wistan* (Lt W.H. Forster) and landed in Freetown.

DEFOE. On 24 September 1942, she was south-west of Rockall when an explosion occurred on board. Caught fire, abandoned and sank. Six died.

DELAMBRE (Captain Pratt). Sailing independently from South America to join a homeward convoy at Freetown when intercepted by the German raider *Thor* (KptzS. Otto Kähler) north-west of Ascension Island on 7 July 1940. After being hit by the third broadside, she stopped and was abandoned. A party from the *Thor* boarded and scuttled her with demolition charges. All 44 crew and 1 passenger were taken prisoner.

OTHER SHIPS SUNK BY THE *THOR* AT THAT TIME

1 July: Kertosono (Du.). Taken to Lorient by a prize crew.

9 July: Bruges (Belg.). Scuttled by the Germans and her crew of 44 taken prisoner.

14 July: Gracefield (Br.). Scuttled and her crew taken prisoner.

16 July: Wendover. See under WATTS, WATTS & CO. LTD.

17 July: Tela (Belg.). Scuttled and her crew of 33 taken prisoner.

The *Thor* was damaged in an engagement with the AMC HMS *Alcantara* on 28 July, but went on to sink the *Kosmos* (Nor.) and the *Natia* before transferring most of her 368 prisoners to the supply ship *Rio Grande* in November.

DEVIS (Captain W. Denson). Sailed from the Clyde and in Convoy KMS.18B which passed Gibraltar on 3 July 1943 to take part in Operation Husky, the invasion of Sicily. On board were Commodore Rear Admiral H.T. England and his staff of 6,264 Canadian and some British troops, army vehicles and ammunition. At approximately 3.45pm on the 5th, she was torpedoed by U.593 (Kptlt Gerd Kelbling) and sank in about 20 minutes in position 37°01′N 04°10′E. Many of the troops were burned or wounded and 51 died. All 47 of the crew, the Admiral and his staff and 237 troops survived, including their OC, Major D.S. Harkness, RCA. Many were picked up from rafts by a rescue tug and all taken to Bougie in Tunisia by the destroyer HMS *Cleveland* (Lt J.K. Hamilton). (For details of other ships sunk in Convoy KMS.18B, see under *City of Venice*, ELLERMAN GROUP.)

LAPLACE (Captain A. MacKellan). Sailing independently and bound for Buenos Aires from Lourenço Marques when torpedoed and sunk by U.159 (Kptlt Helmut Witte) on 29 October 1942 in position 40°35′S 21°35′E. The first torpedo, fired at 9.18pm, failed to sink the ship, but a second one, fired an hour later, finished her off. All 63 abandoned the ship in 3 lifeboats and those in each boat were rescued by different vessels – a South African Air Force crash boat, the US Liberty ship *George Gale*, and the Brazilian *Porto Alegre*. The SAAF boat landed the survivors at Port Elizabeth, while those on the *George Gale* were taken to Aden. The 11 rescued by the *Porto Alegre* (Captain José Francisco Pinto de Medeiros) were still on board when she was torpedoed in the late afternoon of 3 November by U.504 (Krvkpt. Hans-Georg Friedrich Poske) in position 35°27′S 28°02′E. One of the *Porto Alegre*'s crew of 52 was killed, but the others made Port Elizabeth in the ship's lifeboats. No lives were lost on the *Laplace*.

LASSELL (Captain A.R. Bibby). Bound for Rio de Janeiro and Buenos Aires, in Convoy OB.309 which sailed from Liverpool on 12 April 1941 and dispersed on the 19th in position 50°00′N 23°50′W. Sailing independently when torpedoed and sunk by U.107

(Kptlt Günther Hessler) at about 10pm on the 30th in position 12°55′N 28°56′W. An engineer and a greaser were killed in the engine room, but the others got away in 2 lifeboats.

Those in the boat commanded by the 1st Mate, Mr W.H. Underhill, were picked up by the *Egba* in position 10°57′N 29°13′W on 10 May and landed at Freetown. Those in the one commanded by Captain Bibby were picked up by the *Benvrackie* (Captain William Eyton-Jones) on 9 May, but 15 died when she too was torpedoed, by U.105 (Kptlt Georg Schewe) in position 00°49′N 20°15′W, on the 13th. Ten, including Captain Bibby and the survivors of the *Benvrackie*, then endured a further 13 days in a lifeboat before being rescued by the hospital ship HMHS *Oxfordshire* and taken to Freetown. A total of 17 died out of the *Lassell*'s complement of 68. The *Benvrackie* lost 13, but her Master and 44 others were saved. (See also under *Benvrackie*, BEN LINE.)

PHIDIAS (Captain Ernest Parks). In Convoy OB.330 which sailed from Liverpool on 2 June 1941 and dispersed on the 7th. Shortly after midnight on the 8th when in position 48°25′N 26°12′W she was attacked by U.46 (Oblt Engelbert Endrass) but, as the last torpedo possessed by the U-boat hit the ship without exploding, she sank her by gunfire. Eight died. Forty-three were picked up by the *Embassage* and landed at Sydney, Cape Breton.

SWINBURNE. In Convoy OB.290 which sailed from Liverpool on 23 February 1941, rendezvoused with other vessels on the 24th and dispersed on the 27th. When in approximate position 55°N 14°W she was damaged by an enemy aircraft in the forenoon of the 26th and sunk by gunfire from the escort. All survived. (For details of other ships sunk in Convoy OB.290, see under *Mahanada*, BROCKLEBANK LINE.)

WILLIMANTIC (Captain L.O. Everett). Sailing independently and bound for Charleston, South Carolina, when shelled and sunk by U.156 (Krvkpt. Werner Hartenstein) at 3.45am on 24 June 1942 in position 25°55′N 51°58′W. Two Radio Officers were killed when a shell hit the wireless room; 4 others also died and Captain Everett was taken prisoner. The remainder of the 38 crew got away in 2 lifeboats; one under the command of the 1st Mate, Mr Delaney, and the other under the command of the 2nd Mate, Mr Metcalf. Before leaving the scene, Hartenstein apologised for the deaths and gave Mr Metcalf a chart. Those in Mr Metcalf's boat were picked up by the Norwegian ship *Tamerlane* (Captain Kraft) on the 30th, landed in Rio de Janeiro 7 days later and were repatriated to the UK on the *Highland Monarch*. After a 12-day ordeal Mr Delaney's boat landed at St Kitts in the West Indies.

Ships requisitioned by the Royal Navy

VANDYCK. Converted into an Armed Merchant Cruiser in 1939 and became HMS *Vandyck* (Captain G.F.W. Wilson). Engaged in the evacuation of Norway when bombed and sunk off Narvik on 10 June 1940. Seven died and 161 were taken prisoner.

VOLTAIRE. Converted into an Armed Merchant Cruiser in 1939 and became HMS *Voltaire* (A/Captain J.A.P. Blackburn, RN). Bound for Freetown to escort a convoy when sunk by the German raider (KptzS. Otto Kähler) on 9 April 1941 in position 14°30′N 40°30′W. Seventy-five died and 197 were taken prisoner by the *Thor*.

Three sailors drift in the North Atlantic, suffering from shock and exposure after having been torpedoed and machine-gunned. (HMSO)

With no food and only 2 gallons of water, these men drifted for 15 days, using tin lids flashing the sun for distress signals. (HMSO)

After having watched 24 comrades die, these 4 survivors lived for a month in this lifeboat. (HMSO)

It was a raft that saved these men after their ship was torpedoed, their rescue ship bombed and their lifeboat machine-gunned. (HMSO)

These men are rescued from the North Atlantic. (HMSO)

A ship breaking in two after being torpedoed at close range by a surface raider in the South Atlantic. (HMSO)

Witnessing the sinking of a British merchant ship before the guns of the battleship *Graf Spee*. (HMSO)

The open torpedo wound of the *Franche Comte*. (HMSO)

A convoy of 45 ships with escorts move in battle order. (HMSO)

Ohio being towed into Malta with her cargo safe after having been torpedoed and set on fire in the August convoy. (HMSO)

Many passenger ships became troopships in the Second World War, carrying soldiers instead of civilians and painted in battledress. (HMSO)

Athenia. (Clifford M. Johnston collection)

U-boats rescuing survivors of the *Laconia*. (ObltzS. Leopold Schuhmacher)

Red Duster. (HMSO)

THE RISKS THEY RUN FOR YOU

BOMB

SHELL

TORPEDO

MINE

Under the 'RED DUSTER' they sustain our Island Fortress

Nearly one third of the world's Merchant Ships fly the RED ENSIGN

The Casablanca convoy moves eastward across the Atlantic bound for Africa. (NARA)

A convoy crossing the Atlantic, with the Liberty ships visible in this section. (Library of Congress)

Managed for Ministry of War Transport

EMPIRE IBEX (Captain Sweeney). In the Halifax section of Convoy HX.245 which sailed on 25 June 1943. At 5.20pm on 1 July she collided with the Merchant Aircraft Carrier *Empire MacAlpine* when aircraft were landing on the latter's deck. Although her bow was badly damaged, the *Empire MacAlpine* was able to continue with the convoy, but with her engine room flooded and her bulkheads carried away, the *Empire Ibex* was abandoned and subsequently sank on the 3rd in position 53°30′N 36°25′W. All her crew were taken on board the rescue vessel *Perth*.

Lyle Shipping Co.

CAPE CLEAR. Bound for Hampton Roads via the Mediterranean from Basra when in collision with the US Liberty ship *Henry Dearborn* in the Gulf of Suez on 21 August 1944. Sank in position 28°21′N 33°11′E without casualties, and the *Henry Dearborn* survived.

CAPE CORSO (Captain W.C. Montgomery). Bound for Murmansk in Convoy PQ.15 which sailed from Oban on 10 April 1942 and from Reykjavik on the 26th. Struck by an aerial torpedo delivered by a Heinkel 111 at 11.27pm on 2 May and sank in position 73°02′N 19°46′E. Fifty died. Six, including 3 wounded, were picked up by HMS *Badsworth* and HMS *Venomous*. (For further details of Convoy PQ.15, see under *Botavon*, REARDON SMITH LINE.)

CAPE HORN. Bound for Rangoon via the Cape, sailing in Convoy OS.21 which left Liverpool on 4 March 1942 and arrived at Freetown on the 24th. When sailing south in a section of the convoy on the 28th she blew up and sank due to what was believed to be a delayed incendiary exploding in her cargo of ammunition, in position 08°24′S 08°46′W. Cadet O. Kerr, Junior Engineer C. Lowe, 2nd Engineer S.R. Wallace and 1st Radio Officer O. Rowlands are listed on the Tower Hill War Memorial, but they died when the ship was damaged by German planes in Port Said on 14 May 1941. In *Merchant Ships Damaged WWII* the ship is listed under 14 May 1941, but in *Merchant Ship Losses WWII* she is not listed at all. No further details.

CAPE HOWE. Requisitioned by the Admiralty and renamed HMS *Prunella* (A/Cdr E.L. Woodhall). When hunting for U-boats off the south coast of Ireland she was torpedoed by U.28 (Kptlt Günter Kuhnke) at 8.46am on 21 June 1940 and abandoned. Torpedoed again about an hour later and sank in position 49°44′N 08°52′W. Fifty-six died. Twenty-seven in a lifeboat, spotted by a Sunderland of RAF Coastal Command, were picked up by the *Casamance* (Fr.) and landed at Falmouth on the 25th. Thirteen picked up from a raft by the destroyer HMS *Versatile* (Cdr J.H. Jauncey) on the 27th were landed at Devonport on the 28th.

CAPE NELSON (Captain K.M. Mackenzie). Bound for New York from Hull, sailing in Convoy OB.288 which left Liverpool on 18 February 1941 and dispersed on the 22nd in position 59°30′N 21°15′W. Torpedoed by U.95 (Kptlt Jost Metzler) at 0046 hours on the 24th and sank in approximate position 59°30´N 21°00´W. Four died, 34 were picked up by the *Harberton* and landed at Halifax on 4 March. (For details of other ships sunk and damaged in Convoy OB.288 or after dispersal, see under *Sirikishna*, SALVESEN, CHRISTIAN.)

CAPE OF GOOD HOPE (Captain A. Campbell). Sailed independently from New York on 5 May 1942 bound for Basrah and Bandar Shahpur via the Cape. Torpedoed and shelled by U.502 (Kptlt Jürgen von Rosenstiel) at 7.43pm on the 11th and sank in position 22°48´N 58°43´W. All 37 survived. Nineteen in one boat landed at Burgentra near Puerto Plata in the Dominican Republic on the 23rd. Eighteen in another boat landed at Tortola, Virgin Islands, on the 24th.

CAPE RACE (Captain J. Barnetson). Bound for Manchester from Boston, Massachusetts, sailing in Convoy SC.94 which left Sydney, Cape Breton, on 31 July 1942. Damaged by U.438 (Kptlt Rudolf Franzius) at 12.20pm on 8 August and straggling when sunk by U.660 (Oblt Götz Baur) in position 56°45´N 22°50´W. All 51, plus 12 survivors from the *Port Nicholson* which had been sunk by U.87 (Kptlt Joachim Berger) on 16 June, were picked up by the corvettes HMS *Nasturtium* and HMS *Dianthus*. (For details of other ships sunk in Convoy SC.94, see under *Kelso*, ELLERMAN GROUP.)

CAPE RODNEY (Captain P.A. Wallace). Bound for London from Lagos, sailing in Convoy SL.81 which left Freetown on 15 July 1941. Torpedoed by U.75 (Kptlt Helmuth Ringelmann) at 5.20am on 5 August in position 53°26´N 15°40´W. Two days later taken in tow by the tug HMS *Zwarte Zee*, but foundered in position 52°44´N 11°41´W on the 9th. All 39 survived: 36 picked up by corvette HMS *Hydrangea* (Lt J.E. Woolfenden) and landed at Gourock, 3 picked up by the corvette HMS *Zinnia* (Lt Cdr C.G. Cuthbertson) and landed at Londonderry. (For details of other ships sunk in Convoy SL.81 see under *Swiftpool,* ROPNER SHIPPING CO.)

CAPE VERDE (Managed for the MOWT) (Captain J.R. McIntyre). Bound for Cape Town, Trinidad, Baltimore and New York from Suez. Sailing independently when torpedoed and sunk by U.203 (Kptlt Rolf Mützelburg) at 11.05pm on 9 July 1942 in position 11°32´N 60°17´W. Two died. Forty landed at the Bay of St Vincent in the Windward Islands on the 14th.

CAPE YORK. Bound for the UK, sailing in Convoy HX.65 which left Halifax, Nova Scotia, on 12 August 1940. Hit by an aerial torpedo when 10 miles off Kinnaird Head on the 26th and abandoned. Sank the next day in position 57°41´N 01°45´W when under tow off Rattray Head. All survived. (For details of other ships sunk in Convoy HX.65, see under *Empire Merlin*, ROPNER SHIPPING CO.)

Manchester Liners

(PARTLY OWNED BY FURNESS, WITHY)

MANCHESTER BRIGADE (Captain F.L. Clough). Bound for Montreal and commodore ship of Convoy OB.218 which sailed from Liverpool on 24 September 1940. Torpedoed and sunk by U.137 (Oblt Herbert Wohlfarth) at 0050 hours on the 26th in position 54°53´N

10°22′W. Fifty-eight died, including the Master and the entire commodore staff. Four were picked up by French hospital ship *Canada* and landed at Gibraltar. (For details of other ships sunk and damaged in Convoy OB.218, see under *Bassa*, ELDER DEMPSTER LINE.)

MANCHESTER CITIZEN (Captain G.S. Swales). In Convoy ST.71 which sailed from Freetown bound for Lagos on 3 July 1943. Torpedoed by U.508 (Kptlt Georg Staats) at about 2.45am on the 9th. Torpedoed again and sank about an hour and a half later in position 05°50′N 02°22′E. Twenty-eight died. Fifty-three crew and 23 Kroo boys were picked up by the Free French corvette *Commandant Detroyat* and landed at Lagos. The *De la Salle* (Captain J. Le Mancheewere) was also sunk by U.508. Ten died. Two hundred and thirty-nine were picked up by the *Commandant Detroyat* and the *Calabar* and landed at Lagos.

MANCHESTER MERCHANT (Captain F. Struss). Bound for Halifax, Saint John and New York, sailing in Convoy ON.166 which left Liverpool on 11 February 1943. Torpedoed and sunk by U.628 (Kptlt Heinrich Hasenschar) at 8.17am on the 25th in position 45°10′N 43°23′W. Thirty-six died. Thirty-three were picked up by the destroyer HMS *Montgomery* (Lt Cdr W.L. Puxley) and the corvette HMCS *Rosthern* (Lt R.J.G. Johnson) and landed at St John's, Newfoundland. (For details of other ships sunk in Convoy ON.166, see under *Eulima*, SHELL GROUP.)

MANCHESTER REGIMENT (Captain W.E. Raper). In Convoy HXF.11 which sailed from Halifax on 2 December 1939 bound for Liverpool. In collision with the *Oropesa* on the 4th and sank in approximate position 44°30′N 61°52′W. Nine died and 63 were picked up from lifeboats by the *Oropesa* which returned to Halifax. (See also under *Chancellor*, HARRISON LINE.)

MANCHESTER SPINNER (Captain F. Lewis). Together with other vessels, scuttled as a blockship on 7 June 1944 to facilitate the landing of troops during the invasion of Normandy.

New Zealand Shipping Co. Ltd

(OWNED BY P&O)

HURUNUI (Captain B. Evans). Bound for Auckland from Newcastle and Liverpool, sailing in Convoy OA.228 which left Methil on 12 October 1940. Torpedoed and sunk by U.93 (Kptlt Claus Korth) at 0018 hours on the 15th in position 58°58′N 09°54′W. Two died. Seventy-three were picked up by the *St Margaret,* transferred to the sloop HMS *Fowey* (Lt C.G. deL. Bush) and landed at Greenock on the 20th.

OPAWA (Captain W.G. Evans). Bound for the UK, sailing independently from Lyttleton on 6 January 1942. Torpedoed by U.106 (Oblt Hermann Rasch) at 12.10pm on 6 February and abandoned in 4 lifeboats. Shelled by the U-boat and sank at 3pm in position 38°21′N 61°13′W. Two engineers killed by the explosion. It was decided that the lifeboats should make for Bermuda, but due to heavy seas they parted company and 3 of them, containing 54 men, were never seen again. During the evening of the 11th, the 15 in the remaining boat, with Captain Evans in charge, were picked up by the *Hercules* (Du.) and landed at New York on the 13th. Fifty-six died and 15 survived.

OTAIO (Captain G. Kinnell). Bound for Curaçao and Sydney, Australia, sailing in Convoy OS.4 which left Liverpool on 23 August 1941. Torpedoed and sunk by U.558 (Kptlt Günther Krech) at 4.41pm on the 28th in position 52°16′N 17°50′W. Thirteen died. Fifty-eight were picked up by the destroyer HMS *Vanoc* (Lt Cdr J.G.W. Deneys) and landed at Liverpool. (For details of other ships sunk in Convoy OS.4, see under *Saugor*, NOURSE LINE.)

PIAKO (Captain B. Evans, ex-*Hurunui*). Bound independently for Liverpool from Albany in Western Australia. Making for Freetown when torpedoed by U.107 (Kptlt Günther Hessler) at 10.27pm on 18 May 1941 and abandoned. Torpedoed again about 20 minutes later and sank in position 07°52′N 14°57′W. Ten died. Sixty-five, including Captain Evans, were picked up by the sloop HMS *Bridgewater* (Cdr H.F.G. Leftwich) and landed at Freetown.

RANGITANE (Captain H.L. Upton). On 24 November 1940, sailed independently from Auckland bound for the UK via the Panama Canal. At 3.40am on the 27th, when in approximate position 36°S 175°W, intercepted by the German raiders *Orion* (Krvkpt. Kurt Weyher) and *Komet* (KptzS. Robert Eyssen) accompanied by the supply ship *Kulmerland*. Shelled when heard transmitting and, with her wireless room damaged, her steering gear disabled and on fire, Captain Upton stopped the engines and informed the raiders that there were women on board. The firing immediately ceased, a boarding party approached and ordered that the ship be abandoned. Of the 192 crew and 111 passengers, 9 of the former and 7 of the latter were killed.* All surviving crew and passengers were then taken prisoner on board the three German ships before the *Rangitane* was sunk by torpedoes and gunfire.

On 20 December, the surviving passengers, together with those of other ships which the raiders had sunk, were put ashore at the island of Emirau, in the Bismarck Archipelago near Papua New Guinea, and were subsequently taken to Australia on the *Nellore* and *Montoro* in January 1941. All merchant seamen, however, were retained by the German ships and taken to PoW camps in Germany.

Two others died in captivity.

REMUERA (Captain F.W. Robinson). Bound for London, sailing from Wellington on 12 July 1940 and in Convoy HX.65 which left Halifax, Nova Scotia, on 12 August. During the evening of the 24th, the convoy divided into 2 sections, with the *Remuera* proceeding in Convoy HX.65A which consisted of ships bound for ports on the east coast. When about 6½ miles north-east of Kinnaird Head on the 26th, HX.65A was attacked by 4 Heinkel 115 torpedo bombers based at Stavanger and eight Junkers 88s based at Aalsborg. The *Remuera* was hit by an aerial torpedo and sank in position 57°47′N 01°53′W. All 94 were rescued by the Fraserburgh lifeboat. (For details of other ships sunk in Convoy HX.65, see under *Empire Merlin*, ROPNER SHIPPING CO.)

TURAKINA (Captain J.B. Laird). Bound independently for Wellington from Sydney, Australia. Attacked by German raider *Orion* at 5pm on 20 August 1940 when about 260 miles west of Taranaki. Set ablaze by gunfire before being sunk by torpedoes in position 38°33′S 167°12′E. Thirty-six died; 21, including wounded, were taken prisoner by *Orion*. (See *Rangitane*.)

Managed for Ministry of War Transport

EMPIRE AVOCET (Captain F. Pover). Bound independently for the UK from Buenos Aires and heading for Freetown when torpedoed by U.125 (Kptlt Ulrich Folkers) at 0035 hours on 30 September 1942. Torpedoed again at 0016 and 0038 hours and sank in position 04°05′N 13°23′W. Two men died in the engine room and Captain Pover and the Chief Engineer, Mr A. Berry, were taken prisoner by the U-boat. Twenty-four in the lifeboat commanded by Mr J.H.E. Clarke, the 1st Mate, were picked up by the corvette HMS *Cowslip* (Lt F. Granger) on 4 October and landed at Freetown the next day. Twenty-three in the other boat, commanded by Mr I.B. Rose, the 2nd Mate, landed 10 miles from Bonthe in Sierra Leone on 7 October; several contracted malaria during their subsequent arduous walk through jungle to reach the town.

EMPIRE MANOR. In Convoy HX.276 which left New York on 21 January 1944 bound for the UK. In collision with the US Liberty ship *Edward Kavanagh* on the 27th. Taken in tow, but abandoned the following day when chemicals in the cargo caught fire and she broke in two. Sunk by the escort in position 43°53′N 53°04′W. None died. The *Edward Kavanagh* succeeded in reaching St John's, Newfoundland.

EMPIRE WHIMBREL (Captain A.E. Williams). Bound independently for the UK from Buenos Aires and making for Freetown when torpedoed twice by U.181 (Krvkpt. Wolfgang Lüth) at 5.56am on 11 April 1943 and abandoned. The U-boat surfaced and questioned the survivors before sinking the ship by gunfire in position 02°31′N 15°55′W. All 53 were picked up by the destroyers HMS *Wolverine* (Lt I.M. Clegg) and HMS *Witch* (Lt Cdr S.R.J. Woods) and landed at Freetown.

SAMSIP (Captain E.A. Quick). Liberty ship bound for Barry from Antwerp when she struck a mine in the River Scheldt on 7 December 1944 and caught fire. Taken in tow by the tug HMS *Sea Giant*, but the attempt to save her failed and she was sunk by gunfire, being a danger to shipping. Seven died and the remaining 34, all of whom were injured to varying degrees, were picked up from the oily water by MTB753 and taken to Ostend.

Nourse Line

BHIMA. Torpedoed and sunk by the Japanese submarine I-65 (Lt Cdr Harada Hakue) on 20 February 1942 in position 07°47′N 73°31′E. All 70, including two passengers, were picked up from lifeboats 3 days later.

GANGES (Captain J.T. Vivian). On 6 April 1942, bombed by planes from the heavy cruiser *Chokai*, part of the Japanese Central Group operating in the Indian Ocean, and sank in position 17°48′N 84°09′E. The 1st Radio Officer M.J. Murphy, the 2nd Radio Officer W. Reilly, the 4th Engineer Mr R.G. Keir and 12 Lascars died. Survivors reached land after 24 hours in the boats. (For other ships sunk by the Japanese at this time, see under *Dardanus*, HOLT, ALFRED, & CO.)

INDUS (Captain C.E. Bryan). Bound for Fremantle from Safaga and Colombo when intercepted and shelled by the German raider *Thor* (KptzS. Günther Gumprich) on 20 July 1942. Returned the fire as she tried to escape and transmitted a QQQQ message. Abandoned after her stern gun and radio room were put out of action and her bridge was on fire; sank in position 26°44′S 82°50′E. Twenty-three died. Forty-nine, taken prisoner on board the *Thor*, were transferred to the *Tannenfels* on 29 August and landed at Bordeaux on 2 November.

JHELUM (Captain L.W. Newman). Bound for Oban from Izmir, Turkey, and Cape Town, sailing in Convoy SL. 68 which left Freetown on 13 March 1941. Torpedoed and sunk by U.105 (Kptlt Georg Schewe) at 10pm on the 21st in approximate position 21°N 25°W. Eight died. Forty-nine landed at St Louis in Senegal and interned by the Vichy French authorities. (For details of other ships sunk in Convoy SL.68, see under *Benwyvis*, BEN LINE.)

JUMNA. Bound for Calcutta via Freetown, sailing in Convoy OB.260 which left Liverpool on 16 December 1940 and dispersed on the evening of the 19th. Sunk by the German cruiser *Admiral Hipper* (Konteradmiral (Kadm.) Wilhelm Meisel) during the forenoon on Christmas Day in position 44°51′N 27°45′W. All 64 crew died as did 43 Lascar passengers who had survived the sinking of the *Planter* in Convoy SL.53. (See under *Planter*, HARRISON LINE.)

SAUGOR (Captain J.A.A. Steel). Bound for Freetown and Calcutta from London in Convoy OS.4 which left Liverpool on 23 August 1941. Torpedoed and sunk by U.557 (Oblt Ottokar Arnold Paulssen) at about 1.30am on 27th in position 53°36′N 16°40′W. Fifty-nine died. Twenty-three were picked up by the rescue ship *Perth* (Captain K. Williamson) and landed at Greenock the following day.

OTHER SHIPS SUNK IN CONVOY OS.4

Embassage (Captain E. Kiddie). By U.557. Thirty-nine died. Three picked up by the destroyer HMCS *Assiniboine* (Cpt. G.C. Jones) and landed at Greenock.

Otaio. See under NEW ZEALAND SHIPPING CO. LTD.

Segundo (Nor.) (Captain Karsten B. Wilhelmsen). By U.557. Seven died, including Gudrun Torgersen, the wife of the 1st Mate). Twenty-seven picked up by the sloop HMS *Lulworth* (Lt Cdr C. Gwinner).

Tremoda (Captain J.S. Bastian). By U.557. Thirty-two died. Twenty-one picked up by the Free French minesweeper *Chevreuil* and landed at Kingston, Jamaica.

SUTLEJ. Bound for Aden and Fremantle from Kosseir in Egypt when torpedoed and sunk by the Japanese submarine I-37 (Lt Cdr Hajime Nakagawa) on 26 February 1944 in position 08°00′S 70°00′E. The submarine fired on the survivors in boats, on wreckage and in the water. Five were rescued after 42 days in a lifeboat and 18 after being on 2 rafts for 49 days. Fifty died. (See under *British Chivalry*, BRITISH TANKER CO. LTD, and *Centaur*, HOLT, ALFRED, & CO.)

Orient Line

ORAMA (Captain F.G. Sherburne). Requisitioned as a troopship in 1940. Sent to aid the evacuation of troops of the British Expeditionary Force from Norway, but returned without troops as she was found surplus to requirements. At dawn on 8 June 1940, in company with the hospital ship *Atlantis*, the tanker *Oil Pioneer* and the MS trawler HMS *Juniper* (Lt Cdr G.S. Grenfell), she was intercepted by the German cruiser *Admiral Hipper* (KptzS. Hellmuth Heye) and a destroyer. Ordered to abandon ship, when she was in the process of complying, a faulty elevator mechanism caused a torpedo from the *Hipper* to destroy one of the lifeboats, killing its 19 occupants. Sank in position 67°44′N 03°52′E and 280 were taken to Germany as PoWs. The *Oil Pioneer* and HMS *Juniper* were also sunk. Twenty died from the *Oil Pioneer* and 1 was picked up by the *Hipper* from a Carley float. Thirty-one died and 4 were taken prisoner from HMS *Juniper*.

ORCADES (Captain C. Fox). Requisitioned as a troopship in 1939. Bound independently for the UK from Suez, sailing from Cape Town on 9 October 1942. Torpedoed three times by U.172 (Kptlt Carl Emmermann) between 11.23am and 11.30am on the 10th. Forty-eight died when boat 12a came to grief while being launched, but 20 boats cleared the ship. As the ship was still seaworthy and able to proceed at 5 knots, Captain Fox and 54 crew remained on board in an attempt to save her, but 2 more torpedoes broke her back and she eventually sank in position 31°51′S 18°30′E. The remaining crew then got away in the last 4 boats. The Polish ship *Narwik* had already rescued the other survivors when she approached the 4 boats at midnight, but as it was dangerous for her to stop, Captain Fox warned her against it. Captain Zarwarda of the *Narwik* ignored the warning and spent an hour picking them up. All were landed at Cape Town on the morning of the 12th. Forty-eight died and 1,026 survived.

ORFORD. Requisitioned as a troopship in 1939. In Marseille on 1 June 1940 when bombed by the Luftwaffe, set on fire and later beached. Fourteen died. Refloated in 1947 and broken up at Savona.

ORONSAY (Captain N. Savage). Requisitioned as a troopship in 1939. Bound independently for the UK from Cape Town when torpedoed by the Italian submarine *Archimede* (C.C. Guido Saccardo) at 5.20am on 9 October 1942 and sank in position 04°29′N 20°52′W when a fourth torpedo struck her about 2½ hours later. As the ship's aerial was brought down, no SSSS message was transmitted and this hampered the search for survivors. After being spotted by a Sunderland flying boat on the 15th, survivors were picked up from 8 lifeboats by the destroyer HMS *Brilliant* (Lt Cdr A.G. Poe) the following day and landed at Freetown on the 17th. Returning to the search on the 20th, HMS *Brilliant* picked up more survivors from 2 lifeboats and rescued a total of 382. Sixty-three were picked up from a lifeboat by the Vichy French sloop *Dumont D'Urville* (Capitaine de Frégate Toussaint de Quievrecourt) on the 21st and taken to Dakar where they were interned. Five died when torpedoed.

Pacific Steam Navigation Co. (PSNC)

(OWNED BY ROYAL MAIL)

LA PAZ. Unescorted and bound for Valparaiso when torpedoed by U.109 (Kptlt Heinrich Bleichrodt) at 11.36pm on 1 May 1942 in position 28°15′N 80°20′W. Sank in shallow water, beached and her cargo salvaged. Subsequently repaired and sold to the US War Shipping Administration. All 57 on board survived.

OROPESA (Captain H.E.H. Croft). Requisitioned as a troopship in 1939. Sailed independently from Cape Town on Christmas Day 1940 bound for the UK. Torpedoed three times by U.96 (Kptlt Heinrich Lehmann-Willenbrock) between 4am and 6am on 16 January 1941 and sank in position 56°28′N 12°00′W. One hundred and six died. One hundred and forty-three were picked up by the rescue tugs HMS *Superman* and HMS *Tenacity* and the destroyer HMS *Westcott* (Lt Cdr W.F.R. Segrave) and landed at Liverpool.

Peninsular & Oriental Steam Navigation Co. (P&O)

COASTER

ESTON (Captain Herbert Harris). A straggler from Convoy FN.81 and on passage from Hull to Blyth when on 28 January 1940 she was sunk in position 55°03′N 01°24′W by a mine laid by U.22 (Kptlt Karl-Heinrich Jenisch). All 18 died.

CARGO SHIPS

ALIPORE (Captain Ernest Lee). Bound independently for New York from Alexandria via Cape Town and Trinidad, off the coast of British Guiana when torpedoed by U.516 (Krvkpt. Gerhard Wiebe) at 11pm on 29 September 1942. The first torpedo narrowly missed her stern, but a second one struck her starboard side causing a boiler to explode, flooding the engine room and killing everyone in it. Many of the crew took to rafts before being transferred to the 2 lifeboats which got away and made sail for the coast. At noon the next day the boats were sighted by the fishing schooner *United Eagle* which towed them to Georgetown. After being subjected to gunfire from the U-boat, the *Alipore* sank in position 07°09′N 54°23′W shortly after 4am on the 30th. Ten died. Seventy-three survived.

JEYPORE (Captain Thomas Stevens). Commodore ship of Convoy SC.107 which sailed from New York on 24 October 1942 bound for Liverpool. Torpedoed and sunk by U.89 (Krvkpt. Dietrich Lohmann) shortly before 10pm on 3 November in position 55°30′N 40°16′W. One died. Ninety were picked up by the US Navy tugs *Uncas* and *Pessacus*

OTHER SHIPS SUNK IN CONVOY SC.107

Dalcroy (Captain J. Johnson). By U.402 (Kptlt Baron Siegfried von Forstner). All 49 picked up by the *Stockport*.

Daleby. See under ROPNER SHIPPING CO.

Empire Antelope (Captain W. Slade). By U.402. All 50 picked up by the *Stockport*.

Empire Leopard (Captain J. Evans). By U.402. Thirty-nine died. Three picked up by the *Stockport*.

Empire Lynx (Captain T. Muitt). Sunk by U.132 (Kptlt Ernst Vogelsang). All 43 picked up by the *Titus* (Du.) and landed at Liverpool on the 10th.

Empire Sunrise (Captain A. Hawkins). Damaged by U.402. Sunk by U.84 (Kptlt Horst Uphoff). All 51 picked up by the *Stockport*.

Hahira (US) (Captain J. Elliott). Sunk by U.521. Three died and 53 picked up by the *Stockport*.

Hartington (Captain M. Edwards). Damaged by U.522 (Kptlt Herbert Schneider) and U.438 (Kptlt Rudolf Franzius). Sunk by U.521 (Kptlt Klaus Bargsten). Twenty-four died. Twenty-four picked up by the destroyer HMS *Winchelsea* (Lt Cdr G.W. Gregorie) and landed at St John's, Newfoundland.

Hatimura (Captain W. Putt). Torpedoed by U.132 and sinking when torpedoed again by U.442 (Frgkpt. Hans-Joachim Hesse). U.132 was standing by the burning ship; when she blew up, the U-boat was lost with all hands. Four died. Eighty-six picked up by the tugs *Pessacus* and *Uncas* and transferred to the *Stockport*.

Hobbema (Du.) (Captain A. van Duin). Sunk by U.132. Twenty-eight died. Sixteen picked up by the *Pessacus* and *Uncas*.

Maritima (Captain A. Phelps-Mead). Sunk by U.522 (Kptlt Herbert Schneider). Thirty-two died. Twenty-seven picked up by the corvette HMCS *Arvida* (Lt A.I. MacKay) and landed at Londonderry.

Mount Pelion (Gr.). Sunk by U.522. Seven died and 32 survived.

Parthenon (Gr.). Sunk by U.522. Six died and 23 survived.

Rinos (Gr.) By U.402. Eight dead and 23 survivors.

and transferred to the rescue ship *Stockport* (Captain Ernest Fea) which landed them at Reykjavik on 8 November.

LAHORE (Captain Geoffrey Stable). Homeward bound from Calcutta, sailing from Freetown in Convoy SL.67 on 1 March 1941. Torpedoed by U.124 (Kptlt George-Wilhelm Schlulz) at about 6am on the 8th when in position 20°51′N 20°32′W. On fire and with her pumps unable to control the inflow of water, she was abandoned the next morning. All 82 were picked up by the destroyer HMS *Forester* (Lt Cdr E.B. Tancock) and landed at Gibraltar on the 16th. (For details of other ships sunk in Convoy SL.67, see under *Nardana*, BRITISH INDIA STEAM NAVIGATION CO.)

NAGPORE (Captain Percy Tonkin). Bound for Liverpool, commodore ship of Convoy SL.125 which sailed from Freetown on 16 October 1942. Torpedoed and sunk by U.509 (Krvkpt. Werner Witte) shortly after 10pm on the 28th when in position 31°30′N 19°35′W. Twenty died. Thirty-four were picked up by the corvette HMS *Crocus* (T/Lt J.F. Holm) and landed at Liverpool on 9 November. The 19 men in No 4 boat were not so fortunate, as when launched the boat smashed against the ship's side and the rudder was lost so that the boat could not be steered and lost touch with the others. However, with the 4th Engineer Mr J.J. Marshall in charge, it reached La Orotave in the Canary Islands after 2 weeks adrift.

OTHER SHIPS SUNK IN CONVOY SL.125

27 October:

Anglo Maersk (Captain M. Walløe Valsberg). A straggler. Damaged by U.509 on the 26th. Sunk by U.604 (Kptlt Horst Höltring). All 36 reached Canary Islands.

Pacific Star. See under BLUE STAR LINE.

Stentor. See under HOLT, ALFRED, & CO.

29 October:

Hopecastle (Captain Dugald McGilp). Damaged by U.509 on the 28th. Sunk by U.203. (Kptlt Hermann Kottmann). Five died. Twenty-one rescued by the *Mano* and landed at Greenock on 9 November. Sixteen landed at Funchal, Madeira, by the *Baron Elgin*.

30 October:

Baron Vernon (Captain Peter Liston). See under HOGARTH, H. & CO./BARON LINE.

Brittany (Captain William Dovell). By U.509. All 40 crew and 3 passengers picked up by HMS *Kelantan*. (As the *Kelantan* did not carry a doctor, her Chief Steward attended to the sick and wounded, and due to the large number of survivors she had on board, she soon ran out of food.)

Bullmouth. See under SHELL GROUP.

Corinaldo. See under DONALDSON LINE.

Président Doumer. See under BIBBY LINE.

Silverwillow. See under SILVER LINE.

31 October:

Tasmania. See under BROCKLEBANK LINE.

OBSERVATIONS ON CONVOY SL.125

The Allied invasion of North Africa was about to begin and although the Germans did not know what was going on, they had noticed an increase of activity around Gibraltar and transferred U-boats from the Azores area to form the Streitax group near Freetown. When the attack on SL.125 began, the Torch convoys of the invasion forces were already at sea, but instead of locating them the U-boats found SL.125, allowing the more valuable Torch convoys to get through.

There has been much speculation as to whether this was by chance or design, cynics suggesting that SL.125 was deliberately sacrificed for the greater benefit. The statement made by Admiral Reyne after the war can be interpreted to support this view: 'It was the only time in my career that I had been congratulated by the Admiralty for losing a large number of ships.'

PESHAWUR (Captain J.C. Mellonie). In convoy JC.30 and on passage from Swansea to Calcutta via Trincomalee when torpedoed and sunk in the Bay of Bengal by the Japanese submarine RO-111 (Lt Cdr Nakamura Naozo) on 23 December 1943 in position 11°11′N 80°11′E. All 134 were picked up by the minesweeper HMAS *Ipswich* and landed at Madras.

SHILLONG (Captain James Hollow). Bound for the UK in Convoy HX.231 when torpedoed by U.635 (Oblt Heinz Eckelmann) at 10.15pm on 4 April 1943. Well down by the head, she was abandoned and sank about 3 hours later in position 57°10′N 35°30′W when U.630 (Oblt Werner Winkler) put a second torpedo into her. As there was half a gale blowing and the seas were mountainous most took to a raft, but when it was swamped and overturned 3 times only 11 succeeded in staying on it. The Master, 1st Mate, Cadet G. Francis and an Asian died during the freezing and stormy night. No 3 lifeboat, with Cadet Coleman in charge, had succeeded in getting away and during the night a destroyer approached saying that she would return to pick them up but never did. When they sighted the raft at about 9am, the surviving 7 on it, and their stores, were taken on board. U.635 was sunk on the 6th by the frigate HMS *Tay*. All died.

The account of the ordeal undergone by those in the lifeboat, given in *Business in Great Waters* by George F. Kerr, is a dreadful one. When the boat was eventually sighted by a Catalina and a destroyer came to their rescue at dusk on their 8th day, only 7 of the original complement of 38 were still alive: Cadets Clowe and Moore, and DEMS gunners Petty Officer Hadley, Barnes, Stevens, French and Theobald. But the bitter cold and continuous soakings had taken their toll, so that they were unable to board the destroyer without help. Only Clowe, French and Stevens left hospital with all their limbs intact. Moore had both his legs and most of his fingers amputated. Hadley and Theobald lost both their legs and Barnes's feet were amputated. They were the only survivors of *Shillong*'s complement of 78.

OTHER SHIPS SUNK IN CONVOY HX.231

5 April:

British Ardour (Captain Thomas Copeman). Torpedoed by U.706 (Krvkpt. Alexander von Zitzewitz) and scuttled by the destroyer HMS *Vidette* (Lt Cdr R. Hart) and the corvette HMS *Snowflake* (Lt Cdr Chesterman). All 62 picked up by the *Snowflake* and landed at Londonderry on the 9th.

Vaalaren (Swed.). Left the convoy when the attack began and sunk by U.229 (Oblt Robert Schetelig). All 38 died.

6 April:

Blitar (Du.) (Captain W.E. van der Knip). Left the convoy when the attack began and sunk by U.632 (Krvkpt. Hans Karpf). Twenty-six of her crew of 62 died. U.632 subsequently sunk by depth charges from an RAF Liberator and all 48 died.

Sunoil (US) (Captain Sedolf Berg Heggelund). Straggling with engine trouble when damaged shortly before midnight on the 5th by U.563 (Kptlt Götz von Hartmann). Sunk by U.530 (Kptlt Kurt Lange) and all 69 died.

Waroonga (Captain Charles Taylor). Had been damaged by U.630 and was scuttled by the corvette HMS *Loosestrife* (Lt A.A. Campbell). Of her complement of 132, 13 crew and 6 passengers died. The survivors were picked up by the *Loosestrife* and the *Joel Roger Poinsett* (US) and landed at Londonderry on the 9th.

SOMALI. On the first stage of a voyage to Hong Kong, commodore ship of Convoy FN.442 which left Southend on 25 March 1941 bound for Methil. Attacked by Heinkel 111s on the afternoon of the 25th, struck by 3 bombs and set on fire. The crew fought hard to control the fire, but when they failed to do so they and the passengers were taken off by armed trawler HMT *Pelican* at 10pm on the 26th. Early on the 27th the Holy Island, North Sunderland and Boulmer lifeboats arrived on the scene and 2 crewmen were put on board the burning ship to help connect a towline to the ocean-going tug *Sea Giant*. After doing so they were returned to their lifeboat and at 9.30am the *Sea Giant* set off for the Farne Islands where the salvage officer and 2 crewmen of the salvage vessel *Iron Axe* were put on board the *Somali* by the Boulmer lifeboat *Clarissa Langdon*. The *Sea Giant* then resumed the tow and at midday the salvage officer from the *Iron Axe* was taken off by the *Clarissa Langdon* and returned to his vessel.

It was the intention to transfer the tow to the *Iron Axe*, but when this was about to take place there was a tremendous explosion on board the *Somali* which blew off her bow, showering the lifeboats with debris, injuring several men, causing structural damage around the village of Beadnell, about 1½ miles away, and even breaking windows in Seahouses, about 5 miles distant. The *Clarissa Langdon* was about 200 yards away when the explosion occurred, but although she was thrown into the air and some of her crew injured, Coxswain James Campbell succeeded in proceeding through the smoke to rescue the 2 men still on board the stricken ship. As the *Clarissa Langdon* was leaving at full speed, however, her propeller fouled on a piece of wreckage and she had to be towed clear by the North Sunderland lifeboat *W.B.A.* (Coxswain Dawson). The *Somali* sank in position 55°33′N 01°36′W and, miraculously, only one crewman died.

SOUDAN. Sunk by a mine when off Cape Agulhas on 15 May 1942 and the crew got away in 3 lifeboats. The occupants of 2 of them were picked up within 40 hours, but it was 6 days later when the 31 in the remaining boat, commanded by the 2nd Mate, were picked up by the *Clan Murray*.

SURAT (Captain Thomas Daniel). Homeward bound from Karachi and sailing unescorted when attacked by U.103 (Krvkpt. Viktor Schütze) north-west of Freetown at 11.45pm on 5 May 1942. A single torpedo fired at her missed, but when 2 more were fired shortly after

5am on the 6th, one hit her stern and brought her to a halt. However, it took another 2 to sink her and she went down in position 08°23′N 15°13′W. Four died. Sixty-one were picked up by the hopper barge *Foremost 102* and taken to Freetown.

Passenger Ships (converted to troopships)

CATHAY (Captain D.M. Stuart). Went to Algiers in Torch Convoy KMF.1A and then on to Bougie. While disembarking troops on 11th November 1942 she came under attack from German aircraft. The raids lasted from 1.30pm until dusk and the ship was so badly damaged that she was abandoned at 7pm. About 3 hours later a delayed action bomb exploded in her galley. This started a fire which led to ammunition exploding at 7am on the 12th, and with her stern blown off she sank to the bottom about an hour later. As the ship was out in the bay, the survivors took to the boats and although ordered to head for the BI ship *Karanja* which had also landed troops, some made for the shore. Many of the survivors of the *Cathay* were therefore on the *Karanja* when she too was bombed and sunk at dawn on the 12th. Those from both ships joined the hundreds of survivors in the École Supérieure where they remained until boarding the *Strathnaver* (Captain E.M. Coates) during yet another air raid for the passage home. No details of casualties. (See also under *Karanja*, BRITISH INDIA STEAM NAVIGATION CO.)

ETTRICK (Captain John Legg). During the late afternoon of 15 November 1942, sailed from Gibraltar in Convoy MKF.1YG bound for the UK. Shortly after 4am the following day she was torpedoed and sunk by U.155 (Krvkpt. Adolf Cornelius Piening) in position 36°13′N 07°54′W. Twenty-four died and the remaining 312 were picked up by the Norwegian destroyer HNoMS *Glaisdale* which carried them back to Gibraltar for repatriation to the UK on the *Mooltan*.

OTHER SHIPS ATTACKED IN CONVOY MKF.1YG

HMS *Avenger* (Captain A.P. Colthurst). The 'Woolworth' Escort Carrier. Torpedoed by U.155 at the same time as the *Ettrick*, blew up and sank within minutes. Twelve picked up by the *Glaisdale*. Five hundred and fourteen died.

USS *Almaack* (Cdr Thomas R. Cooley). Damaged by U.155. Four died and another 4 in her engine room badly burned. One hundred and ninety-three transferred to the *Glaisdale* and the others were still on board when the tug *Jaunty* brought the ship into Gibraltar on the 17th.

NARKUNDA (Captain L. Parfitt). Sailed from the Clyde in a KMF convoy (perhaps KMF.4) and arrived in Bougie on 14 November 1942. With her troops disembarked into barges, she had just rounded the headland on her way back to Algiers when bombed and sunk by German aircraft. Thirty-one died. Others got away in the lifeboats and were picked up by the minesweeper HMS *Cadmus*.(Lt Cdr J.B.G. Temple).

STRATHALLAN (Captain J. Biggs). Commodore ship of Convoy KMF.5A when torpedoed and sunk by U.562 (Kptlt Horst Hamm) at about 2.30am on 21 December 1942 in position

36°52′N 00°34′W. The torpedo struck the engine room, killing 4 men. The 248 Queen Alexandra nurses and 4,408 British and American troops were ordered to take to the lifeboats and rafts, but when it was decided that the ship might be saved the evacuation was stopped after about 1,300 had left. She was then taken in tow by HMS *Laforey* (Capt. R.M.J. Hutton), but the tug HMS *Restive* (Lt D.M. Richards) had replaced her when the situation became serious enough to warrant the transfer of the remainder of the troops and 396 crew to HMS *Panther* (Lt Cdr Viscount Jocelyn) and HMS *Pathfinder* (Cdr E.A. Gibbs). The Master, Commodore, OC troops and 70 crew were still on board, however, when at about 1.15pm oil came into contact with the boilers, the ship was set ablaze and the order to abandon ship was given. HMS *Restive* continued to tow the burning ship for a further 14 hours, but she capsized and sank off Oran at about 4am the next day. All the survivors were taken to Oran, those who had been in the lifeboats and on rafts by HMS *Verity* (Lt J.C. Rushbrooke), the remainder of the troops by HMS *Panther*, and the crew by HMS *Laforey*. Six of the crew and 5 others died and the surviving troops went on to Algiers on the *Duchess of Richmond*.

VICEROY OF INDIA (Captain S.H. French). Went to Algiers in Torch Convoy KMF.1A and having disembarked her troops was returning independently to the UK, carrying only a few hospital cases and some naval and army staff. Torpedoed and sunk by U.407 (Kptlt Ernst-Ulrich Brüller) at 4.28am on 11 November 1942 in position 36°24′N 00°35′W. Four died. Survivors were picked up by the destroyer HMS *Boadicea* (Lt Cdr F.C. Brodrick) and landed at Gibraltar.

Ships requisitioned by the Royal Navy

HMS COMORIN (Armed Merchant Cruiser) (Captain J.I. Hallett). Together with the destroyer HMS *Lincoln* (Cdr G.B. Sayer), escorting a convoy from the UK to Freetown when fire broke out in her engine room on 6 April 1941. When the fire went out of control she signalled to the *Glenartney* (Captain D.L.C. Evans) to stand by her. One hundred and four were rescued by the *Glenartney* and 121 by the *Lincoln* before the destroyer HMS *Broke* (Cdr B.G. Scurfield) arrived to assist. It was dark by this time and as there were no lifeboats left, those still on board had to jump down onto her deck and some were lost by falling between the two ships. With a gale blowing and high seas running, it was difficult for the *Broke* to remain alongside the burning ship, but although damaged by the encounters, she closed time and time again and succeeded in rescuing 180. The blazing hulk was torpedoed and sunk the next day by HMS *Broke* in position 54°34′N 21°20′W. Twenty died and 401 were rescued.

HMS MATA HARI (1,020-ton ex-coaster and anti-submarine ship) (Captain A.C. Carston). With Singapore under siege by the Japanese, she sailed from there at 7.30pm on 13 February 1942 with 483 on board, including 132 women and children, nurses, Royal Marines and men of the Argylls. As almost all her native crew had elected to remain in Malaya, survivors of the *Prince of Wales* and the *Repulse* had taken their place. Her orders were to make for Batavia (Djakarta), but after successfully negotiating a minefield, surviving attacks by Japanese bombers and endeavouring to evade the enemy, she was caught by their warships in the Banka Strait at about 3am on the 15th. No lives were lost during this nightmare passage, but many were destined to die in captivity.

HMS RAJPUTANA (Armed Merchant Cruiser) (Captain F.H. Taylor). On patrol in the Denmark Strait when struck by a torpedo fired by U.108 (Kptlt Klaus Scholtz) at about 7.45am on 13 April 1941. Three men in her engine room were killed and the ship set on fire, but it took another torpedo, fired at 9.30am, to sink her in position 64°50′N 27°25′W. Forty died and later in the day an RAF Sunderland spotted the lifeboats. In about an hour the destroyer HMS *Legion* (Cdr R.F. Jessel) picked up the 283 survivors and landed them at Reykjavik the same evening.

HMS RAWALPINDI (AMC) (Captain E.C. Kennedy). On patrol north of the Faroe Islands when she encountered the German battle cruisers *Scharnhorst* and *Gneisenau*, at dusk on 23 November 1939. The repeated signals from the *Scharnhorst* to abandon ship were ignored and the *Rawalpindi* opened fire, with a hit made on the *Gneisenau* before being sunk in position 63°40′N 12°31′W by the cruisers' superior firepower. Two hundred and fifty-nine died. Thirty-seven were taken prisoner. Ten picked up from a lifeboat by the requisitioned P&O liner AMC HMS *Chitral* were landed in Glasgow a week later.

Port Line

PORT AUCKLAND (Captain A.E. Fishwick). Bound for Avonmouth from Brisbane, sailing in the Halifax Section of Convoy SC.122 on 8 March 1943 and which joined the main New York Section on the 9th. Struck by two torpedoes fired by U.305 (Kptlt Rudolf Bahr) shortly after 11pm on the 17th and sunk by a third torpedo from the same U-boat at 0017 hours on the 18th in position 52°25′N 30°15′W. Eight died. One hundred and ten, including 10 RAF passengers, were picked up by the corvette HMS *Godetia* (Lt M.A.F. Larose) and landed at Gourock.

OTHER SHIPS SUNK IN CONVOY SC.122

Alderamin (Du.). By U.338 (Kptlt Manfred Kinzel). Fifteen died. Forty-nine picked up by the corvette HMS *Saxifrage* and the rescue ship *Zamalek* (Captain O.C. Morris) and landed at Gourock on the 22nd.

Carras (Gr.). Damaged by U.666 (Oblt Herbert Engel) and sunk by U.333 (Oblt Werner Schwaff). All 34 survived. *Clarissa Radcliffe*. See under RADCLIFFE SHIPPING CO.

Fort Cedar Lake (Captain C.L. Collings). Damaged by U.338 and sunk by U.665 (Oblt Hans-Jürgen Haupt). All 50 picked up by the *Zamalek*. (All 46 crew of U.665 died when she was depth-charged and sunk by the RAF on the 22nd.)

Granville (Pan.) (Captain Friedrich Matzen). By U.338. Thirteen died, including 10 engine room staff. Thirty-four picked up by the corvette HMS *Lavender* (Captain L.G. Pilcher) and landed at Liverpool on the 23rd.

King Gruffydd (Captain H. Griffiths). By U.338. Twenty-four died and 25 picked up by the *Zamalek*.

Kingsbury (Captain W. Laidler). By U.338. Four died and 44 rescued by the *Zamalek*.

Zouave (Captain W.H. Cambridge). By U.305. Thirteen died, some trapped in the engine room. Thirty got away in a lifeboat and picked up by HMS *Godetia*.

PORT BRISBANE (Captain H. Steele). West of Cape Leeuwin and homeward bound from Adelaide via Durban on 19 November 1940 when alerted to the presence of an unidentified merchantman by a QQQQ message transmitted by the *Maimoa* which was subsequently sunk. An attempt was made to clear the area, but the raider, which turned out to be the *Pinguin* (KptzS. Ernst-Felix Krüder), caught up with her at 9.45pm on the 21st. After a warning shot was fired across her bows the *Port Brisbane* made off at full speed, at the same time transmitting a QQQQ message until her radio room was destroyed and she was set on fire by shelling. She was then abandoned and sunk. One died. Sixty men and a woman were taken on board the *Pinguin* from 2 lifeboats and the following day the heavy cruiser HMAS *Canberra* (Captain H.B. Farncomb), searching for the raider, picked up 28 survivors from a third lifeboat which had escaped in the darkness. (See under *Nowshera*, BRITISH INDIA STEAM NAVIGATION CO.)

PORT DENISON (Captain J.B. Bradley). Bound for New Zealand, commodore ship of Convoy OA.220 which left Methil on 26 September 1940. Bombed by a German plane when 6 miles north-east of Peterhead and sank the following day in approximate position 57°38′N 01°36′W. Sixteen died and 67 survived.

PORT GISBORNE (Captain T. Kippins). Bound for Belfast and Cardiff from Auckland, sailing in Convoy HX.77 which left Halifax, Nova Scotia, on 30 September 1940. Torpedoed and sunk by U.48 (Kptlt Heinrich Bleichrodt) shortly after 10pm on 11 October in position 56°38′N 16°40′W. Twenty-six died when No 3 lifeboat capsized. Those in No 4 boat were picked up by rescue tug HMS *Salvonia* (Lt G.M.M. Robinson) on the 22nd, while those in No 2 boat were rescued by the *Alpera* on the 24th and landed at Greenock. Twenty-six died and 38 survived.

OTHER SHIPS SUNK IN CONVOY HX.77

Brandanger (Nor.) (Captain E.J. Andresen). By U.48. Six died. Sixteen picked up from a lifeboat and a raft by the corvette HMS *Clarkia* (Lt Cdr F.J.G. Jones) and landed at Liverpool on 15 October. Eight picked up by the *Clan Davanger* (Nor.) (Captain E.K. Karlsen). By U.48. Eighteen died. Twelve reached Broadhaven, Pembrokeshire, in a lifeboat on the 18th.

Macdonald (Captain A. Mackinley) on the 16th and landed at Liverpool on the 19th.

Pacific Ranger. See under FURNESS, WITHY GROUP.

Saint Malo (Can.). By U.101. (Kptlt Fritz Frauenheim). Twenty-eight died. Sixteen picked up by HMS *Salvonia* on the 22nd.

Stangrant (Captain E.D. Rowlands). By U.37 (Kptlt Victor Oehrn). Nine died. Twenty-nine rescued by an RAF Sunderland flying boat and landed at Oban.

PORT HARDY (Captain J.G. Lewis). In Convoy HX.121 which sailed from Halifax on 16 April 1941 bound for the UK. Torpedoed by U.96 (Kptlt Heinrich Lehmann-Willenbrock) at 7.25pm on the 28th and sank some hours later. One died. Ninety-seven were picked up by the rescue ship *Zaafaran* (Captain C.K. McGowan) and landed at Greenock on 1 May.

OTHER SHIPS SUNK IN CONVOY HX.121

Caledonia (Nor.) (Captain Ragnvald Andresen). By U.96. Twelve died and 25 picked up by the *Zaafaran*.

Capulet (Captain E.H. Richardson). Damaged by U.552 (Oblt Erich Topp) on 28 April and abandoned. Sunk by U.201 (Oblt Adalbert Schnee) on 2 May. Nine died. Eighteen picked up by the destroyer HMS *Douglas* (Cdr W.E. Banks) and landed at Londonderry. Seventeen picked up by the *Zaafaran*.

Nerissa. See under FURNESS, WITHY GROUP.

Oilfield (Captain L.R. Andersen). By U.96. Forty-seven died. Eight picked up by the ASW trawler HMS *St Zeno* (Lt J.K. Craig) and landed at Londonderry.

PORT HOBART (Captain G.S. Hall). Bound for New Zealand via the Panama Canal, sailing in Convoy OB.239 which left Liverpool on 4 November 1940. Left the convoy on the 20th and sailing independently when intercepted by the pocket battleship *Admiral Scheer* (KptzS. Theodor Krancke) towards noon on the 24th in position 24°44′N 58°21′W. The *Port Hobart*, which failed to identify the warship, immediately transmitted an RRRR message and then added 'opened fire on me' when a shot was fired across her bow. Heard by a US ship, the message was relayed to the Royal Navy in Bermuda. When the ship eventually complied with the order to stop, a boarding party was sent from the *Scheer*. All 73 were transferred to the warship and after an attempt to scuttle her failed, she was sunk by shelling. The prisoners were subsequently transferred to other ships and landed at Bordeaux on 1 March 1941.

PORT HUNTER (Captain J.B. Bradley). Bound for Auckland via Durban, sailing in Convoy OS.33 which left Liverpool on 1 July 1942 bound for Freetown. Left the convoy on the 11th and proceeding independently when torpedoed and sunk by U.582 (Krvkpt. Werner Schulte) at 1.47am on the 12th in approximate position 31°N 24°W. Ammunition in her cargo exploded and she sank within 2 minutes. Eighty-nine died, including Captain Bradley, who had survived the sinking of the *Port Denison*. Three of the crew, who had been sleeping on the upper deck aft, were blown into the water. Clinging to debris, they were spotted by the *City of Windsor* and subsequently picked up by the frigate HMS *Rother*

(Lt Cdr R.V.E. Case) at about 8.30am. (For details of other ships sunk after dispersal from Convoy OS.33, see under *Cortona*, DONALDSON LINE.)

PORT MONTREAL (Captain J.G. Lewis, ex-*Port Hardy*). Sailing independently and on passage from Halifax, Nova Scotia, bound for Melbourne via the Panama Canal when she picked up 43 survivors from the Honduran ship *Tela* (Captain J. Shiell) which had been torpedoed and sunk by U.504 (Krvkpt. Hans-Georg Friedrich Poske) on 8 June 1942. Torpedoed and sunk by U.68 (Krvkpt. Karl-Friedrich Merten) at noon on the 10th in position 12°17'N 80°20'W. All 88 on board got away in 4 lifeboats. They were picked up by the Colombian schooner *Hiloa* on the 16th and landed at Cristobal the next day. Eleven died when the *Tela* was torpedoed and 2 more died in the *Port Montreal*'s lifeboats. All 45 of the *Port Montreal*'s complement survived.

PORT NAPIER. Under construction in June 1940 when requisitioned by the Admiralty and completed as the minelayer HMS *Napier*. Tied up to the pier at Kyle of Lochalsh on the night of 27 November 1940 when she went on fire. Towed across the narrow channel towards Skye after an attempt to extinguish the fire failed, as the position was serious with 550 mines on board. When about 300yd off Skye there was an explosion and she sank in about 20 metres of water. Fortunately, however, none of the mines had exploded and during 1956–57 the Navy recovered most but not all of them. No lives lost.

PORT NICHOLSON (Captain H.C. Jeffrey). Sailed from Halifax in Convoy XB.25 on 14 June 1942 bound for New York and Wellington via the Panama Canal. Torpedoed twice at about 4.15am on the 16th by U.87 (Kptlt Joachim Berger) and 85 crew members transferred to the corvette HMCS *Nanaimo* (Lt T.J. Bellas). As the ship remained afloat when daylight came, Captain Jeffrey, the Chief Engineer Lt J.M. Walkley and 3 ratings of the *Nanaimo* boarded to assess the damage. Rough seas broke the bulkheads when they were on board and she went down by the stern in position 42°11'N 69°25'W. The boarding party descended into their lifeboat but it was overturned by the suction of the sinking ship and only 2 of the ratings were recovered. Six died and 85 survived. Twelve survivors of the *Port Nicholson* were returning to the UK on the *Cape Race*, in Convoy SC.94, when she was torpedoed by U.660 (Oblt Götz Baur) on 10 August. All again survived. The US ship *Cherokee* (Captain T.E. Brown) was also sunk by U.87. Forty-four were picked up by the *Norlago* and landed at Provincetown, Massachusetts. Thirty-nine picked up by the USCGC *Escanaba* were landed at Boston. Eighty-six died.

PORT TOWNSVILLE. Bound for Melbourne from Bristol on 3 March 1941 when struck by a bomb from a German plane off St David's Head, Pembrokeshire. All 67 crew and 9 passengers abandoned the ship and a French escort vessel took them to Milford Haven. The *Port Townsville* sank the next day in position 52°05'N 05°24'W. Two passengers died, Mr and Mrs Frank Berger.

PORT VICTOR (Captain W.G. Higgs). Sailing independently and bound for Buenos Aires from Liverpool when struck by a torpedo fired by U.107 (Kptlt Harald Gelhaus) at 0030 hours on 1 May 1943. While the lifeboats were being launched, 3 more torpedoes struck the ship and she sank shortly after 0045 hours in position 47°49'N 22°02'W. SSSS messages, which continued to be sent until she went down, were heard by the sloop

HMS *Wren* (Lt Cdr R.M. Aubrey) which picked up 85 crew and 60 passengers and carried them to Liverpool. Fourteen crew and 5 passengers died.

PORT WELLINGTON (Captain T.E. Oliver). In the Indian Ocean, bound independently for Durban and the UK from Adelaide when shelled at about 10.30pm on 30 November 1940 by the German raider *Pinguin* (KptzS. Ernst-Felix Krüder). The 1st Radio Officer A.F. Haslam was killed in the radio room and Captain Oliver was so severely wounded that the 1st Mate Mr F.W. Bailey took command and ordered 'Abandon ship'. Eighty-eight crew and passengers took to the lifeboats and were picked up by the raider which, after taking stores from the ship, sank her the next day. The prisoners, together with those from the *Port Brisbane*, were among the 400 subsequently transferred to the captured Norwegian tanker *Storstad* which landed them at Bordeaux on 5 February 1941. Captain Oliver died on board the *Pinguin*. No details of further casualties. (See also under *Nowshera*, BRITISH INDIA STEAM NAVIGATION CO.)

Managed for Ministry of War Transport

FORT STIKINE (Captain A.J. Naismith). Bound for Karachi and Bombay, and with 1,400 tons of explosives and over £1 million of gold bullion among her cargo, sailing in Convoy OS.69/KMS.43 which left Liverpool on 23 February 1944. On 5 March, the KMS.43 section, which she was in, detached from OB.69 and reached Gibraltar on the 6th where it joined other ships coming from the USA before proceeding into the Mediterranean. Two days later the convoy was attacked by 4 Focke-Wulf 200 Condors, but no ships were sunk and on reaching Port Said the *Fort Stikine* continued independently through the Suez Canal and the Red Sea, arriving at Karachi on 30 March. Crated gliders and Spitfires were discharged while other cargo was loaded to fill the vacant space. This included 8,700 bales of raw cotton beneath which were placed 1,000 drums of lubricating oil, some of which were leaking. This was, of course, extremely dangerous with explosives in the same hold. Captain Naismith objected, but his objections were ignored.

The *Fort Stikine* sailed in convoy from Karachi on 9 April and arrived in Bombay (now Mumbai) on the 12th. Because it was wartime, she did not fly the red flag to show that she carried a dangerous cargo, nor were the explosives discharged in the roads, and a pilot took her to No 1 berth in Victoria Dock. Shortly after 1.30pm on the 14th, smoke was seen in No 2 hold. The stevedores hastily left the hold, but although water was poured down it, cotton continued to smoulder and the fire brigade was summoned. As they were not told that there were explosives in the hold, only two 2 engines were sent, but when the news eventually reached them, another 8 were dispatched. As the situation deteriorated, even more hoses were played down the hold and the firemen were standing in near-boiling water. At 3.15pm the explosives caught fire and black smoke rose from the hold, but the firemen continued with their work until a huge flame rose above the height of the mast. The orders to 'Get clear' and 'Abandon ship' were given. Men jumped into the water or onto the quay where some sustained broken limbs. The first explosion occurred at 4.06pm and the second at 4.33pm. Two hundred and thirty-one people in the docks were killed, while another 476 were injured. Outside the port, 500 were killed and 2,408 injured.

Captain Naismith, the 1st Mate Mr W.D. Henderson and the 2nd Cook Mr A.K. Jopp were killed, but the others in the crew survived.

The port of Bombay was devastated. In addition to the *Fort Stikine*, the *Baroda, Fort Crevier, General Van Der Heijden* (Du.), *General Van Swieten* (Du.), *Tinombo* (Du.), *Graciosa* (Nor.), *Iran* (Pan.), *Jalapadma, Kingyuan* and *Rod El Farag* (Egypt) were destroyed and 16 more ships seriously damaged. It took almost 8,000 men 7 months to get the port back into operation. Sabotage was not suspected and the fire on the *Fort Stikine* may have been caused by the internal combustion of raw cotton stored above the explosives.

Radcliffe Shipping Co.

CLARISSA RADCLIFFE (Captain S.G. Finnes). Bound for Barrow-in-Furness with a cargo of iron ore, sailing from New York on 5 March 1943 in Convoy SC.122. Owing to bad weather, straggling from the convoy when torpedoed and sunk by U.663 (Kptlt Heinrich Schmid) at 3.40pm on the 18th in approximate position 42°00′N 62°00′W. All 55 died. (For details of other ships sunk in Convoy SC.122, see under *Port Auckland*, PORT LINE.)

ETHEL RADCLIFFE. Bound for London from Saint John, New Brunswick, sailing in Convoy SC.26 which left Halifax, Nova Scotia, on 20 March 1941. Dispersed from the convoy when torpedoed by an E-boat near No 6 buoy Great Yarmouth on the 17th and beached north of North Pier, Gorleston. Later bombed and became a total loss, but about 2,000 tons of wheat was salvaged. All 40 survived.

LLANARTH (Captain J.J. Perry). Bound independently for Melbourne from Aberdeen and Leith when torpedoed by U.30 (Kptlt Fritz-Julius Lemp) at 2am on 28 June 1940, and sank 2½ hours later in position 47°39′N 10°17′W. All 35 survived. Sixteen were picked up on the 30th by the corvette HMS *Gladiola* (Lt Cdr H.M.C. Sanders) and the remaining 19 by a Spanish trawler which landed them at San Sebastian.

LLANASHE (Captain J. Parry). Bound independently for Cape Town from Basrah, Bandar Abbas and Port Elizabeth when torpedoed and sunk by U.182 (Kptlt Asmus Nicolai Clausen) on 17 February 1943 in position 34°00′S 28°30′E. Thirty-three died. Mr S.P. Lloyd, the 1st Mate, and 8 others were picked up from a lifeboat by the *Tarakan* (Du.) on the 28th, transferred to British warships and landed at Cape Town on 4 March.

LLANCARFAN. Bound for Lisbon from Glasgow when bombed and sunk 2 miles south of Cape St Vincent on 30 May 1943. No further details.

LLANDILO (Captain W.R.B. Burgess). Loaded a military cargo in New York. Sailed independently from Trinidad on 9 October 1942 bound for Saldanha Bay, Durban and Bombay. Torpedoed and sunk by U.172 (Kptlt Carl Emmermann) at 9.43pm on 2 November in position 27°03′S 02°59′W. Twenty-four died. Twenty were picked up by the *Olaf Bergh* (Nor.) on the 7th and landed at Port of Spain, Trinidad, on the 26th.

LLANFAIR (Captain W. Evans). Bound for Avonmouth from Mackay in Queensland, sailing in Convoy SL.41 which left Freetown on 25 July 1940. Straggling when torpedoed and sunk by U.38 (Kptlt Heinrich Liebe) at 3.19pm on 11 August in position 54°48′N 13°46′W. Three died. Thirty were picked up by the *California* (US).

LLANISHEN (Captain J.E. Thomas). In Convoy OA.203 which sailed from Methil on 22 August 1940. Attacked by German bombers when about 20 miles south-east of Duncansby Head at about 10pm the following day and sank in position 58°17′N 02°27′W. Eight died. Twenty-eight survived. The *Beacon Grange* was damaged. (See also under *Makalla*, BROCKLEBANK LINE.)

LLANOVER (Captain L.A. Osborne). Bound for Halifax, sailing in Convoy ONS.92 which left Loch Ewe on 6 May 1942. Torpedoed by U.124 (Kptlt Johann Mohr) at 2.22am on the 12th and scuttled by the corvette HMCS *Arivida* (T/Lt A.I. MacKay) in position 52°50′N 29°04′W. All 46 were picked up by the rescue ship *Bury* (Captain L.E. Brown) and landed at St John's, Newfoundland, on the 16th.

OTHER SHIPS SUNK IN CONVOY ONS.92

Batna. See under STRICK LINE.

Cocle (Pan.). By U.94 (Oblt Otto Ites). Five died. Thirty-eight picked up by the *Bury*, but one man died of his injuries.

Cristales (Captain H. Roberts). By U.124. Thirty-seven picked up by HMCS *Shediac*. Forty-five picked up by the USCGC *Spencer* and landed at Boston. None died.

Empire Dell (Captain H. Mackinnon). By U.124 at the same time as the *Llanover*. Two died. Twenty-five picked up by the corvette HMCS *Shediac* (Lt J.E. Clayton), 21 by the *Bury* and all landed at St John's.

Mount Parnes (Gr.). Torpedoed by U.124 at the same time at the *Cristales*, but scuttled by the escort. All 33 rescued.

Tolken (Swed.). Torpedoed at 6.18am and 10.20am on the 13th by U.94. All 34 picked up by the *Bury*.

LLANWERN (Captain D. James). Sailed from Newport, Monmouthshire, to join Convoy OB.290 which left Liverpool on 23 February 1941. When the convoy was attacked by U.47 (Krvkpt. Günther Prien) and Focke-Wulf 200 Condors on the 26th the *Llanwern* was bombed and sank in position 56°17′N 17°06′W. Twenty-five died and 12 survived. (For details of other ships sunk in Convoy OB.290, see under *Mahanada*, BROCKLEBANK LINE.)

VERA RADCLIFFE. Sunk to form part of Gooseberry harbour No 4 at Juno Beach (between Saint-Aubin-sur-Mer and Courseulles-sur-Mer) during the Normandy landings in June 1944.

Reardon Smith Line

BARRDALE (Captain F.J. Stirling, ex-*Jersey City*). Sailed independently from New York on 9 May 1942 bound for Cape Town, Basrah and Abadan. Torpedoed by U.156 (Kptlt Werner Hartenstein) at 9.04pm on the 17th and sank within 10 minutes in position 15°15′N 52°27′W. DEMS Gunner C. Murray, Maritime Regiment Royal Artillery, died. Fifty-two were picked up by the *Rio de Iguazu* (Arg.) and landed at Pernambuco.

BARRWHIN (Captain T.S. Dixon). Bound for London, sailing in Convoy HX.212 which left Halifax on 18 October 1942. At about 11pm on the 27th, when the convoy was south-east of Cape Farewell, the southernmost point of Greenland, U-boats began an attack which continued for the next 2 days. At about 5.30pm on the 29th, the *Barrwhinn* picked up 60 survivors of the *Kosmos II*, but she was torpedoed and sunk by U.436 (Kptlt Günther Seibicke) at 9.18pm the same day in position 55°02′N 22°45′W. Twenty-four died, including 12 from the *Kosmos II*. Forty-two crew and 48 survivors of the *Kosmos II* were picked up from rafts by the corvette HMCS *Kenogami* (Lt P.J.B. Cook) the next morning and landed at Londonderry.

OTHER SHIPS SUNK IN CONVOY HX.212

Bic Island (Can.) (Captain J. Brown). By U.224 (Oblt Hans-Carl Kosbadt). All 165 on board died.

Kosmos II (Nor.) (Captain W. Kihl). Damaged by U.606 (Oblt Hans-Heinrich Döhler) on the 28th. Straggling and on fire when sunk by U.624 (Kptlt Graf Ulrich von Soden-Fraunhofen) shortly after 3am on the 29th. Fifty-two died, including the 12 picked up by the *Barrwhin*.

Gurney E Newlin (US) (Captain Herman Leon Dahlhof). Damaged by U.436 and abandoned. Sunk by U.606. Sixty died. Twelve picked up by HMCS *Alberni* and 44 by the *Bic Island*.

Pan-New York (US) (Captain H.V. Thompson). Badly damaged by U.624 and sunk by the corvettes HMCS *Rosthern* (T/Lt R.J.G. Johnson) and HMCS *Summerside* (T/Lt F.O. Gerity). Forty-two died. Thirteen picked up by HMCS *Rosthern*, but one died later. Two picked up by HMCS *Summerside*.

Sourabaya (Captain W. Dawson). By U.436. Eighty-one picked up by the corvettes HMCS *Alberni* (Lt A.W. Ford) and HMCS *Ville de Quebec* (Lt Cdr D.G. Jeffrey) and landed at Liverpool on 2 November. Seventy-seven picked up by *the Bic Island*.

(*Frontenac* (Nor.) (Captain W. Thorsen). Badly damaged by U.436, but succeeded in reaching Lamlash.)

BRADFYNE (Captain R.G. Vanner). Bound for Belfast from Montreal, sailing in Convoy SC.11 which left Sydney, Cape Breton, on 9 November 1940. Torpedoed and sunk by U.100 (Kptlt Joachim Schepke) at 1.17am on the 23rd in position 55°04′N 12°15′W. Thirty-nine died. Four were picked up from a lifeboat by the *Norse King* (Nor.) 2 days later and landed at Belfast.

OTHER SHIPS SUNK IN CONVOY SC.11 – ALL BY U.100 ON 23 NOVEMBER

Bruse (Nor.) (Captain Ole Brekke). Sixteen died. Five picked up by the destroyer HMCS *Skeena* (Lt Cdr J.C. Hibbard) and landed at Gourock on the 25th. Broke in two but after part, containing lumber, remained afloat and was subsequently towed to the shore.

Bussum (Du.) (Captain L. Wulp). All 29 picked up by the destroyer HMCS *Ottawa* (Cdr E.R. Mainguy).

Justitia (Captain D.L. Davies). Thirteen died. Twenty-six picked up by sloop HMS *Enchantress* (Cdr A.K. Scott-Moncrieff) and landed at Liverpool.

Leise Mærsk (Captain P.K. Mortensen). Seventeen died. Seven picked up by a Dutch salvage tug and landed at Campbeltown.

Ootmarsum (Du.) (Captain J. de Vries). With a cargo of iron ore, sank in seconds and all 25 died.

Salonica (Nor.) (Captain Ole G. Økland). Nine died. Nine rescued by HMCS *Skeena* and 7 by HMS *Enchantress*.

(The *Alma Dawson*, also in the convoy and bound for Ipswich, struck a mine and sank on the 24th, west of Islay in position 55°32′N 06°44′W. All 35 picked up by the *Spurt* (Nor.).)

BRADFORD CITY (Captain H. Paul). Independently bound for the UK from Port Louis, Mauritius, via Cape Town and Freetown when torpedoed 3 times and sunk by U.68 (Krvkpt. Karl-Friedrich Merten) at 6.54am on 1 November 1941 in position 22°59′S 09°49′E. When all 45 had abandoned the ship in 2 lifeboats, Merten enquired if they had water and gave them a course for the nearest land. The boats became separated, but both landed in Namibia where one group was spotted several days later by an SAAF plane and all were subsequently rescued.

BRADGLEN (Captain W. Lawday). Bound for London from Jacksonville, Florida, sailing in Convoy HX.146 which left Halifax on 21 August 1941. Struck a mine and sank 2 miles from B.3 Buoy off Barrow Deep in the Thames estuary on 19 September. Nine died. Survivors were picked up by HMS *Vivian* and landed at Sheerness.

CORNISH CITY. Bound for Aden and Suez, sailing from Durban on 22 July 1943 in Convoy DN.53. Dispersed from the convoy when torpedoed and sunk by U.177 (Krvkpt. Robert Gysae) at 9am on the 29th in position 27°20′S 52°10′E. Thirty-seven died. Six were picked up from rafts by the destroyer HMAS *Nizam* (Cdr C.H. Brooks) and landed at Port Louis, Mauritius.

DALLAS CITY (Captain Shalton). Sailed in Convoy OA.178 which left Southend on 3 July 1940. When south-east of Portland Bill on the afternoon of the 4th, struck by 3 bombs delivered by a 'Stuka' dive bomber. Severely damaged, she collided with the *Flimstone* and was abandoned. Some reports claim that all were rescued by the destroyer HMS *Shikari*, but a cook who was wounded states that they were picked up from 2 lifeboats by the damaged

Antonio. The *Dallas City* was still on fire the next day when taken in tow by a tug, but the attempt to save her failed. Several other ships were sunk and damaged in the attacks.

FRESNO CITY (I) (Captain R.A. Lawson). In Convoy HX.84 which sailed from Halifax on 28 October 1940 bound for the UK. The convoy was intercepted by the German pocket battleship *Admiral Scheer* (KptzS. Theodor Krancke) at 4.30pm on 5 November and she sank 7 ships, including the *Fresno City.* One man died, Mr D.R.H. Smith, and she sank the next day in position 51°47′N 33°29′W. Survivors were picked up the next day by the *Gloucester City* and landed at St John's, Newfoundland.

OTHER SHIPS IN CONVOY HX.84 SUNK BY THE SCHEER ON THE SAME DAY

Maidan. See under BROCKLEBANK LINE.

Beaverford. See under CANADIAN PACIFIC.

HMS *Jervis Bay.* See under SHAW SAVILL & ALBION.

Kenbane Head (Captain T.F. Milner). Twenty-three died.

Mopan. See under ELDERS & FYFFES.

Trewellard (Captain L. Daniel). Sixteen died. Twenty-five picked up by the *Gloucester City.*

(Other ships were damaged, including the *San Demetrio.* See under *Maidan.*)

FRESNO CITY (II) (Captain R.A. Lawson). Bound for Liverpool, sailing in Convoy HX.232 which left New York on 1 April 1943. Torpedoed and damaged at about 4.45am on the 12th by U.563 (Kptlt Götz von Hartmann). Straggling when torpedoed and sunk by U.706 (Kptlt Alexander von Zitzewitz) at 1.40pm in position 54°15′N 30°00′W. All 45 were picked up by the corvette HMS *Azalea* (Lt G.C. Geddes) and landed at Gourock.

OTHER SHIPS SUNK IN CONVOY HX.232

Edward B. Dudley (US) (Captain G.D. Hillary). By U.615 (Kptlt Ralph Kapitzky). Cargo of ammunition exploded. All 69 died.

Pacific Grove. See under FURNESS, WITHY GROUP.

Ulysses (Du.) (Captain H. Jonkman). By U.563. All 41 picked up by HMS *Azalea.*

HOUSTON CITY. Arriving from Rosario with a cargo of grain when she struck a mine north-east of the East Oaze Light Vessel in the Thames estuary on 21 October 1940. Beached and declared a total loss. No further details.

JERSEY CITY (Captain F.J. Stirling). Bound for Baltimore from Newport, Monmouthshire, sailing in Convoy OB.191 which left Liverpool on 30 July 1940. Torpedoed and sunk by U.99 (Kptlt Otto Kretschmer) at 1.24pm on the 31st in position 55°47′N 09°18′W. Two died. Forty-three were picked up by the *Gloucester City*, transferred to HMS *Walker* (Lt Cdr A.A. Tait) and landed at Liverpool. U.99 damaged the *Alexia*, *Lucerna* and *Strinda* (Nor.), but all reached Milford Haven unaided.

KING CITY (Captain H.W. Marshall). Bound for Singapore from Cardiff with a cargo of coal when sunk by the German raider *Atlantis* (KptzS. Bernhard Rogge) on 24 August 1940 in position 16°53′S 65°17′E. Four deck apprentices and a cabin boy were killed and the remaining 38 crew taken prisoner taken on board the *Atlantis* where one died while being operated on. Together with survivors from other vessels, those from the *King City* were transferred to the captured Yugoslav ship *Durmitor* on 26 November. (See under *Athelking*, ATHEL LINE.)

NEW WESTMINSTER CITY (Captain W.J. Harris). Bound for Murmansk in Convoy PQ.13 which sailed from Loch Ewe on 10 March 1942 from Reykjavik on the 20th and arrived on the 31st. Bombed and sunk in Murmansk on 3 April. Two died and 50 survived. Salvaged post war.

SHIPS SUNK IN PQ.13

Bateau (Pan.) (Captain Johan A. Haltlid). Sunk by the German destroyer Z26 on the 29th. Thirty-nine died and 7 became PoWs. Z26 was subsequently sunk by the cruiser HMS *Trinidad* (Captain L.S. Saunders).

Effingham (US) (Captain C.H. Hewlett). Torpedoed and sunk by U.435 (Kptlt Siegfried Strelow) on the 30th. Twelve died and 31 survived.

Empire Ranger (Captain M.E. Sadler). Bombed and sunk on the 28th. All 55 became PoWs.

Empire Starlight. See under ROPNER SHIPPING CO.

Induna (Captain W.N. Collins). Torpedoed and sunk by U.376 (Friedrich Karl Marks) on the 30th. Thirty-one died and 28 survived.

Raceland (Panamanian flag, but not a Panamanian on board) (Captain Sverre Brekke). Bombed and sunk on 28th. Thirty-two died. Twelve became PoWs.

(Owing to frostbite, many of those who survived had limbs amputated. For example, 6 of the survivors of the *Raceland* lost both legs.)

PRINCE RUPERT CITY. Bound for the St Lawrence from Hull and in Convoy EC.26 which left Southend on 29 May 1941. Damaged by German aircraft when 13 miles north-east of Cape Wrath on 2 June. Abandoned and sank in position 58°46′N 04°41′W. Four died and 40 survived. The *Fernbank* (Nor.) (Captain Johan Severin Nygaard) was damaged, but made it to Aberdeen.

QUEBEC CITY (Captain W.C. Thomas). Bound independently for the UK from Alexandria and Cape Town. Heading for Freetown when torpedoed and sunk by gunfire by U.156 (Krvkpt. Werner Hartenstein) at 3.46pm on 19 September 1942 in position 02°12′S 17°36′W. Five died. Forty-one were picked up by the destroyer HMS *Decoy* (Lt Cdr G.I.M. Balfour) and landed at Freetown.

QUEEN CITY (Captain G. Hornsby). Sailed independently from Bombay (now Mumbai) bound for the UK via Cape Town and Trinidad, sailing from Cape Town on 30 November 1942. Torpedoed and sunk by gunfire by the Italian submarine *Enrico Tazzoli* (C.C. Carlo Fecia di Cossato) on 21 December when east of Para, Brazil, in position 00°49′S 41°34′W. Five died. Steward J.F. Osborne taken prisoner. Forty landed from lifeboats near São Luís, Maranhão, Brazil.

SACRAMENTO VALLEY (Captain H.L. Sharp). Bound for Pernambuco from Cardiff, sailing in Convoy OB.324 which left Liverpool on 18 May 1941 and dispersed on the 27th in position 53°00′N 29°30′W. Torpedoed and sunk by U.106 (Kptlt Jürgen Oesten) at 5.03am on 6 June in position 17°10′N 30°10′W. Three died. Thirty-nine were picked up by the *Caithness* and landed at Freetown on the 14th. Seven others picked up by the *Stanvac Cape Town* (Pan.) on the 24th were landed at Aruba on 3 July. The *Elmdene* (Captain E. Fear), also dispersed from Convoy OB.324, was torpedoed and sunk by U.103 (Krvkpt. Viktor Schütze) on the 8th. All were picked up by the *Carlton* and landed at Cape Town.

SANTA CLARA VALLEY. Bombed and sunk in Nauplia Bay, Greece, on 23 April 1941. Seven died. Raised and towed to Trieste to be scrapped in 1952.

TACOMA CITY. Sunk by parachute mine which exploded beneath her when in the Formby Channel of the River Mersey on 13 March 1941. Four died; 41 were picked up by a motorboat from the training ship HMS *Conway* and transferred to other larger boats for landing.

VANCOUVER CITY (Captain H.C. Egerton). Independently bound for the UK from Suva in Fiji when torpedoed and sunk by U.28 (Oblt Günter Kuhnke) at 10am on 14 September 1939 in position 51°23′N 07°03′W. Three died. Thirty-two were picked up by the Dutch tanker *Mamura* and landed at Liverpool.

VERNON CITY (Captain M.D. Loutit). Bound for Montevideo, dispersed from Convoy OS.49 when torpedoed and sunk by U.172 (Kptlt Carl Emmermann) at 6.43am on 28 June 1943 in position 04°30′S 27°30′W. All 52 were picked up by the *Aurora M* (Braz.) and landed at Pernambuco on 4 July.

VICTORIA CITY (Captain A. Longstaff). Bound for London with a cargo of steel, sailing in the New York section of Convoy HX.90 which left on 17 November 1940 and rendezvoused with the other sections on the 24th. Straggling when torpedoed by U.140 (Oblt Hans-Peter Hinsch) at 9.42pm on 3 December and sank within 15 seconds in position 55°12′N 10°20′W. All 43 died. (For details of other ships sunk and damaged in Convoy HX.90, see under *Tasso*, ELLERMAN GROUP.)

WILLAMETTE VALLEY. Requisitioned by the Admiralty and renamed HMS *Edgehill* (Cdr R.E.D. Ryder), a decoy ship with concealed armament and a buoyant cargo to help keep her afloat. Torpedoed 3 times by U.51 (Kptlt Dietrich Knorr) between 0016 and 0124 hours on 29 June 1940 and sank in position 49°27′N 15°25′W. Sixty-seven died and 24 survived.

Managed for Ministry of War Transport

BOTAVON (Captain J.H.R. Smith). Commodore ship bound for Murmansk in Convoy PQ.15 which sailed from Oban on 10 April 1942 from Reykjavik on the 26th and arrived on 5 May. In position 73°02′N 19°46′E at 11.27pm on 2 May when severely damaged by an aerial torpedo and abandoned. Wreck sunk by the destroyer HMS *Badsworth* (Lt G.T.S. Gray) the next day. Twenty-one died. Commodore Captain H.J. Archer and Yeoman of Signals A.R. Marriott were picked up by ASW trawler HMS *Cape Palliser* and the others by either HMS *Badsworth* or the ASW trawler HMS *Chiltern* (Skipper A. Mair). A total of 137 were picked up from the *Botavon*, *Jutland* and *Cape Corso* by HMS *Badsworth* and HMS *Chiltern*.

OTHER SHIPS SUNK IN CONVOY PQ.15

Alcoa Cadet (US). Sunk by a mine after arrival in Murmansk. One died.

Cape Corso. See under LYLE SHIPPING CO.

Jastrzab (Pol.) (Cdr Boleslaw Romanowski). Submarine detected outside her allotted patrol area by the minesweeper HMS *Seagull* and the Norwegian destroyer *St Albans*. Believing her to be a U-boat, mistakenly sank her. Five died.

Jutland (Captain J. Henderson). Severely damaged by an aerial torpedo on the 2nd and abandoned. One passenger died. Sixty-two picked up by HMS *Chiltern* and landed at Murmansk. Wreck sunk by U.251 (Kptlt Heinrich Timm) on the 3rd.

HMS *Punjabi*, one of the warships providing distant cover for the convoy, sunk after colliding with the battleship HMS *King George V* in dense fog on 1 May. Forty-nine died and 209 were rescued. The bow of HMS *King George V* was severely holed.

(HMS *Cape Palliser* was damaged and one German plane shot down.)

BOTUSK. In Convoy HX.103 which sailed from Halifax on 15 January 1941 bound for the UK. Struck a mine and sank 6 miles north-east of Rona Island, about 44 miles north of the Butt of Lewis, on the 31st. Four died. Eleven were rescued by the corvette HMS *Verbena* (Lt Cdr D.A. Rayner) and landed at the Clyde the next day. The *Emmaplein* (Du.) (Captain S. Plantenga) also sunk by a mine. All 34 were rescued by the cable ship *Ariel* and two corvettes. The convoy ran into a British minefield.

CAROLINA THORDÉN (Ex-Finnish). Independently bound for New York from Petsamo when badly damaged in an air attack by German Heinkel bombers off the Faroe Islands on 26 March 1941. One passenger died. Eight passengers were picked up by the *Venezuela* (Swed.) bound for Rio de Janeiro and died, together with her crew of 41, when she was torpedoed and sunk by U.123 (Kptlt Karl-Heinz Moehle) on 17 April. No information regarding other survivors. Beached in Thorshaven Bay and subsequently sunk as a blockship at Scapa Flow. Raised and scrapped in 1949.

EMPIRE CARIBOU (Captain B.E. Duffield). Bound for Boston, Massachusetts, sailing in Convoy OB.318 which left Liverpool on 2 May 1941. Torpedoed and sunk by U.556 (Kptlt Herbert Wohlfarth) at 7.52am on the 10th in position 59°28′N 35°44′W shortly after dispersal of the convoy. Thirty-four died. Eleven were picked up by the destroyer HMS *Malcolm* (Cdr C.D. Howard-Johnston), and landed at Reykjavik. (For details of other ships sunk before and after the dispersal of Convoy OB.318, see under *Ixion*, HOLT, ALFRED, & CO.)

EMPIRE JAGUAR (Captain H.T. Thomas, ex-*Empire Toucan*). Bound for Philadelphia from Cardiff, sailing in Convoy OB.252 which left Liverpool on 30 November 1940 and dispersed in bad weather on 4 December. Torpedoed and sunk by U.103 (Krvkpt. Viktor Schütze) at 1.32am on the 9th when in position 51°34'N 17°35'W. All 37 died.

OTHER SHIPS SUNK AFTER DISPERSAL OF CONVOY OB.252

Farsum (Du.) (Captain B. Jansma). By U.99 (Kptlt Otto Kretschmer). Sixteen died. Nineteen eventually picked up from a lifeboat by the destroyer HMS *Ambuscade* (Lt Cdr R.A. Fell), but 4 died from frostbite.

Silverpine. See under SILVER LINE.

Skrim (Nor.) (Captain Max Emil Gran). Never seen after 4 December; all 21 died. U.43 (Oblt Wolfgang Lüth) sank an unidentified ship on the 6th which is thought to have been her.

EMPIRE KESTREL. In Convoy UGS.13 which sailed from Hampton Roads, Virginia, on 27 July 1943. Sunk by an aerial torpedo from an Italian plane piloted by Tenente (Lt) Vezio Terzi on 16 August when off the coast of Algeria in position 37°10'N 04°35'E. Nine died and 30 survived. The RFA *Oligarch* was damaged, but succeeded in reaching Alexandria.

EMPIRE TOUCAN (Captain H.T. Thomas). Bound independently for Port Sulphur, Louisiana, from Garston when she came under gunfire from U.47 (Kptlt Günther Prien) at 5.15am on 29 June 1940. Torpedoed 20 minutes later and broke in two in position 49°20'N 13°52'W. First Radio Officer M.R. Gerard, 2nd Radio Officer E.R. Campbell and Fireman F. Roberts died. Thirty-one were picked up by the destroyer HMS *Hurricane* (Lt Cdr H.C. Simms) which sank the fore part of the ship.

FORT MÉDINE (Captain Louis Rabour). Bound for Port Talbot from Wabana in Newfoundland with a cargo of iron ore, having crossed the Atlantic in Convoy SC.21 which sailed from Halifax on 31 January 1941. Struck a mine in the Bristol Channel on 20 February, broke in two and sank in position 51°35'N 03°56'W. Captain Rabour was seriously injured and died 2 days later. Forty-six survived.

OTHER SHIPS SUNK IN CONVOY SC.21

Alnmoor (Captain A. Edwards). Straggling in a gale when torpedoed and sunk by U.123 (Kptlt Karl-Heinz Moehle) at 0038 hours on the 15th. All 55 died.

Belcrest. Straggling when torpedoed and sunk by the Italian submarine *Michele Bianchi* on the 14th. All 36 died.

Elisabeth Marie (Trawler). Straggling when sunk by aircraft on 14 February. One died. Twenty-four survived.

Middleton. Sunk on the 18th in collision with the *Tungsha* (Nor.), which was not in the convoy. None died.

FORT MUMFORD (Captain J.H.R. Smith, ex-*Botavon*). On her maiden voyage, bound for Alexandria from Vancouver and Lyttleton, New Zealand, bunkered at Colombo and sailed from there on 15 March 1943. Torpedoed and sunk by the Japanese submarine I-27 (Lt Cdr Toshiaki Fukumura) on the 20th in approximate position 10°N 71°E. Survivors machine-gunned in the lifeboats. Fifty-two died. The sole survivor was DEMS Gunner H. Bailey, picked up by an Arab dhow and landed at Mikindani in Tanganyika (now Tanzania). After sinking the *Kedive Mail* on 12 February 1944, I-27, still commanded by Fukumura, was sunk by the destroyers HMS *Paladin* and HMS *Petard*. All died.

FORT NORFOLK (Captain G. Hornsby). Leaving the anchorage at Juno Beach, Normandy, when she struck a mine at 8.17am on 24 June 1944. Seven engine room staff and RN DEMS Gunner A.J. Paterson, C/JX 291281, died. The remaining 65, including 6 injured, were picked up from a lifeboat and the water by motor launches, transferred to the Norwegian destroyer *Stord* and landed at Portsmouth that night.

MYSON (Ex-French). Sailed in Convoy OB.294 which left Liverpool on 5 March 1941 and dispersed in position 51°29'N 20°30'W on the 9th. Sunk by the German battleship *Gneisenau* (flagship of Admiral Günther Lütjens) south-east of Cape Race at 1.25pm on the 16th in approximate position 42°N 43°W. All 43 were taken prisoner. (For details of the many ships sunk and captured by the *Scharnhorst* and the *Gneisenau* after dispersal of the convoy, see under *British Strength*, BRITISH TANKER CO. LTD.)

Ropner Shipping Co.

AINDERBY (Captain G.R. Cobb). Bound for the Tyne from Santos and sailing independently when torpedoed and sunk shortly before 11pm on 10 June 1941 by U.552 (Oblt Erich Topp) in position 55°30'N 12°10'W. Twelve died. Twenty-nine were picked up by the destroyer HMS *Veteran* (Cdr W.E.J. Eames) and landed at Greenock.

ALDERPOOL (Captain T.V. Frank). Bound for Hull from New York, sailing in Convoy SC.26 which left Halifax, Nova Scotia, on 20 March 1941. Torpedoed by U.46 (Oblt Engelbert Endrass) at 0042 hours on 3 April and abandoned. Sunk by U.73 (Kptlt Helmut Rosenbaum) at 3.28am. All 41 were picked up by the *Thirlby*, which was damaged about 5 hours later by U.69 (Kptlt Jost Metzler) but succeeded in reaching Loch Ewe. Two of her crew died.

OTHER SHIPS SUNK IN CONVOY SC.26

2 April:

British Reliance. See under BRITISH TANKER CO. LTD.

3 April:

British Viscount. See under BRITISH TANKER CO. LTD.

Indier (Belg.) (Captain J. Onghena). By U.73. Forty-two died. Four picked up and landed at Liverpool.

Leonidas Z Cambanis (Gr.). By U.74 (Kptlt Eitel-Friedrich Kentrat). Two died and 27 survived.

Westpool. See under ROPNER SHIPPING CO.

(The AMC HMS *Worcestershire* was damaged by U.74 (Kptlt Eitel-Friedrich Kentrat) on the 3rd.)

4 April:

Athenic (Captain E.W. Agnes). By U.76 (Kptlt Friedrich von Hippel). All 40 picked up by the corvette *Arbutus* (Lt A.L. Warren) and landed at Liverpool.

Harbledown (Captain G. Jones). By U.94 (Kptlt Herbert Kuppisch). Sixteen died. Twenty-three picked up by HMS *Veteran* (Cdr W.T. Conchman) and landed at Liverpool.

Helle (Nor.) (Captain Karl Jørgensen). By U.98 (Kptlt Robert Gysae). All 24 picked up by HMS *Havelock*.

Welcombe (Captain R.E. Johnson). By U.98. Twenty died and 21 picked up by HMS *Havelock*.

17 April:

Ethel Radcliffe. See under RADCLIFFE SHIPPING CO.

ASHBY (Captain T.V. Frank). Bound for Pepel, Sierra Leone, and in Convoy OS.12 which sailed from the UK on 18 November 1941. Developed engine trouble and straggled from the convoy. Torpedoed by U.43 (Kptlt Wolfgang Lüth) at about 7.30pm on the 30th in position 36°54′N 29°51′W. Sank within minutes and 17 died. After a week in a lifeboat, Captain Frank, who had survived the sinking of the *Alderpool*, and 27 others landed at Fayal in the Azores and were eventually taken to Lisbon. (See also under *Thornliebank*, WEIR, ANDREW, & CO./BANK LINE.)

BOULDERPOOL. In ballast and in a coastal convoy bound for the Tyne from London when attacked by German E-boats on 7 March 1941. Torpedoed by S.61 near Cromer in position 52°58′N 01°28′E. Broke in two, the fore part sank and the stern grounded on Scroby Sands. All survived. The *Kenton* and *Corduff* were also sunk with the loss of 4 and 7 lives respectively.

CARPERBY (Captain F. Gardiner). Bound for Buenos Aires and dispersed from Convoy ON.66 which sailed from Liverpool on 13 February 1942. Torpedoed and sunk by U.558 (Kptlt Victor Vogel) at 2am on 1 March in position 39°57′N 55°40′W. All 40 died. *Empire Hail* (Captain R. Jones), also dispersed from the convoy, was torpedoed and sunk by U.94 (Oblt Otto Ites) on 24 February. All 49 died.

CRITON (Captain Gerald Dobeson). Formerly a Vichy French ship captured by the AMC HMS *Cilicia* on 9 May 1941 and taken to Freetown. With a scratch crew of Distressed British Seamen (DBS), sailed from Freetown in Convoy SL.78 on 18 June, but unable to maintain convoy speed, was returning to Freetown unescorted when intercepted by the Vichy French warships *Air France IV* and *Edith Germaine*. Sunk by the *Air France IV* on the 21st and the crew taken to Conakry after which they suffered the worst treatment meted out to British merchant seamen by the Vichy French, serving the longest period of internment in French West Africa and not arriving home until 15 January 1943. Three died during internment and a fourth later died from an illness contracted during it. Although the French never apologised for the treatment of the internees, they made a reparations payment to the British Government. The payment, however, was not passed on to those involved.

OTHER SHIPS SUNK IN CONVOY SL.78

27 June:

Empire Ability. See under ELDER DEMPSTER LINE.

Oberon (Du.) (Captain E.O.J. Jans). By U.123 (Kptlt Reinhard Hardegen). Six died and 28 picked up.

P.L.M. 22 (Ex-French) (Captain Yves Le Bitter). By U.123. Thirty-two died. Twelve picked up by the corvette HMS *Armeria* (Lt Cdr H.M. Russell), transferred to the corvette HMS *Asphodel* (Lt Cdr K.W. Steward) and landed at Freetown on 4 July.

River Lugar (Captain W. Frame). By U.69. Thirty-eight died and 6 picked up by HMS *Burdock*.

29 June:

River Azul (Captain T.V. Sutherland). By U.123. Thirty-three died. Nine picked up by the AMC HMS *Esperance Bay* (Capt. G.S. Holden) and landed at Scapa Flow.

George J. Goulandris (Gr.). By U.66 (Krvkpt. Richard Zapp). Two lifeboats were provisioned by the U-boat and all 28 survived.

Kalypso Vergotti (Gr.). By U.66. Cargo of iron ore and sank within a minute. Although the U-boat saw men alive in the water, all 36 died.

30 June:

Saint Anselm (Captain T. Ross). By U.66. Thirty-four died. Eighteen picked up by the AMC HMS *Moreton Bay* (Captain C.C. Bell) and landed at Freetown on 13 July. Fifteen others picked up by the *Tom* (Sp.) and landed at Buenos Aires.

DALEBY (Captain J.E. Elsdon). In Convoy SC.107 which sailed from Halifax on 24 October 1942. Torpedoed and sunk by U.89 (Krvkpt Dietrich Lohmann) at 10.35pm on 4 November in position 57°24′N 35°54′W. All 47 were picked up by the Icelandic ship *Brúarfoss* and landed at Reykjavik. (For details of other ships sunk in Convoy SC.107, see under *Jeypore*, P&O.)

FIRBY (Captain T. Prince). Sailing independently and bound for Churchill in Hudson Bay when sunk by gunfire and torpedoed by U.48 (Kptlt Herbert Schultze) at 3.40pm on 11 September 1939 in position 59°40′N 13°50′W. All 34 were picked up by the destroyer HMS *Fearless* (Cdr K.L. Harkness) and landed at Scapa Flow the next day.

FISHPOOL (Captain Cole). In Syracuse, Sicily, loaded with ammunition and drums of petrol brought from Alexandria when German planes attacked the port on 26 August 1943. Struck amidships and abandoned; blew up after receiving 2 more direct hits. Twenty-eight died and 18 survived.

HAWNBY. On passage from the Tyne to Gibraltar when sunk by a mine on 20 April 1940 in position 51°32′N 01°13′E. All 39 were rescued by MTB4. The *Mersey* (Captain W. Rockett) was also sunk by a mine on the same day. Fourteen died and 7 were taken to Ramsgate.

HAXBY (Captain C. Rundell). Bound for Corpus Christi in Texas, sailing from the Clyde on 8 April 1940 and joined Convoy OG.25 which formed at sea on the 10th. Dispersed from the convoy and sailing independently when intercepted and sunk by the German raider *Orion* (Krvkpt. Kurt Weyher) on the 24th in position 31°30′N 51°30′W. Seventeen died and 24 were taken on board the *Orion*, but together with other prisoners were transferred to the Norwegian ship *Tropic Sea* (Captain Henrik Nicolaysen) after she was captured on 18 June. Under a prize crew and heading for Bordeaux, the *Tropic Sea* was intercepted and scuttled by the submarine HMS *Truant* (Lt Cdr H.A.V. Haggard) on 3 September in the Bay of Biscay. The *Truant* carried 25 of the released prisoners to Gibraltar, while a Sunderland Flying Boat of Coastal Command rescued some Norwegians. Twenty-one others were landed from a lifeboat at Corunna in neutral Spain on the 7th. The prize crew also landed in Spain, from where they were repatriated to Germany.

HERONSPOOL (Captain S.E. Batson). Bound for Montreal from Swansea, sailing in Convoy OB.17 which left Liverpool on 9 October 1939 and dispersed on the 12th. Sailing independently when torpedoed and sunk by gunfire from U.48 (Kptlt Herbert Schultze) shortly after 1am on the 13th in position 50°13′N 14°48′W. The entire crew were picked up by the *President Harding* (US) and landed at New York. U.48 also sank the *Louisiane* (Fr.) on the 13th. One died and the remainder were picked up by the *Imogen*.

The *Stonepool* (Captain A. White), also dispersed from Convoy OB.17, was damaged by gunfire from U.42 (Kptlt Rolf Dau) at 8.30am on the 13th in position 48°40′N 15°30′W. Forced to dive quickly to escape the returned gunfire, the U-boat's gun crew were thrown into the water but she surfaced shortly afterwards to retrieve them. Meanwhile, the *Stonepool* transmitted an SSSS message. This brought the destroyers HMS *Ilex* (Lt Cdr P.L. Saumarez) and HMS *Imogen* (Cdr E.B.K. Stevens) to her assistance, and at about 7pm they located and sank the U-boat. Twenty-five of the U-boat's crew died and 17 were picked up by the *Ilex*. (See also *Stonepool*, below.)

HINDPOOL (Captain M.V.A. Tinnock). Bound for Middlesbrough from Pepel, sailing from Freetown in Convoy SL.67 on 1 March 1941. Torpedoed and sunk by U.124 (Kptlt Georg-Wilhelm Schultz) at about 6am on the 8th in position 20°51′N 20°32′W. Twenty-eight died. Six were picked up by the destroyer HMS *Faulknor* (Capt. A.F. de Salis) and landed at Gibraltar on the 16th. Six others picked up by the *Guido*. (For details of other ships sunk in Convoy SL.67, see under *Nardana*, BRITISH INDIA STEAM NAVIGATION CO.)

KIRKPOOL (Captain Kennington). Bound for Montevideo, sailing independently from Durban on 31 March 1942. Intercepted, shelled and torpedoed by the German raider *Thor* (KptzS. Günther Gumprich) at about 8pm on 10 April 1942 and abandoned. Seventeen died and the others were picked up from the water by the *Thor* before she sank the ship with another torpedo.

On board the *Thor*, the survivors joined those from the *Wellpark*, *Willesden* and the *Aust* (Nor.) and later by those from the Australian ship *Nankin*, sunk on 10 May. The *Thor* subsequently rendezvoused with the *Dresden* and all the women and children from the *Nankin*, plus the wounded and some seamen, were transferred to her. On 14 May, the remainder of the prisoners were transferred to the *Regensburg* which, with 200–300 prisoners on board, called at various ports in the Dutch East Indies before heading for Yokohama where she arrived on 7 July. All the prisoners were then transferred to the German ship *Ramses* where they remained in the custody of German guards until handed over to the Japanese on 25 August. At all times the prisoners were well treated by the Germans, but it was a very different story when they were under the Japanese, where they remained until they were brought home by both air and sea at the end of the war. Many, however, did not survive the ordeal and, like Captain Kennington, died in captivity.

LACKENBY (Captain W.A. Allen). Bound for London, sailing in Convoy SC.117 which left New York on 12 January 1943. Straggling when torpedoed and sunk by U.624 (Kptlt Graf Ulrich von Soden-Fraunhofen) on the 25th in position 55°N 37°50′W. All 44 died. The *Mount Mycale* (Gr.), also straggling from the convoy, was torpedoed and sunk by U.413 (Kptlt Gustav Poel) on the 22nd. No survivors.

MANSEPOOL (Captain H. R. Clark). Bound for Halifax, Nova Scotia, from Cardiff, sailing in Convoy OB.289 which left Liverpool on 20 February 1941. Torpedoed and sunk by U.97 (Kptlt Udo Heilmann) shortly after 2am on the 24th in position 61°10′N 11°55′W. Two died. Seventeen were picked up by the corvette HMS *Petunia* (Lt Cdr G.V. Legassick) and 22 by the *Thomas Holt*. The 22 were subsequently transferred to the *Petunia* which landed all the survivors at Stornoway on the 27th.

OTHER SHIPS SUNK AND DAMAGED IN CONVOY OB.289 – ALL BY U.97

British Gunner (Captain J.W. Kemp). Three died and 41 picked up by the *Petunia*.

G.C. Brøvig (Nor.). Damaged but reached Stornoway with the assistance of the *Petunia*.

Jonathan Holt (Captain W. Stephenson). Fifty-one died. Three picked up by the *Petunia*. Three others picked up by the rescue ship *Copeland* (Captain W.J. Hartley) and landed at Greenock.

OTTERPOOL (Captain T. Prince). Bound for Middlesbrough from Bône, sailing in Convoy HGF.34 which left Gibraltar on 13 June 1940. Torpedoed and sunk by U.30 (Kptlt Fritz-Julius Lemp) at 2.12am on the 20th in position 48°45′N 08°13′W. Twenty-three died. Fifteen were picked up by the sloop HMS *Scarborough* (Cdr C.T. Addis) and landed at Liverpool. (For details of other ships sunk in Convoy HGF.34, see under *British Monarch*, BRITISH TANKER CO. LTD.)

PIKEPOOL. Bound for Barry from Glasgow when sunk by a mine 23 miles ESE of the Smalls Light, Pembrokeshire, on 22 November 1940. Seventeen died, but no further details.

REEDPOOL (Captain W.J. Downs). Sailing independently and bound for Fernandina, Florida, from Massawa via Cape Town and Trinidad on 13 September 1942 when she picked up 16 survivors from the *Medon* (Captain S.R. Evans) sunk by the Italian submarine *Reginaldo Giuliani* (C.F. Giovanni Bruno) on 10 August. At 8.15pm on 20 September she herself was torpedoed and sunk by U.515 (Kptlt Werner Henke) in position 08°58′N 57°34′W. Six of her crew died while Captain Downs was taken prisoner and subsequently landed at Lorient. The remaining 50, including the 16 from the *Medon*, were picked up from a lifeboat by the schooner *Millie M Masher* (Captain F. Barnes) and landed at Georgetown in British Guiana on the 24th. (See under *Medon*, HOLT, ALFRED, & CO.)

ROMANBY (Captain H. Nicholson). Sunk in Narvik harbour on 10 April 1940 and her crew of 34 taken prisoner. After being forced to march to the Swedish border in extremely cold weather they were interned in Gothenburg, but 2 years later, Captain Nicholson and 13 others sailed on 2 Norwegian ships trying to reach the UK. Their attempt was unsuccessful and resulted in them being taken to the Milag Nord camp in Germany as PoWs. Captain Nicholson died in the camp on 28 December 1942, but others were repatriated in April 1945.

ROXBY (Captain G. Robinson). Bound for Halifax, Nova Scotia, from Cardiff, sailing in Convoy ON.142 which left Liverpool on 30 October 1942. Straggled, torpedoed and sunk by U.613 (Kptlt Helmut Köppe) at 3.40pm on 7 November in position 49°35′N 30°32′W. Thirty-four died. Thirteen were picked up by the *Irish Beech* and landed at St John's, Newfoundland. The *Glenlea* (Captain J.R. Nicol), also a straggler from ON.142, was sunk on the same day by U.566 (Kptlt Gerhard Remus). Forty-four died. Captain Nicol was taken prisoner and subsequently landed at Brest. Four were rescued from a lifeboat 3 weeks later by the *Thorstrand* (Nor.) and landed at New York.

RUSHPOOL (Captain W.G. Stewart). Bound for Belfast from Saint John, New Brunswick, sailing in Convoy SC.19 which left Halifax, Nova Scotia, on 12 January 1941. Straggled, torpedoed and sunk by U.94 (Kptlt Herbert Kuppisch) at about 3am on the 30th in position 56°N 15°42′W. All 40 were picked up by the destroyer HMS *Antelope* (Lt Cdr R.T. White) and landed at Greenock.

OTHER SHIPS SUNK IN CONVOY SC.19

Aikaterini (Gr.). By U.93 (Kptlt Claus Korth). All 30 survived.

Sesostris (Egyp.) By U.106 (Oblt Jürgen Oesten). No survivors.

King Robert (Captain L. Trail). By U.93. All 42 picked up by the destroyer HMS *Anthony* (Lt Cdr V.C.F. Clark) and ASW trawler HMS *Lady Madeleine* (Lt P.H. Potter) and landed at Gourock.

W.B. Walker (Captain M.B. Simpson). By U.93. Four died. Forty-three picked up by HMS *Anthony* and HMS *Antelope* but transferred to the ASW trawler HMS *Arab* which landed them at Gourock.

West Wales (Captain F.C. Nicholls). By U.94. Sixteen died. Twenty-one picked up by the *Antelope* and *Anthony*.

SALMONPOOL (Captain C. Yare). Seized in Narvik on 15 April 1940 and the crew of 37 taken prisoner. Renamed *Putzig* and sailed under the German flag until retaken in 1945. Renamed *Empire Salmonpool* and managed by Ropner until sold in 1947.

SEDGEPOOL (Captain R.B. Witten). Bound for Manchester from Montreal, sailing in Convoy SC.7 which left Sydney, Cape Breton, on 5 October 1940. Torpedoed and sunk at about 2am on the 19th by U.123 (Kptlt Karl-Heinz Moehlein) in position 57°20′N 11°22′W. Three died. Thirty-six were picked up by the rescue tug HMS *Salvonia* (Lt G.M.M. Dickinson) and landed at Gourock.

OTHER SHIPS SUNK AND DAMAGED IN CONVOY SC.7

16 October:

Trevisa (Can.) (Captain R.C. Stonehouse). By U.124 (Kptlt Georg-Wilhelm Schulz). Seven died. Fourteen picked up by the corvette HMS *Bluebell* (Lt Cdr R.E. Sherwood) and landed at Gourock on the 20th.

17 October:

Aenos (Gr.). By U.38 (Kptlt Heinrich Liebe). Four died. Twenty-five picked up by the *Eaglescliffe Hall* (Can.) and landed in Gourock the following day.

Languedoc (Captain J. Thomson). By U.48 (Kptlt Heinrich Bleichrodt). All 39 picked up by HMS *Bluebell*.

Scoresby (Captain L.Z. Weatherill). By U.48. All 39 picked up by HMS *Bluebell*.

18 October:

Beatus (Captain W.L. Brett). By U.46 (Oblt Engelbert Endrass). All 37 picked up by HMS *Bluebell*.

Blairspey. Damaged by U.101 (Kptlt Fritz Frauenheim).

Boekelo (Du.). Damaged by U.100 (Kptlt Joachim Schepke).

Carsbreck. Damaged by U.38 (Kptlt Heinrich Liebe).

Convallaria (Swed.). By U.46. Crew picked up by the sloop HMS *Fowey* (Lt C.G. deL. Bush) and landed at Greenock.

Creekirk (Captain E. Robilliard). By U.101. All 36 died.

Empire Miniver (Captain R. Smith). By U.99. Three died and 35 picked up by HMS *Bluebell*.

Fiscus (Captain E. Williams). By U.99. Thirty-eight died and a man was later found on floating debris and taken into a lifeboat containing men from the *Snefjeld* (Nor.). All rescued by the corvette HMS *Clematis* (Cdr Y.M. Cleeves) on the 23rd.

Gunborg (Swed.). By U.46. All 23 picked up by HMS *Bluebell*.

Niritos (Gr.). By U.99. One died and 27 survived.

19 October:

Assyrian (Captain R.S. Kearon). By U.101. Seventeen died. Thirty-four picked up by the sloop HMS *Leith* (Cdr R.C. Allen) and landed at Liverpool.

Blairspey. Straggling when damaged by U.100, but her cargo of timber kept her afloat and she was towed to the Clyde on the 25th.

Boekelo (Du.). By U.123 when stopped to pick up survivors of the *Beatus*. All 25 picked up by HMS *Fowey*.

Clintonia. See under STAG LINE.

Empire Brigade (Captain S.W. Parks). Six died and 35 picked up by HMS *Fowey*.

Shekatika (Captain R. Paterson). By U.123 (Kptlt Karl-Heinz Moehle). All 36 picked up by HMS *Fowey*.

Snefjeld (Nor.) (Captain Finn Skage). By U.99. All 21 picked up by HMS *Clematis*.

Soesterberg (Du.). By U.101. Six died and 19 picked up by HMS *Leith*.

Thalia (Gr.). By U.99. Twenty-two died and 4 survived.

SOMERSBY (Captain J.W. Thompson). Bound for Hull, sailing in Convoy SC.30 which left Halifax, Nova Scotia, on 29 April 1941. Straggling when torpedoed and sunk by U.111 (Kptlt Wilhelm Kleinschmidt) at 11.41am on 13 May in position 60°39′N 26°13′W. All 43 were picked up by the *Marika Protopapa* (Gr.) and landed at Loch Ewe. (For HMS *Salopian*, also sunk in Convoy SC.30, see under *Shropshire*, BIBBY LINE.)

STONEPOOL (Captain J.H. Nicholson). Bound for Avonmouth from Montreal, sailing in Convoy SC.42 which left Sydney, Cape Breton, on 30 August 1941. Torpedoed and sunk by U.207 (Oblt Fritz Meyer) at 2.45am on 11 September in position 63°05′N 37°50′W. Forty-two died. Seven were picked up by the corvette HMCS *Kenogami* (Lt Cdr R. Jackson) and landed at Loch Ewe.

OTHER SHIPS SUNK IN CONVOY SC.42

9 September:

Empire Springbuck (Captain W. O'Connell). By U.81 (Kptlt Friedrich Guggenberger). All 42 died.

10 September:

Empire Hudson (Captain J.C. Cooke). By U.82 (Oblt Siegfried Rollmann). Four died. Sixty-three picked up by the *Baron Ramsay* and the *Regin*.

Muneric (Captain F. Baker). By U.432 (Oblt Heinz-Otto Schultze). All 63 died.

Sally Maersk (Captain J.K. Lindberg). By U.81. All 34 picked up by HMCS *Kenogami*.

Stargard (Nor.) (Captain Lars Larsen). By U.432. Two died. Nine rescued from the ship by the *Regin* (Nor.) and landed at Loch Ewe. Six picked up from a lifeboat by a corvette and landed at Reykjavik on the 13th.

Thistleglen. See under ALBYN LINE.

Winterswijk (Du.) (Captain J. de Groot). By U.432. Twenty died. Thirteen picked up by a corvette and landed at Gourock.

11 September:

Berury (Captain F.J. Morgan). By U.207. One died. Forty-one picked up HMCS *Kenogami* and the corvette HMCS *Moosejaw* (Lt F.E. Grubb).

Bulysses. See under SHELL GROUP.

Empire Crossbill (Captain E.R. Townsend). By U.82. All 49 died.

Garm (Swed.). By U.432 (Oblt Heinz-Otto Schultze). Six died. Fourteen picked up from lifeboats by the *Bestum* (Nor.) and landed at Reykjavik.

Gypsum Queen (Captain A.J. Chapman). By U.82. Ten died. Twenty-six picked up by the *Vestland* (Nor.) and landed at Belfast.

Scania (Swed.). Damaged by U.82 and abandoned. Sunk by U.202 (Kptlt Hans-Heinz Linder). All 24 rescued.

16 September:

Jedmoor. See under RUNCIMAN, WALTER, & CO. LTD/MOOR LINE LTD.

19 September:

Baron Pentland. See under BARON LINE.

(*Tahchee*, damaged by U.652 on the 10th, was towed to Reykjavik by HMCS *Orillia*.)

SWAINBY (Captain H. Thompson). In Convoy ON.25 which sailed from Methil on 5 April 1940 bound for Norway via Kirkwall, but ordered to return when Norway was invaded by Germany on the 9th. Sailing independently bound for Kirkwall when torpedoed and sunk by U.13 (Kptlt Max-Martin Schulte) shortly after 5.30pm on 17 April 1940 in position 61°00′N 00°50′W. All 38 reached Norwick Bay in Shetland by lifeboat.

SWIFTPOOL (Captain H.R. Clark). Bound for Middlesbrough and in Convoy SL.81 which sailed from Freetown on 15 July 1941. Torpedoed and sunk by U.372 (Oblt Heinz-Joachim Neumann) at about 2am on 5 August in position 53°03′N 16°00′W. Forty-two died, including Captain Clark who had survived the sinking of the *Mansepool* 5 months earlier. Two were picked up by HMS *Bluebell* (Lt Cdr R.E. Sherwood) and landed at Greenock.

OTHER SHIPS SUNK IN CONVOY SL.81

Belgravian (Captain R.S. Kearon). See under ELLERMAN GROUP.

Cape Rodney. See under LYLE SHIPPING CO.

Harlingen (Captain J. Willingham). By U.75. Three died. Thirty-nine picked up by HMS *Hydrangea*.

Kumasian (Captain W.E. Pelisser). See under UNITED AFRICA CO. LTD.

THIRLBY (Captain P.E. Birch). Bound for Halifax, Nova Scotia, from New York to join Convoy SC.66 which left Halifax on 23 January 1942. Torpedoed and sunk by U.109 (Kptlt Heinrich Bleichrodt) at about 8.15am on the 23rd in position 43°20′N 66°15′W. Five died. Forty-one, including the US pilot, were picked up by the *Belle Isle* (US) and landed at Halifax.

TROUTPOOL (Captain Muitt). Bound for Glasgow from Rosaria, struck by 2 mines when leaving Belfast Lough on 20 July 1940. Eleven died and the wreck was blown up because it was a hazard to shipping.

ULLAPOOL. In Convoy SC.23 which sailed from Halifax on 18 February 1941. Arrived in the River Mersey on 13 March, where she struck a mine off Princes Stage and broke in two. Fifteen died and 23 survived.

WANDBY (Captain J. Kenny). Bound for Middlesbrough from Victoria, British Columbia, via the Panama Canal. In company with 9 other ships, she sailed from Bermuda on 6 October 1940 to join Convoy HX.79 which was to leave Halifax, Nova Scotia, on the 8th. Torpedoed by U.47 (Kptlt Günther Prien) shortly before midnight on the 19th and abandoned, but owing to her cargo of timber did not sink until the 21st in position 56°45′N 17°07′W. All 34 were picked up by the ASW trawler HMS *Angle* (Lt A.N. Blundell) and landed at Belfast on the 26th.

OTHER SHIPS SUNK IN CONVOY HX.79

19 October:

Bilderdijk (Du.). By U.38 (Kptlt Heinrich Liebe). All 39 picked up by the minesweeper HMS *Jason* (Cdr H.G.A. Lewis) and landed at Methil on the 24th.

Matheran (Captain J. Greenhall). By U.38. Nine died. Seventy-two picked up by the *Loch Lomond* and all survived when she was sunk early the next morning.

Ruperra. By U.46. Thirty died. Seven picked up by the *Induna* and landed at Methil.

Uganda (Captain C. Mackinnon). By U.47. All 40 picked up by HMS *Jason*.

20 October:

Caprella. See under SHELL GROUP.

Janus (Swed.). By U.46 (Oblt Engelbert Endrass). Four dead. Thirty-three picked up by the corvette HMS *Hibiscus* (Lt Cdr R. Philipps).

La Estancia (Captain J. Meneely). By U.47. One died. Seven picked up by the *Induna*. Twenty-six picked up by the corvette HMS *Coreopsis* (Lt Cdr A.H. Davies) and landed at Methil.

Loch Lomond (Captain W.J. Park). By U.100 (Kptlt Joachim Schepke). One died. One hundred and eleven picked up by the minesweeper HMS *Jason* (Lt Cdr R.E. Terry) and landed at Methil.

Shirak (Captain L.R. Morrison). Damaged by U.47, sunk by U.48 (Kptlt Heinrich Bleichrodt). All 37 picked up by the ASW trawler HMS *Blackfly* (Lt A.P. Hughes) and landed at Belfast.

Sitala. See under SHELL GROUP.

Whitford Point (Captain J.E. Young). By U.47. Thirty-seven died. Three picked up by the trawler *Sturdee* and landed at Londonderry.

(*Athelmonarch*. Damaged by U.47.)

WARLABY (Captain S.H. Murray). Bound for the UK from Alexandra, sailing from Freetown as commodore ship of unescorted Convoy SL.64S which left Freetown on 30 January 1941. Sunk by the heavy cruiser *Admiral Hipper* (Kadm. Wilhelm Meisel) on 12 February in position 37°12′N 21°20′W. Thirty-six died and 3 were picked up.

OTHER SHIPS SUNK IN CONVOY SL.64S

By the Hipper:

Borgestad (Nor.) (Captain Lars Grotnæss). All 31 died, including the 21-year-old wife of the 1st Mate.

Derrynane. All 37 died.

Oswestry Grange. Five died. Thirty-seven picked up by the *Lornaston* and landed at Madeira.

Perseus (Gr.). Fourteen died and 22 survived.

Shrewsbury. Twenty died and 19 survived.

Westbury. Five died and 33 survived.

(The *Lornaston* and *Clunepark* were damaged.)

By U.48 (Kptlt Herbert Schultze):

Nailsea Lass (Captain T.L. Bradford). Straggling when torpedoed and sunk by U.48 (Kptlt Herbert Schultze) at 9.45pm on 24 February about 60 miles south-west of the Fastnet. Captain Bradford, 1st Mate A. Hodder and Cabin Boy Edward Dicks taken on board the U-boat, but the latter returned to the lifeboat after medical treatment. Mr E.J. Knight, the 2nd Mate, and 18 others landed at Ballyoughtragh, Co. Kerry, on the 26th, while the 3rd Mate and 9 others landed near Berehaven, Co. Cork. Five died from exposure in the lifeboats. The Royal Navy ocean boarding vessels *Camito*, *Corinthian*, *Cavina* and *Maron* were sent to pick up survivors, but no further details.

WILLOWPOOL (Captain N.J. Oliver). Bound for Middlesbrough from Bône with a cargo of iron ore. Dispersed from Convoy HG.9 when on 10 December 1939 she struck a mine laid by U.20 (Oblt Karl-Heinz Moehle) and sank in position 52°53′N 01°51′E about 3 miles east of the Newarp Lightship off Great Yarmouth. All 36 were picked up by the Gorleston lifeboat.

Managed for Ministry of War Transport

EMPIRE ARNOLD (Captain F. Tate). Bound for Alexandria from New York via Trinidad and Cape Town and dispersed from Convoy E.6 when torpedoed and sunk by U.155 (Kptlt

Adolf Cornelius Piening) at 4.15pm on 4 August 1942 in position 10°45′N 52°30′W. Nine died and Captain Tate was taken prisoner by the U-boat. Fifty-one were picked up from a lifeboat by the *Davanger* (Nor.) on the 12th and landed at Georgetown, British Guiana (now Guyana), on the 14th.

EMPIRE BISON (Captain W.H Harland). Bound for the Clyde from Baltimore, sailing in Convoy HX.82 which left Halifax, Nova Scotia, on 20 October 1940. Straggling when torpedoed and sunk by U.124 (Kptlt Georg-Wilhelm Schulz) shortly after 7am on 1 November 1940 in position 59°30′N 17°40′W. Thirty-one died. Four were picked up by the *Olga S* (Dan.) and landed at Gourock. The *Rutland* (Captain R.N. Sinclair), also a straggler, was sunk the previous evening by U.124. All 24 died.

EMPIRE DRYDEN (Captain R. Powley). Bound for Alexandria via the Cape, sailing independently from New York on 17 April 1942. Torpedoed and sunk by U.572 (Kptlt Heinz Hirsacker) shortly after 3am on the 20th in position 34°21′N 69°00′W. Twenty-six died. Twenty-five were picked up by the *Monarch of Bermuda* and landed at Bermuda.

EMPIRE MERLIN (Captain D.W. Simpson). Bound for Hull from Port Sulphur, Louisiana, sailing in Convoy HX.65 which left Halifax on 12 August 1940. Torpedoed and sunk by U.48 (Krvkpt. Hans Rudolf Rösing) at 2.45am on the 25th in position 58°30′N 10°15′W. Thirty-five died. The sole survivor, Ordinary Seaman John Lee, was picked up by the corvette HMS *Godetia* (Lt Cdr G.V. Legassick) and landed at Methil.

OTHER SHIPS SUNK IN CONVOY HX.65

24 August:

La Brea (Captain G.E. Firth). By U.48. Two died. Fourteen landed at Islivig Bay, Isle of Lewis, and 17 landed at South Uist.

25 August:

Athelcrest. See under ATHEL LINE.

Fircrest (Captain R.H. Tuckett). By U.124. All 39 died.

Harpalyce (Captain W.J. Rees). By U.124 (Kptlt Georg-Wilhelm Schulz). Forty-two died. Four picked up by the armed trawler *Fort Dee* and landed at Kirkwall.

Pecten (Captain H.E. Dale). By U.57 (Oblt Erich Topp). Forty-nine died. Eight picked up by the rescue ship *Torr Head* but transferred to the armed trawler HMS *Robina* and landed at Methil.

(*Stakesby*. Damaged by U.124. Towed to Stornoway and sank in shallow water. Raised in January 1942, repaired and re-entered service as the *Empire Derwent* in 1943. All 30 survived.)

26 August:

Cape York. See under LYLE SHIPPING CO.

Remuera. See under NEW ZEALAND SHIPPING CO. LTD.

EMPIRE MOONBEAM (Captain G.S. Hewison). Bound for Norfolk, Virginia, via New York, sailing in Convoy ON.127 which left Liverpool on 4 September 1942. Straggling when torpedoed and damaged by U.211 (Kptlt Karl Hause) shortly after 1am on the 12th and sunk 4 hours later by U.608 (Kptlt Rolf Struckmeier) in position 48°55'N 33°38'W. Three died. Fifty-two were picked up by the corvette HMCS *Arvida* (Lt A.I. MacKay) and landed at St John's, Newfoundland, on the 15th.

OTHER SHIPS SUNK IN CONVOY ON.127

10 September:

Elisabeth van Belgie (Belg.). By U.96 (Oblt Hans-Jürgen Hellriegel). One died and 49 survived.

Sveve (Nor.) (Captain Harald Hasen). By U.96. Scuttled by the corvette HMCS *Sherbrooke* (Lt J.A.M. Levesque) which landed all the crew of 39 at St John's on the 16th.

11 September:

Empire Oil (Captain E. Marshall). Damaged by U.659 (Kptlt Hans Stock) at 9.10pm on the 10th and abandoned. Sunk by U.584 (Kptlt Joachim Deecke) at 1.47am on the 11th. All 53 survived: 19 picked up by the destroyer HMCS *Hindanger* (Nor.) (Captain Otto Olsvik). By U.584. One died. Forty picked up by corvette HMCS *Amherst* (T/Lt H.G. Denyer).

St Croix (Lt Cdr A.N. Dobson) and landed at St John's on the 15th; 34 picked up on the 14th by the destroyer HMCS *Ottawa*, but 18 died when she herself was sunk.

12 September:

Hektoria (Captain F.A. Gjertsen). Damaged by U.211 (Oblt Karl Hause) and sunk by U.608 (Oblt Rolf Struckmeier). One died and 85 picked up by HMCS *Arvida*.

13 September:

Stone Street (Pan.) (Captain Harald Anderson). By U.594 (Oblt Friedrich Mumm). Thirteen died and Captain Anderson taken prisoner by the U-boat. Thirty-nine picked up by the *Irish Lark* on the 19th and landed at Saint John, New Brunswick, on the 22nd.

14 September:

HMCS *Ottawa*. (A/Lt Cdr Clark A. Rutherford). By U.91 (Kptlt Heinz Walkerling). One hundred and thirty-seven died. Sixty-seven picked up by the corvette *Celandine* (Lt Collings) and the *Arvida* and landed at St John's.

SHIPS DAMAGED IN CONVOY ON.127

Daghild (Nor.) (Captain Olaf K. Egidius). By U.404 on the 12th.

F J Wolfe. By U.96 on the 10th.

Fjordaas (Nor.) (Captain Peder N.A. Saltnes). By U.218 (Oblt Richard Becker) on the 11th.

Marit II (Nor.) (Captain Herman Williamson). By U.404 (Kptlt Otto von Bülow) on the 11th. Two died.

EMPIRE RAINBOW (Captain J. Kenney). Bound for Halifax from Avonmouth via Belfast Lough, sailing in Convoy ON.113 which left Liverpool on 17 July 1942. Torpedoed and damaged by U.607 (Kptlt Ernst Mengersen) at about 8am on the 26th and sunk by U.704 (Horst Wilhelm Kessler) about 10 minutes later in position 47°08′N 42°57′W. All 47 were picked up by the destroyer HMS *Burnham* (Cdr T. Taylor) and the corvette HMCS *Dauphin* (Lt R.A.S. MacNeil) and landed at St John's. (U.90 (Hans-Jürgen Oldörp) was sunk by the destroyer HMCS *St Croix* (A/Lt Cdr A.H. Dobson) on the 24th. All 44 died.)

OTHER SHIPS SUNK IN CONVOY ON.113

25 July:

Broompark. See under DENHOLM, J. & J., LTD.

29 July:

Pacific Pioneer. See under FURNESS, WITHY GROUP.

(*British Merit*. Damaged by U.552 on the 25th. One died and 1 seriously injured.)

EMPIRE STARLIGHT (Captain W.H. Stein). Bound for Murmansk and in Convoy PQ.13 which sailed from Loch Ewe on 10 March 1942, from Reykjavik on the 20th and arrived on the 31st. She made it to the port but was sunk during an air raid on 3 April after discharging her cargo. One died and 67 survived. Raised after the war and converted into a storage barge. (For details of ships sunk in Convoy PQ.13, see under *New Westminster City*, REARDON SMITH LINE.)

FORT PELLY. Sailed from Alexandria on 6 July 1943 to support the invasion of Sicily which had begun on the 10th. Arrived at Augusta on the 18th, but sunk 2 days later by German aircraft. Thirty-six died. No further details.

SAMSUVA (Captain C.H. Churchill). Bound for the UK from Archangel, sailing in Convoy RA.60 which left Kola Inlet on 29 September 1944. Torpedoed on the 29th by U.310 (Kptlt Wolfgang Ley) and broke in two. Scuttled by the destroyers HMS *Musketeer* (Cdr R.L. Fisher) and HMS *Bulldog* (Lt Cdr C.G. Walker) in position 72°58′N 23°59′E. Three died. Fifty-seven were picked up by the rescue ship *Rathlin* (Captain A. Banning) which reached the Clyde on 5 October.

(*Edward H. Crockett* (Captain A. Baldi). Torpedoed at the same time by U.310. Abandoned and sunk by gunfire from HMS *Milne* (Captain M. Richmond). One died. Sixty-seven were picked up by the rescue ship *Zamalek* which reached the Clyde on 5 October.)

Royal Mail Line

ARABY. Sunk by an acoustic mine 9 cables west of the Nore Light Vessel on 27 December 1940. Six died, but no further details.

BRITTANY (Captain W.W. Dovell). Bound for Liverpool from Buenos Aires, sailing from Freetown in Convoy SL.125 on 16 October 1942. Torpedoed by U.509 (Oblt Werner Witte) at midnight on the 29th in position 33°29′N 18°32′W. Fourteen died. Forty-three were picked up by the auxiliary patrol ship HMS *Kelantan* (Lt A.E. Jones) and landed at Gourock on 8 November. (For details of other ships sunk in Convoy SL.125, see under *Nagpore*, P&O.)

CULEBRA (Captain G.D. Bonner). Bound for Bermuda and Jamaica, sailing in Convoy ON.53 which left Liverpool on 2 January 1942 and dispersed on the 19th. From about 6pm on the 25th she fought a gun battle with U.123 (Kptlt Reinhard Hardegen) and was abandoned after the stern gun received a direct hit. Hardegen provided the lifeboats with buckets, provisions, a knife to open tinned food, and a course for Bermuda before sinking the ship in position 35°30′N 53°25′W. All 45 crew survived the shelling, but the lifeboats were never seen again.

OTHER SHIPS SUNK AFTER DISPERSAL OF CONVOY ON.53

Maro (Gr.). Shelled and sunk by U.552 (Kptlt Erich Topp). No survivors.

Vassilios A. Polemis (Gr.) (Captain Vassilios N. Michas). Torpedoed and sunk by U.333 (Kptlt Peter-Erich Cremer). Twenty-one died. Twelve, suffering from frostbite, picked up by the *Leonidas N. Condylis* (Gr.) (Captain Tatakas) and landed into Halifax Infirmary on the 27th.

Empire Wildebeeste (Captain H.C. Stewart). Nine died. Twenty-two picked up by the destroyer USS *Lang* (Lt Cdr E.A. Seay) and landed at Bermuda.

Icarion (Gr.) (Captain Panagis Dracatos). Torpedoed and sunk by U.754 (Kptlt Hans Oestermann). Nine died, including 1 in the lifeboat in which 19 others reached Newfoundland on the 28th.

EMPIRE BITTERN. (Managed for the MOWT.) On 23 July 1944, scuttled as a blockship to become part of Gooseberry 3 harbour, created to facilitate the landing of troops at Gold Beach, Normandy.

HIGHLAND PATRIOT (Captain R.H. Robinson). Bound for Glasgow from Buenos Aires and sailing independently when torpedoed twice by U.38 (Kptlt Heinrich Liebe) at 6.47am on 1 October 1940. Abandoned when sunk by a third torpedo in position 52°20′N 19°04′W. Three died. One hundred and forty were picked up by the sloop HMS *Wellington* (Cdr R.E. Hyde-Smith) and landed at Greenock.

LOCHAVON (Captain C.E. Ratkins). In unescorted Convoy KJF.3 and bound for Liverpool from Vancouver when torpedoed and sunk by U.45 (Kptlt Alexander Gelhaar) on 14 October 1939 in position 50°25′N 13°10′W. All were picked up by the destroyer HMS *Ilex* (Lt Cdr P.L. Saumarez) and landed at Plymouth. Seven died on the *Bretagne* (Fr.) when she too was torpedoed and sunk by U.45. On the same day, all 38 died on the U-boat when she was depth-charged and sunk by the destroyers HMS *Inglefield*, HMS *Ivanhoe* and HMS *Intrepid*.

LOCHGOIL. Damaged by a mine in the Bristol Channel on 6 October 1939. Beached at Mumbles and declared a total loss, but repaired and returned to service as the *Empire Rowan* in 1940. The *Empire Rowan* (owned by the MOWT) was in Convoy KMS.11G which sailed from the Clyde on 14 March 1943. North-west of Bône on the 27th, she was struck by an aerial torpedo delivered by an Italian plane and sank in position 37°16′N 06°54′E. Three died and several were injured. The *Prins Willem III* (Du.), also in the convoy, was struck by an aerial torpedo on the 26th. She was taken in tow the next day by the tug *Hengist*, but capsized and sank. Eleven died.

LOCHKATRINE (Captain P. Cooper). In Convoy ON.115 which sailed from Liverpool on 24 July 1942 bound for the US. Torpedoed and sunk at about 3am on 3 August by U.552 (Kptlt Erich Topp) in position 45°52′N 46°44′W. Nine died. Eighty-one were picked up by the destroyer HMCS *Hamilton* (Lt Cdr N.V. Clark) and the corvette HMCS *Agassiz* (A/Lt Cdr B.D.L. Johnson) and landed at Halifax.

OTHER SHIPS SUNK IN CONVOY ON.115

Arletta (Captain G.W.S. Rogers). Straggling when torpedoed and sunk by U.458 (Oblt Kurt Diggins) at 4.15pm on the 5th. Thirty-six died. Five rescued from a lifeboat by the Coast Guard ship USS *Menemsha* on the 20th and landed at Boston on the 25th.

Belgian Soldier (Belg.) (Captain H. Sanglier). Torpedoed and damaged by U.553 (Krvkpt. Karl Thurmann) at 4am on the 3rd. Straggling when torpedoed and sunk by U.607 (Kptlt Ernst Mengersen) at 2.30am on the 4th. Twenty-one died and 39 survived.

(*G.S. Walden*. Damaged by U.552 when she sank the *Lochkatrine*. None died.)

NALON. Bound for the UK from Cape Town, sailing in Convoy SL.52F which left Freetown on 22 October 1940. At about 10am on 6 November, when the convoy was off the west coast of Ireland, it was attacked by German bombers. A near miss holed the *Nalon* below the waterline and tugs were sent to tow her in, but she sank in approximate position 53°57′N 15°31′W before they arrived. All 72 were picked up by the destroyer HMS *Viscount*.

NATIA. Bound independently for Buenos Aires from the UK when intercepted and sunk by the German raider *Thor* (KptzS. Otto Kähler) on 8 October 1940. One died and 84 were taken on board the *Thor* where a severely injured man died and was buried at sea. With the exception of 4 masters, all *Thor*'s 364 prisoners were transferred to the *Rio Grande* (which had been renamed *Belgrano*) in mid-November and landed at Bordeaux on 13 December for transportation to prison camps in Germany. During her cruise, which began from Kiel in June 1940 and ended in Hamburg in April 1941, *Thor* sank 12 ships.

NAVASOTA (Captain C.J. Goble). Bound for Buenos Aires from Liverpool, sailing in Convoy OB.46 which left Liverpool on 3 December 1939. Torpedoed at 2.40pm on the 5th by U.47 (Kptlt Günther Prien) in position 50°43′N 10°16′W. Thirty-seven died. Thirty-seven were picked up by the destroyer HMS *Escapade* (Cdr H.R. Graham). Eight picked up by the *Clan Farquhar* were landed at Cape Town.

NEBRASKA (Captain B.C. Dodds). Bound for Buenos Aires and dispersed from Convoy OS.71 which sailed from Liverpool on 14 March 1944. Torpedoed and sunk by U.843 (Kptlt Oskar Herwartz) on 8 April in position 11°55′S 19°52′W. Two died and 66 survived. One lifeboat landed at Bahia and another at Recifé on the 22nd. Those in a third boat were picked up by the *Kindat* and landed at Freetown.

PAMPAS (Captain E.B. Ingram). Convoy MW.10, composed of the *Pampas*, HMS *Breconshire* (Captain C.A.G. Hutchinson), *Clan Campbell* and the Norwegian ship *Talabot* (Captain Albert Toft), sailed from Alexandria on 20 March 1942 bound for beleaguered Malta. From the 22nd, it suffered continual attacks by large numbers of Italian and German planes and only the *Pampas* and the *Talabot* succeeded in reaching Valletta.

The convoy dispersed on the 22nd, with each merchantman being accompanied by a destroyer. The next day the *Clan Campbell* was 20 miles from the port when she was sunk. The *Breconshire* was 8 miles from the port on the 24th when she was disabled. Owing to heavy seas, she could not be towed into Grand Harbour, but was taken to a bay on the S side of the island where she was bombed and sunk on the 27th. When over 300 bombers attacked Grand Harbour on the 26th, the *Pampas* was sunk and the *Talabot* so severely damaged that she was scuttled in case her cargo of ammunition exploded. Between them, they had been able to discharge only a few hundred tons of their cargoes. The Royal Navy lost the destroyers HMS *Legion* and HMS *Southwold*, while a cruiser and 2 destroyers were damaged. (See also under *Clan Campbell*, CLAN LINE and *Breconshire*, HOLT, ALFRED, & CO.)

SABOR (Captain P.M. Burrell). Sailing independently and bound for Rio de Janeiro from Port Said, Mombasa, Tamatave, Durban and Cape Town when torpedoed shortly after 3am on 7 March 1943 by U.506 (Kptlt Erich Würdemann). She was struck by a second torpedo at 5.32am and sank in position 34°30′S 23°10′E. Six engine room staff died. Fifty-two were picked up by a South African Air Force rescue launch and landed at Mossel Bay. One survivor later died from his injuries.

SAMBRE (Captain E.B. Ingram). Bound for Philadelphia, sailing in Convoy OB.188 which left Liverpool on 23 July 1940. Torpedoed and sunk by U.34 (Kptlt Wilhelm Rollmann) at 3am on the 27th in position 56°37′N 17°53′W. All 48 were picked up by the destroyer HMS *Winchelsea* (Lt Cdr W.A.F. Hawkins) and landed at Liverpool. (For details of other ships sunk in Convoy OB.188, see under *Thiara*, SHELL GROUP.)

SARTHE (Captain C.E. Mason). Bound independently for Rio de Janeiro from Port Said, Aden and Lourenço Marques when torpedoed and sunk by U.68 (Krvkpt. Karl-Friedrich Merten) at 10pm on 8 October 1942. All 57 were picked up the next day by the armed trawler HMSAS *Vereeniging* and landed at Simonstown.

SIRIS (Captain H. Treweeks). Bound for Rio de Janeiro, sailing in Convoy OS.33 which left Liverpool on 1 July 1942 bound for Freetown. Dispersed from the convoy when torpedoed at 4.13am on the 12th by U.201 (Kptlt Adalbert Schnee) and sunk by gunfire at 6.26am in position 31°20′N 24°48′W. Twenty-eight were picked up from a lifeboat by the corvette HMS *Jonquil* (Lt Cdr R.E.H. Partington) on the 21st, transferred to the sloop HMS *Ibis* (Cdr H.M. Darell-Brown) and landed at Milford Haven on 5 August. Twenty-seven landed at the Cape Verde Islands, but 3 died after landing. (For details of other ships sunk after dispersal from Convoy OS.33, see under *Cortona*, DONALDSON LINE.)

SOMME (Captain C. Prosser). Bound for Bermuda, sailing in Convoy ON.62 which left Liverpool on 1 February 1942. Dispersed from the convoy when torpedoed by U.108 (Krvkpt. Klaus Scholtz) at 11.27pm on the 18th and abandoned in 3 lifeboats. Sunk by a second torpedo at 11.38pm in position 35°30′N 61°25′W. The lifeboats were never seen again. All 48 died. The *Biela* (Captain D. Anderson), also dispersed from Convoy ON.62, was torpedoed and sunk at about midnight on the 14th by U.68 (Kptlt Robert Gysae). All 49 died.

Runciman, Walter, & Co. Ltd/Moor Line Ltd

ALNMOOR (Captain A. Edwards). Bound for Glasgow from New York, sailing in Convoy SC.21 which left Sydney, Cape Breton, on 31 January 1941. Straggling due to a gale when torpedoed by U.123 (Kptlt Karl-Heinz Moehle) at 0038 hours on 15 February and sank in position 55°40′N 25°15′W. All 55 died.

BLYTHMOOR. Loading iron ore in Narvik when the Germans invaded Norway on the night of 8/9 April 1940. The crew were taken prisoner and the ship sunk on the 10th either by destroyers of the Royal Navy or the Germans. (See under *Mersington Court*, COURT LINE and *Romanby*, ROPNER SHIPPING CO.)

CASTLEMOOR (Captain R. Lisle). Bound for Middlesbrough, sailing in Convoy HX.20 which left Halifax on 16 February 1940. Last seen by the *Merchant Royal* when about 800 miles west of Ushant on the 25th, and, as no U-boat claimed sinking her, it was considered that she was lost by 'marine causes'. All 42 died.

DALEMOOR. On 15 January 1945, she struck a mine off the Humber and sank in position 53°22′N 00°50′E. None died.

EASTMOOR (Captain J.B. Rodgers). Bound independently for the UK from Savannah and Halifax when torpedoed by U.71 (Kptlt Walter Flachsenberg) at about 4am on 1 April 1942 and sank in position 37°33′N 68°18′W. Sixteen died, including Captain Rodgers who had survived the sinking of the *Pearlmoor*. Thirty-six were picked up by the *Calgary* and landed at Cape Town.

GLENMOOR (Captain J. Young). Bound for Alexandria from Cardiff, sailing in Convoy OB.248 which left Liverpool on 23 November 1940 and dispersed on the 26th. Torpedoed and sunk by U.103 (Krvkpt. Viktor Schütze) shortly before 8pm on the 27th in position 54°35′N 14°31′W. Thirty-one died. Two were picked up by the destroyers HMS *Harvester* (Lt Cdr M. Thornton) and HMS *Havelock* (Lt Cdr E.H. Thomas) and landed at Liverpool.

OTHER SHIPS SUNK AND DAMAGED AFTER THE DISPERSAL OF CONVOY OB.248

Irene Maria (Captain A.P. Evers). Sunk by U.95 (Kptlt Gerd Schreiber). All 25 died.

Ringhorn (Nor.) (Captain Torger N. Humlevik). Damaged by U.52 (Kptlt Otto Salman). Abandoned, but reboarded and arrived at Belfast Lough on 1 December.

JEDMOOR (Captain R.C. Collins). Bound for Glasgow from Santos, sailing in Convoy SC.42 which left Sydney, Cape Breton, on 30 August 1941. Torpedoed and sunk by U.98 (Kptlt Robert Gysae) at about 11.15pm on 16 September in approximate position 59°N 10°W. Thirty-one died. Three were picked up by the *Knoll* (Nor.) and 2 by the *Campus*. (For details of other ships sunk in Convoy SC.42, see under *Stonepool*, ROPNER SHIPPING CO.)

NORTHMOOR (Captain A. Peters). Bound for Durban and Buenos Aires, sailing in Convoy LMD.17 which left Lourenço Marques on 16 May 1943. Torpedoed and sunk by U.198 (KptzS. Werner Hartmann) at 2.12pm on the 17th in position 28°27′S 32°43′E. Twelve died. Twenty-seven were picked up by the ASW trawler HMS *Loman* (Lt R.C. Warwick) and landed at Durban.

ORANGEMOOR (Captain R.E. Richardson). With a cargo of iron ore from Bône, sailing in Convoy HG.31 which left Gibraltar on 23 May 1940. Torpedoed by U.101 (Kptlt Fritz Frauenheim) at about 2pm on the 31st and sank in position 49°43′N 03°23′W. Eighteen died. Twenty-two were picked up by the *Brandenburg* and landed at London.

PEARLMOOR (Captain J.B. Rodgers). Bound for Methil and Immingham from Pepel, Sierra Leone, sailing in Convoy SL.38 which left Freetown on 1 July 1940. Straggling when torpedoed by U.62 (Oblt Hans-Bernhard Michalowski) at 6.28pm on the 19th, broke in two and sank in position 55°23′N 09°18′W. Thirteen died. Twenty-six were landed at Gola Island, Co. Donegal.

VINEMOOR (Captain D.J. Jones). Bound for Naura in the South Pacific from Manchester, sailing in Convoy OB.188 which left Liverpool on 23 July 1940. Torpedoed by U.34 (Kptlt Wilhelm Rollmann) at 2.47pm on the 26th and sank the next day in position 55°25′N 16°25′W. All 32 were picked up by the corvette HMS *Clarkia* (Lt Cdr F.J.G. Jones) but transferred to the *Hollinside* and landed at Liverpool. (For details of other ships sunk in Convoy OB.188, see under *Thiara*, SHELL GROUP.)

YORKMOOR (Captain T.H. Matthews). Bound independently for New York, sailing from St Thomas, Virgin Islands, on 23 May 1942. Intercepted by U.506 (Kptlt Erich Würdemann) at about 3am on the 28th and kept up a running battle with the U-boat until abandoned at 3.45am. Captain Matthews was questioned by the U-boat before it left and the ship sank at 4.20am in position 29°30′N 72°29′W. Seventeen in the lifeboat commanded by the 1st Mate were picked up by the *Laguna* during the 31st and landed at Charleston, South Carolina, the next day. After being spotted by a plane, the 28 in Captain Matthews' boat were picked up a US Coast Guard cutter on 4 June and landed at Morehead City, North Carolina. None died or injured.

ZURICHMOOR (Captain J.H. Anderson). Bound for St Thomas, sailing independently from Halifax on 21 May 1942. Torpedoed twice by U.432 (Kptlt Heinz-Otto Schultze) at 0024 hours on the 23rd and sank within a minute and half in position 39°30′N 66°00′W. All 45 died.

Managed for Ministry of War Transport

EMPIRE ADVENTURE (Captain T.O. Phinn). Bound for Wabana, Bell Island, Province of Newfoundland and Labrador, from the Tyne, sailing in Convoy OB.216 which left Liverpool on 19 September 1940 and dispersed in position 53°00′N 17°05′W on the 23rd. Torpedoed by U.138 (Oblt Wolfgang Lüth) at 2.27am on the 21st when in position 55°48′N 07°22′W and sank on the 23rd while being towed to the Clyde by the tug HMS *Superman*. Twenty-one died. Eighteen were picked up by the *Industria* (Swed.) and landed at Belfast. (For details of other ships sunk in Convoy OB.216, see under *City of Simla*, ELLERMAN GROUP.)

EMPIRE BEAUMONT. In Convoy PQ.18 which left Loch Ewe on 2 September 1942. Hit by an aerial torpedo delivered by a Heinkel 111 at 3.15pm on the 13th in position 76°10′N 10°05′E. On fire and abandoned, and sank about 3 hours later. Five died and 35 were picked up by the minesweeper HMS *Sharpshooter* (Lt W.L. O'Mara). (For details of other ships sunk in Convoy PQ.18, see under *Atheltemplar*, ATHEL LINE.)

EMPIRE BLESSING. Struck a mine in the River Schelde on 19 March 1945 and sank in position 51°24′N 03°17′E. None died.

EMPIRE DAWN (Captain W.A. Scott). Bound for Trinidad from Durban when intercepted by the German raider *Michel* (KptzS. Helmuth von Ruckteschell) on 12 September 1942. Although the ship signalled that she had stopped and was being abandoned, the raider continued to shell and machine-gun her, killing 20 of her 44 crew; she sank in position 32°27′S 03°39′W. The survivors were taken on board the *Michel*, but it would appear that one man died as they were transferred from her to the *Tannenfels* on the 21st, and only 23 disembarked when she docked at Tanjung Priok, Batavia. There they were handed over to the Japanese and subsequently became PoWs in Japan. (See also under *Lylepark*, DENHOLM, J. & J., LTD, *Patella*, SHELL GROUP, *Gloucester Castle*, UNION-CASTLE LINE and *Arabistan*, STRICK LINE.)

EMPIRE STATESMAN (Captain J. Brown). Bound for Middlesbrough from Pepel with a cargo of iron ore, sailing in Convoy SLS.56 which left Freetown on 19 November 1940. Began straggling on the 21st and torpedoed and sunk by U.94 (Kptlt Herbert Kuppisch) at 7.12pm on 11 December in position 53°40′N 17°00′W. All 32 died. The *Calabria* (Captain D. Lonie), also a straggler from the convoy, was torpedoed 3 times by U.103 (Krvkpt. Viktor Schütze) at about 9pm on the 8th and sank in position 52°43′N 18°07′W. The ship carried Indian seamen who were to serve on other ships and all 360 on board died.

OCEAN VAGABOND (Captain J.W. Smith). Bound for Hull from Wabana, Newfoundland, sailing in Convoy SC.115 which left New York on 27 December 1942. Straggling when torpedoed 3 times by U.186 (Kptlt Siegfried Hesemann) between 0033 and 0145 hours on 11 January 1943 and sank in position 57°17′N 20°11′W. The 1st Radio Officer, J.F. Wilson, died. Forty-six were picked up by the destroyer HMS *Wanderer* (Lt Cdr D.H.P. Gardiner) and landed at Liverpool.

SAMSELBU. Bound for England from Antwerp on 19 March 1945 when she struck a mine off the coast of Belgium and sank in position 51°23′N 03°06′E. None died.

Salvesen, Christian

FLOATING FACTORIES

All Salvesen's whale factory ships, converted into tankers, were lost.

NEW SEVILLA (Captain Richard Chisholm). In Convoy OB.216 and on passage from Liverpool to Antarctica when just after 9pm on 20 September 1940 she was torpedoed by U.138 (Oblt Wolfgang Lüth), about 50 miles north-west of Rathlin Island, on the north-eastern coast of Ireland. As the vessel remained afloat she was taken in tow, but sank off the Mull of Kintyre the following evening. Two died. Twenty-three were picked up by the corvette HMS *Arabis* and landed at Liverpool. The Icelandic trawler *Belgaum* rescued 44 but transferred them to the *Industria* (Swed.) which already had 215 others on board and took them to Belfast. (For details of other ships sunk in Convoy OB.216, see under *City of Simla*, ELLERMAN GROUP.)

SALVESTRIA (Captain J.C. Jamieson). Sank 2¾ miles from Inchkeith in the Firth of Forth on 27 July 1940 after setting off an acoustic mine when fully loaded and heading for Rosyth. Ten died.

SOURABAYA (Captain W.T. Dawson). Bound for the UK in Convoy HX.212 when torpedoed and sunk by U.436 (Kptlt Günther Seibicke) shortly after 11pm on 27 October 1942 in position 54°32′N 31°02′W. The Master, 36 crew members, 24 passengers, 16 DBS passengers and 4 gunners were picked up by the corvettes HMCS *Alberni* (Lt A.W. Ford) and HMCS *Ville de Quebec* (Lt Cdr D.G. Jeffrey) and landed at Liverpool on 2 November. Twenty-six crew, 31 passengers, 16 DBS passengers and 4 gunners had the misfortune of being rescued by the *Bic Island* as there were no survivors when she too was torpedoed. (For details of other ships sunk in Convoy HX.212, see under *Barrwhin*, REARDON SMITH LINE.)

SOUTHERN EMPRESS (Captain Olaf Hansen). Bound for the UK in Convoy SC.104 when torpedoed at 8.21pm on 13 October 1942 by U.221 (Oblt Hans-Hartwig Trojer). Torpedoed again at 11.25pm and sank 5 minutes later in position 53°40′N 40°40′W. Survivors were picked up by the Norwegian corvette *Potentilla* but later transferred to the Norwegian tanker *Suderoy* which had 71 survivors on board when she arrived in the Clyde. Out of the 126 on board, 48 were lost: 24 crew, 4 DEMS gunners and 20 DBS passengers.

OTHER SHIPS SUNK IN CONVOY SC.104

Ashworth (Captain W. Mouat). By U.221. All 49 died.

Empire Mersey (Captain Felix de Bastarrechea). By U.618 (Oblt Kurt Baberg). Sixteen died and 39 picked up by the *Gothland*.

Fagersten (Nor.) (Captain Sverre Langfeldt). By U.221. Nineteen died and 10 picked up by HMS *Potentilla*.

Nellie (Gr.). By U.607 (Kptlt Ernst Mengersen). Thirty-two died and 5 picked up by the *Gothland*.

Nikolina Matkovic (Yugo.) By U.661 (Oblt Erich Lilienfeld). Fourteen died and 21 survived.

Senta (Nor.) (Captain Conrad Rustad). By U.221. All 35 died.

Susana (US) (Captain Jose Ayesa). By U.221. Thirty-eight died. Twenty-one picked up by the rescue ship *Gothland*. (Captain J.M. Hadden) and landed at Gourock on the 21st.

SOUTHERN PRINCESS (Captain H. Neilson). Survived the ordeal of Convoy HX.212 and bound for the UK in Convoy HX.229 when torpedoed and sunk by U.600 (Krvkpt. Bernhard Zurmühlen) at about 6am on 17 March 1943 in position 50°36′N 34°30′W. Four crew members and 2 passengers were lost. The Master, 59 crew, 7 DEMS gunners and 27 passengers were picked up by the *Tekoa* and landed at Liverpool. (For details of other ships sunk in Convoy HX.229, see under *Canadian Star*, BLUE STAR LINE.)

STROMBUS (Captain Hjalmar Nilsen) (Owned by Norwegian subsidiary A/S Sevilla). On 26 October 1940, she had a pilot on board and was about to sail for Antarctica. Adjusting her compasses off Swansea when an acoustic mine exploded near her stern, damaging steam pipes and causing water to enter the engine room. Taken in tow by the tug *Victor*, but ran aground and most of the crew taken ashore by HMS *Silja*. After 2 tugs made an unsuccessful attempt to tow her during the early hours of the 28th, the pilot and 13 others were taken off by the *Victor* and landed in Swansea. Captain Nilsen and 1st Mate Osvald Wilhelmsen remained on board throughout that day, but during a storm on the 30th she broke in two. The 2nd Engineer, Alfred Monsen, was injured, but none died. Raised and broken up in Briton Ferry in 1942.

Tanker

PEDER BOGEN (Captain W.T. Dawson). On 19 March 1942 sailed from Port of Spain in Trinidad to join a convoy at Halifax for the UK when torpedoed twice by the Italian submarine *Morosini* (C.C. Athos Fraternale) during the late afternoon of the 23rd in approximate position 24°43′N 57°44′W. An SSSS message intimated that she was being abandoned and, after being subjected to gunfire, she sank the following day. The 22 in the boat commanded by Captain Dawson were picked up by the *Gobeo* (Sp.) on the 27th and landed at Lisbon on 12 April. The 32 in the 1st Mate's boat were picked up by the *Rio*

Gallegos (Arg.) on the same day and landed at New York on 31 March. The *Peder Bogen* carried 1 passenger, the Radio Officer of the *Melpomene* (Captain A. Henney) sunk by the Italian submarine *Giuseppe Finzi* (Capitano di Vascello (Capt.) Ugo Giudice) on 6 March, and he was among those in Captain Dawson's boat. All survived.

Whale catchers requisitioned by the Royal Navy and serving as minesweepers

HMS SANTA. Struck a mine when west of Maddalena, Sardinia, and sank on 23 November 1943. No further details.

HMS SEVRA. Struck a mine and sank off Falmouth on 6 November 1940. No further details.

HMS SHERA. Bound for Murmansk in Convoy PQ.12 when she capsized in heavy seas and pack ice in the Barents Sea on 9 March 1942. No further details other than that there were some survivors.

HMS SHUSA. Transferred into the Soviet Navy, foundered and sank in the Barents Sea on 20 November 1942. No further details.

HMS SOTRA. Torpedoed and sunk off Bardia, Libya, by U.431 (Kptlt Wilhelm Dommes) on 29 January 1942. All the crew, including 6 Norwegians, were killed when she exploded.

HMS SOUTHERN FLOWER. Torpedoed and sunk by U.1022 (Kptlt Hans-Joachim Ernst) off Reykjavik on 3 March 1945 in position 64°05′N 23°15′W. No further details.

HMS SOUTHERN PRIDE. Based at Freetown when she became stranded near the port on 16 June 1944 and became a total loss.

HMS SULLA. Transferred into the Soviet Navy and part of the escort of Convoy PQ.13 when, on passage to Murmansk, she went missing on 25 March 1942. At 10.36am on the 30th U.456 (Kptlt Max-Martin Teichert) torpedoed and sank a straggling ship in the Barents Sea in position 70°28′N 35°44′E which may have been her, but it is possible that she capsized due to icing up in a gale which scattered the convoy. No survivors.

HMS SVANA. Sunk by Italian aircraft off Alexandria on 8 April 1942. No further details.

Managed by Salvesen for St Helier Shipowners Ltd until May 1941

SVEND FOYN (Br.). (Whale Factory ship). Bound for Liverpool in Convoy HX.229, sank after striking an iceberg when 70 miles south of Cape Farewell on 19 March 1943. One hundred and ninety-five were lost and 152 rescued by the USCGC *Algonquin*.

Cargo ships

ALBUERA. Bound for the Tyne from Chatham, New Brunswick. Sunk by an E-boat when 2 miles south-west of Lydd Light Float in the Strait of Dover on 24 June 1940. Seven died. Twenty-nine were rescued by the *Merope* (Du.) which transferred them to ASW trawler HMS *Grimsby Town*.

BRANDON (Captain R. Chisholm). Bound for Port Everglades from Cardiff. Straggling from Convoy OB.48 when torpedoed and sunk by U.48 (Kptlt Herbert Schultze) at 11.55am on 8 December 1939 in position 50°28′N 08°28′W, 80 miles south-east of the Fastnet Rock. Nine died. The Master and other survivors were picked up by the Belgian trawlers *Marie*

Jose Rosette and *Tritten* and landed at Milford Haven. (For the *San Alberto*, also in Convoy OB.48, see SHELL GROUP.)

FINTRA (Captain R.J. Roll). Bound independently for Algiers from Philippeville (Skikda), and with 340 tons of ammunition in her cargo, when torpedoed and sunk by U.371 (Kptlt Waldemar Mehl) at 12.50pm on 23 February 1943 in position 36°57′N 03°41′W. Twelve died. Twenty-three survived.

GLEN FARG (A Norwegian Line ship registered in the UK) (Captain R. Hall). On passage to Methil and Grangemouth from Folden Fjord when torpedoed and sunk by gunfire by U.23 (Kptlt Otto Kretschmer) at 4.45pm on 4 October 1939 in position 58°52′N 01°31′W. One died. Sixteen were picked up by the destroyer HMS *Firedrake* (Lt Cdr S.H. Norris) and landed at Scapa Flow the following day.

GLITRA (A fleet collier at Scapa Flow). Bombed and sunk 3 miles south-east of Grim Ness, South Ronaldsay, Orkney, on 30 January 1940. No survivors.

SAGANAGA (Captain A.W.D. Mackay). At anchor in the roads at Wabana, Newfoundland, when torpedoed by U.513 (Krvkpt. Rolf Rüggeberg) at 4.12pm on 5 September 1942. With a cargo of iron ore, she sank in 3 minutes. Thirty died. Fourteen were rescued by a Customs launch and landed at Lance Cove, Bell Island. About half an hour later, the Canadian ship *Lord Strathcona* was torpedoed by the same U-boat. But although she was also laden with iron ore and sank in under 1½ minutes, all 44 on board escaped because they had prepared to abandon ship on witnessing the fate of the *Saganaga*.

SHEKATIKA (Captain R. Paterson). Bound for Hartlepool from Gaspé, Quebec, sailing in Convoy SC.7 which left Sydney, Cape Breton, on 5 October 1940. At 8.21pm on the 18th when in position 57°12′N 11°08′W, 90 miles ESE of Rockall, and romping from the convoy, she was struck amidships by a torpedo fired by U.123 (Kptlt Karl-Heinz Moehle). Seven minutes later U.123 put another torpedo into her, but as she remained afloat U.99 (Kptlt Otto Kretschmer) fired yet another torpedo into her and the crew took to the rafts. At 11.17pm, a fourth torpedo was fired into her by U.100 (Kptlt Joachim Schepke), but it took a fifth, from U.123, fired into her engine room at 3.17am on the 19th, before she slowly sank. All 36 on board were picked up by the sloop HMS *Fowey* (Lt C.G. deL. Bush) and landed at Greenock on the 20th. The reason that the *Shekatika* was so difficult to dispose of was no doubt due to the fact that her cargo, in the holds and on deck, was pit props. (For details of other ships sunk in Convoy SC.7, see under *Sedgepool*, ROPNER SHIPPING CO.)

SIRIKISHNA (Captain R. Paterson). Bound for Halifax from Barry, commodore ship of Convoy OB.288 which left Liverpool on 18 February 1941 and dispersed on the 22nd in position 59°30′N 21°15′W. Torpedoed by U.96 (Kptlt Heinrich Lehmann-Willenbrock) at 2.20am on the 24th and again about 6 hours later. Broke in two and sank in approximate position 58°N 21°W. All 43 died.

OTHER SHIPS SUNK AFTER DISPERSAL OF CONVOY OB.288

Anglo Peruvian (Captain C.M. Quick). By U.96. Twenty-nine died. Seventeen picked up by the *Harberton* and landed at Halifax on 4 March.

Cape Nelson. See under LYLE SHIPPING CO.

HMS *Manistee* (An ocean boarding vessel) (Lt Cdr E.H. Smith). Damaged by U.107 (Kptlt Günther Hessler) on the 23rd. Sunk by U.107 on the 24th. All 141 died.

Huntingdon. See under FEDERAL STEAM NAVIGATION CO.

Linaria. See under STAG LINE.

Marslew (Captain H.R. Watkins). By U.95 (Kptlt Jost Metzler). Thirteen died. Twenty-three picked up by the *Empire Cheetah*.

Svein Jarl (Nor.) (Captain M. Marsteen). By U.69 (Kptlt Gerd Schreiber). All 22 died.

Temple Moat (Br.) (Captain T. Ludlow). By U.95. All 42 died.

Wayngate (Captain S.G. Larard). By U.73 (Kptlt Helmut Rosenbaum). All 41 picked up by the Free French destroyer *Léopard* and landed at Greenock on 28 February.

SHIPS DAMAGED IN AIR ATTACK ON THE 22ND BEFORE DISPERSAL

Keila. Returned to port under escort.

Kingston Hill (Captain W.E. Niven). Towed to Loch Ewe by the rescue tug HMS *Thames*. Captain Niven was the sole casualty.

Managed for Ministry of War Transport

ALGARVE (Ex-Danish) (Captain J.N. Mikkelsen). Sunk by an E-boat off Sheringham, Norfolk, on 19 February 1941. All 25 died.

CROWN ARUN (Captain Hugh Leaske). Bound for the UK from Gaspé, Quebec, sailing in Convoy HX.71 which left Halifax on 5 September 1940. Torpedoed, shelled and sunk by U.99 (Kptlt Otto Kretschmer) at about 8.30am on the 17th when in position 58°02′N 14°18′W, north of Rockall. All 25 picked up by the destroyer HMS *Winchelsea* (Lt Cdr W.A. Hawkins) and landed at Liverpool. Another casualty of Convoy HX.71 was the *Tregenna*, sunk by U.65 (Hans-Gerrit von Stockhausen). Thirty-three died. Four were picked up by the *Filleigh* and landed at Avonmouth.

DAPHNE II. Damaged by an E-boat off the Humber on 18 March 1941. Taken in tow, but broke in two and sank. Survivors landed at Hartlepool.

EMPIRE BRUCE (Captain J. Edwards). Bound independently for Freetown from Buenos Aires and about 100 miles from her destination when torpedoed and sunk by U.123 (Oblt Horst von Schroeter) on 18 April 1943. All 49 were picked up by the minesweeper HMS *MMS-107* (Skipper H.J. Craven).

EMPIRE DUNSTAN (Captain N. Ramsay). On 18 November 1943, had dispersed from Convoy KMS.31 and on passage to Brindisi from Bône, carrying landmines, when torpedoed and sunk in the Ionian Sea in position 39°24′N 17°40′E by U.81 (Oblt Johann-Otto Krieg). Two died. Forty were picked up by the *Lom* (Nor.) and landed at Taranto. (For details of ships sunk in Convoy KMS.31, see under *Birchbank*, WEIR, ANDREW, & CO./BANK LINE.)

EMPIRE HERITAGE (Captain J. Jamieson). Bound for the UK in Convoy HX.305. Torpedoed and sunk by U.482 (Kptlt Hartmut Graf von Matuschka, Freiherr von Toppolczan und

Spaetgen) when NNE of Tory Island off the north-western coast of Ireland at about 6am on 8 September 1944. When the rescue ship *Pinto* was taking men from the stricken ship she was herself torpedoed by U.482. It is believed that out of her complement of 77 crew, 11 DEMS gunners and 73 DBS passengers, 52, 8 and 53 respectively were lost, but these figures may be somewhat inaccurate as sources differ. Twenty-five crew, 3 DEMS gunners, 20 DBS passengers and one signalman, together with 21 survivors from the *Pinto,* were picked up by the trawler HMS *Northern Wave* (Lt F.J.R. Storey) and landed at Londonderry.
EMPIRE KINGSLEY (Captain D. Hunter). In Convoy TBC.103 and sailing in ballast from Ghent to Manchester on 22 March 1945 when torpedoed and sunk by U.315 (Oblt Herbert Zoller) off Botallack Head in Cornwall in position 50°08′N 05°51′W. Eight died. Forty-seven were rescued by the trawler HMS *Fir* (Lt W.H. Buley) which transferred them to the Sennen lifeboat.
(The **ELSWICK PARK, VINLAKE, BECHEVILLE, INGHAM, FLOWERGATE, SALTERGATE** and **NJEGOS** were all scuttled as blockships during the Normandy landings in 1944, but raised and broken up after the war.)

Shaw Savill & Albion

(FURNESS, WITHY HAD A CONTROLLING INTEREST)

CERAMIC (Captain H.C. Elford). Bound for Sydney, Australia, via St Helena and Durban, sailing from Liverpool in Convoy ON.149 on 26 November 1942 and dispersed from it on 2 December. Torpedoed and sunk by 5 torpedoes from U.515 (Kptlt Werner Henke) on 7 February in position 40°30′N 40°20′W. Out of her complement of 657, only Sapper Eric Munday of the Royal Engineers survived, being taken prisoner by the U-boat. (For other ships sunk after dispersing from Convoy ON.149, see under *Henry Stanley*, ELDER DEMPSTER LINE.)
JERVIS BAY (Captain E.S. Fogerty Fegen, RN). Managed by the Company until requisitioned by the Admiralty and converted into an AMC, HMS *Jervis Bay*. She was the only ship escorting Convoy HX.84 when it was intercepted by the pocket battleship *Admiral Scheer* (Captain Theodor Krancke) on 5 November 1940. Engaged the *Scheer* and sank with the loss of 190 men. Sixty-five were picked up by the Swedish ship *Stureholm* (Captain Sven Olander). Many on HMS *Jervis Bay* were the Company's men who had transferred into the Royal Navy by signing T.124 articles. (For more details, see under *Maidan*, BROCKLEBANK LINE and *Fresno City (I)*, REARDON SMITH LINE.)
MAIMOA (Captain H.S. Cox). Bound for Durban and the UK from Fremantle and sailing independently in the Indian Ocean on 21 November 1940 when attacked by a plane from the raider *Pinguin* (KptzS. Ernst-Felix Krüder) which dropped a message ordering her stop and deliberately broke the main aerial in order to prevent transmission. The aerial, however, was quickly repaired and a QQQQ message transmitted. The *Pinguin* then shelled the ship

and she was scuttled after the crew had abandoned her. The 87 crew were taken prisoner on board the *Pinguin* but later transferred to the captured Norwegian tanker *Storstad* which, with a prize crew commanded by Oblt Levit, arrived at Bordeaux on 5 February 1941. (See under *Nowshera*, BRITISH INDIA STEAM NAVIGATION CO.)

When being taken to Germany, Mr E. Howlett and Mr R. Dunshea, the 4th and 5th Engineers, jumped off the train with two other officers. In two separate pairs they reached Marseille and then Spain. Mr Dunshea and his companion arrived back home in June 1941, but Mr Howlett and his companion were imprisoned and not released until June 1942.

MATAKANA. In bad weather, lost by grounding on the Plana Cays Islands in the Bahamas on 1 May 1940. All 78 rescued by the *Panama* (US).

TAIROA (Captain W.B. Starr). Bound for London from Brisbane when intercepted by the *Admiral Graf Spee* (Captain Hans Langsdorff) in position 21°38′S 08°13′E on 3 December 1939. Shelled and sunk by torpedo after her crew had been transferred to the warship. On 6 December, the *Graf Spee* met the *Altmark* (Captain Dahl) and transferred most of her Merchant Navy prisoners to her, but some of the *Tairoa*'s men were retained on the *Graf Spee* so that they were released in Montevideo after the Battle of the River Plate which took place on the 13th. Those on the *Altmark* were released by a boarding party from the destroyer HMS *Cossack* (Captain P. Vian) on 16 February 1940 when she illegally intercepted the prison ship in Norwegian territorial waters. The *Cossack* docked at Leith the next day.

WAIMARAMA (Captain R.S. Pearce). In Convoy WS.21S (Operation Pedestal) which sailed from the UK on 2 August 1942 and from Gibraltar on the 10th. From the evening of the 11th, until its remnants reached Malta on the 14th, the convoy suffered constant air and sea attacks. The *Waimarama* was hit by 4 bombs at about 8am on the 13th. With cased aviation spirit in her cargo, there was an explosion which brought down one of the attacking planes and she sank in minutes. Eight-three died and 18 were rescued by the destroyer HMS *Ledbury* (Lt Cdr R.P. Hill).

OTHER SHIPS SUNK IN CONVOY WS.21S

Almeria Lykes (US). None died.

Clan Ferguson. See under CLAN LINE.

Deucalion and *Glenorchy*. See under HOLT, ALFRED, & CO.

Dorset. See under FEDERAL STEAM NAVIGATION CO.

Santa Elisa (US). Four died.

Wairangi and *Empire Hope*. See below.

SHIPS THAT GOT THROUGH

Brisbane Star. Damaged. One died.

Melbourne Star.

Ohio. Tanker so severely damaged that she sank on arrival. No details of other casualties. (See below, under SHELL GROUP.)

Port Chalmers.

Rochester Castle. Despite being hit by an aerial torpedo.

WARSHIPS SUNK

HMS *Cairo*. Cruiser – 26 died.

HMS *Eagle*. Aircraft carrier – 160 died.

HMS *Foresight*. Destroyer, damaged and scuttled – 5 died.

HMS *Manchester*. Cruiser, damaged and scuttled – 150 died.

WARSHIPS DAMAGED

The aircraft carrier HMS *Indomitable* and the cruisers *Kenya* and *Nigeria.* No details of casualties.

WAIOTIRA (Captain A.V. Richardson). Sailing independently and bound for the UK from Auckland via the Panama Canal when damaged shortly after 10pm on 26 December 1940 by 2 torpedoes fired by U.95 (Kptlt Gerd Schreiber) in position 58°05′N 17°10′W. The U-boat made off because British destroyers were in the area, but at about 1.45am on the 27th, U.38 (Kptlt Heinrich Liebe) came across the stationary ship and sank her. One died and the remaining 89 were picked up by the destroyer HMS *Mashona* (Cdr W.H. Selby) and landed at Greenock the next day.

WAIRANGI (Captain H.R. Gordon). In Convoy WS.21S (Operation Pedestal). Torpedoed by an E-boat during the early morning of 13 August 1942 and, with her engine room flooded and her pumps useless, scuttled and abandoned. All rescued by the destroyer HMS *Eskimo* (Cdr E.G. Le Geyt). (See under *Waimarama* above.)

WAIWERA (Captain C.M. Andrews). Sailing independently and bound for Liverpool from Auckland via the Panama Canal when torpedoed and sunk by U.754 (Kptlt Hans Oestermann) shortly after 6am on 29 June 1942 in position 45°49′N 34°29′W. Eight died. Seventy-nine crew and 18 passengers were picked up from 2 lifeboats and rafts by the Norwegian ship *Oregon Express* (Captain Ragnar M. Walsig) and landed at New York.

ZEALANDIC (Captain F.J. Ogilvie). Bound independently for Australia from Liverpool when torpedoed by U.106 (Kptlt Jürgen Oesten) at 0045 hours on 17 January 1941. An SSSS message was transmitted but the ship continued on its way until a second torpedo struck and sank her in position 58°28′N 20°43′W. The U-boat's crew witnessed the survivors abandon the ship in 3 lifeboats, but they were never seen again. All 67 crew and 6 passengers died.

Managed for Ministry of War Transport

COMMISSAIRE RAMEL (Captain R. McKenzie). A requisitioned French ship bound for the UK from Sydney, Australia, when shelled and sunk by the raider *Atlantis* (KptzS. Bernhard

Rogge) on 20 September 1940 in position 28°25′S 74°27′E. Three engine room staff were killed, but the remaining 63 men got away in 3 lifeboats and were picked up and landed in Italian Somaliland where they were interned until released by British Forces in February 1941.

EMPIRE HOPE (Captain G. Williams). In Convoy WS.21S (Operation Pedestal). With high octane gas and explosives among her cargo, was so badly damaged by near misses and 2 direct hits during an air attack at about 8pm on 12 August 1942 that she was abandoned. Most of the survivors were taken on board the destroyer HMS *Bramham* (Lt E. Baines) which then sank the burning ship. Others were rescued by the destroyer HMS *Penn* (Lt Cdr J.H. Swain). None died. (See under *Waimarama* and *Wairangi* above.)

EMPIRE TRADER (Captain E.T. Baker). Bound for New York to load for New Zealand, sailing in Convoy ON.166 which left Liverpool on 11 February 1943. Straggled and torpedoed by U.92 (Kptlt Adolf Oelrich) at about 10.30pm on the 21st in position 48°25′N 30°10′W. Abandoned the next day, but stayed afloat and although the corvette HMCS *Dauphin* (Lt Cdr R.A.S. MacNeil) tried to sink her, she was seen again on the 23rd. All 106 picked up by the rescue ship *Stockport* (Captain T.E. Fea) but transferred to the *Dauphin* which landed them at St John's, Newfoundland. (For details of other ships sunk in Convoy ON.166, see under *Eulima*, SHELL GROUP.)

Shell Group

(INCLUDING ANGLO-SAXON AND EAGLE OIL OPERATED AS SEPARATE COMPANIES BUT OWNED BY SHELL)

AFRICA SHELL (Captain P.G. Dove). Intercepted, and sunk after abandoned, by the pocket battleship *Admiral Graf Spee* (KptzS. Hans Langsdorff) on 15 November 1939 in position 24°41′S 35°00′E. A German party boarded and took possession of all the ship's food and wine. The 27 crew, ordered into the lifeboats, landed in Portuguese East Africa. Captain Dove, taken prisoner on board the *Graf Spee*, was released in Montevideo after the Battle of the River Plate which took place on 13 December. None died.

AGNITA. Independently bound for Caripito in Venezuela from Freetown when intercepted by the German raider *Kormoran* (KptzS. Theodor Detmers) on 22 March 1941 in position 03°20′N 23°48′W. Crew of 38 were taken prisoner on board the raider before she was scuttled.

ALBERTA (Fr.). Seized by the Vichy French and renamed *Alabeta*. Torpedoed by the submarine HMS *Torbay* (Lt Cdr A.C.C. Miers) off Cape Helles, Turkey, on 6 June 1941. Sunk by gunfire on the 9th in approximate position 40°02′N 26°11′E.

ALDEGONDA (Du.). Requisitioned by the Royal Netherlands Navy as an auxiliary tanker and renamed *TAN 5*. Scuttled at Soerabaja on 2 March 1942. Salvaged by the Japanese and renamed *Akebono Maru*. Returned to owners after the war.

ALEXIA. Damaged by U.99 (Kptlt Otto Kretschmer) on 2 August 1940 and again by U.510 (Frgkpt. Karl Neitzel) on 10 August 1943. Requisitioned by the Royal Navy and became the Merchant Aircraft Carrier HMS *Alexia*. Transferred to Shell France after the war and renamed *Ianthina*.

AMBO (Du.). Formerly the *Jane Maersk*. Seized by the Royal Netherlands Navy at Tarakan in Borneo on 10 May 1940 because Denmark had been occupied by the Germans. Used as an auxiliary tanker and renamed *TAN 8*. Scuttled at Soerabaja on 2 March 1942, but raised by the Japanese and sailed as the *Teikai Maru* until bombed and sunk by US planes on 30 December 1944 in position 17°13N′ 119°20′E.

ANADARA (Captain W.T. Walmsley). Bound for Curaçao from Heysham and the Clyde, sailing in Convoy ON.67 which left Liverpool on 14 February 1942. Torpedoed twice by U.558 (Kptlt Günther Krech) at 9.50am on the 24th. Straggling when torpedoed again and subjected to gunfire by U.587 (Kptlt Ulrich Borcherdt). Sank in position 43°57′N 44°45′W. All 62 died.

OTHER SHIPS SUNK IN CONVOY ON.67

Adellen (Captain J. Brown). By U.155 (Kptlt Adolf Cornelius). Thirty-six died. Twelve picked up by the corvette HMCS *Algoma* (Lt J. Harding), transferred to the rescue ship *Toward* (Captain A.J. Knell) and landed at Halifax on 1 March.

Eidanger (Captain Johan Kjærstad) (Nor.). By U.558. All 39 picked up by the *Toward*.

Empire Celt (Captain E. McCready). By U.158 (Kptlt Erwin Rostin). Six died. Twenty-three picked up by the Canadian rescue ship *Citadelle* and 24 by the ASW trawler HMS *St Zeno* (Lt J.K. Craig) and landed at St John's, Newfoundland, on the 27th.

Finnanger (Captain Bernt Thorbjørnsen) (Nor.). By U.158. All 39 died.

Inverarder (Captain A.G. Robins). By U.558. All 42 picked up by the *Empire Flame* but transferred to the *Toward*.

Sama (Captain Ingold Just) (Nor.). By U.155. Three drifted off on a small raft and were never seen again and 1, on a small raft, was crushed to death between the raft and the destroyer USS *Nicholson* (Cdr J.S. Keating) which rescued 20 survivors.

White Crest (Captain G. Joures). By U.162 (Kptlt Jürgen Wattenberg). All 47 died.

(*Diloma*. Damaged by U.158.)

ANASTASIA (Du.). Scuttled off Tanjung Priok on 3 March 1942 to avoid capture by the Japanese. Raised by them and sailed as the *Takekuni Maru* until sunk on 10 September 1944 by a mine laid by the submarine HMS *Porpoise* (Lt Cdr H.B. Turner).

ANGELINA (Du.). Scuttled off Soerabaja on 2 March 1942 to avoid capture by the Japanese. Raised by them and sailed as the *Anjo Maru* until torpedoed and sunk by the submarine USS *Bonefish* (Lt Cdr L.L. Edge) in the South China Sea on 28 September 1944.

APOLLONIA (Du.). (Captain P. Scholl). Sunk by two German destroyers between The Lizard and Wolf Rock at about 1am on 25 November 1940. Many were severely wounded and 13 Chinese crew died.

ARINIA (Captain B.B. Bannister). On 19 December 1940, laden with oil from Aruba, dropped anchor 5 miles ESE of Southend Pier to await the opening of the dock gates at the Isle of Grain. The engines were then shut down, but as this also switched off the anti-magnetic system a nearby mine was drawn into her and exploded. Sixty died, including the pilot, Mr W.H. Hopkins, and 2 survived.

AUGUSTINA (Du.) (Captain A.J. Moerman). Sailed from Tanjung Priok on 27 February 1942 in an attempt to reach Australia. The Master had orders to scuttle the ship if she were in danger of falling into the hands of the Japanese, so when a Japanese destroyer stopped her on 1 March the sea valves were opened and the crew left in 2 lifeboats.

Aware of the scuttling, the Japanese commander ordered Captain Moerman and the 1st Engineer to return to save their ship, but on doing so they found it impossible. The Japanese commander then ordered the lifeboats away from his ship and had his men slaughter their occupants with gunfire. When the Japanese whaler carrying Captain Moerman and the 1st Engineer came alongside the destroyer, a sailor jumped into it and killed them both. Mr L. Meyer, the 3rd Engineer, escaped by swimming under the water and, as he was naked, he reboarded the *Augustina* to retrieve clothes when the destroyer had gone. He then entered an undamaged lifeboat in which he drifted until picked up by another Japanese destroyer on the night of 3/4 March. He was first taken to Macassar and eventually to Japan where he remained a prisoner until released on 12 September 1945. Thirty were massacred. Mr Meyer, and two Chinese who swam ashore, survived.

AURIS. Independently bound for Gibraltar from Trinidad when torpedoed at 8.45pm and again at 9.25pm, and sunk by the Italian submarine *Leonardo da Vinci* (C.C. Ferdinando Calda) on 28 June 1941 in position 32°27′N 11°57′W. Her SSSS transmissions were received in Gibraltar and HMS *Farndale* (Cdr S.H. Carlill), escorting Convoy HG.66, was ordered to the scene. She picked up 25 from two rafts and from the sea. Thirty-two died, including 4 picked up by HMS *Farndale*.

BULLMOUTH (Captain J. Brougham). Bound for the Tyne, sailing in Convoy SL.125 which left Freetown on 16 October 1942. Damaged by U.409 (Oblt Hanns-Ferdinand Massmann) at 0021 hours on the 30th and became a straggler. Sunk at 1.40am by U.659 (Oblt Hans Stock). Seven got away on a raft which they could not paddle and which just drifted until it landed on Bugio Island, south-east of Madeira, at 1am on 6 November. However, 1st Mate B.F. Dickinson and Donkeyman J.B. Smith died after landing. Forty-nine died and 5 survived. (For details of other ships sunk in Convoy SL.125, see under *Nagpore*, P&O.)

BULYSSES (Captain B. Lamb). Bound for Stanlow, sailing in Convoy SC.42 which left Sydney, Cape Breton, on 30 August 1941. Torpedoed and sunk by U.82 (Oblt Siegfried Rollmann) at 1.51am on 11 September in position 62°40′N 38°50′W. One died. Sixty were picked up by the *Wisla* (Finn.) and landed at Liverpool. (For details of other ships sunk in Convoy SC.42, see under *Stonepool*, ROPNER SHIPPING CO.)

CAPRELLA (Captain P. Prior). Bound for the Mersey from Curaçao, sailing from Halifax, Nova Scotia, in Convoy HX.79 on 8 October 1940. Torpedoed by U.100 (Kptlt Joachim Schepke) at 0015 hours on the 20th and abandoned in position 56°37′N 17°15′W. One died. Fifty-two were picked up by the ASW trawler HMS *Lady Elsa* (Lt J.G. Rankin) and landed at Londonderry. The drifting wreck, with only 15 metres of her bow above water, was last seen on the 22nd. (For details of other ships sunk in Convoy HX.79, see under *Wandby*, ROPNER SHIPPING CO.)

CARDITA (Captain J.O. Evans). Bound for Shellhaven from Curaçao, sailing in Convoy HX.166 which left Halifax on 21 December 1941. Straggling when torpedoed by U.87 (Kptlt Joachim Berger) at 7.54 pm on the 31st in position 59°18′N 12°50′W and sank on 3 January. Twenty-seven died. Thirty-three were picked up by the destroyers HMS *Onslow* (Captain H.T. Armstrong) and HMS *Sabre* (Lt P.W. Gretton) and landed at Reykjavik.

CHAMA (Captain H.S. Sivell). Bound for New York, sailing in Convoy OG.56 which left Liverpool on 17 March 1941. Dispersed from the convoy at 8pm on the 23rd. Torpedoed and sunk by U.97 (Kptlt Udo Heilmann) at 11.26pm that same day in position 49°35′N 19°13′W. All 59 died.

OTHER SHIPS SUNK AFTER DISPERSAL FROM CONVOY OG.56

Hørda (Nor.) (Captain O. Lind). By U.97. All 30 died.

Agnete Maersk. By Italian submarine *Veniero* (C.C. Manlio Petroni). All died.

CIRCE SHELL (Captain J.T. Sinclair) (RFA). Bound for Trinidad, sailing in Convoy OB.60 which left Liverpool on 26 January 1942. Dispersed from the convoy when torpedoed by U.161 (Kptlt Albrecht Achilles) at 9.13pm on 21 February, but did not sink. Because 3 planes arrived at the scene, the U-boat waited until nightfall before it again torpedoed her at 1.14am, and she sank in position 11°03′N 62°03′W. One died. Fifty-seven were picked up by the tug *Busy* and landed at Port of Spain on the 23rd.

OTHER SHIPS SUNK FROM CONVOY OB.60 (APART FROM FFL *ALYSSE*, ALL WERE DISPERSED)

FFL *Alysse* (LV Pepin Lehalleur). A French corvette. By U.654 (Oblt Ludwig Forster) on 9 February. Thirty six died. Thirty-four picked up by the corvettes HMCS *Moosejaw* (T/Lt H.D. Campsie) and HMCS *Hepatica* (T/Lt T. Gilmour) and landed at St John's, Newfoundland, on the 11th. The *Alysse* sank on the 10th when being towed by HMCS *Hepatica*.

Empire Fusilier (Captain W. Reid). By U.85 (Oblt Eberhard Greger) on 9 February. Nine died. Thirty-eight picked up by the corvette HMCS *Barrie* (Chief Skipper G.N. Downey) and landed at Halifax, Nova Scotia.

Macgregor (Captain W.G. Todman). By U.156 (Kptlt Werner Hartenstein) on 27 February. One died. Thirty picked up by a San Domingo Coast Guard cutter and landed at Puerto Plata, Dominican Republic.

Meropi (Gr.). By U.566 (Kptlt Dietrich Borchert) on 15 February. Twenty-six died and 14 rescued.

CLEA (Captain W.G. Boyt). Bound for Loch Ewe and Scapa Flow from Curaçao, sailing in Convoy HX.106 which left Halifax on 30 January 1941. Straggling when torpedoed and sunk by U.96 (Kptlt Heinrich Lehmann-Willenbrock) at 3.08pm on 13 February in position 60°25′N 17°10′W. All 59 died. The *Arthur F Corwin* (Captain J.L. Gant), also straggling from Convoy HX.106, was damaged by U.103 (Krvkpt. Viktor Schütze) and sunk by U.96. All 46 died.

CONCH (Captain C.G. Graham). Bound for the Tyne from Trinidad, sailing in the Bermuda section of Convoy HX.90 which rendezvoused with the Halifax and Sydney, Cape Breton, sections on 24 November 1940. Torpedoed by U.47 (Kptlt Günther Prien) at 5.25pm on 2 December and straggling when torpedoed twice by U.95 (Kptlt Gerd Schreiber) between 9.05 and 9.32am on the 3rd. Abandoned when sunk at about 11pm that day by U.99 (Kptlt Otto Kretschmer) in position 54°21′N 19°30′W. All 53 were picked up by the destroyer HMCS *St Laurent* (Lt H.S. Rayner) and landed at Greenock. (For details of other ships sunk in Convoy HX.90, see under *Tasso*, ELLERMAN GROUP.)

CONUS (Captain C. Asquith). Bound for Curaçao, sailing in Convoy OB.304 which left Liverpool on 30 March 1941 and dispersed on 4 April in position 62°20′N 20°15′W. During the evening of the 4th, torpedoed 3 times by U.97 (Kptlt Udo Heilmann) and sank in position 56°14′N 31°19′W. All 59 died, so it was not until after the war that relatives learned of their fate. In his book *Upon Their Lawful Occasions*, Vernon G.A. Upton states that so many ships sailing independently were lost with all hands that the only possible explanation is that their lifecraft were deliberately destroyed by the U-boats.

CORBIS (Captain S.W. Appleton). Independently bound for Cape Town from Abadan via Bandar Abbas when torpedoed four times and sunk by U.180 (Kptlt Werner Musenberg) at about 4am on 18 April 1943 in position 34°56′S 34°03′E. Fifty died. Ten drifted in a lifeboat for 13 days before being rescued by an SAAF crash launch and landed at East London.

DARINA (Captain J.M. Cuthill). Bound for Galveston, Texas, sailing in Convoy ON.93 which left Liverpool on 8 May 1942 and dispersed on reaching position 38°55′N 42°43′W on the 17th. Torpedoed by U.158 (Kptlt Erwin Rostin) at 10pm on the 20th in position 29°17′N 54°25′W. Three boats got away and the U-boat shelled the ship while the 1st Mate's boat returned to collect the Master, Chief Engineer and a seaman who had been left on board. Six died at the time, but others of the 50 rescued later died of their wounds. Those in the Master's boat were picked up by the tanker *British Ardour* and landed at Charleston, South Carolina, on the 27th. Those in the 3rd Mate's boat were picked up by the *Exanthia* (US) on the 26th and landed at Norfolk, Virginia. Those in the 1st Mate's boat were picked up by the *Dagrun* (Nor.) on the 26th and landed at Cape Town on 23 June.

The *Norland* (Nor.) (Captain E. Christoffersen), also dispersed from Convoy ON. 93, was torpedoed and sunk by gunfire by U.108 (Krvkpt. Klaus Scholtz) on 20 May. All 48 hands were rescued, and 14 picked up on the 25th by the *Polyphemus* (Du.) (Captain C. Koningstein) again survived when she was torpedoed and sunk by U.578 (Krvkpt. Ernst-August Rehwinkel) on the 27th. (See under *Polyphemus*, Dutch Blue Funnel, HOLT, ALFRED, & CO.)

DELPHINULA. Ran aground at entrance to Alexandria harbour on 9 May 1943 when arriving from Haifa. Petrol vapour surrounded the tanker when 2 tugs arrived to refloat her at 6am on the 18th and when this was ignited, either by a spark or flame on the ship herself or because one of the tugs had open fires, there was an explosion and a fire on board. The tugs also caught fire and all 3 vessels were abandoned. Several died and survivors were rescued from the water. Broke in two on 21 July and declared a total loss.

DIALA (Captain H.J.A. Peters). Bound for Los Angeles from Stanlow, sailing in Convoy ON.52 which left Liverpool on 31 December 1941 and dispersed on 11 January 1942. Torpedoed and severely damaged by U.553 (Kptlt Karl Thurmann) at 11.17pm on the 15th and abandoned in position 44°50′N 46°50′W. Fifty-seven died. Eight were picked up by the *Telefora de Larrinaga* and landed at New York. (See also under *Athelcrown*, ATHEL LINE.)

OTHER SHIPS SUNK AND DAMAGED AFTER THE DISPERSAL ON CONVOY ON.52

Nylot (Nor.) (Captain A.P. Andersen). By U.87 (Kptlt Joachim Berger) on the 17th. Twenty died. Twenty-one survivors landed at Halifax by the destroyer HMCS *St Clair* (A/Lt Cdr D.C. Wallace).

Toorak damaged by U.86 (Kptlt Walter Schug) on the 16th. None died.

DONAX (Captain J.M. Cuthill, ex-*Darina*). Sailed in Convoy ON.139 which left Liverpool on 16 October 1942 bound for New York. Torpedoed by U.443 (Oblt Konstantin von Puttkamer) at 9.45pm on the 22nd in position 49°51′N 27°58′W. Taken in tow by the tugs HMS *Nimble* and HMS *Marauder* (Lt F. Jennings) but sank in position 48°04′N 24°41′W on the 29th. None died. Thirty-eight were rescued by the corvette HMCS *Drumheller* (T/Lt L.P. Denny) and landed at St John's, Newfoundland. Ten were rescued by HMS *Nimble* and landed at Greenock, and 15 by a British destroyer.

OTHER SHIPS SUNK IN CONVOY ON.139

Primrose Hill (Captain M.D. Mackenzie). By UD.5 (Kpt. Bruno Mahn) when dispersed from the convoy. Three died. Forty-six picked up by the *Sansu* and landed at Freetown.

Winnipeg II (Captain O.F. Pennington). By U.443. All 192, including 68 passengers, picked up by the corvette HMCS *Morden* (T/Lt J.J. Hodgkinson) and landed at St John's, Newfoundland, on the 25th.

DONOVANIA (Captain D.B. Edgar). Independently bound for Trinidad from Lagos when torpedoed and sunk by U.160 (Oblt Georg Lassen) at 10.29am on 21 July 1942 in position 10°56′N 61°10′W. Five died. Forty-five were picked up by British MTBs and the destroyer USS *Livermore* and landed at Port of Spain.

DORSANUM. Seized while under construction in Hamburg in 1939. Sold to the Soviet Union in 1940 and renamed *Komsomolets*.

DORYSSA (Captain W. Fraser). Bound for Abadan, sailing from Cape Town on 24 April 1943, in ballast and unescorted. Torpedoed by the Italian submarine *Leonardo da Vinci* (T.V. Gianfranco Gazzana-Priaroggia) at 7.20pm on the 25th in position 37°03′S 24°04′E and sank when a second torpedo struck. Fifty-three died. Nine in No 3 boat, commanded by the 3rd Mate, Mr Quick, were picked up by HMSA patrol boat *Southern Barrier* on the 30th and landed at Cape Town on 4 May. (See also under *Manaar (II)*, BROCKLEBANK LINE.)

DOSINIA. Struck by a mine, broke in two and sank off Southport on 26 October 1940. All rescued, but no further details.

ELUSA (Du.) (Captain J.J. Beckeringh). Bound for the Clyde from Curaçao, sailing in Convoy HX.126 which left Halifax on 10 May 1941. Torpedoed and set ablaze by U.93 (Kptlt Claus Korth) at 5.29am on the 21st in position 59°00′N 38°05′W. Five died. Captain Beckeringh, who had remained on board, was picked up by a destroyer, together with 48 others from three lifeboats, and all were landed at Reykjavik on the 25th. The *Elusa* eventually sank in position 58°30′N 38°10′W.

OTHER SHIPS SUNK IN CONVOY HX.126

Barnby (Captain A.J. Gale). By U.111 (Kptlt Wilhelm Kleinschmidt). Two died. Forty-four landed at Reykjavik.

British Security. See under BRITISH TANKER CO. LTD.

Cockaponset (Captain B. Green). By U.556 (Kptlt Herbert Wohlfarth). All 41 picked up by the rescue tug *Hontestroom* (Du.) and landed at Reykjavik on the 27th.

Darlington Court. See under COURT LINE.

Harpagus (Captain J.V. Stewart). Returning to station when torpedoed by U.109 (Krvkpt. Hans-Georg Fischer). Fifty-eight died, including 26 from the *Norman Monarch*. Forty picked up by the destroyer HMS *Burnham* (Cdr J. Bostock) and landed at Reykjavik.

John P. Pedersen (Nor.) (Captain Hans A. Nilsen). By U.94. One died when the torpedo struck and 21 in a lifeboat were never heard of again. Sixteen in another lifeboat picked up by the *Hontestroom* on the 23rd.

Norman Monarch (Captain T.A. Robertson). By U.94 (Kptlt Herbert Kuppisch). All 48 picked up by the *Harpagus*.

Rothermere. See under DONALDSON LINE.

EULIMA (Captain F.W. Wickera). Sailed in Convoy ON.166 which left Liverpool on 11 February 1943 bound for New York. Sunk by 2 torpedoes and gunfire from U.186 (Kptlt Siegfried Hesemann) during the evening of the 23rd in position 46°48′N 36°18′W. Sixty-two died. The sole survivor was Mr J. Campkin, the 3rd Mate, who was taken prisoner by the U-boat and landed at Lorient on 5 March.

OTHER SHIPS SUNK IN CONVOY ON.166

21 February:

Empire Trader. See under SHAW SAVILL & ALBION.

Stigstad (Nor.) (Captain Odd Petersen). Straggled. Damaged by U.332 (Oblt Eberhard Hüttemann) and sunk by U.603 (Oblt Hans-Joachim Bertelsmann). Three died. Thirty-four picked up from a lifeboat by the trawler *Thomas Boot* (Skipper A. Howie) on 7 March and landed at Valentia.

22 February:

Chattanooga City (US) (Captain R.C. Forbes). Sunk by U.606 (Oblt Hans-Heinrich Döhler). All 58 picked up from 4 lifeboats and a raft by the corvette HMCS *Trillium* (Lt P.C. Evans) but the 11 armed guards transferred to the UCGC Spencer and all landed at St John's, Newfoundland.

Empire Redshank. See under DONALDSON LINE.

N.T. Nielsen Alonso (Nor.) (Captain Johan Bjerkholt). Badly damaged by U.92 and abandoned. Sunk by U.753 (Frgkpt. Alfred Manhardt von Mannstein). Three men in the engine room died. Fifty picked up by USCGC *Campbell* (Cdr James Hirshfield) but transferred to the Polish destroyer *Burza* (Lt Cdr Wojewodzki) and landed at St John's on the 27th.

23 February:

Expositor (US). Straggled. Damaged by U.606 late on the 22nd and abandoned. HMCS *Trillium* tried to sink her, but U.303 (Kptlt Karl-Franz Heine) succeeded on the 23rd. Survivors picked up by the *Trillium*. Nine died. Shortly after her attack, U.606 was depth-charged and sunk by the destroyer USS *Campbell* and the Polish destroyer *Burza*. Thirty-six died and 11 survived.

Glittre (Nor.) (Captain Ivar Kvadsheim). Badly damaged by U.628 (Kptlt Heinrich Hasenschar) and abandoned. Sunk by U.603. Three died. Thirty-four picked up by the corvette HMS *Dianthus* (Lt Cdr C.E. Bridgman) and landed at St John's on the 26th.

Hastings (US) (Captain R.O. West). Sunk by U.186 (Kptlt Siegfried Hesemann). Nine died. Fifty-three picked up by the corvette HMCS *Chilliwack* (Lt L.L. Foxall) and landed at St John's.

Stockport. When trying to catch up with the convoy after transferring the survivors of the *Empire Trader* to HMCS *Dauphin*, sunk by U.604 (Kptlt Horst Höltring). All 64 died.

Winkler (Pan.) (Captain A. Gasso). Straggling when damaged by U.223 (Kptlt Karl-Jürg Wächter) and sunk by U.628. Nineteen died and the remaining 32 picked up by HMS *Dianthus*.

24 February:

Ingria (Nor.) (Captain Fredrik Ditlefsen). Badly damaged by U.600 (Krvkpt. Bernhard Zurmühlen) and abandoned. Sunk by U.628 and all 39 picked up by the corvette HMCS *Rosthern* (Lt R.J.G. Johnson).

Jonathan Sturges (US) (Captain Thorbjorn Leerberg). Straggling when sunk by U.707 (Oblt Günter Gretschel). The survivors in one lifeboat were picked up by the destroyer USS *Belknap* on 12 March and landed at St John's. Those in another boat were picked up on 5 April by U.336 (Kptlt Hans Hunger), taken to Brest and then to a PoW camp at Bremen. The third boat, with Captain Leerberg and 16 others on board, was never seen again. Fifty-one died and 24 survived.

25 February:

Manchester Merchant. See under MANCHESTER LINERS.

(*Madoera* (Du.) (Captain J. Lassche). Damaged by U.653 (Kptlt Gerhard Feiler) at about 1.15am on the 24th and abandoned. When daylight came and the ship was still afloat, Captain Lassche, the Chief Engineer and 13 others reboarded and, with only one boiler working, they brought the ship into St John's on 1 March. Those in one of the lifeboats were picked up on 12 March by the USS *Belknap* and landed at Argentia in Newfoundland on the 14th. A second boat containing the 2nd Engineer, Mr G. van der Vuurst, 2 Dutch greasers and several Lascars was found by U.591 (Kptlt Hans-Jürgen Zetzsche). Mr van der Vuurst was taken prisoner, but later transferred to U.758 (Kptlt Helmut Manseck) which reached Bordeaux on 30 March. U.753 (Frgkpt. Alfred Manhardt von Mannstein) came across the third boat, containing 6 Dutchmen and 29 Lascars, on 27 February but took off only the Dutchmen who were landed at La Pallice. The 2 Dutch greasers and all the Lascars left in the 2 lifeboats by U.591 and U.753 were never seen again. Sixty died and 26 survived.)

EULOTA (Du.) (Captain B. Elzinga). Bound for Curaçao from Rotterdam when torpedoed by U.28 (Kptlt Günter Kuhnke) at 3.17am on 11 March 1940 in position 48°35′N 08°22′W. Abandoned but reboarded and on fire when spotted by a plane which directed HMS *Broke* (Cdr B.G. Scurfield) and HMS *Wild Swan* (Lt Cdr J.L. Younghusband) to the scene. All 42 were rescued and the still-floating bow section was sunk by the destroyers.

FIONA SHELL. In Gibraltar on the night of 19/20 September 1941 when sunk by human torpedoes operating from the Italian submarine *Sciré* (Cdr Prince Junio V.S. Borghese). One died. The *Denby Dale* and the *Durham* were also sunk, and the 6 crewmen of the torpedoes escaped by swimming to Spain.

GENOTA (Du.). Captured by the Japanese raider *Aikoku Maru* on 9 May 1942, when in the Mozambique Channel in position 17°40′S 76°20′E. Named changed to *Ōse*, but no further details.

GOLD SHELL. Approaching the Scheldt on 16 April 1945 when sunk by a mine. A lifeboat from the *Portia*, manned by her 2nd Mate D. Davidson and four other volunteers, braved the burning sea and picked up five DEMS gunners who had been blown clear. The gunners were subsequently landed at Antwerp. Thirty-five died. Twenty-nine survived, including the gunners. Among the survivors was her newly promoted Chief Engineer, W.W. Burns, who was permanently disfigured and blinded.

HARPA (Captain C.A. Howarth). Bound for Tanjung Priok when sunk by a British mine in the Singapore Strait on 27 January 1942. Thirty-four of her 41 crew died. (Four engineer officers had already been killed when she was bombed in Port Swettenham/Port Kelang on 22 December.)

HAVRE (Captain G.C. Pearson). In Convoy AT.49, bound for Tobruk from Alexandria when torpedoed and sunk by U.81 (Kptlt Friedrich Guggenberger) at 2.18am on 10 June 1942 in position 31°10′N 28°36′E. Twenty died. Thirty were picked up by the armed trawler HMS *Parktown* and landed at Mersa Matruh in Egypt.

OTHER SHIPS SUNK IN CONVOY AT.49

Athene (Nor.) (Captain T. Tharaldsen). By U.559 (Kptlt Hans Heidtmann). Fourteen died. Seventeen, some badly burned, picked up by the escorts.

Brambleleaf (Captain H.A. Shacklock). Badly damaged by U.559 and abandoned. Seven died. Fifty-three picked up by the Greek destroyer RHS *Vasilissa Olga* (Lt Cdr G. Blessas) and landed at Alexandria. Reboarded and towed to Alexandria where she was used as an oil storage hulk.

HERBORG (Nor.) (Captain J.O. Westad). With a cargo of crude oil, sailing from Abadan on 29 May 1942 bound for Fremantle. Captured by the German raider *Thor* (KptzS. Günther Gumprich) on 19 June in approximate position 26°S 77°E. All the crew, including 38 Chinese, were taken prisoner. Renamed *Hohenfriedberg* and, under a prize crew commanded by Oblt Rudolf Gerwin, sailed to Batavia (Djakarta) and then to Japan. Spotted by a USAAF B-24 when bound for France on 20 February 1943 and scuttled when intercepted by HMS *Sussex* in position 41°45′N 20°58′W.

HORN SHELL (Captain A. MacDougall). Bound independently for Trinidad from Gibraltar when struck by 4 torpedoes fired by the Italian submarine *Barbarigo* (C.C. Francesco Murzi) at about 9pm on 26 July 1941 in position 33°23′N 22°18′W. Those in No 1 lifeboat, with the Master in charge, were picked up by the *Cuyaba* (Braz.) on 8 August and landed at Pernambuco. No 2 boat, with the 1st Mate in charge, was never seen again. Those in No 3 boat, with the 2nd Mate in charge, were picked up by the *Africa Occidental* and landed at St Vincent in the Cape Verde Islands, while those in No 4 boat, with the 3rd Mate F. Harvey, in charge, were picked up by the *Maria Leonor* (Port.) on the 14th but transferred to the destroyer HMS *Avondale* on the 19th. Seventeen died, including Mr Walker, the 1st Radio Officer, who died in No 4 boat, and 40 were rescued.

IRIS (Du.). Requisitioned by the Royal Netherlands Navy as an auxiliary tanker and renamed *TAN 9*. Scuttled in the River Musi, Plaju, Sumatra, on 15 February 1942 but salvaged by the Japanese and renamed *Kikusui Maru*. In a convoy when torpedoed by the submarine USS *Snook* (Lt Cdr G.H. Browne) on 24 October 1942 in position 19°26′N 118°15′E and sank the next day.

JAN CARSTENSZ (Du.). Sunk on 31 March 1942 at Ambon by the Netherlands East Indian Army to prevent her falling into the hands of the Japanese.

J.H. MENTEN (Du.). Scuttled as a blockade ship at Macassar on 2 March 1942.

JOSEFINA (Du.). Requisitioned by the Royal Netherlands Navy as an auxiliary tanker and renamed *TAN 6*. Scuttled at Soerabaja on 2 March 1942 but salvaged by the Japanese and renamed *Yosei Maru*. Torpedoed and sunk by the submarine USS *Baya* (Lt Cdr B.C. Jarvis) on 13 May 1945 in position 06°18′S 111°11′E.

JUNO (Du.). Requisitioned by the Royal Netherlands Navy as an auxiliary tanker and renamed *TAN 2*. Scuttled at Soerabaja on 2 March 1942 but salvaged by the Japanese and renamed *Yuno Maru*. On 30 April 1945, struck a mine laid by the submarine USS *Guitarro* (Lt Cdr T.B. Dabney) and sank in position 01°00′S 104°186′E.

JUSTINA (Du.). Bound for Curaçao from Maracaibo, sank in the Caribbean on 23 September 1944 after colliding with the tanker *Yamhill* (US). No further details.

KASUARIS (Du.). A 340-ton tanker scuttled at Soerabaja on 2 March 1942 to avoid capture by the Japanese.

LETICIA (Captain J.J.T. Gilde) (Du.). Sailing independently and bound for the UK from Curaçao and Trinidad when torpedoed by U.47 (Kptlt Günther Prien) at 5.5pm on 27 June 1940 in position 50°11′N 13°15′W. The U-boat surfaced, but refrained from sinking the ship by shellfire until she was abandoned. Prien gave dry clothing and schnapps to three men whom the U-boat picked up from the sea and provided the lifeboats with first aid materials, sausages and wine. Two died. Twenty-eight, including the seriously wounded 2nd Mate, were picked up the same evening by the destroyer HMS *Hurricane* (Lt Cdr H.C. Simms) and landed at Plymouth on the 29th.

LUCRECIA (Du.) (Captain C. Smith). Sailing independently and bound for Falmouth from Aruba when torpedoed by U.34 (Kptlt Wilhelm Rollmann) at 7.14am on 7 July 1940 in position 49°50′N 08°07′W. Two died. Survivors were picked up by the *Alfarrarede* (Port.).

MAGDALA (Du.). Bound for Stanlow, sailing in ballast from Reykjavik in Convoy RU.150 on 15 January 1945 and never heard of again.

MAJA (Captain W.C. Robinson). Unescorted and bound for Reykjavik from Swansea and Belfast when torpedoed and sunk by U.1055 (Oblt Rudolf Meyer) on 15 January 1945 in position 53°40′N 05°14′W. Twenty-five died. Forty were picked up by the Belgian trawler *Hendrik Conscience* and landed at Holyhead.

MAMURA (Du.) (Captain P. Dobbenga). Sailing independently and bound for Halifax from Houston and New York when torpedoed twice and sunk by U.504 (Krvkpt. Hans-Georg Friedrich Poske) at 7.13pm on 26 February 1942 in position 29°00′N 76°20′W. All 49 died.

MANVANTARA (Du.) (Captain W.L. Happee). Packed with refugees, sailed in a convoy which left Singapore at 6.30pm on 13 February 1942 bound for Palembang on Sumatra. Bombed and sunk by Japanese planes in the Banka Strait. Four died. (See under *Merula*.)

MARISA (Du.) (Captain J.C. Landman). Bound independently for Curaçao from Freetown when torpedoed twice by U.107 (Kptlt Günther Hessler) between 0036 hours and 0115 hours on 17 May 1941 in position 06°10′N 18°09′W. Abandoned and sunk by gunfire by the U-boat. Three lifeboats got away. One boat was found on the 20th by the corvette HMS *Columbine* (T/Lt S.J. Lavis) and another by the patrol yacht HMS *Surprise*. The remaining boat landed at French Guinea on the 23rd. Two died and 47 survived.

MERULA (Du.) (Captain G.J. Tapperwijn). Packed with refugees, sailing in the same convoy as the *Manvantara*. Severely damaged by Japanese planes, taken in tow by the tanker

Herborg (Nor.) but later abandoned. Forty-two died. The boom carrier HMS *Bulan* and the frigate HMAS *Toowoomba* rescued the survivors of both tankers and landed them at Tanjung Priok.

MEXPHALTE (Fr.). Seized by the Germans after the occupation of France and renamed *Hedgehog*. Bombed and sunk in Kiel on 16 September 1944, but salvaged. Bombed and sunk, again in Kiel, on 3 April 1945. Again salvaged, and returned to Shell Algiers after the war.

MILO (Du.). A 322-ton tanker scuttled off Tanjung Priok on 2 March 1942 to avoid capture by the Japanese.

MOEARA BOELIAN (Du.). Scuttled off Soerabaja on 6 March 1942.

OCANA (Du.). Bound independently for Halifax from Curaçao when torpedoed by U.552 (Kptlt Erich Topp) at 4.13am on 25 March 1942 in position 42°36′N 65°30′W. Fifty-three died. Four were picked up some hours later by the destroyer USS *Mayo*. The burned-out wreck was sunk by the minesweeper HMCS *Burlington* (Lt J.M. Richardson) on 15 April in position 43°24′N 64°45′W.

OHIO (Managed and owned by the Texas Oil Co.) (Captain D.W. Mason). In Convoy WS.21S (Operation Pedestal) which sailed from Gibraltar on 10 August 1942 bound for Malta. Torpedoed by the Italian submarine *Axum* (T.V. Renato Ferrini) on the 12th while the convoy was being attacked by Junkers 88s. When off the island of Pantelleria a near miss buckled the ship's plates, and when her guns brought down a Junkers 87 it crashed into her starboard side and exploded. After bombs hit the tanker she came to a halt. The story of Operation Pedestal is more comprehensively told elsewhere, but supported by the destroyers HMS *Penn* (Cdr J.H. Swain) and HMS *Ledbury* (Cdr Hill) she arrived in Valletta on the 15th and subsequently broke in two. On 19 September 1946, both halves were towed out to sea and sunk by gunfire. The death toll among both merchant and naval seamen on ships sunk and damaged in the convoy amounted to over 400. (For ships sunk in Operation Pedestal, see under *Waimarama* and *Empire Hope*, SHAW SAVILL & ALBION, *Deucalion* and *Glenorchy*, HOLT, ALFRED, & CO., *Clan Ferguson*, CLAN LINE, and *Dorset*, FEDERAL STEAM NAVIGATION CO.)

OLIVIA (Du.). Intercepted by the German raider *Thor* (KptzS. Günther Gumprich) in the Indian Ocean on 14 June 1942 in approximate position 26°S 77°E. Shelled and became a blazing inferno in which most of the crew died, shocking those who witnessed it on the *Thor*. One man was picked up from the blazing sea by a boat from the *Thor*. One boat, containing 4 Dutch and 8 Chinese, got away. One Dutchman and 7 Chinese died in the boat before it landed at Madagascar on 13 July. Forty-one died. Five survived.

ONOBA (Du.). Damaged in an air raid on Liverpool on 21 December 1940. Sunk by German planes, 140 miles west of Tory Island, Ireland, on 16 January 1941 in position 55°33′N 12°14′W. None died.

OSCILLA (Du.) (Captain M.A.F. Kuypers). Sailed in Convoy ON.71 which left Liverpool on 26 February 1942 and dispersed on 11 March. Bound for Curaçao when torpedoed twice, shelled and sunk by the Italian submarine *Morosini* (C.C. Athos Fraternale) at about 11pm on the 16th, 100 miles north of Bermuda in approximate position 19°N 60°W. Four died and 51 were rescued by the *Explorer* (US). Four officers were subsequently being carried to the UK on the Dutch ship *Leto* (Captain E.H. van der Veen) when she was sunk by U.553 (Krvkpt. Karl Thurmann) on 12 May, and 2 of them were among the 12 who died.

OTINA (Captain G.L. Forrest). Bound for New York from Belfast, sailing in Convoy ON.153 which left Liverpool on 11 December 1942. Straggling when torpedoed twice and sunk by U.621 (Oblt Max Kruschkaat) at 10.21pm on the 20th in position 47°40′N 33°06′W. All 60 died.

OTHER SHIPS SUNK IN CONVOY ON.153

Bello (Nor.) (Captain Trygve Bernt). By U.610 (Oblt Freiherr Walter von Freyberg-Eisenberg-Allmendingen). Thirty-three died. Seven picked up by the corvette HMS *Pink* (Lt R. Atkinson) and landed at St John's on the 29th.

Emile Francqui (Belg.) (Captain F. Paret). By U.664 (Oblt Adolf Graef). Fifty-nine died. Nineteen picked up by HMS *Pink* and the *Saint Bertrand*.

HMS *Firedrake* (Cdr E.H. Tilden). Destroyer. By U.211 (Kptlt Karl Hause). One hundred and seventy died. Twenty-seven picked up by the corvette HMS *Sunflower* (Lt Cdr J.T. Jones) but one died from his wounds.

(*Regent Lion*. Damaged by U.610.)

OVATELLA. Newly built in Odense and seized when the Germans invaded Denmark on 9 April 1940. Renamed *Weissenburg* and used as a supply tanker.

PATELLA (Captain R.M. Barber). Bound for the Cape from Trinidad when shelled by the German raider *Michel* (KptzS. Helmuth von Ruckteschell) on 19 April 1942 about 1,200 miles east of Rio de Janeiro. Three killed, 60 taken prisoner and the ship scuttled by demolition charges. On 8 May, the *Michel* rendezvoused with *Charlotte Schliemann* and all prisoners were transferred to her for transportation to Japan. Captain Barber died in captivity on 16 February 1944 at the age of 39. (See also under *Lylepark*, DENHOLM, J. & J., LTD, *Empire Dawn*, RUNCIMAN, WALTER, & CO. LTD/MOOR LINE LTD, *Arabistan*, STRICK LINE, and *Gloucester Castle*, UNION-CASTLE LINE.)

PAULA (Du.). Requisitioned by the Royal Netherlands Navy and renamed *TAN 1*. Scuttled at Tanjung Priok on 1 March 1942. Salvaged by the Japanese and renamed *Arare Maru*. Found sunk at Singapore at the end of the war. Salvaged and returned to owners.

PECTEN (Captain H.E. Dale). Bound for the Clyde from Trinidad, sailing in Convoy HX.65 which left Halifax, Nova Scotia, on 12 August 1940. Straggling when torpedoed and sunk by U.57 (Oblt Erich Topp) at 7.48pm on 25 August 1940 in position 56°22′N 07°55′W. Forty-nine died. Eight were picked up by the *Torr Head* but transferred to the armed trawler HMS *Robina* and landed at Belfast. (For details of other ships sunk in Convoy HX.65, see under *Empire Merlin*, ROPNER SHIPPING CO.)

PETRONELLA (Du.). Sunk by a mine when on passage from Alexandria to Piraeus on 15 October 1944. Twenty-five died.

PHASIANELLA (Australian). Scuttled at Tanjung Priok on 3 March 1942. Salvaged by the Japanese and renamed *Arukani Maru*. Broken up in China after the war.

PHOBOS (Du.). Damaged by a mine 5 miles east of the North Goodwin Light Vessel on 20 March 1940. When undergoing repairs at Schiedam, she was seized by the Germans when they invaded the Netherlands in May. Operating as the *Thann*, she was mined and sunk in the Baltic on 29 December 1944 in position 54°41′N 12°35′E.

PINNA (Captain W.A. Thomas). Bound for beleaguered Singapore from Pladjoe, near Palembang in Sumatra, when attacked by Japanese planes during the afternoon of 3 February 1942. The crew's accommodation received a direct hit, but the ship was able to continue. Machine-gunned and bombed in Singapore harbour the next day and sank. Survivors were picked up from a lifeboat and a raft by HMS *Bulan* and taken ashore in her launch. Twenty died and others, including the wounded Master, were taken prisoner when Singapore fell to the Japanese, but a few escaped and eventually reached the UK.

PLEIODON. Captured by the Japanese in Singapore on 15 February 1942 and renamed *Nansei Maru*. Sunk by the submarine USS *Ray* (Lt Cdr W.T. Kinsella) in the China Sea at about 2pm on 18 August 1944 in position 08°39′N 116°39′E.

POMELLA. Bound for Portsmouth, sailing from Milford Haven in Convoy WP.183 on 7 July 1942. Seven *schnellboote* (E-boats), led by Krvkpt. Klaus Feldt, attacked the convoy in Lyme Bay shortly after midnight on the 9th. Torpedoed twice and sunk by S-67 (Kptlt Felix Zymalkowski). No further details.

OTHER SHIPS SUNK IN CONVOY WP.183

D/S *Røsten* (Nor.) (Captain Tolle Tollisen). By S-109 (Cdr Dross). Six died, including the Master, British Mess Boy Eluina Varipati and DEMS Gunner A. Graham, RN (D/JX 290984). Twelve survived, including a British DEMS gunner. See *Gripfast* below.

D/S *Kongshaug* (Nor.) (Captain Einar Apeland). By S-48 (Kptlt Götz Freiherr von Mirbach). Eight died, including Signalmen C.W.J. Healey, RN (C/JX 232566) and W.B. Tremorrow RN (C/JX 171121). Fourteen, including the British commodore, and an RN DEMS signaller landed at Portsmouth by the destroyer HMS *Brocklesbay* (Lt Cdr E.G. Pumphrey).

HMT *Manor* (Skipper B. Pile). By S-63. Second Hand C.H.J. Foal, picked up by the HMT *Ruby*, was the sole survivor.

Reggestrom (Du.). By S-50.

D/S *Bokn*. (Nor.) (Captain Adolf O. Mæle). By S-70 (Lt Klose). Twelve died, including DEMS gunners D. Hezelgrave, RN (P/JX 263494) and C.F.H. Davis, RN (P/JX 333292). Four survivors landed at Portsmouth.

Gripfast. Sunk later in the day by German planes. Seven died, including 5 survivors she had picked up from the D/S *Røsten*.

POSEIDON (Du.). A small tanker of 696 tons, scuttled off Tjilatjap, Java, on 6 March 1942 to avoid capture by the Japanese. Raised by them and sailed under the name *Hosei Maru* until sunk by gunfire from the RNN submarine O-19 (Lt Cdr J.F. Drijfhout van Hoof) on 10 April 1945 in position 5°25′S 106°39′E.

ROSALIA (Du.) (Captain J. van der Linden). Unescorted and bound for Curaçao from Maracaibo when torpedoed by U.615 (Kptlt Ralph Kapitzky) at 2am on 28 July 1943 in position 12°07′N 69°13′W. Broke in two, caught fire and sank at 4.25am. Twenty-three died. Thirteen were picked up by the submarine chaser HNMS H-8 and the rescue boat *MBR-50*.

ROTULA (Du.). Bound for Swansea from Curaçao, sailing in Convoy SC.22 which left Halifax on 8 February 1941. Bombed by German planes on 1 March and abandoned in position 52°20′N 05°29′W. Sixteen died and 32 survived. The wreck was sunk by an armed trawler. The *Kervégan* (Fr.), also in the convoy, foundered on 9 February. All died.

Although not sunk when in the convoy, the Norwegian tanker *Mexico* (Captain Godtfred Sandnes) did not reach her destination as she was sunk by a mine near the Thames estuary on 6 March when in coastal Convoy FS.427. Ten died and 20 were picked up by the destroyer HMS *Witherington*.

SAN ALBERTO (Captain G. Waite, later Master of the *San Demetrio* when in the Jarvis Bay Convoy, and of the *San Ernesto*). Bound for Trinidad from the Clyde, sailing in Convoy OB.48 which left Liverpool on 6 December 1939. Torpedoed by U.48 (Kptlt Herbert Schultze) at 7.10am on the 9th in position 49°20′N 09°45′W and broke in two. The fore part sank and the ship was abandoned, but as the after part remained afloat it was reboarded and the crew provided with hot meals. With the weather continuing to worsen, the lifeboats could not be hoisted and were eventually smashed. At dawn the next day the Belgian tanker *Alexandre André* arrived at the scene and 3 seamen, who succeeded in reaching her by diving into the rough sea, were taken to Weymouth. The destroyer HMS *Mackay* (Cdr G.H. Stokes) arrived at 11pm but it was the next morning before the 35 remaining men could be transferred to her and the stern section sank shortly afterwards. HMS *Mackay* took the survivors to Liverpool. One died. (For the *Brandon*, also in Convoy OB.48, see under SALVESEN, CHRISTIAN.)

SAN ALVARO (Captain G.A.H. Knott). Bound for Suez via Aden from Abadan in Convoy PA.69 when torpedoed by U.510 (Oblt Alfred Eick) on 22 February 1944 and abandoned in position 13°46′N 48°49′E. One died. Fifty-two were picked up by HMAS *Tamworth* (Lt F.E. Eastman) which sank the burning wreck.

OTHER SHIPS SUNK AND DAMAGED IN CONVOY PA.69 BY U.510

E.G. Seubert (US) (Captain I. Boklund). Six died. Sixty-four picked up by the minesweeper HMAS *Tamworth* and corvette HMIS *Orissa* and landed at Aden on the 24th.

Erling Brøvig (Nor.) (Captain R.V. Jacobsen). Damaged and towed to Aden. None died.

SAN ARCADIO (Captain W.F. Flynn). Sailed unescorted from Houston bound for Halifax to join a convoy to the Mersey. Torpedoed twice by U.107 (Oblt Harald Gelhaus) at 4.45pm on 31 January 1942 in position 38°10′N 63°50′W. Torpedoed again about 2 hours later and sank. Forty-one died, including Captain Flynn who had survived the sinking of the *San Tiburcio*. Nine were picked up by a US flying boat and landed at Bermuda.

SAN CALISTO (Captain A.R. Hicks). Bound for Houston and on passage from Hull to Southend to join a convoy when struck by 2 mines as she altered course to pass the Tongue Light Vessel shortly after noon on 2 December 1939. Six died; 8 seriously injured and survivors landed at Margate.

SAN CASIMIRO (Captain H.R. Shotton). Bound for Curaçao, sailing in Convoy OB.294 which left Liverpool on 5 March 1941 and dispersed in position 51°29′N 20°30′W on the 9th. Shelled, damaged and captured by the *Gneisenau* on the 15th in position 39°58′N 43°19′W. The Master and two DEMS gunners were transferred to the warship, while the others remained prisoners of the German prize crew. An RRRR message had been transmitted and, 5 days later, a single plane circled the ship. The Chief Steward Mr Hoggett and the cook, who had the freedom to move about the ship, hastily prepared a thick paste of flour and water and spelt out the letters SOS, 6ft high on the poop deck. Shortly after this, the prisoners were informed that the ship was to be scuttled, but while this was being done and the wireless room was ablaze more planes arrived and the warships HMS *Renown* and HMS *Ark Royal*, from which they had flown, appeared on the scene. The planes were firing at the ship when she was abandoned. The German prize crew and the prisoners were taken into the care of the Royal Navy and the blazing tanker sunk by HMS *Renown* on the 20th in position 45°12′N 19°42′W. (For details of the many ships sunk and captured by the *Scharnhorst* and the *Gneisenau*, see under *British Strength*, BRITISH TANKER CO. LTD.)

SAN CONRADO. On 9 March 1941 was sailing in the Bermuda section of Convoy HX.114 which joined up with the main (Halifax) section at sea bound for the UK. Attacked by German aircraft when about 10 miles off the Smalls on 1 April. Bombed and machine-gunned, taken in tow, bombed again and sank the next day. None died.

OTHER SHIPS SUNK AND DAMAGED IN CONVOY HX.114

Hidlefjord (Nor.) (Captain H. Gullestad). Bombed and abandoned. Twenty-nine died. Five rescued by the *York City* and landed at Milford Haven.

Kaia Knudsen (Nor.) (Captain J. Fagerland). Damaged. One died and several seriously wounded.

SAN DELFINO (Captain A.E. Gumbleton). Bound for Halifax and Hull, sailing independently from Houston on 3 April 1942. Torpedoed seven times by U.203 (Kptlt Rolf Mützelburg) between 3.47am and 5.08am on the 10th and sank in position 35°35′N 75°06′W. Twenty-eight died. Twenty-two were picked up by the ASW trawler HMS *Norwich City* (Lt L.H. Stammers) and landed at Morehead City, North Carolina.

SAN DEMETRIO (Captain C. Vidot). On passage from Baltimore to Halifax and sailing independently to join a convoy for the UK when torpedoed and sunk by U.404 (Kptlt Otto von Bülow) at 2.16am on 16 March 1942 in position 37°03'N 73°50'W. Nineteen died. Thirty-two were picked up by the *Beta* (US) on the 18th and landed at Norfolk, Virginia.

SAN EMILIANO (Captain J.W. Tozer). Bound for Suez via the Cape, sailing in Convoy E.7 which left Trinidad on 6 August 1942 and dispersed at 3am on the 8th. Torpedoed twice by U.155 (Kptlt Adolf Cornelius Piening) at about 9.30pm on the 9th in position 07°22'N 54°08'W, abandoned, and sank at 7am the next day. Only one lifeboat, with the 1st Mate T.D. Finch in charge, got away from the blazing tanker, and Mr Finch was making to return to collect Captain Tozer and the Chief Steward Mr C.D. Bennell when the former forbade him to do so as it would endanger the boat. After picking up men from the sea, the boat contained 12 men. Apprentice D.O. Clarke, 2nd Mate R. Hudson, a steward, and a greaser, all badly burned, died in the boat before it was spotted by a plane which dropped supplies. Forty died and 8, some of whom were badly injured, were picked up by the US troopship *General Thomas S. Jessop* during the evening of the 10th and landed at Paramaribo at 11am on the 11th.

SAN ERNESTO (Captain G. Waite). Bound independently for Bahrain from Sydney, Australia, when torpedoed by the Japanese submarine I-37 (Cdr Kiyonori Otani) on 15 June 1943 in position 09°18'S 80°20'E. Abandoned as a second torpedoed struck her. The submarine surfaced and machine-gunned the ship, but 3 lifeboats got away. Those in the Master's boat were picked up on the 23rd by a merchant ship bound for Australia. Twenty-eight days later the other two boats, commanded by the 2nd and 3rd Mates, landed at the Maldives. One was killed and 1 died of exposure. The *San Ernesto* drifted 2,000 miles to Pulau Nias, an island off the coast of Sumatra, and was broken up by the Japanese.

SAN FABIAN (Captain L.G. Emmott). Bound for the UK from Curaçao and in Convoy TAW.15 when torpedoed and sunk by U.511 (Kptlt Friedrich Steinhoff) at 6.29am on 27 August 1942 in position 18°09'N 74°38'W. Twenty-six died. Thirty-three were picked up by the destroyer USS *Lea* and the patrol craft USS PC-38 and landed at Guantanamo Bay.

OTHER SHIPS SUNK BY U.511 – TORPEDOED AT THE SAME TIME AS THE
SAN FABIAN

Esso Aruba (Captain F. Pharr). Damaged, but made it to Guantanamo Bay under her own power at 10pm the next day. None died.

Rotterdam (Du.) (Captain W. de Raat). Ten died. Thirty-seven picked up by the submarine chaser USS *SC-522*.

SAN FERNANDO (Captain A.R. Buckley). Bound for Milford Haven from Curaçao, sailing in Convoy HX.49 which left Halifax on 9 June 1940. Torpedoed by U.47 (Kptlt Günther Prien) at 8.07pm on the 21st in position 50°20'N 10°24'W. Taken in tow by tugs, but sank the next day. All 49 were picked up by the sloops HMS *Fowey* (Cdr H.B. Ellison) and HMS *Sandwich* (Cdr M.J. Yeatman) and landed at Plymouth.

OTHER SHIPS SUNK IN CONVOY HX.49

Eli Knudsen (Nor.) (Captain M. Midbøe). Dispersed from the convoy when torpedoed by U.32 (Oblt Hans Jenisch). All 37 picked up by HMS *Sandwich* and landed at Liverpool.

Moordrecht (Du.) (Captain I. Hutjes). Dispersed from the convoy on the 18th and torpedoed by U.48 (Krvkpt. Hans Rudolf Rösing) on the 20th. Twenty-five died. Four picked up from a lifeboat by the *Orion* (Gr.) on the 23rd and landed at Liverpool on the 29th.

Randsfjord (Nor.) (Captain H. Pedersen). By U.30 (Kptlt Fritz-Julius Lemp). Four died. Twenty-nine picked up by the *Port Hobart* after 36 hours in a lifeboat and landed at Glasgow on the 25th.

SAN FLORENTINO (Captain R.W. Davis). Bound for Curaçao from the Clyde and in Convoy OB.19 which sailed from Liverpool on 21 September 1941. Dispersed from the convoy and sailing independently when torpedoed and severely damaged at 7.45pm on 1 October by U.94 (Oblt Otto Ites) in position 52°50′N 34°40′W. Struck by 2 more torpedoes about 2½ hours later, but proceeded on her way until she began to break in two in the early hours of the 2nd when yet a fourth torpedo was put into her. The protracted nature of the attacks was due to the U-boat having to avoid the fire from the ship's solitary 4.7in gun. As an SSSS message had been transmitted, the corvettes HMCS *Alberni* (Lt Cdr G.O. Baugh) and HMCS *Mayflower* (Lt Cdr G. Stephen) arrived. The latter, which picked up 33 from the lifeboats and 2 who had clung to the half-submerged stern section for 15 hours, took them to St John's, Newfoundland. The former sank the stern section. Twenty-three died.

OTHER SHIPS SUNK IN CONVOY OB.19

Empire Wave (Captain C.P. Maclay). By U.562 (Oblt Horst Hamm). Twenty-nine died. Thirty-one picked up by the Icelandic trawler *Surprise* and landed at St Patrick's Fjord, Iceland.

Hatasu (Captain W.J. Meek). By U.431 (Kptlt Wilhelm Dommes). Forty died. Seven picked up after 7 days in a lifeboat by the destroyer USS *Charles F. Hughes* and landed at Reykjavik.

SAN GERARDO (Captain S. Foley). Sailing independently and bound for Halifax from Curaçao when torpedoed and sunk by U.71 (Kptlt Walter Flachsenberg) at 10.22pm on 31 March 1942 in approximate position 36°N 67°W. Fifty-one died. Six were picked up by the *Regent Panther* and landed at Halifax.

SAN TIBURCIO (Captain W.F. Flynn). Bound for Invergordon from Scapa Flow when she struck a mine at 8.10pm on 4 May 1940 in position 57°46′N 03°45′W. Broke in two and sank. All 40 were picked up by the ASW trawler HMS *Leicester City* (T/Lt A.R. Cornish) and landed at Invergordon.

SAN VICTORIO (Captain S. Perry). On her maiden voyage and independently bound for Freetown from Aruba when torpedoed and blown up by U.155 (Kptlt Adolf Cornelius Piening) at 2.17am on 17 May 1942 in position 11°40′N 62°33′W. Fifty-two died. The sole survivor, DEMS gunner A. Ryan of a maritime regiment of the Royal Artillery, blown over the side from the poop, was picked up by the patrol yacht USS *Turquoise* and landed at Trinidad.

SCALARIA (Captain J. Waring). Loading at the Egyptian oil terminal of Ras Gharib on the Red Sea when attacked by German aircraft at about 11pm on 19 October 1942. Struck by an aerial torpedo and bombs, and sank in shallow water. Eleven died. Survivors, including many wounded, were picked up by a motor launch.

SEMIRAMIS (Du.). Scuttled near Palembang on 12 February 1942. Salvaged by the Japanese and sailed as the *Kyoko Maru* until torpedoed and sunk by the submarine USS *Ray* (Lt Cdr B.J. Harral) in the Flores Sea on 27 December 1943 in position 05°00′S 121°22′E.

SHELBRIT I (Captain W. Martin). In the Moray Firth bound for Inverness from Grangemouth when, at about 8am on 19 September 1940, she exploded, caught fire and sank in position 57°39′N 03°56′W. It was assumed that she struck a mine. All 21 died.

SHELL 4 (Fin.). Bombed and sunk by German planes near Oritsaari, USSR, on 17 June 1944. No further details.

SHU KWANG. Requisitioned by the Royal Navy as anti-submarine vessel HMS *Shu Kwang*. Bombed and sunk by Japanese planes south of Bintan Island, Dutch East Indies, on 14 February 1942 in position 00°42′N 104°30′E when attempting to reach Tanjung Priok with refugees from Singapore. Twenty died. Two hundred and seventy-three survived; some were rescued by the palm oil carrier *Tanjong Pinang* and landed at Tembilahan, Sumatra. Salvaged by the Japanese and renamed *Fukuan Maru*. Hit a mine on 23 December 1944 and sank in the Berhala Strait in approximate position 00°34′S 104°17′E. Again with refugees on board, the *Tanjong Pinang* was sunk by gunfire from a Japanese submarine on the 17th with great loss of life.

SIMNIA (Captain J.R. Anderson). Bound for Curaçao, sailing in Convoy OB.294 which left Liverpool on 5 March 1941 and dispersed on the 9th in position 51°29′N 20°30′W. Proceeding independently when attacked by the *Gneisenau* at 3.30pm on 15 March 1941 in position 40°28′N 43°30′W. Received 5 directed hits and abandoned by all but the Master and a few others. All, however, were taken on board the warship before she sank the *Simnia*. Many prisoners were subsequently transferred to the infamous *Altmark*, now under a different name, but Captain Anderson and Captain Shotton of the *San Casimiro* remained on the *Gneisenau* until she docked in Brest on 22 March. Three died on the *Simnia* which was sunk later on the same day that the *San Casimiro* was captured (see above). (Operating together, the *Gneisenau* and the *Scharnhorst*, under the command of Admiral Günther Lütjens, sank 15 ships. For details, see under *British Strength*, BRITISH TANKER CO. LTD.)

SITALA (Captain J.L. Morgan). Bound for Manchester from Curaçao, sailing from Halifax, Nova Scotia, in Convoy HX.79 on 8 October 1940. Torpedoed by U.100 (Kptlt Joachim Schepke) at 0015 hours on the 20th and abandoned in position 56°37′N 17°15′W. One died. Forty-three were picked up by HMS *Lady Elsa* and landed at Belfast. (For details of other ships sunk and damaged in Convoy HX.79, see under *Wandby*, ROPNER SHIPPING CO. See also under *Caprella* above.)

SUMATRA. Sunk by the Royal Navy in Hong Kong on 20 December 1941 to avoid capture. Salvaged by the Japanese and renamed *Sumatra Maru*. Sunk in Phuket harbour, Thailand, by Chariot-manned torpedoes launched 6 miles out by the submarine HMS *Trenchant* (Lt Cdr A.R. Hezlet) on 27 October 1944.

TELENA (Captain H.F. Gosling). Bound independently for Pauillac, on the Gironde, from Tripoli in Lebanon when, at 7.14am on 29 May 1940, U.37 (Kptlt Victor Oehrn) fired three warning shots across her bows and then at the ship when her radio was used. On fire when abandoned in position 42°15′N 09°04′W and ran aground in shallow water. Eighteen died. Eighteen were picked up by the Spanish trawlers *Buena Esperanza* and *Jose Ignacio de C* and landed at Mari and El Grove near Vigo. The wreck was seized, salvaged and repaired by Spain, and sailed under the name *Gerona* until broken up in 1975.

TEMBUSU (Du.). A 344-ton tanker scuttled off Soerabaja on 2 March 1942 to avoid capture by the Japanese.

THIARA (Captain R.W. Thompson). Bound for Curaçao and in Convoy OB.188 which sailed from Liverpool on 23 July 1940. Torpedoed and sunk by U.34 (Kptlt Wilhelm Rollmann) at 3.13am on the 27th in position 56°37′N 17°56′W. Twenty-five died. Thirty-six were picked up the destroyer HMS *Winchelsea* (Lt Cdr W.A.F. Hawkins) and landed at Liverpool.

OTHER SHIPS SUNK IN CONVOY OB.188 – ALL BY U.34

Accra. See under ELDER DEMPSTER LINE.

Sambre (Captain E.B. Ingram). All 48 picked up by HMS *Winchelsea*.

Vinemoor (Captain D.J. Jones). All 32 picked up by HMS *Clarkia* but transferred to the *Hollinside* and landed at Liverpool.

TORINIA (Captain H. Jackson). Bound for the Clyde, sailing in Convoy HX.72 which left Halifax on 9 September 1940. Torpedoed and damaged by U.100 (Kptlt Joachim Schepke) on the 21st in position 54°55′N 18°17′W. Scuttled by the destroyer HMS *Skate* (Lt F.B. Baker). All 55 were picked up by the *Skate* and landed at Londonderry on the 23rd. (For details of other ships sunk in Convoy HX.72, see under *Scholar*, HARRISON LINE.)

TRICULA (Captain O.E. Sparrow). Bound for Cape Town, sailing in a convoy which left Trinidad on 1 August 1942 and dispersed on the morning of the 3rd. Torpedoed by U.108 (Krvkpt. Klaus Scholtz) at 10.20pm that same day in position 11°35′N 56°51′W and sank in less than a minute. Forty-seven died. Eleven were picked up from rafts by the *Rio San Juan* (Arg.) and landed at Fernando, Cuba.

TURBO (Captain J.B. Jones). Sailed from Haifa during the evening of 19 August 1942 bound for Alexandria. Attacked by two Italian planes at 5.45pm the next day. Struck by an aerial torpedo, but managed to travel slowly to Port Said where she arrived on the 21st and discharged her cargo. Because she was severely damaged it was decided that the *Gladys*

Moller should tow her to Karachi to be used as an oil storage hulk. Under tow on 4 April she broke in two in the Red Sea about 15 miles north of Ras Banas, Egypt. The after part sank, but the bow section was later sunk by gunfire as it was a danger to shipping. No information regarding casualties.

Managed for Ministry of War Transport

EMPIRE SPENSER (Captain J.B. Hodge). Bound for Stanlow from Curaçao, sailing in Convoy HX.217 which left New York on 27 November 1942. Torpedoed twice and sunk by U.524 (Kptlt Freiherr Walter von Steinaecker) shortly after 2am on 8 December in position 57°04′N 36°01′W. One died. Fifty-seven were picked up by the rescue ship *Perth* (Captain K. Williamson) and landed at Greenock on the 13th.

OTHER SHIPS SUNK IN CONVOY HX.217

Charles L.D. (Captain D.E. Canoz). By U.553 (Krvkpt. Karl Thurmann. Thirty-six died and 12 picked up by the Perth. See under UNION-CASTLE LINE.

James McKay (US) (Captain H.N. Olsen). By U.600 (Kptlt Bernhard Zurmühlen) when straggling. Two lifeboats got away, but were never seen again. All 62 died.

EMPIRE NORSEMAN (Captain W.S. Smith). Bound for Curaçao from Greenock and in Convoy UC.1 when torpedoed and damaged by U.382 (Kptlt Herbert Juli) at 10.14pm on 23 February 1943. Torpedoed and severely damaged a few minutes later by U.202 (Kptlt Günter Poser) and abandoned. Sunk at 11.45pm by U.558 (Kptlt Günther Krech) in position 31°18′N 27°20′W. All 53 were picked up by the sloop HMS *Totland* (Lt Cdr L.E. Woodhouse) but transferred to the *Maaskerk* (Du.) and landed at Trinidad.

Silver Line

SILVERAY (Captain H. Green). Bound for Halifax and New York, sailing in Convoy ON.55 which left Liverpool on 8 January 1942 and dispersed on the 26th in position 44°25′N 51°19′W. Between 4.27am and 5.07am on 4 February, she was torpedoed 3 times by U.751 (Kptlt Gerhard Bigalk) and sank in position 43°54′N 64°16′W. Eight died. Thirty-five were picked up by the USCGC *Campbell* and landed at Argentia, Newfoundland. Six picked up by the Canadian motor fishing vessel *Lucille M* were landed at Lockeport, Nova Scotia.

SHIPS SUNK IN CONVOY ON.55 ON 14 JANUARY

Chepo (Pan.). By U.43 (Kptlt Wolfgang Lüth). Seventeen died and 21 survived.

Empire Surf (Captain A. Sandham). By U.43. Forty-seven died. Six picked up by the corvette HMS *Alisma* (Lt Cdr M.G. Rose) and landed at Londonderry.

SILVERBEECH (Captain T.G. Hyem). Bound for Freetown and Lagos, sailing in Convoy OS.44 which left Liverpool on 6 March 1943. Collided with the *Djambi* on the 13th and put into Gibraltar for repairs. Proceeding in Convoy RS.3 when torpedoed and sunk by U.172 (Kptlt Carl Emmermann) on the 29th in position 25°30′N 15°55′W. Fifty-nine died. Eight were picked up by the tug *Empire Ace* and landed at Bathurst.

OTHER SHIPS SUNK IN CONVOY RS.3

Lagosian. See under UNITED AFRICA CO. LTD.

Moanda (Belg.) (Captain J. Heusers). By U.167 (Kptlt Kurt Sturm). Twenty-nine died and 27 survived.

SILVERBELLE (Captain H. Rowe). Bound for Liverpool from Durban, sailing in Convoy SL.87 which contained 11 ships and left Freetown on 14 September 1941. Torpedoed by U.68 (Krvkpt. Karl-Friedrich Merten) at 2.23am on the 22nd. Taken in tow, in succession, by the sloop HMS *Gorleston* (Cdr R.W. Keymer), the Free French sloop *Commandant Duboc* and the ASW trawler HMS *Lady Shirley* (Lt Cdr A.H. Callaway), but sank on the 29th in position 26°30′N 23°14′W. All 60 were picked up by the escort. (For details of other ships sunk in Convoy SL.87, see under *Dixcove*, ELDER DEMPSTER LINE.)

SILVERCEDAR (Captain T. Keane). Bound for Liverpool from New York, and laden with explosives, sailing in Convoy SC.48 which left Sydney, Cape Breton, on 5 October 1941. Torpedoed and blown up by U.553 (Kptlt Karl Thurmann) at 8.15am on the 15th in position 53°36′N 29°57′W. Twenty-two died. Twenty-six were picked up by the Free French corvette *Mimosa* (Captain Roger Birot) and landed at Reykjavik. (For details of other ships sunk in Convoy SC.48, see under *Empire Heron*, WEIR, ANDREW, & CO./BANK LINE.)

SILVERFIR (Captain J. Thompson). Bound for New York from Manchester, sailing in Convoy OB.294 which left Liverpool on 5 March 1941 and dispersed in position 51°29′N 20°30′W on the 9th. Sunk by the *Scharnhorst* on the 16th in position 43°40′N 43°57′W. One died and 40 taken prisoner. (For details of the many ships sunk and captured by the *Scharnhorst* and the *Gneisenau*, see under *British Strength*, BRITISH TANKER CO. LTD.)

SILVERLAUREL (Captain J. Duncan). Bound for Falmouth and Hull from Duala in Convoy BTC.10 when torpedoed and sunk by U.486 (Oblt Gerhard Meyer) on 18 December 1944 in position 50°07′N 04°40′W. All 65 were picked up by the *Monkstone* and landed at Plymouth.

SILVERMAPLE (Captain W.C. Brydson). In Convoy STL.12 which left Freetown on 22 February 1944 bound for Takoradi and Lagos. Torpedoed and sunk by U.66 (Oblt Gerhard Seehausen) on the 26th in position 04°44′N 03°20′W. Seven died. Fifty-seven were picked up by the patrol vessel HMS *Kildwick* (Lt P. Pannell) and landed at Takoradi the following day.

SILVERPALM (Captain R.L. Pallett). Bound for Glasgow from Calcutta, sailing from Freetown on 31 May 1941. She may have been the ship torpedoed and sunk by U.371 (Kptlt Heinrich Driver) at 3.26am on 12 June in position 56°10′N 24°30′W. Last seen on 1 June, and on 15 July a lifeboat containing 8 bodies was sighted by the trawler *Cave*. All

68 died. Some sources claim that she was sunk by U.101 (Kptlt Ernst Mengersen) on 9 June in position 51°00′N 26°00′W, but she is not listed among the ships sunk by that U-boat.

SILVERPINE. Bound for New York, sailing in Convoy OB.252 which left Liverpool on 30 November 1940 and dispersed on 4 December. Torpedoed and sunk by the Italian submarine *Argo* (T.V. Alberto Crepas) on the 5th in position 54°14′N 18°08′W. Thirty-six died and 19 survived. (For details of other ships sunk after dispersal of Convoy OB.252, see under *Empire Jaguar*, REARDON SMITH LINE.)

SILVERWILLOW (Captain R.C. Butler). In Convoy SL.125 which sailed from Freetown on 16 October 1942 bound for Liverpool. Torpedoed and damaged by U.409 (Oblt Hanns-Ferdinand Massmann) at 11.28pm on the 30th. Abandoned on 5 November and subsequently sank in position 37°24′N 10°45′W. Six died. Sixty-one were picked up by the auxiliary patrol vessel HMS *Kelantan* (Lt A.E. Jones) and landed at Gourock on 8 November. (For details of other ships sunk in Convoy SL.125, see under *Nagpore*, P&O.)

SILVERYEW (Captain J. Smith). Bound independently for London from Calcutta when torpedoed and sunk by U.106 (Kptlt Jürgen Oesten) at 0036 hours on 30 May 1941 in position 16°42′N 25°29′W. Captain Smith died. Fifty-three, in a lifeboat, landed at San Antonio, Cape Verde Islands.

Stag Line

J. ROBINSON & SONS, NORTH SHIELDS

CLINTONIA (Captain T.H. Irvin). Bound for Manchester from St Francis, Nova Scotia, sailing in Convoy SC.7 which left Sydney, Cape Breton, on 5 October 1940. Torpedoed by U.99 (Kptlt Otto Kretschmer) at about 4am on the 19th and straggling when sunk by gunfire from U.123 (Kptlt Karl-Heinz Moehle) about an hour later in position 57°10′N 11°20′W. One died and 35 were picked up by the corvette HMS *Bluebell* (Lt Cdr R.E. Sherwood) and landed at Gourock. (For other ships sunk in Convoy SC.7, see under *Sedgepool*, ROPNER SHIPPING CO.)

EUPHORBIA (Captain T. Hilton). Bound for Lynn, Massachusetts, from Swansea, sailing in Convoy OB.256 which left Liverpool on 8 December 1940 and dispersed on the 12th in position 59°04′N 15°30′W. Torpedoed and sunk by U.100 (Kptlt Joachim Schepke) shortly before 8pm on the 14th when WSW of Rockall. All 34 died. The *Kyleglen* (Captain T. Storer), also dispersed from Convoy OB.256, was torpedoed and sunk by U.100 on the 14th. All 36 died.

GARDENIA. Bound for Middlesbrough from Casablanca, off Cromer on 12 March 1940 when she struck a mine and sank in position 53°04′N 01°33′E. All 33 were picked up by the ASW trawler HMS *Viviana*.

LINARIA (Captain H.T. Speed). Bound for Halifax from the Tyne, sailing in Convoy OB.288 which left Liverpool on 18 February 1941 and dispersed on the 22nd in position 59°30′N

21°15′W. Torpedoed and sunk by U.96 (Kptlt Heinrich Lehmann-Willenbrock) at 1.16am on the 24th in approximate position 61°N 25°W. All 34 died. (For other ships sunk after dispersal of Convoy OB.288, see under *Sirikishna*, SALVESEN, CHRISTIAN.)

Strick Line

ARABISTAN (Captain E.R. Barrett). On passage from Cape Town to Trinidad and south of St Helena on 14 August 1942 when shelled at point-blank range by the raider *Michel* (KptzS. Helmuth von Ruckteschell) and sank within minutes. Fifty-nine died. Mr Edwin Goodridge, her Chief Engineer and sole survivor, spent the night hanging on to an upturned, wrecked lifeboat and was picked up by the *Michel* the following morning. Along with some 300 survivors of other ships sunk by the *Michel*, Mr Goodridge was subsequently transferred to the supply tanker *Charlotte Schliemann* where the prisoners were inadequately fed and housed down a small, rat-infested hold. The *Charlotte Schliemann* landed 40 survivors at Singapore on 30 September and reached Yokohama on 19 October. Mr Goodridge was repatriated from Japan when the war ended. In 1946, Ruckteschell was convicted of war crimes and incarcerated in Fuhlsbüttel prison in Hamburg. He died in 1948, shortly after hearing that he was to be released due to a heart condition. (See also under *Lylepark*, DENHOLM, J. & J., LTD, *Patella*, SHELL GROUP, *Empire Dawn*, RUNCIMAN, WALTER, & CO. LTD/MOOR LINE LTD, and *Gloucester Castle*, UNION-CASTLE LINE.)

ARMANISTAN (Captain C.R. Knight). Bound for Basrah from Antwerp and joined Convoy OG.16 which formed at sea on 31 January 1940. Torpedoed and sunk by U.25 (Krvkpt. Viktor Schütze) at 2.32pm on 3 February in position 38°15′N 11°15′W. All were picked up by the *Monte Abril* (Sp.) and landed at Tenerife.

BALTISTAN (Captain J.H. Hedley). In Convoy OB.290 which sailed from Liverpool on 23 February 1941. Torpedoed and sunk on the 27th by the Italian submarine *Michele Bianchi* (C.C. Adalberto Giovannini) in position 51°52′N 19°55′W. Fifty-one died and 18 survived. (For details of other ships sunk in Convoy OB.290, see under *Mahanada*, BROCKLEBANK LINE.)

BALUCHISTAN (Captain T.H. Farrar). Sailed from Basrah bound independently for the UK via Cape Town and Freetown. Torpedoed 3 times and then sunk by gunfire by U.68 (Krvkpt. Karl-Friedrich Merten) on the afternoon of 8 March 1942 in position 04°13′N 08°32′W. Three died. Sixty-eight landed near Cape Palmas, Liberia.

BANDAR SHAHPOUR (Captain W.A. Chappell). Bound for the UK from Abadan, sailing from Takoradi to Freetown in Convoy TS.37 when torpedoed and sunk by U.515 (Kptlt Werner Henke) at about 11pm on 30 April 1943 in position 07°15′N 13°49′W. One died. Seventy-seven were picked up by the ASW trawler HMS *Birdlip* (Lt E.N. Groom) and landed at Freetown the following day. (For details of other ships sunk in Convoy TS.37, see under *Nagina*, BRITISH INDIA STEAM NAVIGATION CO.)

BATNA (Captain R.M. Potts). Bound for Halifax, sailing in Convoy ONS.92 which left Loch Ewe on 6 May 1942. Torpedoed and sunk by U.94 (Oblt Otto Ites) at 3.51am on the 13th in position 52°09′N 33°56′W. One died. Forty-one were picked up by the rescue ship *Bury* (Captain L.E. Brown) and landed at St John's, Newfoundland, on the 16th. (For details of other ships sunk in Convoy ONS.92, see under *Llanover*, RADCLIFFE SHIPPING CO.)

CAMERATA. At anchor at Gibraltar when sunk by a limpet mine placed by an Italian frogman on 8 May 1943. Operating from their depot ship *Olterra* at Algeciras, frogmen also sank the *Mahsud* and so severely damaged the US Liberty ship *Pat Harrison* that she became a total loss. Two died on the *Pat Harrison*. None died on the *Camerata*.

FLORISTAN. Bound for the Persian Gulf from Manchester, sailing in Convoy OS.17 which left Liverpool on 18 January 1942. Lost the convoy due to gale force winds, heavy rain and poor visibility. The Master decided to head for Oban, but the ship ran aground on Kilchiaran Reef off the south-western coast of Islay at about 9pm on the 19th in position 55°48′N 06°28′W. All rescued. The *Mobeka* (Belg.) (Captain Lauwereins), also in Convoy OS.17, ran aground at Carskey Bay, Mull of Kintyre, on the 19th. Forty-four were rescued by the Campbeltown lifeboat *Duke of Connaught* and all survived.

GUELMA. Bound for Pepel from Madeira when torpedoed and sunk by the Italian submarine *Alessandro Malaspina* (T.V. Giuliano Prini) on 15 July 1941 in position 30°44′N 17°33′E. All 41 were rescued by the submarine HMS *Thunderbolt* (Lt C.C. Crouch) on the 17th. No further details. HMS *Thunderbolt* was formerly HMS *Thetis* which failed to resurface during her trial in Morecambe Bay in 1939.

HAMLA (Captain W.A. Shute). Sailed unescorted from Rio de Janeiro on 18 August 1942 bound for the UK via Trinidad and Freetown. Torpedoed twice by U.506 (Kptlt Erich Würdemann) at 11.37pm on the 23rd, exploded and sank immediately, with a cargo of manganese ore, in approximate position 04°N 13°W. All 38 died.

MEDJERDA (Captain C.E. Banks). Bound for Middlesbrough via Freetown, sailing from Pepel in Sierra Leone on 7 March 1941. Sailed from Freetown in Convoy SL.68 which left on the 13th. Straggling when torpedoed by U.105 (Kptlt Georg Schewe) at 4am on the 18th and sank, with a cargo of iron ore, within half a minute in approximate position 17°N 21°W. All 54 died. (For details of other ships sunk in Convoy SL.68, see under *Benwyvis*, BEN LINE.)

NIGARISTAN. In Convoy HX.150 which sailed from Halifax, Nova Scotia, on 16 September 1941 bound for the UK. Abandoned when her coal bunkers went on fire in the early hours of the 24th and, in spite of a gale blowing and high seas running, all her 63 crew were picked up from the lifeboats by the destroyer USS *Eberle* (Lt Cdr E.R. Gardner).

REGISTAN (Captain C.S. Bartlett). Bound independently for Philadelphia from Basrah when torpedoed and sunk by U.332 (Kptlt Johannes Liebe) at 1.12am on 29 September 1942 in position 12°37′N 57°10′W. Sixteen died. Thirty-eight were picked up the next day by the *Rio Neuquen* (Arg.) and landed at Pernambuco in Brazil on 11 October.

SELVISTAN (Captain G.E. Miles). Bound for Halifax, sailing in Convoy ONS.5 which left Liverpool on 21 April 1943. Torpedoed and sunk by U.266 (Kptlt Ralf von Jessen) at 9.50pm on 5 May in position 53°10′N 44°40′W. Six died. Forty were picked up by the frigate

HMS *Tay* (Lt Cdr R.E. Sherwood) and landed at St John's, Newfoundland. (For details of other ships and U-boats lost in Convoy ONS.5, see under *Dolius*, HOLT, ALFRED, & CO.)

SHAHRISTAN (Captain E.H. Wilson). Bound for Basrah, sailing in Convoy OS.1 which left Liverpool on 24 July 1941. Dispersed from the convoy when torpedoed and sunk by U.371 (Kptlt Heinrich Driver) at 1.38am on the 30th in position 35°19′N 23°53′W. Sixty-five died. Thirty-three were picked up by the *Campeche* (Sp.). Thirty-seven picked up by the corvette HMS *Sunflower* (Lt Cdr J.T. Jones) were landed at Ponta Delgada in the Azores. Six were picked up by the AMC HMS *Derbyshire* (Captain E.A.B. Stanley) and landed at Gourock. Mr Goodridge was one on the survivors – see *Arabistan* above. (For details of other ships sunk and damaged in Convoy OS.1, see under *Botwey*, HENDERSON LINE.)

TABARISTAN (Captain T. Dunn). Bound independently for the UK from Basrah when torpedoed twice and sunk by U.38 (Kptlt Heinrich Liebe) at 11.50pm on 29 May 1941 in position 06°32′N 15°23′W. Twenty-one died. Thirty-nine were picked up by the ASW trawler HMS *Bengali* (T/Lt R.L. Petty-Major) and the armed trawler HMS *Turcoman* (Skipper F.C. Butler), and landed at Freetown.

TAFNA (Captain R.C. Newlands). Bound for London from Beni Saf, Algeria, with a cargo of iron ore when torpedoed and sunk at 11.19am on 24 October 1939 by U.37 (Krvkpt. Werner Hartmann) in position 35°44′N 07°23′W. Two firemen/trimmers died. Thirty-one were picked up by the destroyer HMS *Keppel* (Captain F.S.W. de Winton) and landed at Gibraltar.

THALA. Bound for the Tees from Pepel, sailing in an SL convoy from Freetown. Ran aground on the rocky islet of Hartamul, a mile south of Rubha Melvick on South Uist on 8 February 1941. No further details.

Managed for Ministry of War Transport

FORT HOWE (Captain W. Williams). After taking part in Operation Avalanche, the invasion of the Italian mainland, she joined Convoy MKS.26 bound for the UK. Torpedoed and sunk by U.410 (Oblt Horst-Arno Fenski) at 0005 hours on 1 October 1943 in position 37°19′N 06°40′E. Two DEMS gunners died. Sixty-seven were picked up by the corvettes HMS *Spiraea* (Lt A.H. Pierce) and HMS *Alisma* (Lt G. Lanning) which landed them at Bougie and Algiers respectively. The tanker *Empire Commerce* (Captain J.L. Fitzpatrick) (Hadley Shipping Co. Ltd) was torpedoed by U.410 at the same time and broke in two. All 51 were picked up by HMS *Alisma* and landed at Algiers. The rear section sank but the forward section remained afloat. The Royal Navy tried to sink it, but when this failed it was towed to a beach at Algiers where it was gutted by fire.

Union-Castle Line

CHARLES L.D. (Managed for the MOWT) (Captain D.E. Canoz). Bound for Glasgow, sailing in Convoy HX.217 which left New York on 27 November 1942. Torpedoed and sunk by U.553 (Krvkpt. Karl Thurmann) at 9.10am on 9 December in position 59′02′N 30°45′W.

Thirty-six died. Twelve were picked up by the rescue ship *Perth* (Captain K. Williamson) and landed at the Clyde on the 13th. (For details of other ships sunk in Convoy HX.217, see under *Empire Spenser*, SHELL GROUP.)

DROMORE CASTLE. In ballast and bound from London to Leith in Convoy FN.76 when she struck a mine on 12 December 1941 and sank off the Humber estuary. No lives lost.

DUNBAR CASTLE (Captain H.A. Causton). Bound for Beira, sailing from Southend in Convoy OA.69 on 8 January 1940. Struck a magnetic mine the following day when in position 51°23′N 01°34′E. With her back broken, she sank on an even keel in shallow water and was demolished after the war. Nine died, including her Master. Survivors were rescued by the trawler *Calvi* and other small vessels.

DUNDRUM CASTLE. Bound for Alexandria from the UK via the Cape when fire broke out in No 2 hold on 2 April 1943. Abandoned before an explosion occurred and she sank in position 14°37′N 42°23′E. All were rescued by the *Rhona* and landed at Suez.

DUNVEGAN CASTLE. Requisitioned by the Admiralty at the outbreak of the war. Converted into an AMC, HMS *Dunvegan Castle* (Captain H. Ardill), and escorting Convoy SL.43 which sailed from Freetown on 11 August 1940 bound for the UK. During the late evening of the 27th she was struck by 3 torpedoes fired by U.46 (Oblt Engelbert Endrass) and sank the next day in position 55°8′N 9°54′W. On fire and with ammunition exploding, she was abandoned. Twenty-seven died and 192 were picked up by the destroyer HMS *Harvester* (Lt Cdr M. Thornton) and the corvette HMS *Primrose* (Lt Cdr C.B. Sanders) and landed at Gourock on the same day.

GLOUCESTER CASTLE (Captain H.H. Rose). Bound for Cape Town, sailing from Birkenhead on 21 June 1942 and in a convoy until it dispersed on 10 July. Shelled by the German AMC *Michel* (KptzS. Helmuth von Ruckteschell) when sailing independently at 7pm on 15 July and sank within 10 minutes in approximate position 08°00′S 01°00′E.

A shell demolished the bridge and radio room, killing all her deck officers except 2nd Mate R. Pargitter, and as her 3 Radio Officers also died, no distress message was transmitted. Of the 154 people on board, 93 died, including 6 women, 3 men and 2 children who were passengers. The remaining 61, including a woman, an 18-year-old girl and 2 young boy passengers, were taken on board the *Michel* but later transferred to the supply tanker *Charlotte Schliemann*. When the latter eventually sailed, she had some 300 prisoners on board. The women and children were given 2 cabins but the others were housed down a small, rat-infested hold, and all were inadequately fed. The *Charlotte Schliemann* arrived in Singapore on 30 September where 50 prisoners were landed before she sailed for Yokohama, arriving on 19 October. However, a number of her prisoners did not live to be repatriated at the end of the war. (See also under *Lylepark*, DENHOLM, J. & J., LTD, *Patella*, SHELL GROUP, *Arabistan*, STRICK LINE, and *Empire Dawn*, RUNCIMAN, WALTER, & CO. LTD/MOOR LINE LTD.)

LLANDAFF CASTLE (Captain C.J. Clutterbuck). Sailing independently from Mombasa to Dar es Salaam when struck by 2 torpedoes fired by U.177 (Kptlt Robert Gysae) at about 5.30pm on 30 November 1942. Two more torpedoes broke her back and she sank in position 27°20′S 33°40′E. Three crew died. Most of the remaining crew and 150 passengers, including women and children, were rescued by the destroyer HMS *Inconstant* on 2 December and landed at Durban. Two of the lifeboats landed on the coast of Zululand and their occupants brought to Durban by train.

RICHMOND CASTLE (Captain T. Goldstone). Bound for Avonmouth, sailing independently from Montevideo on 18 July 1942. Shortly before 4pm on 4 August she was hit by 2 torpedoes fired by U.176 (Oblt Reiner Dierksen), capsized and sank in position 50°25′N 35°05′W. The survivors got away in 3 lifeboats. Those in the boat containing the Master and 14 others were picked up by the *Irish Pine* (Ir.) (Captain M O'Neill) and landed at Kilrush. The 18 in another boat were rescued by the *Hororater* and landed at Liverpool. The 17 in the 1st Mate's boat endured 12 days afloat before being picked up by the corvette HMS *Sunflower* (Lt Cdr J.T. Jones) and landed at Londonderry on the 16th. Sixteen died. (All 33 on the *Irish Pine* died when she was sunk by U.608 (Oblt Rolf Struckmeier) on 16 November.)

ROTHESAY CASTLE (Captain E.W.H. Furlong). On passage from New York to Glasgow when, on 4 January 1940, she went aground in bad weather at Sanaig Point on the Island of Islay. Because he underestimated the ship's speed and failed to use the patent log and take soundings, Captain Furlong was found responsible for the loss and had his Master's certificate suspended for one year. All the crew were taken off by the tug *Englishman*.

ROWALLAN CASTLE. In Convoy MW.9 which sailed from Alexandria on 12 February 1942 bound for Malta. The heavily escorted convoy left Alexandria in two sections and consisted of only 3 ships: the *Rowallan* in Section 9A, and the *Clan Campbell* and *Clan Chattan* in Section 9B. The air attacks began as the sections were combining late on the 13th. The *Clan Campbell* was seriously damaged, diverted to Tobruk and was escorted back to Alexandria where she arrived on the 16th. The following day the *Clan Chattan*, carrying ammunition, was bombed and set on fire. The destroyer HMS *Southwold* took off 285 crew and passengers, while the destroyers HMS *Avon Vale*, HMS *Beaufort* and HMS *Dulverton* rescued those in the water. At about 3pm the same day the *Rowallan Castle*, also carrying ammunition, was hit. An attempt was made to tow her by the destroyer HMS *Zulu*, but when it was clear that she was sinking, the tow was cast off. After all on board had been taken off by the destroyer HMS *Lance*, she was sunk by gunfire in position 34°54′N 19°40′E. No lives were lost on the *Rowallan Castle* and *Clan Chattan*.

ROXBURGH CASTLE (Captain G.H. Mayhew). Sailing independently and on passage from Glasgow to Buenos Aires when struck by a torpedo fired by U.107 (Kptlt Harald Gelhaus) at about 8.30am on 22 February 1943. The U-boat, which had chased her for 5 hours, put another torpedo into her about 45 minutes later and she sank in position 38°12′N 26°22′W. All 64 were landed at Ponta Delgada in the Azores and carried to Lisbon on the Portuguese ship *Serpa Pinto*.

WALMER CASTLE (Captain G.L. Clarke). Of only 906 gross register tonnage and newly converted into a convoy rescue ship, sailing from Liverpool in Convoy OG.74 on 12 September 1941 bound for Gibraltar. Between the 19th and the 21st she rescued survivors of the *City of Waterford*, *Empire Moat* and *Baltallin*, but when well astern of the convoy later on the 21st she was hit by a bomb from a Focke-Wulf 200 Condor. As the bomb struck the bridge, exploded in the engine room and set her on fire, she was abandoned, and sunk by the escort in position 47°16′N 22°25′W. The Focke-Wulf was shot down by planes from the escort carrier HMS *Audacity* (Cdr D.W. Mackendrick). Eleven died, including her Master, together with 20 out of the 81 she had rescued. Twelve crew and 61 of the rescued survivors were picked up by the corvette HMS *Marigold* (Lt W.S. Macdonald) and the sloop HMS *Deptford* (Lt Cdr H.R. White) and landed at Gibraltar on 28 September.

OTHER SHIPS SUNK IN CONVOY OG. 74

19 September:

City of Waterford (Captain T. Alpin). In collision with the *Thames* (Du.). All 23 rescued by HMS *Deptford* but transferred to the *Walmer Castle* and 5 died when she was sunk.

20 September:

Baltallinn (Captain C.W. Browne). Torpedoed and sunk by U.124 (Kptlt Johann Mohr). Seven died plus 11 more on the *Walmer Castle*. Seventeen picked up by HMS *Deptford*.

Empire Moat (Captain J.F. Travis). Torpedoed and sunk by U.124. All 32 survived, but 5 died on the *Walmer Castle*.

21 September:

Lissa (Captain D. MacQuarrie). Torpedoed and sunk by U.201 (Oblt Adalbert Schee). All 26 died.

Rhineland (Captain J.T. Gilroy). Torpedoed and sunk by U.201. All 26 died.

Runa (Captain H. McLarty). Torpedoed and sunk by U.201. Fourteen died and 9 picked up by HMS *Deptford*.

WARWICK CASTLE (Captain H.R. Leepman-Shaw). Requisitioned as a troopship in 1939 and took part in Operation Torch, the invasion of North Africa. Returning to the UK in Convoy MKF.1X which sailed from Gibraltar on 12 November 1942 she was struck by 3 torpedoes fired by U.413 (Oblt Gustav Poel) between 8.44am and 8.57am on the 14th and sank in position 39°12′N 13°25′W. Of the 462 on board, 96 died, including the Master. The remaining 366 were picked up by the destroyers HMS *Achates* (Lt Cdr A.H.T. Johns) and HMS *Vansittart* (Lt Cdr T. Johnston), the corvette HMCS *Louisburg* (Lt Cdr W.F. Campbell) and the *Leinster*, which landed them at Greenock.

WINDSOR CASTLE (Captain J.C. Brown). Requisitioned as a troopship in 1939 and in Convoy KMF.11 (UK to Mediterranean Fast) which sailed from Greenock on 15 March 1943 bound for Algiers. In the early hours of the 23rd, the convoy was off Cape Ténèz, about 110 miles west of Algiers and in position 37°27′N 00°54′E, when it was attacked by German aircraft. At about 2.35am she was hit by an aerial torpedo delivered by a Junkers 88. One crew member was killed, but as she did not sink until about 3pm, the remaining 289 of her crew and all the 2,699 service personnel on board were rescued by several ships and taken to Algiers.

United Africa Co. Ltd

ASHANTIAN (Captain C. Cartmer-Taylor). Bound for New York and commodore ship of Convoy ONS.3 which left Liverpool on 5 April 1943. Torpedoed and sunk by U.415 (Oblt Kurt Neide) shortly after 8am on 21 April 1943 in position 55°46′N 45°14′W. Sixteen died, including the Master and Commodore Captain Jeffery Elliott, RN. Fifty-one were picked up by the ASW trawler *Northern Gift* (T/A/Lt Cdr A.J. Clemence) but the 3rd Engineer died from exposure before she reached St John's, Newfoundland, on the 25th. (The *Wanstead* was torpedoed at the same time as the *Ashantian*, see WATTS, WATTS & CO. LTD.)

CONGONIAN (Captain George Washington Irvin). Bound independently for Freetown from Liverpool when torpedoed twice and sunk by U.65 (Krvkpt. Hans-Gerrit von Stockhausen) shortly after 6pm on 18 November 1940 in position 8°21′N 16°12′W. Eric Kilgour, the 2nd Mate, died. Thirty-five were picked up by the cruiser HMS *Devonshire* and landed at Freetown on the 29th.

DAHOMIAN (Captain W.L. Taylor). Bound independently for Cape Town from New York and Trinidad when torpedoed and sunk by U.852 (Kptlt Heinz-Wilhelm Eck) on 1 April 1944 in position 34°25′S 18°19′E. Two died. Forty-nine were picked up by the armed whalers HMSAS *Krugersdorp* and HMSAS *Natalia* and landed at Simonstown.

KUMASIAN (Captain W.E. Pelisser). Bound for London and in Convoy SL.81 which left Freetown on 15 July 1941. Torpedoed and sunk by U.74 (Kptlt Eitel-Friedrich Kentrat) at 5.40am on 5 August in position 53°26′N 15°40′W. One died. Fifty-nine were picked up by the corvette HMS *La Malouine* (T/Lt V.D.H. Bidwell) and landed at Liverpool. (For details of other ships sunk and damaged in Convoy SL.81 see under *Swiftpool*, ROPNER SHIPPING CO.)

LAFIAN (Captain E.L. Phillips). Bound for Liverpool from Port Harcourt, sailing in Convoy SL.87 which left Freetown on 14 September 1941. Torpedoed and sunk by U.107 (Krvkpt. Günther Hessler) at 6am on the 24th in position 31°12′N 23°32′W. All 47 were picked up by the sloop HMS *Gorleston* (Cdr R.W. Keymer) and landed at Ponta Delgada, Azores. (For details of other ships sunk in Convoy SL.87, see under *Dixcove*, ELDER DEMPSTER LINE.)

LAGOSIAN (Captain George Washington Irvin, ex-*Congonian*). Bound for Takoradi from Algiers and in Convoy RS.3 when torpedoed and sunk by U.159 (Krvkpt. Kurt Sturm) at 11.47am on 28 March 1943 in position 25°41′N 15°43′W. Eleven died. Thirty-five were picked up by the tug *Empire Denis* and landed at Bathurst. (For other ships sunk in Convoy RS.3, see under *Silverbeech*, SILVER LINE.)

MATADIAN (Captain C.G. Silwyn). Bound independently for the UK from Port Harcourt and Lagos when torpedoed and sunk by U.66 (Oblt Gerhard Seehausen) on 21 March 1944 in position 5°07′N 4°7′E. All 47 were picked up by the motor launch HMS *ML-282* (Sub Lt D.R. Pearson) but transferred to the motor launch HMS *ML-1016* which landed them at Lagos.

NIGERIAN (Captain E.R. Owen). Bound for Trinidad, sailing independently from Takoradi on 22 November 1942. Between 0005 and 0050 hours on 9 December she was torpedoed twice by U.508 (Kptlt Georg Staats) and sank in position 9°17′N 59°00′W. Five died. One

RAF and 3 army officers (passengers) were taken prisoner by the U-boat and landed at Lorient on 6 January 1943. Thirty were picked up by the patrol craft USS PC-624 on the 11th and landed at Moruga Bay, Trinidad. Fifteen picked up by the *Newbrundoc* (Can.) were landed at Georgetown. Seven were picked up by the *Maravi* (Pan.).

ST CLAIR II (Managed for the MOWT) (Captain H. Readman). Bound for Liverpool, sailing in Convoy SL.87 which left Freetown on 14 September 1941 Torpedoed and sunk by U.67 (Kptlt Gunther Muller-Stôckheim) at 0028 hours on the 24th in position 30°25′N 23°35′W. Thirteen died. Twenty-six were picked up by HMS *Gorleston* and 5 by HMS *Lulworth* and landed at Londonderry on 4 October. (See *Lafian* above.)

ZARIAN (Captain W.E. Pelissier, ex-*Kumasian*). Damaged by U.26 (Kptlt Heinz Scheringer) on 1 July 1940. Bound for Takoradi from Leith and in Convoy ON.154 when torpedoed and damaged by U.406 (Kptlt Horst Dieterichs) at 11.17pm on 28 December 1942. Straggling when torpedoed by U.591 (Kptlt Hans-Jürgen Zetzsche) at midnight and sank in position 43°23′N 27°14′W. Four died. Forty-nine were picked up by the destroyer HMS *Milne* (Captain I.M.R. Campbell) and landed at Ponta Delgada in the Azores. (For details of other ships sunk in Convoy ON.154, see under *Baron Cochrane*, HOGARTH, H., & CO./BARON LINE.)

Watts, Watts & Co. Ltd

ASCOT (Captain J.F. Travis). A new ship built in Dundee where the crew signed the articles on 27 November 1942. Sailed in Convoy ON.161 which left Liverpool on 12 January 1943 but detached from the convoy when it was nearing North America and proceeded independently to Durban. Doing only about 7 knots, she did not arrive until late March. From Durban her itinerary is not clear, but in the autumn a passage from the Red Sea to Fremantle took 2 months. Bound independently for Port Louis in Mauritius from Colombo when torpedoed by the Japanese submarine I-37 (Lt Cdr Hajime Nakagawa) at 11.30am on 29 February 1944 in approximate position 05°′S 63°′E. Four died and 52 abandoned ship in lifeboats and on a raft. The submarine surfaced and when her medical officer failed in his attempt to get the Master to declare himself, warning shots were fired over the heads of the survivors. Captain Travis then revealed his identity and was taken on board the submarine, but after an interrogation, during which the palms of his hands were slashed, he was thrown into the water.

Before and after shelling the ship and setting her on fire, the Japanese used machine guns, rifles and pistols to shoot at the survivors, while the submarine used its propellers to destroy the lifeboats and upset the raft. I-37 eventually departed and it was dark when 17-year-old A.H. Taylor found that his companions on the raft were 18-year-old Harry Fortune, 3 ABs (1 wounded) and 2 gunners (1 wounded). Mr Taylor witnessed their ship sink and the next day they were joined by Bill Hughson, another gunner, who had feigned dead in the remains of a lifeboat. After more than 2 days without food and with very little water they were picked up by the *Straat Soenda* (Du.) during the late afternoon of 3 March and taken to Aden. (See also under *Sutlej*, NOURSE LINE, *British Chivalry*, BRITISH TANKER CO. LTD, and *Centaur*, HOLT, ALFRED, & CO.)

BLACKHEATH (Captain J.N. Garrett). Bound for Augusta and Ancona from Greenock and Manchester, sailing in the combined Convoys OS.102/KMS.76 which left Liverpool on 2 January 1945. Torpedoed by U.870 (Krvkpt. Ernst Hechler) shortly after 4pm on the 10th in position 35°49′N 06°03′W. Beached two miles south of Cape Spartel, Morocco, broke in two and declared a total loss. All 51 were picked up by the frigate HMS *Ballinderry* (Lt Cdr E.F. Aitken) and the patrol vessel HMS *Kilbernie* (Lt C.T. Letts) and landed at Gibraltar.

DARTFORD (Captain S. Bulmer). Bound for Sydney, Cape Breton, from the Tyne and Oban, sailing in Convoy ON.100 which left Liverpool on 2 June 1942. Torpedoed and sunk by U.124 (Kptlt Johann Mohr) at 6.12am on the 12th in position 49°19′N 41°33′W. Thirty died. Seventeen were picked up by the rescue ship *Gothland* (Captain J.M. Hadden) and landed at Halifax on the 17th.

OTHER SHIPS SUNK IN CONVOY ON.100

Empire Clough (On her maiden voyage) (Captain Felix de Bastarrechea). By U.94 (Oblt Otto Ites). Five died. Thirty-two picked up by the corvette HMS *Dianthus* (Lt Cdr C.E. Bridgman) and landed at St John's, Newfoundland. Twelve picked up by the Portuguese trawler *Argus* and landed at Greenland on the 26th.

FFL *Mimosa* (French corvette) (Captain Roger Birot). By U.124. Fifty-nine French, including Captain Birot, and 6 British died. Four French picked up by the destroyer HMCS *Assiniboine* (Cdr J.H. Stubbs).

Pontypridd (Captain H.V.B. Morden). Torpedoed twice by U.569 (Kptlt Hans-Peter Hinsch) and abandoned. Two died and Captain Morden taken prisoner. Torpedoed and sunk by U.94. Forty-five picked up by the corvette HMCS *Chambly* (Cdr J.D. Prentice) and landed at St John's.

Ramsay (Captain B.F.R. Thomas). By U.94. Forty died. Eight picked up by the corvette HMS *Vervain* (Lt H.P. Crail) and landed at St John's.

DEPTFORD (Captain J.W. Ferguson). Bound independently for Middlesbrough from Narvik when torpedoed and sunk by U.38 (Kptlt Heinrich Liebe) at 3.28pm on 13 December 1939 in position 62°15′N 05°08′E, about a quarter of a mile from Honningsvaak. With a cargo of iron ore, she sank within 5 minutes and Captain Ferguson, 29 crew and 2 Norwegian pilots died. Four were picked up by the Norwegian fishing vessel *Firda* and 1, plus 2 bodies, by the *Nordnorge* (Nor.). All brought to Leikanger and then to Bergen via Maalöy.

DULWICH. Cut off by the German advance through France, she was beached and set on fire by her crew on 9 June 1940 near Villequier on the Seine. Raised by the Germans in 1942 and renamed *Holtenau,* but bombed and sunk by the RAF near Calais on 17 October in that same year.

TEDDINGTON. Bound for Ceylon (Sri Lanka) from London. Torpedoed by German E-boat E.51 off Cromer in position 53°03′N 01°35′E on 17 September 1941. Taken in tow, but went ashore at Overstrand the next day, broke her back and declared a total loss. All rescued.

TOTTENHAM. Bound for Alexandria via the Cape, sailing in Convoy OB.327 which left Liverpool on 28 May 1941 and dispersed on 1 June in position 52°42′N 22°18′W. Intercepted by the German raider *Atlantis* (KptzS. Bernhard Rogge) disguised as the *Tamesis* (Nor.) on 17 June and a warning shot fired across her bow. Returned the fire while a QQQQ message was transmitted so that the *Atlantis* then shelled her. Struck by a torpedo while being abandoned and subsequently sunk by gunfire in position 07°39′S 19°12′W. The occupants of a lifeboat were picked up by the raider, but Rogge refused the Master's request to continue the search for the other boat as he was anxious to leave the area in case the QQQQ message had been received. The prisoners on the *Atlantis* were later transferred to another ship, which is likely to have been the supply ship *Tannenfels*, and taken to Germany. The 17 in the second lifeboat were never seen again, but about 2 months later the waterlogged and empty boat was washed up on the shore near Rio de Janeiro.

WANSTEAD (Captain W.B. Johnston). Bound for New York from the Tyne and Oban, sailing in Convoy ONS.3 which left Liverpool on 5 April 1943. Torpedoed by U.415 (Oblt Kurt Neide) shortly after 8am on 21 April 1943 in position 55°46′N 45°14′W. On fire when abandoned, but did not sink until a second torpedo was put into her by U.413 (Kptlt Gustav Poel) at 1.45pm. Two died. Forty-eight were picked up by the ASW trawler *Northern Gift* (T/A/Lt Cdr A.J. Clemence), and the corvette HMS *Poppy* (Lt N.K. Boyd), and landed at St John's. (The *Ashantian* was torpedoed at the same time as the *Wanstead*, see UNITED AFRICA CO. LTD.)

WENDOVER. Bound independently for Buenos Aires when intercepted and shelled by the German raider *Thor* (KptzS. Otto Kähler) on 16 July 1940 in position 23°08′S 34°49′W. Mr C.W.A. O'Donnell, her 1st Radio Officer, responded by transmitting a QQQQ message until he was killed by a direct hit to the radio room. The ship was then stopped and abandoned. A boarding party from the *Thor* set demolition charges, but when this caused her only to capsize she was sunk by gunfire. Two died, but of the 39 picked up by the *Thor*, 2 more died from their wounds. (For other ships sunk by the *Thor* at that time, see under *Delambre*, LAMPORT & HOLT LINE.)

WILLESDEN. Bound for North Africa from St Thomas in the West Indies when a plane bearing US markings but really from the German raider *Thor* (KptzS. Günther Gumprich) flew over her on 1 April 1942 and brought down her main transmitting aerial with a hook. The DEMS gunners, using the antiquated 4in gun on the poop, fired at the plane but only succeeded in wounding the Observer. The *Thor* then appeared and, while shelling the ship, ordered the crew to abandon her. The shelling ceased while she was being abandoned and she was then sunk in approximate position 16°00′S 16°00′W. Five died.

The wounded among the 42 survivors were taken to the *Thor's* sick bay while the remainder were put into an 18ft by 12ft room already occupied by the survivors of the *Wellpark* where they were subsequently joined by those of the *Aust* (Nor.) and the *Kirkpool*. On 4 May, somewhere in the Indian Ocean, all survivors were transferred to the supply ship *Regensburg* where they were treated well and whose crew provided them with food and waved goodbye when they left her in Yokohama harbour on 7 July. The crew were transferred to the *Ramses* before being handed over to the Japanese on 25 August and taken to Kamasaki and Fukushima PoW camps. Those who survived this ordeal were released when the Japanese surrendered on 2 September 1945. (See also under *Kirkpool*, ROPNER SHIPPING CO.)

Weir, Andrew, & Co./Bank Line

ALYNBANK. Sunk on 9 June 1944 to form part of Gooseberry harbour No 3 (off Gold Beach at Arromanches) at the time of the Normandy Landings.

ARAYBANK. Badly damaged and run ashore after being bombed by German planes in Suda Bay, Crete, on 3 May 1941. Bombed again on the 16th and on fire with her cargo of ammunition exploding when abandoned. Raised and repaired in 1947. Sold to Achille Lauro and renamed *Napoli*. No information regarding her crew.

AYMERIC (Captain S. Morris). In Convoy ONS.7 which sailed from Liverpool on 7 May 1943 bound for Halifax, Nova Scotia. Torpedoed and sunk by U.657 (Krvkpt. Heinrich Göllnitz) at about 2.30am on the 17th in position 59°42′N 41°39′W. Eleven were picked up by the rescue ship *Copeland* (Captain W.J. Hartley) and 14 by the trawler HMS *Northern Wave* (Lt J.P. Kilbee), but 6 died on the *Copeland* and 7 on the *Northern Wave*. All transferred to the *Copeland* and landed at Halifax on the 25th. Fifty-three died and 12 survived. The *Aymeric* had a Lascar crew. The frigate HMS *Swale* (Lt Cdr J. Jackson) subsequently located U.657 by ASDIC and destroyed her with depth charges and hedgehogs. All 47 on board died.

BIRCHBANK. Bound for an unknown port in the Mediterranean, sailing in Convoy OS.57 which left Liverpool on 27 October 1943. Joined Convoy KMS.31 at Gibraltar on 10 November. A German air attack began at 6.20pm the next day when the convoy was north-east of Oran. The *Birchbank* was struck by an aerial torpedo and sank in position 36°13′N 00°06′W. The Senior 2nd Engineer Mr J.G. Parkinson and DEMS Gunner S. Dugdale, RN (D/JX 339287) died, and 65 were rescued.

OTHER SHIPS SUNK BY AIRCRAFT IN CONVOY KMS.31

Carlier (Belg.) (Captain Frankignoul). Sixty-seven died. Twenty-four picked up by the destroyer USS *Trippe* and landed at Oran.

Indian Prince. See under Prince Line, FURNESS, WITHY GROUP.

Josiah Parker (US). Damaged, but continued in the convoy.

Nivose (Fr.). Damaged, but did not sink until she collided with another ship. None died.

SUNK BY SUBMARINE

Empire Dunstan (Captain N. Ramsay). Sunk by U.81 (Oblt Johann-Otto Krieg) on the 18th in position 39°24′N 17°40′E after she had dispersed from the convoy. Two died and 40 survived.

CEDARBANK (Captain W.J. Calderwood). Bound from Aberdeen to Aandalsnes in Norway, and 1 of the 3 merchant ships in Convoy AP.1, when torpedoed and sunk by U.26 (Kptlt Heinz Scheringer) at 7.49am on 21 April 1940 in position 62°49′N 04°10′E. Fifteen died. Thirty were picked up by the destroyer HMS *Javelin* (Cdr A.F. Pugsley) and landed at Aalesund.

CONGELLA (Captain S.W. Folster). Bound for Mombasa, sailing independently from Colombo at 6am on 21 October 1943. At 9.30am on the 24th a lookout in the crow's nest spotted the periscope of a submarine, and a wireless message was sent to alert the authorities. Shelled by the Japanese submarine I-10 (Cdr Kinzo Tonozuka) from 7.45pm onwards and sank in position 1°02′N 71°14′E. Three damaged lifeboats were successfully launched. The 14 in the boat, commanded by 2nd Mate A.B. Skinner and fired at by the submarine, were picked up by the whaler HMS *Okapi* (Cdr Simpson) at 2.30am on the 26th and landed at Addu Atoll in the Maldives on the 27th. The boat commanded by Apprentice I.A. Clark and containing 19 others, was spotted by an RCAF Catalina flying boat on the 27th and, together with another Catalina, landed on the sea and took the survivors to Addu Atoll. The boat containing the Chief Engineer and 11 others was never seen again. Twenty-eight died and 34 survived.

ELMBANK (Captain H.T. Phillips). Sailed from Cowichan, British Columbia, and in Convoy HX.72 which left Halifax on 9 September 1940 bound for the UK. Torpedoed by U.99 (Kptlt Otto Kretschmer) at 4.47am on the 21st and dropped behind the convoy. She was shelled by U.99 about an hour later and, after an interval, U.99 and U.47 (Kptlt Günther Prien) both shelled and set on fire the now abandoned ship which was finally sunk by a second torpedo from U.99 in position 55°20′N 22°30′W. One died. Fifty-five were picked up by the *Pikepool* and landed at St John's, Newfoundland. (For details of other ships sunk in Convoy HX.72, see under *Scholar*, HARRISON LINE.)

FOYLEBANK. Requisitioned by the Admiralty in 1939 and converted into the anti-aircraft ship HMS *Foylebank*, she was in Portland Harbour, Dorset, when attacked by a squadron of German Junkers 87 'Stuka' dive bombers during the morning of 4 July 1940 and sank the next day. Seventy-two died and 220 survived.

INCOMATI (Captain S. Fox). Bound for the Middle East via Durban and sailing independently when torpedoed and sunk by U.508 (Kptlt Georg Staats) at about 8am on 18 July 1943 in position 03°09′N 04°15′E. One crew member died. One hundred and nine crew and 112 passengers were picked up by the destroyer HMS *Boadicea* (Lt Cdr F.C. Brodrick) and the sloop HMS *Bridgewater* (Cdr N.W.H. Weekes) and landed at Takoradi.

LARCHBANK (Captain W.A. McCracken). Bound for Colombo and Calcutta from Baltimore. Torpedoed by the Japanese submarine I-27 (Lt Cdr Toshiaki Fukumura) on

9 September 1943 and sank within minutes in position 07°38′N 74°00′E. Forty-six died and 30 survived.

OAKBANK (Captain J. Stewart). Bound for the UK from Demerara and sailing independently when torpedoed and sunk by U.507 (Krvkpt. Harro Schacht) on 27 December 1942 in position 00°46′S 37°58′W. Captain Stewart and Apprentice Ian H. Innes-Sim were taken prisoner by the U-boat and lost when it was depth-charged and sunk by a US Catalina on 13 January 1943 with the loss of all hands. Thirty-two were picked up by the Brazilian ship *Commandate Ripper* and landed at Recifé on 3 January. One rescued by the Argentinian tanker *Juvenal* and 2 landed on the coast near Para on the 15th. Twenty-seven died and 35 survived.

SPEYBANK (Captain A. Morrow). Bound for New York from Cochin, India, when captured by the German raider *Atlantis* (KptzS. Bernhard Rogge) in the Indian Ocean on 31 January 1941. Her crew were taken on board the raider but transferred to the supply ship *Tannenfels* (Captain Stroheim) on 21 March; disguised as the Norwegian ship *Tarrongo*, she reached Bordeaux on 20 April. On 12 May, the prisoners left for Germany in cattle trucks. (See under *Mandasor*, BROCKLEBANK LINE.)

Under a prize crew the *Speybank* reached Bordeaux on 10 May. Renamed *Doggerbank*, she was used as an auxiliary minelayer by the Germans but eventually mistakenly sunk by U.43 (Oblt Hans-Joachim Schwantke) shortly before 10pm on 3 March 1943 in position 29°10′N 34°10′W.

SPRINGBANK. Requisitioned by the Admiralty and converted into a fighter catapult ship, HMS *Springbank* (Captain C.H. Goodwin) was part of the escort of Convoy HG.73 which sailed from Gibraltar on 17 September 1941 bound for the UK. Shortly after 2am on the 27th she was torpedoed by U.201 (Oblt Adalbert Schnee) in position 49°09′N 20°10′W. The majority of the survivors were rescued by the corvette HMS *Jasmine* (Lt Cdr C.D.B. Coventry) which subsequently sank the vessel. Others were rescued by the corvettes HMS *Hibiscus* (Lt H. Roach), which carried them by to Gibraltar, and HMS *Periwinkle* (Lt Cdr P.G. MacIver), which landed them at Milford Haven.

OTHER SHIPS SUNK IN CONVOY HG.73

Avoceta (Captain H. Martin). By U.203 (Kptlt Rolf Mützelburg). One hundred and twenty-three died and 43 survived. Forty rescued by HMS *Periwinkle* and landed at Milford Haven. The Bosun and 2 Arab firemen picked up by the *Cervantes*.

Cervantes (Captain H.A. Fraser). By U.124. Eight died and 32, including the 3 from the *Avoceta*, picked up by the *Starling* and landed at Liverpool on 1 October.

Cortes (Captain D.R. McRae). By U.203. All 42 died.

Empire Stream (Captain S.H. Evans). By U.124 (Kptlt Johann Mohr). Eight died and 27 picked up by the corvette HMS *Begonia* (Lt Cdr H.B. Phillips) and landed at Milford Haven.

Lapwing (Captain T.J. Hyam). By U.124. Twenty-six died and, together with 9 survivors of the *Petrel*, 8 reached Slyne Bay, in Co. Galway, on 9 October.

Margareta (Captain H. Pihlgren). By U.201. All 34 picked up by HMS *Hibiscus* and landed at Gibraltar.

Petrel (Captain J.W. Klemp). By U.124. Twenty-two died, while the Master and 8 others landed at Slyne Bay with the survivors of the *Lapwing*.

Siremalm (Nor.) (Captain H. Svendsen). By U.201. All 27 died: 20 Norwegians, 3 Finns, 1 Swede and 3 British.

Varangberg (Nor.) (Captain E.S. Stenersen). By U.203. Twenty-one died. Six picked out of the sea by a corvette and landed at Milford Haven.

TEESBANK (Captain W.G. Loraine). Sailing independently and bound for Demerara from Port Said via Port Elizabeth when torpedoed and sunk by U.128 (Kptlt Ullrich Heyse) at about 6am on 5 December 1942 in position 03°33′N 29°35′W. One died and the other 60 got away in 2 lifeboats. On 9 December, U.461 (Krvkpt. Wolf-Harro Stiebler) intercepted the boats, provided them with food, took Captain Loraine prisoner and eventually docked in St Nazaire on 3 January 1943. Forty-one were picked up by the *Bessemer* (US) and landed at Rio de Janeiro on 22 December. Nineteen picked up by the *East Wales* were landed at Natal, Brazil, on 23 December.

TESTBANK. In Bari, Italy, when the fully illuminated port was attacked by 105 German bombers at about 7.30pm on 2 December 1943. Sunk when the nearby ammunition ship *John L. Motley* (US) blew up, destroying other ships and causing massive damage to the port. The 3rd Engineer, Mr Norman Taylor, and the 4th Engineer, who both suffered concussion and minor injuries, were the only survivors.

OTHER SHIPS SUNK IN THE RAID

John Harvey (US). Mustard gas escaped from her cargo, resulting in many deaths.

Barletta (It.), *Bollsta* (Nor.), *Devon Coast* (Br.), *Fort Athabasca* (Can.), *Fort Lajoie* (Can.), *Frosinone* (It.), *Inaffondabile* (It.), *John Bascom* (US), *Joseph Wheeler* (US), *Lars Kruse* (Br.), *Lom* (Nor.), *Norlom* (Nor.), *Puck* (Pol.) and *Samuel J. Tilden* (US).

Seven more ships were severely damaged, in the region of 800 people died, and the port remained closed until February 1944.

THORNLIEBANK (Captain S. Letton). Bound for the Middle East via Freetown and in Convoy OS.12 which sailed from the UK on 18 November 1941. Shortly after 4am on the 29th she was struck by 2 torpedoes fired by U.43 (Kptlt Wolfgang Lüth) and blew up in position 41°50′N 29°48′W. All 75 on board died. (For the *Ashby*, also in Convoy OS.12, see ROPNER SHIPPING CO.)

THURSOBANK (Captain R.B. Ellis). Sailing independently and bound for Alexandria from New York via Cape Town when torpedoed by U.373 (Kptlt Paul-Karl Loeser) shortly after 5am on 22 March 1942. Struck by a second torpedo about half an hour later and sank in position 38°05′N 68°30′W. Thirty died and 26 were picked up on the 25th by the Norwegian tanker *Havsten*. On their arrival in Halifax on the 28th, the Chinese were arrested for mutiny in the lifeboat.

TIELBANK (Captain W. Broome). Bound for Oban from Kakinada in India via Durban, sailing from Freetown in Convoy SL.67 on 1 March 1941. Torpedoed and sunk by U.124 (Kptlt Georg-Wilhelm Schulz) at about 6am on the 8th in position 20°51′N 20°32′W. Four died and 62 were picked up by the destroyer HMS *Forester* (Lt Cdr E.B. Tancock) and landed at Gibraltar on the 16th. (For details of other ships sunk in Convoy SL.67, see under *Nardana*, P&O.)

TINHOW (Captain P.H. Aydon). Bound for Calcutta via Beira, sailing from Durban in Convoy DN.37. After the convoy had dispersed, she was torpedoed and sunk by U.181 (Krvkpt. Wolfgang Lüth) shortly after 4am on 11 May 1943 in position 25°15′S 33°30′E. Twenty-five crew and 50 passengers died. After clinging to upturned lifeboats and anything which floated for over 48 hours, 132 were picked up by Portuguese fishing boats which landed them at Lourenço Marques on the 13th.

TRENTBANK. Sailed from Gibraltar in Convoy KMS.3 on 22 November 1942 bound for Bône in Algeria. Struck by an aerial torpedo when the convoy was attacked about 10 miles north of Cape Ténèz on the 24th. Abandoned and blew up. Two died and 75 survived. (For details of other ships sunk in Convoy KMS.3, see under *Grangepark*, DENHOLM, J. & J., LTD.)

TYMERIC (Captain T. Fraser). Bound for Buenos Aires and in Convoy OB.244 which sailed from Liverpool on 17 November 1940. Torpedoed by U.123 (Kptlt Karl-Heinz Moehle) at about 8.15am on the 23rd and sank within 20 minutes in position 57°00′N 20°30′W. Seventy-one died. Five were picked up by the sloop HMS *Sandwich* (Cdr M.J. Yeatman) and landed at Liverpool.

OTHER SHIPS SUNK IN CONVOY OB.244

Anten (Swed.) By U.123. One died and 32 picked up by HMS *Sandwich*.

Daydawn (Captain James Horsfield). By U.103 (Krvkpt Viktor Schütze). Two died and 36 picked up by the corvette HMS *Rhododendron* (Lt Cdr W.N.H. Faichney).

King Idwal (Captain R. Storm). By U.123. Twelve died and 28 picked up by HMS *Sandwich*.

Oakcrest (Captain S.G. Dyer). By U.123. Thirty-five died and 6 landed on the Isle of Barra.

Victoria. By U.103. All 27 survived.

WEIRBANK (Captain D.A.B. Reid). Sailing independently and bound for New York from Alexandria via Durban and Trinidad when torpedoed and sunk by U.66 (Kptlt Friedrich Markworth) at 0040 hours on 28 July 1942 in position 11°29′N 58°51′W. One died and 66 landed at Tobago.

WILLOWBANK (Captain D. Gillies). Bound for Hull from Durban, sailing in Convoy SL.34 which left Freetown on 31 May 1940. Torpedoed and sunk by U.46 (Oblt Engelbert Endrass) at 9.38pm on 12 June in position 44°16′N 13°54′W. All 51 were picked up by the

Swedru. The *Barbara Marie* (Captain A.S. Smith) was sunk at the same time by the same U-boat. Thirty-two died and 5 were picked up by the *Swedru*.

Managed for Ministry of War Transport

EMPIRE ATTENDANT (Captain T. Grundy). Bound for Karachi via Durban, sailing in Convoy OS.33 which left Liverpool on 1 July 1942 bound for Freetown. Dispersed from the convoy when torpedoed and sunk by U.582 (Kptlt Werner Schulte) at 3.30am on 15 July 1942 in position 23°48′N 21°51′W. All 59 died. (For details of other ships sunk after dispersing from Convoy OS.33, see under *Cortona*, DONALDSON LINE.)

EMPIRE CITY (Captain B.H. Jackson). In Convoy DKA.21 and bound for Port Said via Lourenço Marques and Aden when torpedoed and sunk by U.198 (Oblt Burkhard Heusinger von Waldegg) on 6 August 1944 in position 11°33′S 41°25′E. Twelve died and 58 were landed at Pekawi in Mozambique. U.198 was sunk 6 days later by the frigate HMS *Findhorn* (Lt Cdr J.C. Dawson) and the sloop HMIS *Godavari* (A/Cdr A.B. Goord) with the loss of all 66 hands.

EMPIRE HERON (Captain J.D. Ross). Bound for Manchester from Freeport, Texas, and in Convoy SC.48 which sailed from Sydney, Cape Breton, on 5 October 1941. Torpedoed and sunk by U.568 (Kptlt Joachim Preuss) at about 1.15am on 16 October 1941 in position 54°55′N 27°15′W. All 43 died.

OTHER SHIPS SUNK IN CONVOY SC.48

16 October:

Barfonn (Nor.) (Captain E.E. Vorberg). By U.432 (Oblt Heinz-Otto Schultze). Two picked up by the corvette HMCS *Baddeck* (T/Lt A.H. Easton) and 24 by the corvette HMCS *Wetaskiwin* (Lt Cdr G.S. Windeyer).

Bold Adventure (Pan.) By U.553. Seventeen died and 17 picked up by HMCS *Wetaskiwin*.

Erviken (Nor.) (Captain P. Heesch). By U.558 when picking up survivors from the *W.C. Teagle*. Twenty-five died and 14 picked up from a raft by two corvettes. Two more died; probably picked up by HMS *Broadwater* and lost when she was sunk.

Evros (Gr.). By U.432. Thirty died and 2 survived.

HMS *Gladiolus* (Corvette) (Lt Cdr Harry M.C. Sanders). By U.558. No survivors.

Ila (Nor.) (Captain T. K. Johnsen). By U.553 (Kptlt Karl Thurmann). Fourteen died. Nine clung to wreckage and an overturned lifeboat for 3 hours before being picked up by the Free French corvette *Mimosa* (Captain Roger Birot) but 2 more died from exposure before she reached Reykjavik.

Rym (Nor.) (Captain C. Rustad). By U.558. She had slowed down to help rescue survivors of *W.C. Teagle* but was hastening to catch up with the convoy again when the *Erviken* was seen to be hit. All 21 survived. Captain Rustad and 3 others remained on board to try to save the ship but eventually joined the others on HMS *Veronica*.

Silvercedar. See under SILVER LINE.

W.C. Teagle (Captain H.R. Barlow). By U.558 (Kptlt Günther Krech). Forty died and 10 picked up by the destroyer HMS *Broadwater*, but 9 of those were lost when she was sunk the next day. Radio Officer N.D. Houston, picked up by the corvette HMS *Veronica* (Lt Cdr D.F. White) and landed at Londonderry on the 19th, was the sole survivor.

18 October:

HMS *Broadwater* (Lt Cdr W.M.L. Astwood). By U.101 (Kptlt Ernst Mengersen). No survivors.

(The destroyer USS *Kearny* was damaged by U.568 on the 17th.)

EMPIRE MINIVER (Captain R. Smith). Bound for Newport, Monmouthshire, sailing in Convoy SC.7 which left Sydney, Cape Breton, on 5 October 1940. Torpedoed and sunk shortly after 10pm on the 18th by U.99 (Kptlt Otto Kretschmer). Three died and 35 were picked up by the corvette HMS *Bluebell* (Lt Cdr R.E. Sherwood) and landed at Greenock on the 20th. (For details of other ships sunk in Convoy SC.7, see under *Sedgepool*, ROPNER SHIPPING CO.)

EMPIRE STEEL (Captain W.J. Gray). Bound for the UK, sailing unescorted from Baton Rouge on 13 March 1942 to join a convoy at Halifax, Nova Scotia. Torpedoed by U.123 (Kptlt Reinhard Hardegen) at 3am on the 24th and sunk by gunfire in position 37°45′N 63°17′W. Thirty-nine died and 8 were picked up by the US tug *Edmund J. Moran* which was towing the *Robert E Lee* and landed at Norfolk, Virginia.

ILE DE BATZ (Captain A.J. Watts). Sailing independently and bound for the UK from Rangoon via Cape Town and Freetown when torpedoed by U.68 (Krvkpt. Karl-Friedrich Merten) at 6.35am on 17 March 1942. Shelled and sank at about 8am in position 04°04′N 08°04′W. Four died. Thirty-nine landed at Cape Palmas and were brought to Freetown by the corvette HMCS *Weyburn* (Lt Thomas M.H. Golby).

Inver Tankers Ltd

INVERDARGLE (Captain E.M. Skelly). On passage from Trinidad to Avonmouth, having crossed the Atlantic in Convoy HXF.15 which sailed from Halifax on 4 January 1940. Sailing independently up the Bristol Channel when at 4.19pm on the 16th she struck a mine laid by U.33 (Kptlt Hans-Wilhelm von Dresky) and sank in position 51°16′N 03°43′W. All 49 died. On 12 February, U.33 was depth-charged and sunk in the Firth of Clyde by the minesweeper HMS *Gleaner*. Twenty-five died, including von Dresky, and 17 survived.

INVERILEN (Captain J. Mann). Bound for Stanlow, sailing from New York in Convoy HX.224 on 22 January 1943. Torpedoed by U.456 (Kptlt Max-Martin Teichert) and sank in position 56°13′N 20°35′W. Thirty-one died. Sixteen, including 2 DBS, were picked up by the corvette HMS *Asphodel* (Lt G.L. Fraser) and landed at Londonderry.

OTHER SHIPS SUNK IN CONVOY HX. 224

Jeremiah Van Rensselaer (US) (Captain L.W. Webb). Struck by 3 torpedoes fired by U.456 and abandoned by all except one man. Forty-six died and 24, picked up by the rescue ship *Accrington*, were landed at Gourock. A number of men from the USCGC *Ingham* later boarded the Liberty ship and took off the man who had remained behind before scuttling her.

Cordelia (Captain E. Marshall). Straggled from the convoy and sunk by U.632 (Kptlt Hans Karpf). Forty-six died. I.C. Bingham, the Chief Engineer, was the sole survivor because he was taken prisoner by the U-boat which reached Brest on the 14th.

INVERLANE. Bound for Invergordon from Abadan when mined in the North Sea on 14 December 1939 in position 55°05′N 01°07′W. Drifted ashore at Seaburn in Co. Durham where she burned for 5 days. Four crew died and many were injured. In 1944, her fore section was filled with 3,000 tons of rubble and stone before it was towed to Burra Sound in Orkney and sunk as a blockship.

INVERLEE (Captain T.E. Alexander). Bound for Gibraltar from Trinidad and sailing independently when torpedoed and sunk by U.204 (Kptlt Walter Kell) at 3am on 19 October 1941 in position 43°18′N 17°38′W. Twenty-two died and 21 were picked up by the destroyer HMS *Duncan* (Lt Cdr A.N. Rowell) and the armed trawlers HMS *Lady Hogarth* (Lt S.G. Barnes) and HMS *Haarlem* (Lt L.B. Merrick) which landed them at Gibraltar. U.204 was depth-charged and sunk later on the same day by the corvette HMS *Mallow* (Lt W.R.B. Noall) and the sloop HMS *Rochester* (Cdr C.B. Allen). All 46 died.

INVERLIFFEY (Captain W. Trowsdale). Bound for Coryton in Essex from Trinidad and sailing independently when torpedoed, shelled and sunk by U.38 (Kptlt Heinrich Liebe) at 1.50pm on 11 September 1939 in position 48°14′N 11°48′W. All 49 were picked up by the US tanker *R.G. Stewart* but transferred to the *City of Joliet* (US) and landed at Milford Haven.

INVERSHANNON (Captain W.R. Forsyth). Bound for Scapa Flow from Curaçao, sailing from Halifax, Nova Scotia, in Convoy HX.72 on 9 September 1940. Torpedoed at 3.12am and again at 11.42am on the 21st by U.99 (Kptlt Otto Kretschmer). Sixteen died. Seventeen were picked up by the sloop HMS *Flamingo* (Cdr J.H. Huntley) and landed at Londonderry. Fifteen picked up the armed trawler HMS *Fandango* (Lt G.E. Mabbott) were landed at Belfast on 29th. (For details of other ships lost in Convoy HX.72, see under *Scholar*, HARRISON LINE.)

INVERSUIR (Captain R.C. Loraine). Bound for Aruba, sailing in Convoy OB.327 which left Liverpool on 28 May 1941 and dispersed on 1 June. Sailing independently on the 3rd when struck by 3 torpedoes fired by U.48 (Kptlt Herbert Schultze) between 1am and 4am. Finally sunk by 2 torpedoes fired by U.75 (Kptlt Helmuth Ringelmann) shortly before 9pm. All 45 survived. Twenty-four were picked up by the *Para* (Nor.) but transferred to HMS *Corinthian* (Cdr E.J.R. Pollitt) which landed them at Greenock on the 21st. Nine picked up by the destroyer HMS *Wanderer* (Cdr A.F.StG. Orpen) were landed at Holyhead. Twelve were rescued by an unknown ship and landed at Quebec.

OTHER SHIPS SUNK AFTER THE DISPERSAL OF CONVOY OB.327

Eibergen (Du.) (Captain R. Hilbrandie). By U.75. Four died. Thirty-five picked up by a British destroyer but later transferred to a British cruiser which landed them at Gourock.

Michael E (Captain M. Macleod). By U.108 (Kptlt Klaus Scholtz). Three died and 59 picked up by the *Alcinous* (Du.).

Trecarrell (Captain G.G. Barrett). By U.101 (Kptlt Ernst Mengersen). Four died and 43 picked up by the *Cornerbrook* and landed at Halifax, Nova Scotia.

Bibliography

Belt, J.E.B. and H S. Appleyard, *A History of Frank C. Strick and his Many Shipping Enterprises* (Kendal: World Ship Society, 1996).

Blake, G., *The Ben Line: The History of a Merchant Fleet 1825–1955* (London: Thomas Nelson, 1956).

British Vessels Lost at Sea 1939–45 (London: Patrick Stephens, 1983).

British Vessels Lost or Damaged by Enemy Action During the Second World War (London: HMSO, 1947).

Cameron, Ian, *Red Duster, White Ensign (War at Sea)* (London: Futura, 1975).

Carlsen, Neil, *Local Heroes* (London: Futures Publications, 2010).

Cowden, James E. and John O.C. Duffy, *The Elder Dempster Fleet History 1852–1985* (Coltishall: Mallett & Bell, 1986).

Crabb, B.J., *Beyond the Call of Duty* (Donington: Shaun Tyas, 2006).

Cubbin, Graeme, *Harrisons of Liverpool* (Preston: World Ship Society/Ships in Focus Publications, 2003).

Duffy, James P., *Hitler's Secret Pirate Fleet: The Deadliest Ships of WWII* (Westport: Praeger, 2001).

Dull, Paul S., *A Battle History of the Imperial Japanese Navy (1941–1945)* (Annapolis: US Naval Institute Press, 1978).

Elphick, Peter, *Liberty: The Ships that Won the War* (Annapolis: US Naval Institute Press, 2001).

Gibson, J.F., *Brocklebanks 1770–1950* (Liverpool: Henry Young & Sons, 1953).

Hague, A., *The Allied Convoy System 1939–1945* (Annapolis: US Naval Institute Press, 2000).

Haws, D., *Merchant Fleets 6: The Blue Funnel Line* (Pembroke: TCL Publications, 1985).

Haws, D., *Merchant Fleets 11: British India Steam Navigation Co.* (Pembroke: TCL Publications, 1987).

Haws, D., *Merchant Fleets 21: Port Line* (Pembroke: TCL Publications, 1991).

Haws, D., *Merchant Fleets 22: Glen and Shire Lines* (Pembroke: TCL Publications, 1991).

Haws, D., *Merchant Fleets 37: Furness, Withy* (Pembroke: TCL Publications, 2000).

Haws, D., *Merchant Fleets 39: China Navigation Company* (Pembroke: TCL Publications, 2001).

Heaton, P.M., *Lamport & Holt* (Newport: Starling Press, 1989).

Heaton, P.M., *Reardon Smith Line: The History of a South Wales Shipping Venture* (Newport: Starling Press, 1984).

Hickey, V.J., *Time to Go, Sparky* (Gloucester: G.D. Hornby, 1994).

Hope, Stanton, *Tanker Fleet* (London: Anglo Saxon Petroleum Co., 1948).

Howarth, S., *Sea Shell: The Story of Shell's British Tanker Fleets, 1892–1992* (Bradford-on-Avon: Thomas Reed, 1992).

Hutchinson, Roger, *Polly: The True Story Behind Whisky Galore* (Edinburgh: Mainstream, 1990).

Jordan, Roger, *The World's Fleets, 1939* (Annapolis: US Naval Institute Press, 2006).

Kerr, George F., *Business in Great Waters* (London: Faber & Faber, 1951).

Laird, Dorothy, *Paddy Henderson* (Glasgow: George Outram & Co., 1961).

MacLean, A., 'The Arandora Star' in *The Lonely Sea* (London: Collins, 1985).

MacVicar, A., *Salt in my Porridge* (London: Jarrolds, 1971).

McAlister, A. and L. Gray, *H. Hogarth & Sons Limited: Baron Line* (Kendal: World Ship Society, 1976).

Middlemiss, Norman L., *Gathering of the Clans* (Newcastle upon Tyne, Shield, 1988).

Middlemiss, Norman L., *The British Tankers* (Newcastle upon Tyne: Shield, 2005).

Mitchell, W.H. and L.A. Sawyer, *The Empire Ships* (London: Lloyds of London Press, 1990).

Owen, Alun, *The Whalers of Anglesey* (Caernarfon: Gwynedd Archive Services, 1983).

Roskill, S.W., Capt., RN, *A Merchant Fleet in War: 1939–1945* (London: Collins, 1962).

Ruegg, B. and A. Hague, *Convoys to Russia 1941–1945* (Kendal: World Ship Society, 1992).

Slader, J., *The Fourth Service: Merchantmen at War 1939–45* (New York: Brick Tower Press, 1995).

Slavick, Joseph P., *The Cruise of the German Raider Atlantis* (Annapolis: US Naval Institute Press, 2003).

Somner, Graeme, *From 70 North to 70 South* (Edinburgh: Christian Salvesen Ltd, 1984).

Taffrail, *Blue Star Line at War 1939–1945* (London: W. Foulsham, 1973).

Upton, Vernon G.A., *Upon their Lawful Occasions* (Leicester: Matador, 2004).

Waters, Sydney D., *Shaw Savill Line* (Christchurch NZ: Whitcombe & Tombs, 1961).

Young, J., *A Dictionary of Ships of the Royal Navy of the Second World War* (Tucson: Aztex Corporation, 1974).

Zabecki, David T. (ed.), *World War II in Europe*, Vol. 2 (New York, Garland, 1999).

Memoirs of Chunilal Navsaria (a boy travelling unescorted on the *Tilawa*)

Report by HMS *Primrose*'s Commanding Officer

Report No 126 Historical Officer Canadian Military HQ

Report of T.D. Finch, 1st Mate, *San Emiliano*

Report of C.B. Skinner, 2nd Mate, *Congella*

Report of J.E. Wills, 2nd Mate, *Rohna*

Weekly Intelligence Report, 3 January 1941

https://home.roadrunner.com

www.100megsfree3.com

www.aamis.myfastforum.org

www.ahoy.tk-jk.net

www.angelfire.com

www.archive.org

www.archiver.rootsweb.ancestry.com/th/read/MARINERS/

www.awm.gov.au

www.barrowbuiltships.co.uk

www.barrymerchantseamen.org

www.battleofbritain1940.net

www.battleships-cruisers.co.uk

www.bbc.co.uk/history/ww2peopleswar/stories/01/a1954901.shtml (Allan Kerr, Midshipman, HMS *Forfar*)

www.bbc.co.uk/history/ww2 peopleswar/stories (Jackie McCauley)

www.bbc.co.uk/history/ww2peopleswar/categories/c55050/ (Tom Simkins, Hugh Ferguson)

www.benjidog.co.uk

www.best-maritime.info

www.bismarck-class.dk/hilfekreuzer/michel.html

www.bismarck-class.dk/hilfskreuzer/atlantis.html

www.books.stonebooks.com

www.canadaatwar.ca

www.cas.awm.gov.au

www.clydesite.co.uk

www.cnrs-scrn.org

www.cofepow.org.uk

www.combinedfleet.com

www.convoyweb.org

www.convoyweb.org.uk (Billy McGee)

www.crwflags.com

www.daileyint.com

www.dale-coastlands-history.org.uk

www.defence.gov.au/sydneyii

www.docksideinn.nl.ca

www.empressofasia.com

www.en.wikipedia.org/wiki/Convoy_PQ_13

www.fad.co.za/Resources/ovi/ovington.htm

www.familyheritage

www.findarticles.com

www.fortships.tripod.com

www.forum.axishistory.com

www.rootsweb.ancestry.com

www.genforum.genealogy.com

www.geocities.com

www.ghostbombers.com

www.gordonmumford.com
www.gwannon.com
www.iancoombe.tripod.com/id5.html
www.halcyon-class.co.uk
www.helderline.nl
www.history.navy/mil
www.hmsconway.org
www.homepage.ntlworld.com
www.iancoombe.tripod.com
www.ibiblio.org/hyperwar/USN
www.ijnsubsite.info/Commander
www.i-law.com
www.imarest.org
www.kentfallen.com
www.killifish.f9.co.uk/Malta
www.london-gazette.co.uk
www.manchesterliners.co.uk
www.mansell.com
www.mariners-l.co.uk
www.mariners-list.com
www.maritimehistoryofthegreatlakes.ca
www.members.iinet.net.au
www.mercantilemarine.org
www.merchant-navy.net (Billy McGee, David Dicks and C. Louis Basson, *Gloucester
    Castle* survivor)
www.merchantnavyofficers.com
www.microworks.net
www.miramarshipindex.org.nz
www.misquita.in/britannia.melvyn.chap2
www.naval.review.cfps.dal.ca
www.naval-history.net
www.ne-diary.bpears.org.uk
www.news.google.com
www.peterheadlifeboat.co.uk
www.portal.pohub.com
www.red-duster.co.uk
www.regiamarina.net
www.rfa-association.org
www.rhiw.com
www.risdonbeazley.co.uk
www.russianarcticconvoymuseum.co.uk (Thomas Doneghan, AB, SS *Empire Cowper*)
www.scotlandsplaces.gov.uk

www.scotsac.com

www.scottishwargraves.phpbbweb.com

www.seawaves.com

www.shipsnostalgia.com (Hugh MacLean, Radio Officer Ivor Lloyd, SS *Surada*)

www.shipwrecksofegypt.com

www.sites.google.com

www.smesh.co.uk

www.southwestmafia.com

www.sscityofcairo.co.uk

www.submarinersworld.blogspot.com

www.swanseadocks.co.uk

www.theshipslist.com

www.thetimesonline.co.uk

www.thewarillustrated.info

www.trove.nla.gov.au

www.tyneandweararchives.org.uk

www.uboat.net

www.uboatwaffe.net

www.union castle.net

www.uscg.mil/history

www.usmm.org

www.war-experience.org (Christopher Tulitt, David Wilson)

www.warsailors.com

www.worldnavalships.com

www.worldwar2daybyday.blogspot.com

www.wrecksite.eu

www.ww2aircraft.net

www.ww2eagles.blogspot.com

www.ww2talk.com

www.xmasgrupsom.com

www.xplorasub.com

www.yoliverpool.com

Index of Ship Names